The Politics of Cultural Differences

The Politics of Cultural Differences

SOCIAL CHANGE AND VOTER MOBILIZATION
STRATEGIES IN THE POST–NEW DEAL PERIOD

David C. Leege
Kenneth D. Wald
Brian S. Krueger
Paul D. Mueller

PRINCETON UNIVERSITY PRESS
PRINCETON AND OXFORD

Copyright © 2002 by Princeton University Press
Published by Princeton University Press, 41 William Street, Princeton, New Jersey 08540
In the United Kingdom: Princeton University Press, 3 Market Place,
Woodstock, Oxfordshire OX20 15Y

All rights reserved

Library of Congress Cataloging-in-Publication Data

The politics of cultural differences: social change and voter mobilization strategies in the post–New Deal period / David C. Leege, Kenneth D. Wald, Brian S. Krueger, and Paul D. Mueller.
p. cm.
Includes bibliographical references and index.
ISBN 0-691-09152-8 (alk. paper)—ISBN 0-691-09153-6 (pbk.: alk. paper)
1. Voting—United States.   2. Voting research—United States.   3. Politics and culture—United States.   4. Social choices—United States.   I. Leege, David C.   II. Wald, Kenneth D.   III. Krueger, Brian S.   IV. Mueller, Paul D.

JK1967 .P65 2002
324.7'0973–dc21   2001056049

British Library Cataloging-in-Publication Data is Available

This book has been composed in

Printed on acid-free paper. ∞

www.pup.princeton.edu

Printed in the United States of America

10 9 8 7 6 5 4 3 2 1

TO THE MEMORY OF

Warren E. Miller, founder and finder

Contents

Figures and Tables ... ix

Preface ... xi

PART I: *Cultural Theory and Recent American Politics*

CHAPTER ONE
Anomalies of Post–New Deal Politics ... 3

CHAPTER TWO
The Political Mobilization of Cultural Differences ... 13

CHAPTER THREE
General Components of Cultural Theory in Political Conflict ... 39

CHAPTER FOUR
Election Rituals, Ideological Movements, and Group Politics ... 56

CHAPTER FIVE
Psychological Mechanisms and Campaign Strategies ... 83

PART II: *Case Studies of the Political Mobilization of Cultural Differences*

CHAPTER SIX
Cultural Strains in the New Deal Coalition ... 101

CHAPTER SEVEN
A Methodology for Assessing Cultural Politics ... 130

CHAPTER EIGHT
Keeping America Purposeful, Powerful, and Pure ... 158

CHAPTER NINE
Race and the Transformation of the Contemporary Party System ... 179

CHAPTER TEN
Gender, Religion, and the Second Party Transformation ... 203

CHAPTER ELEVEN
Cultural Politics: Some Conclusions and Practical Implications ... 252

References ... 271

Index ... 283

Figures and Tables

Figures

7.1	Partisan Patterns of Entire Population, 1960–1996	134
8.1	Partisan Patterns of White, Non-Latino Catholics, 1952–1996	161
8.2	Partisan Preferences of New Deal and Post–New Deal White, Non-Latino Catholics, 1960–1996	164
8.3	Partisan Patterns of Non-Latino Southern Whites, 1960–1996	169
8.4	Partisan Advantage of Non-Latino Whites by Level of Education, 1960–1996	176
9.1	Partisan Patterns of African Americans, 1952–1996	188
9.2	Partisan Patterns of Working-Class Whites Outside the South, 1960–1996	194
10.1	Gender Gap between Non-Latino, White Men and Women, 1960–1996	219
10.2	Partisan Patterns of All White, Non-Latino Men, 1960–1996	220
10.3	Partisan Patterns of All White, Non-Latino Women, 1960–1996	221
10.4a	Republican Identification by Sex, New Deal Generation, 1960–1996	225
10.4b	Republican Identification by Sex, Post–New Deal Generation, 1960–1996	225
10.5	Partisan Patterns of All White, Non-Latino Housewives, 1960–1996	227
10.6	Partisan Patterns of White, Non-Latino Women in Business or Professional Occupations, 1960–1996	228
10.7	Partisan Vote Yields among White Women, by Generation and Occupational Classification, 1960–1996	229
10.8	Republican Voting Tendencies of Mainline and Evangelical Protestants, 1960–1996	237
10.9	Democratic Partisan Advantage of Catholics and Protestants, 1952–1996	238
10.10	Partisan Patterns of White, Non-Latino Southern Evangelical Protestants, 1960–1996	239

TABLES

7.1	Direction Codes for Second-Order Factors: Democrats/Republicans, 1960–1996	148
7.2	White, Non-Latino Democrats, 1960–1996	150
7.3	White, Non-Latino Republicans, 1960–1996	153
8.1	White, Non-Latino, Catholic Democrats, 1960–1996	165
8.2	White, Non-Latino, Southern Democrats, 1960–1996	172
9.1	White, Non-Southern, Non-Latino, Working-Class Democrats, 1960–1996	196
10.1	Partisanship of Ethnoreligious Tradition, 1960–1996: Party Identification, Party Loyalty, Partisan Vote Yield, and Partisan Advantage	232
10.2	White, Non-Latino, Evangelical Protestant Democrats, 1960–1996	241
10.3	White, Non-Latino, Mainline Protestant Republicans, 1960–1996	244

APPENDICES

Readers can find appendices introduced in chapter 7 at the following website, maintained by Kenneth D. Wald: **http://web.clas.ufl.edu/users/kenwald/**. At the same URL we have located additional tables that are discussed but not presented in chapter 8 (pp. 175–177), chapter 9 (pp. 199–200), and chapter 10 (pp. 229–31).

Preface

Much like a fine wine, a book of this magnitude requires a long gestation. We trace its origin back to the mid-1980s, when Dave Leege and Ken Wald first met and began to exchange thoughts at academic conferences. Both of us shared the feeling that something fundamental was changing in the American political order and were doubtful that scholars in the field of American political behavior could effectively model this change. Work inspired by the Michigan school had by now forgotten chapters 12 and 13 of *The American Voter*, which provided cogent discussion of social identification and the group basis of American politics. Instead, in both its American and exported form, the Michigan model perceived the voter as located somewhere along a left-right axis defined by views about economic issues and the role of government. Work inspired by the competing Rochester school and Anthony Downs's *An Economic Theory of Democracy* developed powerful and parsimonious models of rational behavior by citizens and parties. Yet it seemed to overlook the issues where campaign conflict was strongest and the process by which voters developed their preferences.

Fortunately for our own intellectual development, there were several ongoing strands of research that helped point the way to the theory developed in this book. Strong scholarship was mapping the development of racial conflict and its management by party elites. Another emerging scholarly approach showed that atomistic samples failed to capture the social context of vote choice; primary groups and friendship networks constituted the loci for processing most political communications. Still other research demonstrated the cognitive shortcuts—including group-based heuristics—that voters employ to clarify their social and political worlds. Finally, reanalysis of Michigan datasets suggested that ideological concepts like liberal-conservative had referents based in attitudes toward social change, more so than consistent economic positions.

Challenged by these crosscurrents, Leege and Wald felt it was time to offer a more synthetic approach to understanding a changing political order. The first step was a thematic essay that we, joined by Joel Lieske, presented at the 1989 Midwest Political Science Association meeting and later published in a four-volume, state-of-the-discipline work edited by William Crotty. "Toward Cultural Theories of American Political Behavior" suggested the way cultural theory might help us make sense of American political conflict over religion, race, ethnicity, and class lifestyle.

For the next four years, Leege wrote and rewrote three chapters on a cultural theory that might solve the puzzle of the American electorate since 1968: how could a minority party consistently win the presidency? In 1993 he presented a paper at the American Political Science Association (APSA) meeting entitled "The Decomposition of the Religious Vote, 1960–1992." The paper offered a new measure of partisan loyalty/disloyalty that accounted for turnout and defection within ethnoreligious traditions. In the meantime, he had been impressed by Burnham's dictum that politicians seek to control the size and composition of the electorate, and by Marcus and associates' ideas about the emotions that precipitate turnout, turnout failure, and defection. At this point Wald reentered the conversations, sensing that empirical tests of a theory sketch might be possible.

Both Leege and Wald, among the founding generation of the APSA Section on Religion and Politics, felt that empirical research in the field was too atheoretical and parochial to make an impact on mainstream voting behavior research. Scholars in the emerging gender and politics field expressed similar concerns. Yet, issues addressed by scholars of both gender and religion were central to understanding the emerging forms of cultural politics in the United States. By a stroke of good fortune, the National Election Studies (NES) was trying to develop more adequate measures of religiosity and asked Leege to form a task force. Once piloted, many of their measures became staples on NES into the 1990s. Leege was appointed to its Board of Overseers and eventually became its chair. Three other scholars in some aspect of cultural politics were later added to the board.

Both theory and data for a cultural analysis of American campaigns were taking shape. Nevertheless, six more years of data analysis and rewrites of the empirical chapters transpired before we "got it right." Our fresh legs came in 1998 when Brian Krueger and Paul Mueller, two promising graduate students who enrolled at Notre Dame to study religion and politics with Leege, joined the project as research assistants. Attracted to the power of the theory, the measure of partisan loyalty, and the logic of the factor analyses, but not altogether convinced by our ordinary least squares (OLS) models, they patiently set about to educate us in more defensible analytical strategies. In the process, they learned so much substantively and we learned so much analytically that they became writing partners and eventually co-authors.

We have no illusion that the resulting book is the final word. We offer it as a taste of what political scientists could explain through a cultural theory of American political campaigns. In that sense, it is a manifesto spelling out new ways of understanding an emerging political system. Actually, this general perspective is not so new—historians understood

Preface • xiii

pre–New Deal politics through it—but the theory, rigor, and tools are far different.

A day after Election 2000, Thomas Edsall marveled at how the lines of cleavage evident in exit polls had changed over the last two decades. Perhaps that is why forecasting models performed so poorly in 2000—just as they had in 1988. Cultural politics is different from either the prevailing Michigan or Rochester schools, and it incorporates elite strategies, something missing from the social contextualists of the reconstituted Columbia school. That we mention Edsall is quite appropriate. Astute political journalists during the last two decades have been our inspiration every bit as much as creative political scientists. They see the world in insightful ways. We try to make their vision replicable, to submit it to rigorous tests.

In a book that blends social theory, narrative history, and quantitative analysis, the reader may benefit from some guidance about our method of presentation. The extended sections with text in part 1 are meant to summarize explicitly the key assumptions we have drawn about a topic. These propositions underlie our theory of cultural politics and guided our choice of empirical research strategy. We use italics, as do most authors, to emphasize a word or concept, to call attention to a definition, or to drop an ironic comment here and there. We hope the meaning is clear from the context. Our use of history also bears comment. The second chapter focuses on some of the events and developments in post–New Deal history that caught our attention and prompted us to believe that current theories had to be revised. It links those events to earlier episodes of cultural politics in American life but is not intended as a comprehensive account of this phenomenon. In chapter 6, we provide a rough chronological account of the three major axes of cultural campaigning in the post–New Deal era—nationalism and patriotism, race, and the conflict over gender and religion. This is intended as a guide for readers as they explore the empirical findings in the following three chapters. Each of those chapters briefly recapitulates the story so readers will not lose the thread that ties together the empirical findings. Inevitably, some historical events and developments appear on the stage more than once. We hope that the reason for this is apparent.

This book offers political scientists who puzzle over voters and campaigners a new set of eyes, a fresh perspective. It may be astigmatic but perhaps it corrects for myopia.

• • •

We owe a great debt of gratitude to the many people and institutions that helped us bring this book to fruition. Early on, James Old and

Thomas Trozzolo, Notre Dame graduate students in political science and sociology, respectively, managed NES data. James also conducted the content analysis of campaign themes under Leege's direction. Before becoming full-fledged co-authors, Brian Krueger and Paul Mueller ran and reran NES data through a variety of analytical tools. Patricia Leege cheerfully performed most of the word-processing; what she did not type in the earlier stages of the manuscript was capably done by Cheryl Reed and Nancy McMahon of the College of Arts and Letters Steno Pool. The Institute for Scholarship in the Liberal Arts of the College of Arts and Letters provided summer support for a graduate assistant, and the Graduate School and the Department of Government consistently provided the funds for research assistants during the academic year. Leege is especially grateful for two semester-long sabbatical leaves granted to him at crucial stages in writing the manuscript. Bill Mishler provided a hospitable setting for thinking and writing at the University of Arizona. Wald adds his thanks to Ronald Formisano for some fruitful conversations about the concept of culture. He also benefited from a University of Florida research leave in the early stages of the book.

All of us have appreciated working with our editor, Charles T. Myers, from Princeton University Press. He kept our spirits afloat during the lengthy review process, provided clear feedback on ways to improve the manuscript, in his words, "to turn it into a big book," and became a supportive friend. The editorial staff at PUP, particularly Anita O'Brien, a masterful yet gentle copy editor, and Deborah Tegarden, a wonderfully organized production editor, kept the book on course.

Ideas and tools have received airings in a variety of settings. We have appreciated comments from colloquium participants at the University of Florida, the University of Arizona, Harvard University, and UCLA, from the editors of *Commonweal* magazine, and from discussants at sessions of the Religion and Politics Section of the American Political Science Association, the Society for the Scientific Study of Religion, and the Pew Project on Religion in the Public Square. *Commonweal* gave us permission to use language from Leege's article on the 2000 election in chapter 10. Anonymous reviewers' comments have been invaluable in turning a promising manuscript into a serious book. We alone are culpable for the wrong-headed ideas that remain.

In the end, our greatest debt is to the National Election Studies and to the National Science Foundation, which has continued to fund the discipline's most successful example of big science. Our ideas could not have been tested without reliable, continuous time-series data on the American electorate. Such data make historical interpretation through old and new lenses plausible. From its inception the NES Board of Overseers has stayed in intimate contact with the scholarly community to the extent that design, instrument space, and financial boundaries permitted. Board membership has been remarkably permeable by "outsiders" who configure potential explanations of elections and democratic processes differently from current members.

We trace this model of big science to NES's founder, Warren E. Miller. For nearly four decades, Miller was the discipline's diplomat-without-portfolio, seeking to expand the range of scholarly ideas, tools, resources, and personnel to advance knowledge in American and comparative politics. Seldom were people aware of the many times Warren lost a skirmish to a funder or a professional committee; he always appeared to win in the end because of his indomitable resilience.

Warren and Dave Leege were sometime friends but tough adversaries in the creation of NES. Leege sat on the funder's side of the desk and worked with Warren to fashion a national organization responsive to the scholarly community. It grew from the impossibility of funding the Michigan Studies over the long haul. Ever the clever poker player, Warren learned to take the measure of an opponent. Mutual respect was its product. After Leege left NSF, we often worked shoulder to shoulder on matters of disciplinary resources and structure. We shared not only scholarly hopes but also confidences about meaning in our personal lives. Leege was just one of many who had that privilege, because Warren was possessed of a truly magnanimous spirit. When Leege asked his collaborators whom to recognize in the dedication, they responded: is there any other? And so, we dedicate this book to the model and memory of Warren E. Miller.

PART ONE

Cultural Theory and Recent American Politics

This section develops a cultural theory of American electoral politics and applies it to campaign strategy. Chapter 1 presents the puzzle and discusses limitations in the customary theories that mainstream American voting behavior specialists have developed to understand elections. It previews a theory of cultural conflict and campaign dynamics, lists assumptions, and offers caveats. Chapter 2 initiates development of a cultural theory by looking at recent campaigns. It argues that the political mobilization of cultural differences did not begin with the Republican convention of 1992 but has been characteristic of the politics of the entire post–New Deal period, 1960–1996. The chapter makes rudimentary distinctions between economic and cultural politics and looks to the nature of discourse about "a way of living," *moral order*, as the key to cultural appeals. It suggests what is and what is not cultural politics. It concludes with a discussion of reasons for the rise of cultural politics in recent years and previews the instruments of cultural politics.

Chapters 3, 4, and 5 take us into the components of a cultural theory. Chapter 3 explores the problem of predictability in life and the ways in which culture builds on science and religion to offer solutions to questions of identity, norms, and boundaries in society. It then addresses the uses of politics to resolve competition among values, with attention to the instrumental uses of sanctions, compensations, and ideology. Value differences result from the variety of groups and social identities in any society. Whether political conflict occurs depends on the salience of competing values at different times, group cohesion, and the ambitions of politicians. Social heuristics undergird cultural appeals.

Chapter 4 looks at elections as important rituals in a democracy and describes the president as the most significant cultural icon in the United States. Elections legitimate the ruler-ruled social hierarchy, and campaign rituals are built around symbols that reaffirm collective values and attribute blame for societal dysfunctions. They reduce uncertainty. The campaigners must respond to long-term social change that disturbs the moral order. Typically this is done in relationship to a variety of ideological movements. But campaigners must also respond to sudden or episodic events. The campaign is often a mosaic of symbols that manipulate a group's sense of relative deprivation, structure group consciousness, heighten the perception of threat, offer symbolic and material rewards, hive off parts of the opposition to build a winning coalition, purify an unwieldy coalition, and forestall a nascent coalition.

Chapter 5 explores the psychological mechanisms that operate in political campaigns. It is anchored in the notion that political parties are composed of core groups and "owned" issues. For the most part, party identifications, once established, remain stable through life. But turnout varies, and susceptibility to appeals to defect fluctuates. In any given campaign, voters are cognitive misers, gathering only enough information, often through social attribution, to settle on a course of action. Campaign strategy is a mix of turning out the faithful, discouraging turnout among the opposition, and converting wavering groups among the opposition's identifiers.

Each of these chapters discusses the general contours of the theory, offers illustrations from recent America presidential politics, and concludes with testable propositions and generalizations. Many of the propositions and generalizations will be tested in the three case studies of Part 2. Many will not, but we offer them in the hope that they will stimulate both further research on the cultural politics of the era and the development of additional datasets that will yield fruitful empirical tests.

CHAPTER ONE

Anomalies of Post–New Deal Politics

SCIENTISTS LOVE TO solve puzzles. Over the last three decades, political scientists who examine American voting behavior and party politics have faced an unusual challenge. The tools they have developed to analyze an almost unbroken string of fifty years of data from the National Election Studies have yielded strong, but only partial, solutions. Some pieces interlock, but others do not.

A central political puzzle persists throughout the period we call *post–New Deal*, the period beginning with the presidential election of John F. Kennedy. As we shall see in subsequent chapters, the character of the period was rather different from the period of depression, New Deal, war mobilization, and readjustment. Nearly three decades after Franklin D. Roosevelt's New Deal had realigned the electorate and spent its energies, Democratic party identification remained very high, sometimes doubling Republican identification. Even from 1968 to 1988, the Republican party never constituted a majority of party identifiers, and only among non-Latino whites did the party achieve parity or superiority over the Democrats. Yet Republican presidential candidates won five of those six elections. The one loss was by a very narrow margin in the aftermath of the devastating Watergate scandal. During this entire period, Democrats held solid to massive majorities in the House and lost the Senate only for a brief period. Most observers contend, however, that from the first Nixon administration onward, Republican presidents have defined the *agenda* of American politics, that is, the basic issues and symbols around which political discourse swirls. Curiously, throughout the period, electoral turnout continued to decline, with the exception of a modest recovery in 1992.

In the full period, 1960–1996, Republicans won big, time and again. When they had won as the minority party in the 1950s, it was with a war hero who symbolized unity and normalcy for a nation recovering from the displacements of depression and war; no one knew at first whether he was a Republican or a Democrat, and not many cared. But at the heart of the post–New Deal era, the party won with masterful politicians—*Republican* politicians—like Richard Nixon and Ronald Reagan, and continued with less adept but lifelong politicians like Gerald Ford and George Bush. On the five occasions during the post–New Deal period when Democrats won, three times it was not even by a majority of the popular vote (John F. Kennedy's and both of Bill Clinton's elections). Once it was by a very narrow majority (Jimmy Carter), as the country continued to do penance for the collective shame of Watergate. And only once was it by an overwhelming majority (Lyndon Baines Johnson), as a nation wept for its slain prince. For Republicans, however, landslides and clear majorities routinely described the people's choice. The paradox formed by persistent pluralities in Democratic party identification and Republican presidential victories in the context of declining turnout does not match the expectations of party systems theory (Burnham 1970; Clubb, Flanigan, and Zingale 1980).

Scholarly literature for the period relies on several tools and achieves partial success with the paradox. *Party identification* (for the classic conceptualization, see Campbell et al. 1960) explains many of the Democratic victories but fails to account for sudden declines in turnout by key blocs of party identifiers or the widespread defection of identifiers on a recurring basis. Theories about the *rise of independents* (see De Vries and Tarrance 1972) either are based on a measurement artifact or fail to comprehend the size of political generations. With regard to the former, the proportion of independents in the electorate has not risen appreciably when one considers that independents who "lean" toward a party are often more loyal than weak partisans, and they constitute most of the growth in independents (Weisberg 1980). With regard to the latter, Miller and Shanks (1996) have shown how weaker party identification and lower turnout in the electorate are functions of disproportionate generational replacement, but these are concentrated among the less educated and among people who have not yet reached a stage in the life-cycle where they align. *Realignment theory* looked quite appropriate, given the Nixon and Reagan landslides and the partisan movement of underlying social groups (for a fully developed theory of the processes surrounding partisan alignment, see Beck 1979; for the classic statement, see Key 1955; 1959). Yet scholars have searched in vain for either the cataclysmic event—depression, war—that typically precipitated previous realignments, or even the consistency of voting at lower levels of the ticket that had also accompanied previous realignments (Ladd 1991). *Issue voting* was thought to be on the rise since the 1964 Goldwater candidacy (recent work on issue voting takes most of its cues from Enelow and Hinich 1984; see Key 1966 for one of the earliest and still germane statements about voters and issue voting). Yet it too has floundered: (1) on the low levels of cognition about issue differences; (2) on voters' routinely rejecting a candidate whose issue-positions are more consistent with their own positions than with his or her opponent's positions (Abramson, Aldrich, and Rohde 1994); (3) on the predominance of image appeals to the sectors of the electorate who defect (Levine 1995; Newman 1994); and

(4) on evidence that only small numbers of sophisticated voters can make rational decisions based on "hard issues," but most voters respond to "easy issues," a style of response that lends itself to the cultural politics we will shortly describe (Carmines and Stimson 1980). *Economic interest voting* deriving from *rational choice theory* (see Downs 1957 for the classic statement of the theory) also appears to be a powerful tool. Yet "pocketbook voting," where individuals are directly affected by unfavorable economic conditions, seems less evident than "sociotropic voting," where voters assess the general health of the economy (Kinder and Kiewiet 1981). And often compounded within "economic" language about taxes and benefits are negative symbols of cultural outgroups (Edsall and Edsall 1991; Jacoby 2000) to which the voters are responding. Of the bodies of propositions derived from rational choice theory, perhaps the most powerful has been *retrospective voting*: voters are cognitive misers who ask simply, "How do I feel about the incumbent?" and, if satisfied, seek no information about the challenger (Fiorina 1983). Paradoxically, the objective economic content one may infer from such decisions may be illusory: retrospective voting accounted for Republican victories precisely at the time when the economic well-being of the working and middle class underwent a steady decline, and they were the voters who shifted in a Republican direction. "Good" performance apparently was rationalized from other dimensions of presidential activity.

Thus, the arsenal of tools to understand post–New Deal elections is often powerful but seems to break down at critical points. We think there are forces even more general than those tapped by these tools that can be understood through the explicit use of *cultural theory*. In fact, we think of post–New Deal politics as the epitome of cultural politics.

Toward a Cultural Theory of American Presidential Campaigns

The argument we propose to develop in this book is as follows: People who identify with different social groups often have different, deeply held perspectives not only on how they should live but also on the scope of the political community and its purposes. They have a sense of a legitimate moral order, and they expect other citizens and their government to further that design. They often dislike and distrust groups with rival perspectives, and they even feel that some groups have no right to participate in democratic politics, much less to have their rivals' perspectives become binding on society. Parties become anchored in social groups, and political leaders fashion value and interest coalitions for electoral advantage. Campaign strategies involve intricate plans to mobilize the faithful, demobilize parts of the opposition by sowing the seeds of anxiety, and attract defectors from the opposition through negative symbols of the opposition's leadership. The salience of cultural issues will wax and wane as a function of group identifications, historical events, and coalition needs. Patriotism and nationalism, race, gender, and religion have all been the stuff of one or another campaign in the post–New Deal era. The most efficient campaigns involve themes that bundle several of these cultural bases together in a symbol or code word.

The argument rests on several assumptions. First, at root, political conflict concerns who we are, how we are to behave toward each other, and who or what is not of us (an elegant statement of this position in found in Wildavsky 1987). Other social control mechanisms address these issues, but often they spill over into politics. Seldom is a society sufficiently homogenous and small that divergent views on these cultural matters have not formed. Because citizens think of right and wrong ways of living, because they get enthused and proud, dejected and embarrassed over the course of public life, political elites—i.e., those who seek to lead—will address cultural issues. There is both advantage and risk in doing so. In America, since every presidential outcome is built on an electoral coalition, coalitional structure and loyalty are central to political campaigns. Ambitious elites must solve both the matches and mismatches between group attachments and current party or candidate orientations, mobilizing the electorate along the matches and demobilizing the electorate along the mismatches.

Some observers might argue that there was a declining sense of group identification among Americans during the post–New Deal period. The forces of modernity—mass education, mass communication, geographic and social mobility, economic integration, scientific worldviews—had loosened primal loyalties. Since political conflict may at times reflect such changes and at times lead such changes, it would seem reasonable to expect the attenuation of group bonds. Further, scholars have argued that Americans are less likely nowadays to be "joiners" than they were in Tocqueville's America (Putnam 2000). As a result, they would have fewer connections to the civic and political orders and be less attentive to the importance of participation.

We argue that although there is strong evidence for both of these trends, it nevertheless does not diminish the strength of an argument based on group approaches to politics. For example, Wuthnow (1988) notes the decline of confessional conflict and the rise of ecumenism in a formerly denominational society. Yet he also notes the burgeoning of new groups that transcend old group boundaries, that have articulated a clear set of values, that mobilize passionately for their political agendas, and that know which other groups' values they respect and which they view as a threat. Hunter (1991), in particular, argues that the agenda for conflict between rival groups embraces so much of the way we live and has been contested in public life to the point where it has become a virtual *culture war*. The names and bases of the groups may change, but the phenomena of group identity, loyalty, boundaries, and conflict persist with new bases. Further, Huckfeldt et al. (1995) have argued that informal but regular conversation partners continue to perform all of the mobilization functions attributed to groups. Baumgartner and Leech (1998) document the current relevance of group approaches to political conflict. At both the mass and elite level, Americans continue to differentiate themselves into groups with distinct values and conflicting political agendas.

Some have also questioned whether *group* analyses of party identification and partisan behavior are useful anymore. Again, we contend that such arguments confuse change in the intensity of historic group attachments to a particular party with the question of whether group members have attachments to parties at all. In a monumental study, Petrocik (1981) showed that it was possible to sensitively follow groups that compose electoral coalitions through electoral history. In a long succession of publications, Niemi and associates (cf. Stanley, Bianco, and Niemi 1986) have documented the changing proportions of group members from the original New Deal Democratic coalition who have remained in that coalition; they have also measured the proportion of a party coalition composed by a given group's members. Even when change occurs in a given group, analysis of group coalitions within parties remains productive. Further, Manza and Brooks (1999) trace the manner in which recent voter alignments are based on groups representing different class, religion, and gender locations; group differences that have partisan consequences remain stark.

The propensity for party coalitions to represent group conflicts is a durable feature of American politics long after the advent of modernity. In fact, in the next chapter, we will argue that modernity even heightens the propensity. Chapter 3 will show the various ways in which group membership and group identification function politically. Because political elites think in terms of group orientations, campaigns may make group values salient in any given election. For example, Richard Wirthlin, the polling specialist for the 1980 Reagan campaign, used surveys "to pinpoint . . . the values and aspirations that appealed to our key coalitional groups." Some were Republican groups that needed reinforcement and mobilization, but others were vulnerable Democratic groups that needed persuasion. Once campaign themes were developed and a key-state strategy was in place, tracking polls monitored progress with groups and states, as themes were deployed. One theme, "religious traditionalism," was employed to reinforce and enthuse evangelical Protestants Republicans, at the same time that it tried to discourage and dislodge Catholic Democrats. "Strength of leadership" was aimed at "target groups [that] reflected a high commitment to obedience, honor, and willpower" (1981, 243). Appeals combining these with themes of government-induced economic failure were packaged to reach "the less educated, the less affluent, the blue collar, the union members, and Hispanic voters" and "Catholics" (245). Thus, even when the candidate is not linked by affinal ties to a group, the campaign organization constructs themes that resonate with a group's fears and aspirations.

Another assumption is that, while cultural politics is available and is used by both political parties, it is of particular tactical import for the minority party. If all that the parties did during campaigns was to mobilize their respective coalition groups, the minority party would never win. Instead it must mobilize its own groups and dissemble parts of the majority coalition. In any given election, whether the minority party dissembles its opponent through discouraging turnout or encouraging defection is not essential. It must reduce the majority party's support so that the minority party's numbers exceed the majority party's voters. The mechanisms for accomplishing this are detailed in chapter 4, and the general theory of campaign dynamics is presented in chapter 5. Over the long haul, however, defections are more advantageous. They not only interrupt a learned habitual behavior but develop a new habit—one that may facilitate permanent realignment.

For many, political parties and their standard bearers are the embodiment of "our kind." Reflecting on the early voting studies conducted by the Bureau of Applied Social Research at Columbia University and the Survey Research Center at the University of Michigan, Talcott Parsons observed: "the individual seems to vote, other things being equal, with the people whom he most directly feels to be of his own kind, who are in social status and group memberships like, and hence like-minded with, himself. . . . [T]he question is not so much . . . *for what* he is voting as it is *with whom* he is associating himself in voting" (Burdick and Brodbeck 1959, 96).

The minority party must show disaffected groups in the majority coalition how the dominant groups in their party are no longer of "our kind." In like manner, if the minority strays too far from its own kind in making such claims, the majority party will remind "threatened" groups in the minority party coalition that their leaders no longer represent them or are paying too high a price to broaden the party's base. Again the party hearkens to how culturally strange these new bedfellows are.

As generations pass, and intergenerational family socialization processes decay, the reasons why our kind "belong to party X" are hazy or forgotten; oral history is superceded by current events. Thus, new generations come to evaluate the parties either by current performance or by current cultural cleavages. They lose the party of their forebears and align with a different party (Beck 1979).

Yet another assumption needs to be made explicit: the work of political campaigns is not limited to getting to the polls those already converted. Rosenstone and Hansen (1993, 161) argue that "People participate in electoral politics because someone encourages or inspires them to take part. The very nature of elections motivates political leaders to mobilize public involvement: More votes than the opposition means victory. Accordingly in an election campaign, candidates, political parties, campaign organizations, interest groups, and other activists do their best to muster participants." In general, we support this view; it is well substantiated in the empirical literature. However, in this book we wish to initiate research that argues there are times when campaigners seek to *minimize* turnout. In fact, we have devised a measure of party loyalty that builds in turnout failure as one form of disloyalty, and we then assess the impact of campaign themes, issue positions, and group feelings on the failure to go to the polls. Among some target groups from the opposition party, the rival party's themes attract defectors, but among other groups the themes yield turnout failure. All three—turnout, defection, and abstention—can push a presidential campaign toward its goal of victory on election day. Party elites have been remarkably candid in public talk about "stimulating the base," using "wedge issues" on vulnerable parts of the opposition, and seeking to keep part of the opponent's peripheral and even core constituencies at home (cf. Edsall 1999, A1).

The reader will quickly notice that a disproportionate share of our attention focuses on cultural appeals by the Republican party, as the minority party throughout the post–New Deal. Some observers, however, have claimed that the Republican party became the new majority (or plurality) party during President Reagan's first term. They argue that the proof is either in continued Republican victories or that Democratic defection in presidential contests was so habitual that a system of national Republican and local Democratic identification replaced totally aligned Democrats (see Ladd 1981 for an early formulation of this argument). Joining most voting behavior scholars, we argue to the contrary. The time-series data from NES (see chapter 7), the Gallup organization, the Times-Mirror surveys (Shafer and Claggett 1995), and the macropartisanship studies (MacKuen, Erikson, and Stimson 1989) remove any doubt: however measured, with the exception of one month following the 1994 election, either the majority or more likely the plurality of party identifiers remained Democratic. Although the year 2000 may have ushered in a new era—and the end of the era we have attended—the Republican party has yet to gain the plurality of identifiers, at the same time it controlled both branches of the national government and both branches of the majority of state governments.

One final matter must be addressed before embarking on this study: the reader's possible surmise that this book addresses the darker forces in American politics, that it deals with "demagogic appeals" to "irrational" impulses, that its substance is limited to "negative politics." Political elites, as noted in the earlier quotation from Wirthlin, study the electorate to find out what matters to them and to locate strategically important sectors of the electorate who could determine the outcome in a given presidential election. Our approach does not see their activity as the exploitation of dark psychological forces. We expect politicians to act like politicians. From our observations of them, they operate by three cardinal rules: (1) What a politician wants most is a place in the sun, to be out front, to have the opportunity to make decisions. (2) Most politicians would rather be live politicians than dead statesmen or stateswomen. (3) In politics they will get what they can and tolerate what they must. Paraphrasing old-time journalist John T. McCutcheon, one of our students argued that the term "ambitious politician" is a "repetitive redundancy." In short, this book is couched in *ambition theory* (Schlesinger 1966).

From the other side of the campaign relationship, voters typically do have value cores, and in general ways understand which candidate shares or at least espouses their values (Popkin 1991). Some things bother some voters. Some things are not right. Midlevel managers, downsized out of jobs in the 1980s while young Wall Street arbitrageurs played the merger mania for all it was worth, came to dislike the people who profited from the trickle-down economy; eventually they punished the Reagan-Bush regime. In their minds, these greedy profiteers were not civic-minded Republicans who lived by the rules. Democratic politicians played to their estrangement. In like manner, middle-American Catholic women who had long experienced pay discrimination welcomed ratification of the Equal Rights Amendment. But when the women's movement in the later 1970s enjoined an agenda of ERA, abortion rights, equality of opportunity in the military, and approval of lesbianism as true feminism, these Catholic women hoisted anchor. They listened to Republican politicians who said the values of these feminists are not the values of Catholic mothers and working women. Opponents, of course, will cry foul, charging "class warfare" or "gender bashing," respectively. But among the people who sense something is not right, they do not feel their darkest psychological recesses are being manipulated by cunning politicians. They consider the conflict over values, over the role of government in achieving society's goals, to be real. They consider attention to such themes to be legitimate.

Informally, the gatekeepers in the American political system set up boundaries on cultural content and campaign discourse. When gatekeeper consensus says a boundary has been traversed, political elites backpedal with retracted ads or scapegoating a "distant" organization beyond the control of the central campaign apparatus. The 1988 Bush campaign, particularly the different versions of the Willie Horton ad, is a case in point. (These are discussed in chapter 6.) By informed accounts, Lee Atwater, the campaign manager, knew that the issue was not simply the prison furlough but a racially charged fear of crime, specifically, in his words, "a big black rapist." While the official campaign organization quickly withdrew the original ad and Vice President Bush disavowed it, an even more explicit racial version continued to run in many locales, along with printed material. The press, as one gatekeeper, did not let the public forget this transgression of the boundaries on cultural discourse. While many other ads and speeches with explicit cultural content have aired during the post–New Deal period, none has so clearly made the public aware of legitimate boundaries on campaigners' actions and voters' values, aspirations, and fears.

With these statements of the puzzle, the argument, basic assumptions, caveats, and disclaimers, we now embark on the project. Part 1 will develop a cultural theory of American politics sufficiently, we hope, to understand presidential campaign dynamics. It is not designed to speak directly to the "culture wars" thesis but to social scientists who are trying to make analytical sense of American political campaigns in the post–New Deal period. At the same time, we hope that scholars who contribute to the culture wars literature will find that our analyses give pause for thought. While culture war theory may arguably do a good job of delineating conflicting worldviews, it says very little about the process by which such differences are politicized, and it contributes no empirical tests that would illuminate the *translation* mechanisms. As Elaine Sharp's recent volume (1999) indicates, it is not enough to note the salience of cultural differences and then assume some automatic translation into political positions. What is problematic is the manner in which such differences are placed on the electoral agenda. We are not satisfied with a theory that puts politicization in a black box, drawing a straight line, for example, from religion to culture to politics. Unlike culture war theory, we assume considerable autonomy for the political impulse, an autonomy strong enough to shape any stage of an apparent teleological process. We expect politicians to act like politicians. They recognize that to accomplish any normative purpose for society, they must seek and stay in power. Voters are their resources. To mention two recent examples of the political impulse among apparent ideologues: witness the transformation of the ideologically purist Class of 1994 in Congress into seasoned political survivors by 1998, or the evolution of 1960s' radicals into legislative leaders at the state and federal levels. Both Max Weber and Reinhold Niebuhr urged social scientists to be alert to the autonomy of the political, even within the web of culture.

After a narrative history of the period and an introduction to our analytical tools, Part 2 will present three case studies of cultural political strategies and outcomes, dealing with patriotism and nationalism, race, gender, and religion. The section will conclude with a reiteration of empirical findings and a discussion of the quest for efficient cultural symbols in American presidential campaigns.

CHAPTER TWO

The Political Mobilization of Cultural Differences

MOST POLITICAL SCIENTISTS' understanding of the concept "culture" comes from the anthropological tradition. We strive to move beyond this *static, unitary* conception of culture that largely claims consensus in modern societies. Instead, we argue for a *dynamic, diffuse* definition rooted in the competing notions of how we should and should not live— the moral order. Politics becomes cultural politics when competition over the moral order is at stake in a campaign. Crucially, however, this conception of cultural politics is not limited to a preordained set of "moral issues." Just as science finds its identity in its methodology instead of its subject matter, cultural politics defines itself by the style of argumentation over public policy instead of the type of public policy. In this chapter we outline our understanding of culture, the necessary conditions for cultural politics, and the main mechanisms and forces driving cultural conflict in the post–New Deal era.

On the opening night of the 1992 Republican convention, a speaker told the assembled delegates that the ensuing election "was about who we are . . . what we believe and what we stand for as Americans" (Buchanan 1992). The choice was between the incumbent, "a champion of the Judeo-Christian values and beliefs upon which this America was founded," and a challenger associated with "unrestricted abortion on demand," the "raw sewage of pornography," gay rights, disrespect for marriage and family, and various other insults to America's core values. The forthcoming election was not a mere squabble about who gets what, but a "religious war" for the very soul of America. He enjoined his listeners not just to win the forthcoming election but, far more ambitiously, to join his crusade to "take back our culture and take back our country" from the alien values infecting it.

These charges were echoed three nights later in a defiant acceptance speech by the Republican vice presidential nominee. Dan Quayle told the audience: "The gap between us and our opponents is a cultural divide. It is not just a difference between conservative and liberal. It is a difference between fighting for what is right and refusing to see what is wrong" (Quayle 1992a). The core of the difference between the two sides, he declared, was the pernicious assumption by "Hollywood and the media elite" that all lifestyles were morally equivalent and equally worthy of respect. Rejecting this decadent view, the vice president put himself among those who embraced the "traditional values of middle America," the values he had learned from a small-town childhood "built around family, public schools, Little League baseball and church on Sunday." He predicted the Republican party would win because it alone espoused the institutions and values treasured by the American people. Over the course of the convention, speaker after speaker similarly portrayed the Republican party as the embodiment of America's cultural heritage and cast the Democrats as apostates from those norms.

These comments and similar remarks by other speakers were not isolated afterthoughts or the ravings of marginal figures given national television time to vent their extremist sentiments. Nor was their prominence the product of inattention to details by convention organizers, as some commentators suspected. Rather, they reflected a calculated effort by some in the Republican party to define the 1992 election as a referendum on cultural trends. Recognizing that their White House tenure was endangered by a weak economy and the opposition's persuasive young, yet culturally vulnerable, candidate, these Republicans staked their reelection on a campaign emphasizing fidelity to what was variously called "family" or "traditional" values. The goal, according to one Republican strategist, was to position the Republican candidate "as the proponent of fundamental social norms" regarding sexual behavior, family, and work while painting the Democrats as "advocates of individual fulfillment, without regard to generally held values and beliefs" (Edsall 1992).

We can hear in these comments a sustained effort at *social categorization*, the psychological process by which a party, group, or social movement claims a common identity and asserts privileged cultural or political status. There is a determined effort to claim the moral high ground by insisting that "our" party represents the majority tradition and "they" do not. This is followed by an indictment of "them" for associating with all sorts of disreputable groups and values—in the case of Bill Clinton, the unholy litany of abortionists, gays, radical feminists, and pornographers whom Pat Buchanan imagined at center stage of the Democratic convention. This association was forged symbolically in May, when Dan Quayle demonized television's fictional Murphy Brown for glorifying childbearing out of wedlock, and it was reinforced in August when the Democratic candidate's wife, Hillary Rodham Clinton, was painted as a domineering woman who believed that marriage and family were akin to slavery and the Indian reservation. Finally, the process was connected to politics by the assertion that "their" practices were responsible for "our" problems. By emphasizing alternate lifestyles and apologizing for deviance, "they" had knocked the props out from under "our" culture and encouraged behavior that threatened "our" security and well-being. The strategy of promoting cultural conflict, of demonizing opponents as alien or "the other," could not have been clearer or more deliberate.

The events in Houston that summer revealed with stunning clarity the crucial role of cultural values in America's central political ritual, the nomination and election of the president. A frequent observer of national political conventions thought she had seen in the 1992 campaign the seeds of a new framework for political conflict in America:

> [T]he realignment of the next twenty years will transform the nature of partisan competition from a mere fight for office to a surrogate civil war. Each party, and its candidates, will be the carrier of a conflicting cluster of values. The winner will get to decide the role of government, or each of the many governments in our federal system, in promulgating those values. Culture, not class or economics, will define the great political debates of the 21st century. (Freeman 1993, 27)

While such a monolithic assertion may be overstated, our task in this book is to help understand how and why such cultural divisions have become so prominent in American political life and the role they played in destabilizing the New Deal party system.

CULTURAL POLITICS AS CAMPAIGN STRATEGY

At the outset, we stress two points. First, the cultural dimension of the 1992 campaign was not unique, a single-election phenomenon that can be explained away by the political context of that year. It was a durable strategy that was used with more or less vigor from one election to the next throughout the post–New Deal era. Second, using cultural division as a political tactic is not guaranteed to work. Both these assumptions need to be established in order to justify our belief that cultural politics is an intellectual problem worthy of sustained attention.

The "family values" approach was not pioneered in 1992. Cultural themes have a long history in American political life and have been a staple of political campaigns in the recent past. Indeed, George Bush's deployment of "traditional values" against the Democrats in 1992 drew heavily on the symbols and motif of the Reagan-Bush campaigns of 1980 and 1984 and his own successful election in 1988. When Ronald Reagan first ran for the presidency in 1980, his campaign pursued what was called "a strategy of values" (White 1990). In the same way that the Democrats had come to embody fairness and compassion in the 1930s, deploying these values against successive generations of Republican candidates, Reagan consciously set out to persuade the electorate that his party—not the "mutant" strain of Democrats who had taken over Franklin D. Roosevelt's party—now represented the core values of American culture—family, work, neighborhood, peace, and freedom. The combination of "populist cultural values and nationalistic foreign policy" was thought to be the best way Republicans could detach sizable numbers of erstwhile Democrats from their traditional partisan habits (Shafer 1989). The strategy was renewed in 1984, when Republicans argued that the administration had restored America's pride and self-esteem, and was used to particularly good effect in 1988 when former Vice President Bush ran for the presidency on his own. Faced with widespread public doubts about Bush's strength of character and a Democratic nominee with some record of achievement, the Republican campaign decided to push a number of hot-button issues where Governor Michael Dukakis could be portrayed as a dangerous liberal out of touch with the values of the United States. Thus the Democratic nominee's veto of a bill mandating the Pledge of Allegiance in public schools was framed as unpatriotic; his prison work-release program, cited as evidence of softness on crime and, by implication, a tool of racial minorities, and many other gubernatorial actions were similarly mined for their symbolic utility. So successful was this strategy of "faith, family, flags and furloughs" (White 1990, 154), so much had Republicans "taken custody" of family values, that Dukakis's campaign manager later acknowledged that Democrats were presumed guilty of deviance by the electorate: "It is politically dangerous to take for granted that voters will automatically assume the Democratic candidate holds dear the country's basic values: God, patriotism, family, and freedom. In some historically perverse way, Democrats must—at least for now—work hard to somehow prove they are as politically wholesome and decent as Republicans" (quoted in White 1990, 156).

Actually, the use of cultural approbation in campaigns has an even earlier pedigree. In 1972, for example, George McGovern was memorably portrayed as the candidate of "acid, amnesty, and abortion." Four years earlier, Richard Nixon and George Wallace had successfully linked the Democratic party to vivid and unpopular images of demonstrations, riots, and civil unrest. In turn, Nixon and Wallace drew on the ideas and strategies pursued by Barry Goldwater, the Republican nominee of 1964. The strategy of politicizing cultural and group differences did not begin in 1992 but was "a 30-year, sustained Republican drive to portray Democrats as soft on crime, more sympathetic to perpetrators than victims, anti-military, tax raisers, lobbyists for the welfare state and puppets of black and other minority special-interest groups" (Edsall 1998). In fact, the language of "culture wars" is now employed retrospectively to rationalize some of the abuses of power that led to the downfall of the Nixon Administration; John H. Taylor, executive director of the Nixon Library, argued: "Richard Nixon was a wartime commander-in-chief. *We were in a culture war then*. And what the culture tends to remember as the domestic abuses of Watergate can only be understood in the context of these challenges" (Weiner 1999).

The technique was not limited to Republicans. In 1964 at the height of the civil rights consensus, Lyndon Johnson tarred Barry Goldwater with the endorsement of the Grand Dragon of the Ku Klux Klan. Democrats consistently portrayed Republican leaders as the tools of Wall Street financiers, the enemies of working families. In elections from the late 1980s onward, the Democrats similarly accused Republicans of representing theocrats who intended to undermine the separation of church and state and use government to regulate intimate behavior.

Many historians claim that themes of cultural conflict dominated American political life until the New Deal. In making this claim, these historians explicitly challenge an older historical synthesis that emphasized the paramount role played by questions of national economic policy. They do not deny palpable evidence that political elites debated economic issues but contend that these issues were understood at the grass roots through a cultural matrix (Benson 1961; Formisano 1971; 1983; Hays 1980; Jensen 1971; Kleppner 1970; 1979; McCormick 1974; 1986; Swierenga 1990). As James E. Wright summarized the interaction between these two perspectives, "National political debate may well have focused on economic issues such as the tariff, but community reference groups and cultural values provided the basis for electoral cleavage.... the real issues of politics have been those most significant relative to lifestyle and values: prohibition, public financing or control of sectarian schools, sabbatarian laws, woman suffrage and efforts to hasten or retard ethnic assimilation" (1973, 655).

Even when the issue was ostensibly economic in nature, as in the slavery debate, the citizenry was often encouraged to interpret it in a cultural mode. Slavery could thus be attacked by abolitionists as a sinful and immoral practice that violated fundamental social values, as an assault upon the Northern way of life rooted in free labor, or, by utilizing negative reference groups, as a practice associated with despised blacks and Southerners. By framing the question in such terms, it could easily be assimilated to the preexisting cultural images of the national parties (McCormick 1974). Politicians of the past, no less than their present-day counterparts, understood that voters were most easily mobilized when they believed an issue touched upon basic cultural preferences (Oestreicher 1988). The phenomenon we are investigating, the use of cultural themes and appeals in electoral politics, is not new, and we are merely extending the perspective to contemporary politics.

Like all political plans, the politicization of group differences may or may not work. The provisional consensus from 1992 is that the culture war theme failed the Republicans because it did not secure the reelection of the Bush-Quayle ticket. Some commentators went further, arguing that the bitter tone of many speeches at the Republican convention alienated a number of moderate Republicans, particularly women, and sensitized many voters to be wary of candidates pledging themselves to do cultural battle (Wolfe 1998). That may be why Bush suffered crucial defections to Ross Perot from normally Republican voters far less conservative or militant on social issues than loyalist Republicans (Abramowitz 1995; Ladd 1993; Miller and Shanks 1996). The apparent failure of Republican cultural themes may also be traced to the counterstrategy pursued by Democrats who labored hard to blur the differences between the parties over such contentious issues as abortion, crime, and school prayer and kept the mind of the electorate focused firmly on the state of the national economy. Given this plan of attack, Democratic campaign managers situated the party's nominee firmly in middle America, emphasizing his modest social beginnings, his roots in the South, and his deep attachment to the small-town ethos of America. Voters heard about Bill Clinton's fondness for choir singing and revivalism, and they heard the candidate speak in Biblical language of a "new Covenant" that would bind citizens to government through the principle of moral responsibility. In exploiting Bill Clinton's gubernatorial record, Democrats reminded voters of his "workfare" policies and support for the death penalty, themes likely to appeal to social conservatives (Edsall 1992). Clinton also took the advice of those who urged him to "speak American" by stressing his belief in the uniqueness of the nation, its mission to the world, and its embrace of traditional values (Kusnet 1992). These themes were intended to reassure voters that Clinton was not from the values fringe, to diminish the electoral salience of the cultural divide, and so to enable the Democrats to turn the election into a referendum on the state of the economy and Republican economic management.

To do so, it was also necessary for the Democrats to broaden the meaning attached by the electorate to such potent symbols as "family" and "tradition." In the Republican version, families were threatened most fundamentally by changing social norms. How could young people acquire a belief in the sanctity of marriage and family when the media glorified mindless, irresponsible sex, inflamed men with erotic images, and preached the siren call of moral relativism? How could we expect the poor and downtrodden to work their way patiently out of poverty when young women squandered their youth by having babies, and young men, the fathers of the children born out of wedlock, were encouraged by the government to abdicate parental responsibility? Without strong, two-parent households, the poor would remain trapped in desperate circumstances, unable to emulate the success of previous generations in climbing their way into middle-class status. Referring to the social conditions that explained the Los Angeles riots of 1992, the vice president asserted that "The intergenerational poverty that troubles us so much today is predominantly a poverty of values" (Quayle 1992b). The poor suffered and, by turning to crime, threatened the rest of us—all because of social disorganization stemming from deficient family values. Late in the decade, Republican leaders employed similar logic to assign blame to middle-class families for school shootings in Littleton, Colorado, and other locales.

The Democrats offered an alternative interpretation of what ailed the American family. Exploiting Quayle's attack on single-parent families, Democrats insisted on extending social respect to many types of family units that did not meet the two-parent model. They attributed family breakdown to economic and social barriers. In Bill Clinton's perspective, "we have so many children in so much trouble in so many cities . . . because they have seen so little opportunity, so little responsibility, and so little community that they literally cannot imagine the kind of life we are calling them to lead" (Clinton 1992). To climb out of poverty and achieve stable, two-parent families, the poor needed not just belief in family but the *resources* to realize the vision: generous policies of maternity leave, ample child-care facilities, guaranteed health care, determined antipoverty initiatives, and greater investment in job training and education. Further, Democrats charged, if anybody had abandoned the values that sustained American progress, it was the Republicans. By giving huge tax breaks to the wealthy, finding the funds to bail out profligate savings and loans, preaching "family values" to the poor but not to those who got ahead by deceit and dishonesty, the Republicans had undermined Americans' belief in the value of hard work as the way up the economic ladder. Thus, Democrats attempted to tilt the banner of "family values" in a way that complemented the party's overriding strategic objective of making Bush's economic policies the major issue in the campaign.

The varying power of cultural appeals was dramatically on display in the next three national elections. Just two years after neutralizing the Republican advantage on the moral economy, the Democrats in 1994 found themselves very much on the defensive. President Clinton's campaign pledge to repeal the military's ban on gays offered one promising target in the battle over cultural norms. Clinton also drew fire from gun enthusiasts when he supported a ban on the importation of automatic weapons. He also battled well-publicized charges that he had engaged in extramarital affairs and pushed unwanted sexual attention on female state employees in Arkansas. Collectively, these incidents raised anew public doubts about whether Democrats represented the cultural mainstream, permitting the Republicans to claim the mantle of cultural restoration and to win back many conservative voters who had supported Clinton in 1992. The subsequent collapse of Democratic electoral fortunes in the South was succinctly attributed to "God, gays, and guns," a summary of the party's lapses from moral orthodoxy on several issues that define traditional values.

Beyond simply attacking Clinton, the Republicans offered their own package of cultural values in 1994. Consider the cultural perspective embedded in the proposed changes in public welfare outlined in the "Contract with America." Implicit in the Republican version of welfare reform was the normative image of the desirable family as a heterosexual household with two married parents; families who fit the model were to be provided subsidies in the form of tax credits and other extended benefits. Those who deviated from the standard, such as single women who bore children out of wedlock, were denied aid and tax subsidies and were threatened with the loss of their children. The politicization of moral logic was clear in the comments of a Republican leader on the House floor:

> What the Democrats are defending with the harsh, unreal, and irresponsible talk are programs that are immoral and corrupt. It is immoral to take money from decent, middle-class Americans who work for everything they have and give it to people who think they are owed the money for doing nothing. . . . It is immoral to consign poor people to lives of living hell as government dependents so that politicians and bureaucrats can maintain power. . . . It is corrupt to pick on the most vulnerable people in our society, the children and the poor, to maintain one's own political power base. Yet that is what this debate has revealed about the opponents of welfare reform. (quoted in Edsall 1997, 139–40)

A similar moral calculus was apparent in proposals to abolish the National Endowment for Arts and the Corporation for Public Broadcasting. Though presented publicly as efforts to reduce nonessential government spending, these initiatives were animated by the desire to "defund" agencies perceived to glorify homosexuality, mock religious faith, and desecrate sacred symbols.

As perceived by conservative commentator Fred Barnes (1995), the entire Republican legislative agenda was fueled by a persistent ambition to repeal the 1960s "counterculture," repudiate the bearers of that cultural revolution (variously represented as "McGovernites," "hippies," and "radicals"), and dismantle the programs enacted under their influence. Rather than use government to remedy the consequences of social problems or extend the scope of individual rights, the traditional Democratic strategy, the Republicans saw government as an agent to promote individual and family responsibility. Welfare would be reformed by forcing people off of state support and onto their own resources. Crime would be managed by building more prisons and filling them with criminals serving longer sentences under harsher conditions. The public school system would become a vehicle for moral training. Far from the antistatist perspective of traditional conservatism, this new incarnation perceived government "as an evangelical positive force to raise the level of individual morality" (Edsall 1997, 142).

Many Republicans expected the same cultural themes to bring them the White House two years later. As outlined by House Speaker Newt Gingrich, the grand plan was to portray Bill Clinton as the enemy of the "values majority" in the United States (Thomas 1996a). This proposal was built on the premise of a nation divided into camps of "Clinton liberals" and "the rest of us." "The Clinton liberals are centralized in Washington. The rest of us are back home with our families, relating better to local government and local leaders. The Clinton liberals believe in 'compassionate bureaucracy.' The rest of us believe in a compassionate society filled with good people." Accentuating the value differences, the plan's author contended that the Democrats intended to perpetuate programs "that mire people in poverty, ignorance, addiction, alcoholism and entitlements" while the other camp hoped to "liberate" people to achieve "self-reliance, responsibility, productivity, achievement and the pursuit of happiness." Although faint echoes of this approach could be heard in the stump speech of the Republican nominee later in the fall (Seelye 1996), the strategy failed largely because the Democrats positioned their presidential candidate closer to the center. Having been once burned by Republicans for his support of gay rights, Clinton announced his support for congressional action to ban same-sex marriages. He showed so much enthusiasm for school uniforms, antismoking initiatives, the "V-chip" technology, youth curfews, and sexual abstinence programs that one columnist chided him as a candidate for "Daddy in Chief" (Dowd 1996). And his supporters, particularly women's rights groups, went on the cultural offensive by associating the Republican leadership with "theocrats" who threatened the separation of church and state. Unless Clinton were reelected, they warned, both ends of Pennsylvania Avenue would be turned over to people who wanted to control what went on in people's bedrooms. While advocates of the "values strategy" predictably blamed the Republican defeat on its half-hearted embrace of cultural politics (Thomas 1996b), most commentators believed that Clinton won because of a robust economy and because his skillful co-optation of these issues earned him considerable support from moderate Republicans and Independents.

Clinton's 1996 victory was quickly undermined by allegations of sexual misconduct that began to dominate the evening news. Although many commentators referred to the subsequent Clinton-Lewinsky scandal as a morality play, we view it as another installment of cultural politics. It began with ambitious politicians seeking to restore influence in the wake of a bitter election defeat. In the process, these elites campaigned to focus the political process on behavior that would once have been regarded as private and irrelevant to governance—as it was so regarded for some of Clinton's predecessors from both parties. The effort was driven by activists who had found Clinton morally objectionable since he first emerged as a serious presidential candidate. The strategy was to interpret Clinton's behavior as both symbol and product of the excesses of the 1960s' hedonism.

The "politics of righteousness" that developed during the scandal had at least two noteworthy features that are redolent of cultural politics. First, among the Republican prosecutors in the impeachment trial, there was a palpable need to punish. Clinton had to be held up to scorn, condemned, ridiculed, dismissed from office in disgrace. For all the talk about rule of law, this seemed like an exercise much more steeped in punitiveness than justice. As we shall observe in chapter 3, the moral order is often reaffirmed by the harsh treatment of deviants. By imposing severe sanctions on those who stray, the power of the dominant order is ratified. Second, the affair generated what some regarded as a form of "sexual McCarthyism" that ironically ended the political careers of two prominent Republican congressional opponents and did permanent damage to several others. The theorists whom we examine in chapter 4 note that morally unsettling times often produce urgent calls for cultural purges. The 1990s were certainly unsettling in terms of male-female relationships, with battles of particular ferocity breaking out over sexual harassment in the workplace, marital fidelity, and other domains. Such an atmosphere generates a call for moral clarity that may take the form of scapegoating and other actions intended to reestablish moral order. As if on cue, one of the intellectual leaders of cultural conservatism called Clinton's impeachment "an enormous emetic—culturally, politically, morally" that would "purge us" (quoted in Powell 1998). As we point out in chapter 4, public rituals are often aimed at restoring the moral order in times of great cultural ambiguity.

The Republicans lost badly, partly as a result of their decision to center the 1998 campaign on Clinton's infidelity. Performing well below expectations for an opposition party facing an incumbent in the sixth year of his term, they gained no net Senate seats and managed to lose five seats from their majority in the House of Representatives. Shaken by Democratic counterattacks that portrayed them as vindictive and judgmental, out of touch with public opinion, Republicans pledged to retreat from such efforts in the 2000 campaign.

In fact, the Republican presidential campaign of 2000 did seem to have learned the lessons of the preceding decade. Under the direction of Karl Rove, Governor Bush was made to project a much softer image, and the cultural themes, though present, were advanced in a muted fashion. Bush invoked moral traditionalism primarily through a personal narrative of his wastrel youth, religious conversion, and personal rebirth. Not a family with even passing exposure to religion has failed to number a prodigal in its midst—one who squandered the birthright for a youthful adventure but who had seen the light and come back. His acceptance address and repeated campaign trail references treated religion as a source of character. He reasserted civil religion both as the belief that God had called America to a higher purpose and as the belief that leadership requires personal righteousness. Never far from Bush's own personal example and his pledge to "make you proud of the White House again" were his references to the Clinton White House. Like Jimmy Carter in 1976, every campaign speech included a reference to the lack of integrity or decency in the people's White House. Bush appeared simple, honest, and anchored. He had inoculated his past by the prodigal metaphor.

He was in every respect one of us. He was an oil entrepreneur and a major league baseball owner—a risk-taking businessman and sportsman. He was a middling student, not overwhelmed with learning but a school booster, one of the boys, and a charmer with the girls—one of us. Like both enterprisers and moralists, he considered taxation and government spending the tools that allowed faithless, clueless bureaucrats and judges to order our lives into unfamiliar moral orders. If government is not the enemy, it is our friend only when it allies with endeavors of our private collective choosing. Rove fashioned Bush as a "compassionate conservative," one dedicated to getting the government out of places it did not belong, but still recognizing human need and seeking solutions through public/private partnerships. The "faith-based initiative" became the showpiece of this strategy to occupy the moral center. At the same time that Bush co-opted the language of "leaving no child behind," he continued the uses of code words (see Gilens 1999) to describe his welfare, employment, and minorities policies.

To offset the images of exclusivity and rigidity that he had inherited from previous Republican campaigns and the militant GOP leadership in Congress, the candidate surrounded himself with those outside the party core—African Americans, Latinos, working single mothers, Catholic bishops and priests, even gay leaders. Although some would argue that the effort did not pay dividends in broadening the coalition, that was not the point. The objective was to show that Bush was broad-minded enough to associate with those not like us. Rather than being a cultural warrior or an elitist, he was indeed a compassionate conservative. No one should leave the party because Bush did not care enough for those outside the party.

The Democratic nominee worked equally hard to occupy the same space but was too tarred by his association with Bill Clinton to escape responsibility for what many Americans perceived as a moral failure. An effective vice president with a copious appetite for policy details, Gore had also been the faithful lieutenant when his boss got into trouble. Clinton was a liar, of that the country was convinced. No matter how incredulous Gore had looked in joint public appearances with Clinton, he had not withdrawn support. But now when there were no longer grand high executioners or hypocritical adulterers pursuing Clinton, Gore had to convince the nation he was credible within normal standards of personal integrity.

Gore did have bona fide religious credentials and, like most Americans, believed in God, thought religion was a source of the greatness of America, and went to church sporadically. He had attended divinity school for a time while he tried to make sense of a world that had spun out of intelligibility by the 1960s. Even more, he chose centrist colleague Senator Joseph Lieberman as his running mate. An observant Jew, Lieberman had long been comfortable with discourse that acknowledged both private religion and public effects. Lieberman was one Democrat who did not contribute to a naked public square. He could come to Catholics and racial minorities as one of us, just as he could remind mainline Protestants of the responsibility to demand limits on gratuitous sex and violence in the entertainment industry. He too could talk Tocquevillian in the understanding that democracy does not work well without consensual public morals. Just as Bush's diversity props may have given credibility to his compassionate conservatism, so Gore and Lieberman's facility with God talk—within bounds—may have stanched the flow of some moderately religious but morally respectable people away from the Democrats.

The Democratic campaign also went on the offensive. Gore used the languages of justice and stewardship to castigate: "the richest 1 percent," "big oil," "big polluters," "greedy pharmaceuticals." He kept his ties to black churches and labor union leaders. Although personally hoping the incidence of abortion would be minimal, he reminded feminists that Bush would be choosing judges, and "a woman's right to choose" hung in the balance. He advocated always for "the middle class," "the working families." While the former reminded business and professional women that they would lose control over whether and when during their careers to have a baby, the latter reminded those not benefited by tax policies or the access that comes from campaign contributions that they would lose a friend in the White House.

In the end, fully 44 percent of the voting electorate considered the Clinton sexual peccadilloes important in their vote choice. At least 15 percent of Bush's voters, according to exit polls, were Democratic crossovers. Of those who ranked honesty and trustworthiness more important than issue positions, 78 percent chose Bush and 16 percent Gore. The Republicans managed to avoid the mistakes of the previous elections with a much more sophisticated cultural offensive. This played no small role in their victory (such as it was) in an election when the economy decisively favored the incumbent Democrats.

The results of elections from 1992 through 2000 underline the variability of the values strategy. The political mobilization of cultural differences may work in some contexts and fail in others depending upon the tenor of the times, the skill of the campaign, and other contextual forces. Simply put, what we describe as the politicization of cultural differences is a variable and, as such, should be susceptible to scientific analysis and explanation. That is one task of this book: to set the agenda for understanding the sources and impacts of such a strategy in American electoral politics.

CULTURE IN POLITICS AND POLITICAL SCIENCE

Most anthropological definitions of culture emphasize the unitary, the common qualities of habit and mind, the ways of life that suffuse a society (Reading 1977). When political scientists borrowed the term from anthropology, they similarly appropriated the perspective of culture as a common bond: "political culture" denoted values about government widely diffused among the population under study (Almond and Verba 1963). In the structural-functional framework of scholars who attempted to identify the institutions responsible for the operation and preservation of the political system, culture was normally conceived as a force promoting continuity and equilibrium.[1]

We share with students of political culture a sense that the phenomenon of culture encompasses norms deemed legitimate or authoritative by the arbiters of the society. In the words of Kroeber and Kluckhohn (cited in Gould and Kolb 1964, 165), "the essential core of culture consists of traditional (i.e., historically derived and selected) ideas and especially their attached values." Even more on target, Kluckhohn and Kelley isolated the essential quality of culture as offering "explicit and implicit designs for living" (166), or what has more recently been labeled as the *moral order* (Wuthnow 1987). Geertz (1973) uses the term "template" to describe the ordered life of obligations that culture prescribes.

While we share Geertz's and Wuthnow's interest in the prescriptive

---

[1] The emphasis on stability and continuity is precisely why cultural models are presumed incapable of explaining change (cf. Eckstein 1988). We will deal with the theme later on.

qualities of culture, we join critics who question the unitary nature of culture in society. By asserting a very high level of cultural consensus as the norm in modern societies, assuming that certain core ideas and social values are widely diffused among the entire population, this traditional approach fails to recognize the essential contentiousness that surrounds culture. The mere continuity of a society gives no warrant for assuming that all or most citizens share common values. Rather than taking cultural homogeneity as the norm, recent scholarship has treated culture as "heterogeneous in content and function" (DiMaggio 1997, 267). In deciding on strategies of action, individuals are not constrained by a singular set of values but may pick and choose from a "toolkit of symbols, stories, rituals and world-views" (Swidler 1986, 273). Precisely because there are so many discordant models offering diverse perspectives, the "culture" that individuals construct inside their heads manages to integrate elements from many different worldviews. There are, in other words, multiple sources of cultural norms and values, and the differences among them provide fertile opportunity for political mobilization.

Hence, we want to shift the emphasis of scholarly discourse from cultural consensus to conflicts about the content and meaning of the culture in apparently stable polities. *Cultural conflict* is simply *argument (and associated behavior) about how we should live*, what Wildavsky (1987) called the most fundamental question facing any society. *Political conflicts* warrant the label of *culture conflicts* when they involve disagreement about what the society should or does prescribe as the *appropriate way of life*. It is not just about preference ordering; it deals with what is perceived as right and wrong, us versus them. This approach also entails an emphasis on subcultures, groups that persist within the larger society but maintain their own parochial views of the ordered life. While they may recognize that the claims of society as a whole are legitimate in a pragmatic sense—how else could the subculture persist if the society did not allow it leeway to practice and propound its values—the subculture may still feel that its way of life is superior, ordained of God, or "natural" and may either maintain it in a separatistic manner or propound it in hopes of transforming the larger society.

Often "cultural politics" is equated with a particular subset of political themes—currently, issues of sexual behavior and identity, the social content of mass media, equality of opportunity, the permissible limits of religious expression in public life—and embodied in specific conflicts over abortion, the legal rights of homosexuals, school prayer, free speech, affirmative action, the boundaries between public and private, and so forth. While these controversies certainly warrant the label of cultural issues, cultural politics is not wholly circumscribed by them. In speaking of a cultural approach to politics, we wish to emphasize not just the *sub-*

ject matter of a political debate—particular issues involving abortion, women's rights, school prayer—but rather *any political controversy that turns on conflicts about social values, norms, and symbolic community boundaries.* As we understand cultural politics, the phenomenon is woven into argumentation about public policy on a wide range of subjects. That is, we recognize a *style* or manner in which politics is contested that incorporates cultural argument.

Many political debates that appear to rest on the narrow grounds of self-interest ultimately turn on judgments about the norms and standards that should govern our behavior. For example, the United States began to debate educational standards in the 1980s after alarming statistics about illiteracy had raised fears about the nation's capacity to maintain economic competitiveness. As Carmody and Carmody (1990, 3) observe, deeper reflection suggested that this policy debate was really about priorities in resource allocation—how does our obligation to ensure a productive life for our children compare to the need to defend ourselves against external enemies, combat drug abuse, or assure the elderly of quality medical care? And, "If one continues with questions of this sort, and does not turn aside because of fatigue, fear, or challenges to the superficial thinking that dominates most political activity, one is bound to come upon explicitly religious issues. For what have human beings been given existence? In what terms ought a society to calculate the good life? Who are the models of ripe humanity that one's group ought to follow?" These questions lead inescapably to a larger existential dilemma—does anything matter given the reality of the grave? Thus, because cultural questions are almost invariably at the root of political debates, it is easy to assume that all politics are at base "cultural."

With such an expansive view of the political universe, is there anything that is not somehow a matter of culture? Have we subsumed everything under that label? If the concept of cultural politics is to have any analytic value, it is essential to delimit it. We will spell out in the next two chapters our understanding of the politics of cultural differences, but for now it is necessary to indicate the ways in which we envision such politics and how that style of political conflict differs from other forms of competition.

The Nature of Cultural Conflicts in Politics

Considering how "operationally refractory" the concept of culture has been (Pye 1968), it is not surprising that it is difficult to distinguish between cultural and other types of political conflicts. We make no pretense of drawing a hard and fast line between cultural and noncultural conflicts. As we have argued, *cultural politics is less a set of issues than a style of argumentation that invokes fundamental social values and emphasizes group differences.* In addition, cultural conflicts tend to exhibit certain qualities that distinguish them from other kinds of political debates.

Cultural issues seem to evince the qualities that Carmines and Stimson (1980) designated as "easy" issues. Issues are "easy" for the electorate to comprehend and act upon when they exhibit three qualities. First, easy issues are symbolic rather than technical. They are easy for elites to communicate to voters, and voters may interpret them simplistically. This situation is enhanced when the issue can be portrayed in terms of salient images and symbols, a point we will emphasize in the next chapter. Second, a political question may be said to merit the "easy issue" label when it deals with ends rather than means. A question debated in terms of policy alternatives is unlikely to engage the electorate precisely because it requires a considerable framework of information to decipher. But when the terms of debate arise from "the normative preferences of the mass culture," one needs only to have been socialized in the culture to find the issue compelling. That quality was clearly evident in the debates over constitutional reform in post-Occupation Japan. Relatively abstruse questions about education, police, and labor legislation resonated deeply with conservative activists who, though lacking in ideology, "'feel' deep distrust and even hatred toward what seems to be a destroyer of traditional values" and so interpreted socialist proposals as an assault on the social order (Watanuki 1977). Finally, easy issues tend to be questions that have long been unresolved by the political system. It takes time and simplicity for an issue to penetrate the electorate. When these three conditions are satisfied, as in the case of racial segregation in the 1960s, Carmines and Stimson contend that voters may easily associate positions on the issue with various parties and candidates.

We would add a fourth criterion that seems implicit in the Carmines and Stimson formulation and draws upon an earlier tradition of electoral analysis. Cultural questions are often formulated as *position* rather than *valence* issues. By position issues, we refer to questions where the candidates stake out competing and seemingly incompatible policy preferences and try to maximize the distance between themselves and the opposition. That is, on position issues, candidates may well try to be for something and paint their opponents as against it. This contrasts with valence issues where candidates share the same goal but differ primarily in the means of attaining it. In considering valence issues, voters are encouraged to make their choices depending on which candidate they believe will be more efficient in delivering the policy outcome that all sensible voters desire. By contrast, cultural issues lend themselves well to a polarizing approach that forces candidates to take sides.

Cultural conflicts are often explosive. The defense of certain values escalates to the level of intrinsically evil or intrinsically good. Consider this logic: if abortion is murder, then abortionists are murderers. The defenseless child deserves protection, even if that involves coercive or violent action against its oppressor. Such a rationale has been used to justify bombings of abortion clinics and murders of doctors who terminate pregnancies. The issue might have been defined as follows: Abortion is intrinsically evil because it takes human life at its start, but the creation of that human life should not have occurred in the first place. If it came from rape or incest or some other form of nonconsensual exploitation of the mother, which is also intrinsically evil, we must make a practical judgment in the midst of a moral quandary—sometimes aborting, sometimes preserving the life. And we are obligated to mitigate the conditions that lead to such pregnancies in the future. In both of these instances, intrinsic evil is invoked. But the outcomes are different depending on the objects of protection and the obligation of the bystander.

Cultural conflicts sometimes get cast in such a manner that they are nonbargainable. Such conflicts tax the limits of democratic discourse. If, for example, the "other" has no intrinsic right to human dignity, the vigilante mob, for example, can justify lynching the black civil rights worker or beating to death the gay shiphand; or a temporary congressional majority can both suspend civil liberties and extend the death penalty. Subcultures label "the problem" differently, defining situations according to their respective norms. Nonbargainable language shuts down discourse, an essential tool for community-building. Few democracies survive over the long haul when discourse is lost. The slavery issue, among the many things that separated North from South, was capable of severing the Union. Prohibition yielded disciplined, rich, and politically powerful criminal organizations that rivaled the power of the state and legal institutions in many locales. That is why committed democrats worry about the risks of cultural politics and extend so much effort to transform conflict over absolute positions to conflict over directions and tendencies.

The last point returns us to an important qualification. We think of cultural politics as a style of political conflict that may be present in greater or lesser degree. Of course, some issues by their very nature seem to tap into fundamental social values and lend themselves to a politics of group polarization. But the style is available to be used across a wide range of policy questions. As Carmines and Stimson recognized, the development of racial segregation as an "easy" issue, in contrast to the "hard" issue profile of the war in Vietnam, did not grow out of the issue so much as the manner in which political elites framed the controversy for the mass public. "All issues have intrinsically simple and complex facets; which particular facets predominate at a given time is an empirical question" (81). This is another way of expressing the thought that cultural politics is a variable that differs in intensity across issues and times. That makes it a phenomenon less sharply delimited than conventional accounts imply.

The Resurgence of Cultural Conflicts in Recent American Politics

If the cultural politics that appeared in the 1960s exhibits the same style as the cultural politics of the American past, the specific issues that are debated in such terms do seem to have changed. The social historians whom we referenced above have focused on questions such as prohibition, laws protecting the Sabbath, suffrage extension to women and African Americans, parochial school aid, foreign language instruction, anti-Catholicism, immigration (Swierenga 1977). Many of these issues left the agenda of national politics when they were resolved decisively by legislative action or social change. Some, like immigration and foreign language instruction, have reappeared on the contemporary issue agenda but with different referents. But for the most part, the ethnocultural tensions that subdivided the population by nationality and confessional religion have receded in importance. The complex of issues debated in cultural terms since the 1960s have more often centered on race, gender roles, sexuality, and foreign policy. To explain the recent prominence of these cultural appeals, we need to consider how modernity has recast the very basis of political conflict. The major source of renewed cultural conflict appears to be postmodernism itself.

At the most distant level, the development of cultural politics in America is a response to the influence of the Enlightenment that stimulated confidence in human reason and diminished support for a unitary culture built around revealed truth. At the most proximate level, the apparent intensification of cultural politics in American politics since the 1960s can be understood as the product of calculated actions by political elites. As we have noted, cultural tensions may be widely "available" as potential lines of political cleavage, but they are not made manifest unless someone first takes concrete actions to place them on the national agenda. At the intermediate level, we need to consider the broader social conditions that facilitate cultural politics, the qualities of society that persuade elites that a cultural strategy is likely to pay electoral dividends. In our judgment, the crucial background factors involve: (1) the rapid changes in the social order experienced in World War II and its aftermath, and (2) the evolution of the occupational structure under advanced capitalism.

World War II set in motion the most rapid and massive changes in social relationships heretofore known in the United States. The system linking nuclear and extended families (with their corresponding gender role specializations) to homogeneous neighborhood, church, social, and employment networks was perturbed. Men went off to war. Women went to work outside the home again, in large numbers for the first time since the labor laws of the Progressive era. Courtship was truncated, and changed rules regarding sexuality developed. Modifications in gender roles were blessed by the state as part of the patriotic effort at national mobilization. A gay subculture developed especially in the cities that served as ports for the U.S. Navy.

After the war, men did not return to farm, trade, or factory but went to college on the GI bill, supported by a grateful state. Women returned to bearing large families, but they had tasted the freedoms of new roles. Many old ethnic neighborhoods broke up as the next generation had the wherewithal to move to the suburbs; there, they developed the nuclear family rather than the extended family. The church of primal bond was replaced by the church of psychological need or social function. Massive migrations moved people, white and black, off the farms into the cities and factories. Huge demand for consumer products meant massive expansion in the production sectors. Positive experiences with big science during the war effort threw the state into a patron role, funding the scientific and technological advances located at universities. New or expanded roles for institutions—labor unions, schools and universities, mass media, corporations, professions—made them legitimate claimants for respect and resources and, with that, political competitors. An operative philosophy of liberal individualism or interest-group liberalism replaced more organic and communitarian notions of social relationships. Those philosophers, lawyers, theologians, publicists, and others adept at rationalizing the new relationships became the new gurus.

A generation or so later, much of this was changing again. The nuclear family had also disintegrated. The pill removed many sexual taboos, as sex had fewer apparent consequences. Young women, encouraged by their parents, aspired to higher education and professional advancement the equal of men. Racial minorities and their supporters in the dominant hierarchy mobilized claims for respect, resources, and full citizenship through the civil rights advances of the 1960s. A growing share of state resources was devoted to war preparedness against an external enemy, and both heavy industry and newly emergent high-technology industries devoted their efforts to Cold War weapons production. Consumer needs were by now either satiated or satisfied by cheaper products developed through booming economies outside the United States, particularly along the Pacific rim. With integration into a global economy and the subsequent decline in production, the working middle class and their midlevel managers (Dionne 1996) systematically lost good-paying jobs.

Advances both in education and aspirations stigmatized menial jobs, so that labor markets at that level attracted new migrants, displaced either by war or by limited economic opportunities in their home nations. Longevity was both the product of and a stimulant to advances in health care, and the health sector of the economy grew rapidly; increasingly, health-care institutions laid claim to governmental expenditures. Institutions important before the war or during the immediate postwar declined in importance—church, ethnic neighborhood, industrial labor union. As global economic institutions consolidated, the possibility that central political institutions could make much difference came into question; more people doubted that government had the capacity to solve domestic problems through taxing and spending (Dionne 1996). The struggle—whether over free trade, protectionism, or regional organizations—has only been exacerbated late in the post–New Deal period with the loss of the external Soviet enemy; no longer could the merger of nationalism and internationalism forge a consensus about America's role in the world.

The new social relationships called for a new covenant, and politicians struggled to maintain their known advantages with interest-group liberalism (Lowi 1979), while testing the basis for new majority coalitions. That process of testing has become the dominant agenda of post–New Deal politics in the United States. The interplay among social change, political response, and the struggle to find a new, overarching moral order is particularly evident in the consequences of an evolving occupational structure.

Theorists of postindustrial or postmodern society contend that the contemporary economic system has yielded an occupational structure that differs fundamentally from the patterns of industrial capitalism. Due to increases in the scale of enterprises, rationalization of function, the acceleration of technological innovation, and the growth of the state, modern societies need a large stratum of employees with professional, technical and managerial skills (Burris 1980). In response to these technological, and intellectual demands, institutions of higher education expanded their capacity to produce an ever-increasing supply of people adept at the manipulation of information, knowledge, and symbols. Consequently, the class of people who are recognized as professionals—membership based on advanced education and often regulated by formal-legal criteria—has increased as a proportion of the economically active population; this "knowledge elite" or "new middle class" may even have displaced the "property elite" as the controlling influence in the economy. The process has occurred in most advanced industrial societies, the pace varying depending upon local conditions, but has reached particularly high levels in the United States, which closely resembles the ideal type envisioned by models of postindustrial theory. The high degree of economic concentration, heavy investment in technological development, historic emphasis on scientific management, and cultural belief in education have combined to produce a very large sector of white collar, professional, administrative, and managerial employees.

By virtue of their advanced education, social backgrounds, operational creed, and work experience, the members of the professional and managerial sector are substantially less inclined than the rest of the population—or even affluent members of the business elite—to embrace moral traditionalism. In some accounts, this "new class" is said to promote a radical oppositional culture, departing drastically from the norms and values held dear by most Americans. Early accounts of "new class" theory portrayed this group primarily in terms of its estrangement from the economic system that produced it. The group was so consistently described in these terms that one recent account referred to the settled "fact" that members of the stratum have promoted "the diffusion of a new worldview consisting of values and attitudes hostile to bourgeois-capitalist society" (Lerner, Nagai, and Rothman 1996). This hostility supposedly entails opposition to theistic religion, a preference for hedonism over restraint in personal behavior, and eagerness to embrace alternatives to the traditional family structure (Hunter and Fessenden 1992)—precisely the heresies attributed to the Democrats by the Republican speakers cited at the beginning of this chapter. What makes this stratum so relevant to cultural conflict is its strategic social location. The concentration of such individuals in government agencies, education, and the mass media is said to give them power and platforms to promote their distinctive views. It also promotes an inverted form of class conflict where Americans of lesser educational attainment battle on behalf of the traditional values despised by the "knowledge class."

As is typical of new social theories, the "new class" hypothesis has been stated overbroadly by its strongest advocates. In extreme form, it suggests a conscious conspiracy by a new cultural elite to undermine the inherited culture. It defines as "anticapitalist" a number of social welfare programs—health care, worker security, child allowances—commonly practiced in states with thriving capitalist economies. More fundamentally, the new class hypothesis rests on a remarkably limited base of empirical data. Instead, the data that have been analyzed suggest patterns that undermine the extreme versions of "new class" theory. Brint (1994) has marshaled evidence that members of the intellectual stratum share many fundamental social values with the general population. And instead of constituting an anticapitalist elite, it turns out that people who meet the criteria for membership in the "new class" or its many equivalents are either indistinct from the population in their economic attitudes or, more commonly, even more conservative than the rest of the population on questions of government intervention and regulation of the market. Indeed, many of the values and the operating style of new class activists often fit closely the classic capitalist model of entrepreneurship (Hunter and Fessenden 1992). Furthermore, the new class theorists have never established that members of the so-called new class actually utilize their strategic social location to promote an agenda, or indeed that they even think of themselves as constituting a "group."

Reformulated and pruned of excess, new class theory can help explain the recent intensification of cultural conflict in American politics. That reformulation starts with the recognition that members of this group, as a whole, do differ substantially from the general public on a number of questions related to social norms and mores. Higher education and income, while associated with economic conservatism, are positively associated with liberal social attitudes. People with substantial educational credentials are, as a group, more tolerant than others about extending civil liberties to unpopular groups and much more sympathetic to social movements promoting feminism, gay rights, the prochoice option, and similar causes (Delli Carpini and Sigelman 1986). The products of their labor—such things as television programs, movies, and scholarly research—are evidence of their willingness to entertain ideas and images at variance with traditional notions of morality. While this is hardly the thoroughgoing rejection of capitalism attributed to the new class, it is nonetheless an important social difference from the remainder of society.

In four ways, the prominence of highly educated professionals has stimulated culturally based political conflict. First, the members of this social group play a disproportionately large role in the process of socialization. By virtue of their concentration in schools and the media, members of this "new class" are well-placed to transmit their cultural values to the rest of the population. One does not have to subscribe to the exaggerated view that members of this elite brazenly "brainwash" their naive charges—students and audiences—to recognize that schools and the mass media do indeed convey values that may strike traditionalists as incompatible with their models of good and proper behavior. Second, members of this social category have been instrumental in forming advocacy organizations that promote their relatively liberal social perspectives. As part of the advocacy "explosion" in the 1970s and thereafter, there was a surge in the number of and influence of organized groups promoting such formerly heterodox social values as freedom of reproductive choice, decriminalization of formerly "deviant" if not illegal sexual behavior, extension of civil liberties to all manner of groups, assuring the right of women to full social equality, and other causes that struck at the norms and values of religious traditionalists and cultural conservatives. In another contribution to politics based on cultural differences, the social liberalism of the "new class" has also appeared among clergy and religious leaders, once the guardians of religious tradition and conservative social values. The trend is most dramatic among the mainline Protestant community, organized Jewry, and a generation of Roman Catholic priests and hierarchy. These traditions were infused by a cohort of clergy and religious leaders who had imbibed the spirit of liberation and nonconformity pervading college campuses during the 1960s and 1970s. Those who had looked to religious authority for confirmation of traditional norms and values were instead urged by the new religious elites to put their efforts into the quest for social justice, producing a striking dissonance in many congregations. In milder form, the same pattern began to affect the more theologically traditional denominations. Fourth and finally, the social liberals have raised cultural tensions by their command of society's ultimate means of coercion—the state. By funding the expansion of higher education and policy research, employing many of its graduates, providing indirect tax subsidies to advocacy organizations, and disseminating the results of academic studies, the government appears as an active agent in publicizing the perspectives associated with the new class.

These activities of the symbol-makers came at a time when many citizens saw signs of social disintegration and declining predictability in everyday life all around them—lack of commitment to marriage partners and increasing divorce, children on drugs and engaging in promiscuous sexual activity at precocious ages, marital or sexual problems of the clergy, loss of midlevel job security through corporate merger mania, closing of production plants or loss of high wages "to remain competitive," adjustments to working side-by-side with women and minorities who—rumor had it—got their jobs through quotas rather than merit, and on. They sensed it was difficult to turn to the government for redress—in part because the government was perceived as busily taking away their freedoms through all sorts of regulations and taking away their dollars to give them to some undeserving group, and in part because the government was thought to be owned by the very economic and cultural elites who had undermined the social order in the first place (Edsall and Edsall 1991). To turn to government is to sleep with the enemy.

The collective consequences of these factors, we believe, is a heightened perception by social traditionalists that their values, institutions, and preferred ways of life are under challenge. Where social traditionalists may have once enjoyed a monopoly in their communities, protected from threatening ideas and norms by isolation and insularity, the spread of modernity has seriously breached the walls of these enclaves. With government mandates, court-ordered social programs, state dominance in the educational sphere, omnipresent video images, and other invasive procedures, the advocates of the new morality have directly challenged the social traditionalists in the latter's own milieu. Whether the instrument is the mandatory busing of school children to achieve racial balance, the spread of abortion facilities, a mass media emphasis on sexuality, or school books that break with social tradition, the residents of traditional environments have had to confront a barrage of challenges to their norms and values. And those traditionalists who followed economic opportunity to urban areas found even more direct encounters with disturbing social trends. Short of forming hermetically sealed societies and avoiding contact with the larger culture, in the manner of antimodern groups such as the Amish or ultraorthodox Jewry, it is no longer possible for traditionalists to avoid contact with social practices and norms that run directly counter to their own cultural preferences. While they may minimize the challenge by various means, such as creating "parallel culture" institutions like Christian broadcasting and Christian rock, the intrusiveness of modernizing institutions leaves them no place to hide.

The open challenges to traditional values and widespread perception of the disintegration of the social order may have provided the necessary conditions that encouraged political countermobilization. But as social movement theory has taught us, changing social conditions and a widespread sense of grievance are sufficient only to generate political grievance or sporadic acts of uncoordinated protest. For effective action in defense of the social order, it requires a constituency with political resources. Such countermobilization develops effectively only when it is encased in organizational form. That, in turn, requires a constituency with the resources to prosecute its claims effectively. Ironically, if modernity threatened social traditionalists by promoting challenges to their way of life, it also helped equip them with the skills and instruments of resistance.

As conveyed by H. L. Mencken's devastating reports from Tennessee during the Scopes trial, that classic confrontation between tradition and modernity, the locus of social traditionalism in the United States was portrayed as rural, Southern, poor, uneducated, and fundamentalist. As such, it is difficult to understand how such a marginalized population could launch effective political crusades beyond its own cultural backwaters. Whatever the truth of Mencken's claims at the time he made them, they have long since ceased to apply to the United States.[2] Many of the same social changes that produced the "New Class" have also contributed to the development of an urban, well-educated, affluent, and nationwide constituency for traditionalist moral appeals (Wald 1990). The

---

[2] Lienesch (1997) has shown that social traditionalists, far from being country bumpkins, were already well established in urban areas by the turn of the century and had developed an elaborate organizational network of bible colleges, publishing houses, and broadcast outlets. They already possessed sophisticated means of communication and mobilization.

South has undergone massive social change and, as attested by claims about the "Southernization" or "Dixie-fication" of America, has made its presence felt throughout society by both migration and cultural diffusion. Aided and abetted by these social changes, movements of moral reform have also emerged in urban form to constitute a significant national presence (Lienesch 1997). These efforts rest on organizations with the capacity to identify, target, activate, and mobilize supportive constituencies. The tools of such campaigns range from traditional staples of popular mobilization such as neighborhood canvassing and what has been called kitchen table lobbying, to the decidedly more high-tech tools of television and radio broadcasting, cable television programming, closed-circuit "narrowcasts," direct mail, fax and telephone trees, the Internet, and other instruments of communication. By these means, audiences can be informed about threats to the moral order, induced to support organizations committed to cultural restoration, informed about activities to combat dangerous social trends, and harnessed to mass movements of various kinds. A politics of cultural differences that pitted "us" versus "them" could be launched effectively using all the same types of media mastered by the enemy.

In accounting for the ubiquity of cultural appeals during the post–New Deal era, we should not overlook the role played by empirical research on mass political behavior. The activists who programmed the new technology of voter mobilization often relied on the findings of scholars who provided them with insights about converting grievances into political action. Scholars who examined data from the National Election Studies, a biennial series of election surveys funded by the National Science Foundation, offered important evidence about the factors that moved voters from one candidate to another. Professional pollsters and campaign managers often utilized research on emotions in politics, the attribution of responsibility, the nature of issue-based appeals, the salience of candidate traits, and other such topics as a strategic resource. The breakthrough moment, the Kennedy campaign's reliance on the issue profiles of distinct voter groups, was captured in fictional form in Eugene Burdick's *The 480* (1964). In that novel as well as the earlier *Ninth Wave* (1956), Burdick, a distinguished voting behavior specialist at the University of California at Berkeley, showed how campaign managers systematically exploited the findings of academic work in order to position candidates in a favorable public light and to undermine the standing of party rivals. Some of the leading practitioners of cultural politics were graduates of the elite academic programs that produced the research and, ironically, were strong supporters of continued federal funding for social science research when it came under attack during the Reagan years and again when the Republicans organized the Congress in 1995. Even those who were not formally trained in empirical political research became familiar with trends in scholarly work. In capitalizing on the new tools of persuasion, in attempting to harness social discontent into an effective electoral coalition, cultural warriors could thus draw on a solid corpus of scholarship.

This new political force was first put on display in a variety of local and state campaigns on behalf of such disparate causes as appropriate school textbooks, gay rights legislation, and opposition to the Equal Rights Amendment (Crawford 1980). What might have been a private war or a series of local skirmishes took on a more national cast when Republican party activists undertook a concerted campaign to make their party a home for social traditionalists. During the 1960s and 1970s, the party had made considerable electoral strides by attracting support from normally Democratic voters angry about their party's positions on Vietnam, race, and social order. In the aftermath of the Watergate crisis, which decimated the Republicans, activists sought a new way to make further inroads with what they understood as a wellspring of social conservatism still attached by habit and tradition to the Democratic party. By packaging the cultural issues of concern to religious traditionalists along with the racial and class appeals that seemed to work well among other traditionally Democratic voter groups, these activists hoped to make manifest what they perceived as a latent electoral majority (Blumenthal 1986; Edsall and Edsall 1991; Himmelstein 1990). In like manner, groups who had achieved some advances with their agendas now perceived a condition of threat; a new round of more sophisticated mobilization followed (see Bashevkin 1998; Freeman 1999; Katzenstein and Mueller 1987). This book analyzes how their efforts transformed the New Deal party system.

CHAPTER THREE

General Components of Cultural Theory in Political Conflict

TO APPROACH POLITICS from a cultural perspective presupposes that elections have both manifest and latent functions. On the surface, elections are simply one mechanism for selecting public officials. At a deeper level, the electoral process represents an opportunity for society to define itself. In this sense, elections are *rituals*. Their purpose is to legitimate a social hierarchy. For a variety of reasons, people need a sense of legitimacy surrounding social obligations. When it seems right to do something, they find meaning in a moral order. Functioning properly, then, both the process and the outcome of an election reaffirm an existing moral order or embrace a new one.

Presidential elections are at the center of the American political culture. The president is not only a prime minister but also the head of state. The president sets overall policy direction. Because policy involves a binding allocation of values for the society as a whole, any president is calling for a certain kind of moral order. But the president, in his (or, in the fullness of time, her) persona symbolizes who we are as a people, what we value at this time in our history, and who or what is not of us. In short, the president—from the time of George Washington onward—is our designated cultural icon. Presidential elections are thus the appropriate venue in which to explore the power and significance of cultural appeals and forces.

This chapter is the first of three that attempt to define the rudiments of a cultural theory of American presidential elections. By its very nature, it is a dynamic theory, accounting for stability and change, and subsuming many of our existing theories of electoral dynamics. This chapter explores the basic components of our approach, first, by discussing the nature of culture and its linkage with religion and the concept of 'moral order.' Then, it unpacks the concept of 'politics' by showing how it is intimately bound up with questions of moral order. Because cultural politics is often articulated in terms of groups, we also explore 'groups' as carriers and targets of cultural appeals. The final section of the chapter examines the importance of symbols in the ritualism of the electoral process.

Culture, Religion, and Predictability

Culture is a template for predicting (and explaining) the occurrences of events and for organizing social relationships. Geertz (1973, 49) argues that "Culture is best seen *not* as complexes of *concrete behavior patterns*—customs, usages, traditions, habit clusters—but as a *set of control mechanisms*—plans, recipes, rules, instructions—for the governing of behavior" (emphasis in original).

Culture applies to and, therefore, develops the "natural order." Science, like myth and magic, is a process for teasing order out of events. It hypothesizes the conditions that will precipitate an outcome, prescribes rituals for observing regularities, and establishes rules for concluding within a range of confidence that a given set of observations confirms hypothetical expectations. Armed with such knowledge, it is possible to plan for some outcomes and avoid the consequences of others—from childbirth, influenza epidemics, hurricanes, drought, and famine, to sexually transmitted diseases, gene therapy, de-icing of airplanes, and information highways. Science and technology combine to yield a culture of control, of high predictability in the understanding of "naturally occurring" events. Social arrangements can be ordered accordingly.

Culture also applies to and, therefore, develops social behavior. Culture performs three functions: (1) it offers *identity*, (2) it prescribes *norms* for behavior, and (3) it maintains *boundaries* for relationships (Wildavsky 1987). Culture identifies who exists and who is a potential party to a social relationship. It labels the actors. Further, in ascribing a status to each, culture specifies the proper ways for each to behave. Depending on the culture, actors may be human, other animals, or supernatural. They interact within certain contexts, and the context itself—the environment, the family, the group, the political system—is deemed deserving of a proper kind of behavior. Finally, culture indicates that interactions with people or things outside the prescribed range of action will have consequences, usually dire.

Thinkers, themselves culture creators, have often struggled with the question of what comes to social relationships by nature and what by culture. Aristotle claimed that man is by nature a social animal. Both the psalmist and St. Paul agreed that humans were already at conception antagonistic toward themselves, each other, and God, and in need of redemption. Hobbes was confident that fear would drive humans toward cooperation, but Hume concluded that only the use of force by an initial sovereign could overcome the chaos of a "state of nature." It is interesting to note that not only current psychobiologists and geneticists have contributed to this debate, but historically also the leading religious figures and political philosophers. Whether nature or nurture brings order to social relationships, a succession of culture creators tell the defining story, the myth of the age.

It is perhaps no surprise that, even in an era that relies increasingly on science and technology to understand and tame the natural order, we continue to rely on a broader range of "ways of knowing" for our social identities, norms, and boundaries. Social knowledge appears less deterministic to us than natural knowledge; yet both have the same function of establishing order and predictability.

That is probably why the aspect of culture centering on *social* norms remains so closely affiliated with religious myth. Myth is neither necessarily "true" nor "false." Myth tells a plausible, powerful story, often of human origins and destiny. Consider the problem of a founding myth for the United States. The peoples in the colonies lacked a caste system or a natural nobility and, in fact, rejected the legitimacy of a sovereign power by using the set of transcendent standards elaborated in the Declaration of Independence. Their social conditions reinforced a deep sense of equality and enterprise; any man could become whatever he wanted through individual initiative. Except for those favored by the mercantile system of the sponsoring government, many American immigrants came because the new land was viewed as a receiving (or dumping) grounds. It was a place for those who had run afoul of the law, who would not submit to ecclesiastical order, who wanted to escape conscription to military service, or who could not make a go of it financially where they were. Finally, a wide geographical expanse beckoned, but this land had indigenous peoples on it. The country needed a founding myth to establish a moral political order.

The founding myth that stuck—that created and legitimized a democratic regime—was not the myth of the Virginia philosopher-planters, nor the money-sharp Boston merchants, nor Philadelphia's pragmatic proto-scientists and inventors. It was the Plymouth Bay colony's Pilgrims. They freely compacted; they established order from a position of interpersonal equality under a strict but benevolent God. As this myth was merged with Puritan experience, they had become a chosen people in the wilderness, God's clarion, a city on a hill. When they and their nation acted, then, it was not out of the informed self-interest of planter or merchant or the curiosity of scientist or inventor, but out of the call of their Creator. When their nation failed, it was because they had not measured up to the law of the Lord—whether it be slavery or civil rights, Civil War or Great War, genocide with Indians or infanticide with abortion. Their political discourse was not of tariffs and raw metals but of a Cross of Gold, not of a rival hegemonic power but of an Evil Empire. Such symbolic utterances become the medium for celebrating moral order.

In a nation where church and state are officially separate, religion and politics become the handmaidens to each other. An equalitarian, democratic political order often needs the assistance of religiously grounded myth to enhance its legitimacy. Geertz defines *religion* as "a system of symbols which acts to establish powerful, pervasive, and long lasting moods and motivations in men by formulating conceptions of a general order of existence and clothing these conceptions with such an aura of factuality that the moods and motivations seem uniquely realistic" (1973, 90). Geertz notes that "both what a people prizes and what it fears and hates are depicted in its world view, symbolized in its religion, and in turn expressed in the whole quality of life" (131). Life is not genuine unless lived in the religious way. Politics is not just unless its policies measure up to God's law.

Religion is *collective memory*. It rehearses, retells, the story of a people, but gives it cosmic significance. Religion brings God into their midst. It makes their story both transcendent and immanent. Durkheim argued that "Religious force is only the sentiments inspired by the group in its members, but projected outside the consciousness that experienced them, and objectified" (1965, 261). As Leege has argued elsewhere, "For Durkheim, moral authority is society's projection of its own need for order, stability, and predictability in social interactions. . . . People become something more than ordinary mortals when they share a sacred community. People become empowered, they develop the capacity to *act* in concert. Religions specify what actions to take, and religious beliefs create the obligation to act" (Leege 1993b, 9–10).

A political culture that depends so much on religion for its legitimation will face unusual strains in a country whose motto is "E Pluribus Unum." On the one hand, some will see in that motto the "city on the hill," Zion, a chosen people above all nations set aside for a divinely inspired mission. Others will see in that motto a melting pot that welcomes people from many lands and many religious backgrounds, but expects all to adhere to a common *creed*, that is, both a set of beliefs about what we must all hold in common and a positive perspective on our past as a nation. Still others will see in "E Pluribus Unum" a respect for the cultural differences brought from many lands and religions, differences of outlook by gender, race, or social condition, and an insistence that the processes and policies that emerge from our common set of political structures will also respect our pluralism, while depriving no one of opportunity. The differing perspectives about our national motto are also cultural symbols that presage political conflict over the ordered life, and they anticipate widespread use of religious rationales for the legitimacy of one model of order over another. In a society with so many different cultural perspectives, Ann Swidler (1986) reminds us, the individual is seldom rooted in a singular, all-encompassing worldview but rather enjoys the freedom to select among a wide array or "toolkit" of cultural options. In this way, heterogeneity encourages conflict.

Such conflicts manifest themselves in many ways. In her study of prolife and prochoice activists, Kristen Luker (1984) marvels that what separates each group is a different culture. The prochoice activists subordinate their religious views to norms of equalitarianism, individualism, and utilitarianism. The antiabortion activists, however, center their worldview on God, the afterlife, the sacredness of life even in its earliest manifestation, and the natural order of the family. Neither side shows ability to comprehend the other's values or lifestyles. The pro-choice activists fail to grasp why the anti-abortion activists do not seek meaning in work outside the home, and the latter find it incomprehensible that the former want to remove impediments to self-realization beyond the home. Mansbridge's research (1986) on the rejection of the Equal Rights Amendment, particularly her case study of Illinois, finds similar differences in the sense of moral order. For proponents, men and women are indeed created equal; for opponents, men and women are created to complementary but not equal roles. The resulting sense of moral order not only is different but spills over to the instruments of the state. Legislation or the constitution become the means to resolve which view encodes the legitimate social hierarchy. The predictability of social relationships for the broader society—not just a family or members of a particular church—depends on the outcome.

Conflict is also evident in the alternative scripts used to interrogate recent American history. For one group, the 1960s represents original sin, a period of untrammeled licentiousness. Deploying from Gertrude Himmelfarb's work (1995 among others), they see the sexual revolution as the point of origin for loss of respect for authority and for each other, the rise of self-indulgent individualism, the rapid growth of a class permanently dependent on government handouts, and the rampant spread of crime. Their solutions are threefold: (1) limit governmental activity only to those programs that maintain internal and external order and that nurture self-sufficiency, (2) restore respect for the institutions of civil society that build character, and (3) place into elected and appointed leadership only those men and women who subscribe to this script. A government populated by people who use its power for ends beyond these places shackles on its people and is the principal enemy. A second group looks beyond the sexual revolution of the 1960s to the rights revolution. In their script the economy and society that had evolved after the Civil War had become very unjust, systematically precluding opportunity and mobility from whole classes of people, particularly African Americans and other people of color, and women. The tasks of government, therefore, are threefold: (1) to secure the rights of all people, (2) to create opportunities beyond the strictures of the existing economy, and (3) to regulate exploitation of people and environment. Thus, government is the fulcrum for just change, an engine of progress as it had been at the time of the Civil War and during the Progressive era. Like the first group, they find their symbols deep in the American cultural and political experience. At least three other traditions selectively configure elements of the first two. One stresses the goodness of the American people and is optimistic about the future. It does not see the 1960s as inherently evil or good but does prefer more gradualist and pragmatic solutions to problems of injustice. A second stresses libertarian solutions: leave individuals to their own decisions and they will make rational choices that in the end benefit society. Neither regulation of marketplace, as in the New Deal, nor of private conduct, as advocated by the Religious Right, achieves its purposes. A final script advocates the return to the old moral order, pre-1960s. It assumes that natural elites rise to the top and order society into predictable and beneficent ways. Everyone knows his or her place, whether it be in a racially segregated society, a patriarchal household, or the non-unionized workplace.

Much of the discourse of cultural politics has swirled over the points of conflict among the scripts. Groups adopt ideas and programs. Coalitions form as priority is given to one or another element of a script. Schisms develop and coalitions rupture. Symbols are crafted that sell one or another script to the electorate. At root in cultural politics, the ownership of history becomes a vehicle for realizing personal political ambitions and setting programmatic goals for a society.

This discussion leads to several generalizations and propositions:

1. Since culture concerns moral order, various ways of knowing—science, religion, myth—will be used to define identity, prescribe norms for behavior, and draw boundaries that isolate unacceptable people, ideas, or actions.
2. All societies rely on a range of deep myths of their origin and destiny. Current cultural objectives will be shaped by which of the range of deep myths is dominant at that time.
    A. Political conflict will surround the selection of a dominant deep myth and the meaning of national mottoes or other overarching public symbols.
3. Definition of the public agenda shapes the selection of the range of ideas, issues, and actors that must be taken seriously at that time.
    A. Political conflict will involve actors who specialize in one or

another agenda-definition and will center on both the selection of deep myths and how current issues manifest historic concerns. This is what is meant by "ideas matter."

B. Selection of historical scripts has political consequences.

4. Since the objective of culture is to yield greater predictability of natural phenomena and social relationships, modes of knowing that yield both greater certitude and legitimacy will be used.

A. Religion adds both a transcendent and immanent supernatural dimension to identity, norms, and boundaries and is therefore a powerful instrument for persuasion.

B. Political discourse about moral order will be laced with religious references; further, issues that involve technical differences will often be escalated to their religious meaning, i.e., their consequences for moral order as defined by religious values.

C. In the absence of certitude, continuous definition of social relations by religious values will shape those relations in the defined direction, thus yielding moral order as a self-fulfilling prophecy.

Political Systems, Social Control, and Competition among Values

If culture defines moral order and religion involves collective memory, *politics* is *collective action*. Politics seeks to resolve conflicts over goals and means through collectively binding decisions. In Lasswell's simple terms, politics is who gets what, when, and how (cf. Easton 1953; Lasswell 1958). The political system allocates both material and symbolic values (Lasswell and Kaplan 1950). These allocations reflect social hierarchies, namely, those who get the most of whatever is valued are often the most powerful or prestigious people or groups. Yet because some get and others do not, culture (and religion) must legitimate both the social hierarchy and political institutions. The legitimacy of authority is a central concern for any political system that seeks to endure.

According to Glock (1972), there are three mechanisms for social control that contribute to legitimacy: *sanctions, compensations*, and *ideology*. Sanctions most commonly include informal, internalized instruments such as habit, custom, or mores, but at times they require formal, external instruments such as law, judicial action, and uses of force, including police or military actions. Most political systems rely on extragovernmental institutions such as the family, schools, churches, and voluntary eleemosynary organizations to inculcate the cultural consensus. That is why "family breakdown" or the learning of virtue in schools becomes problematic for a political system. Without self-regulation, enormous demands are placed on legislatures, courts, police, and jails to sanction inappropriate social behavior. Jefferson looked to participation in local self-governance as one of the best training grounds for informal social control; it precipitates awareness of the common good and develops respect for the civic order.

Compensations are another alternative for maintaining legitimacy. A compensation is a safety valve; it deflects attention from opportunity foreclosed by offering other avenues for satisfaction. The most common forms of compensation are thought to be religion, sports and other spectacular forms of heroic entertainment, and drugs. Though postulated as alternatives to politics, each of these avenues to achieving gratification may easily become grist for cultural politics.

The notion that religion is a compensation derives from the world-withdrawal nature and other-worldly hopes intertwined with virtually all religions. "Way over Jordan" or speaking in tongues and chiliastic seizures may offer higher rewards to people who receive few benefits from existing social structures and, therefore, may draw their attention away from the illegitimacy of the polity. However, most religions also propound a socially transforming element. They expect the individual's life to change here and now, and for the individual to evangelize others to that new life. Further, virtually all religions are based in community experience. The community is often affected in one way or another by the state, and the community exerts a collective stimulus toward social action. Thus, the notion that religion is primarily a social safety valve understands little of its transformationist thrusts and communal contexts. For a time it may render its adherents more accepting of the powers that be. The role of the black churches in the civil rights movement, however, is a powerful testimony that religion is not an opiate that masks social injustice (see Lincoln and Mamiya 1990).

The final type of social control is ideology. "Ideology is a vision, a verbal picture of the good society and the principal means of achieving it" (see originally Downs 1957; Leege 1993b, 15). Ideology is an instrument for social change, a plan for a society to become something else. Ideologies range from Nazi or Communist or authoritarian development programs to the more benign shaping of national character through the use of national myths (see Amos 1995, on the cultural uses of Tocqueville's *Democracy in America* at different points in United States history). In the U.S., ideology also becomes entwined in simpler programs such as the war on poverty, the war on illiteracy, the war on whatever.

Ideology is the product of culture creators and the stuff that politicians often manipulate symbolically. The appeals to "Christian civilization" raised by the second Ku Klux Klan in the 1920s, by the "massive resistance" to school integration in Virginia in the 1960s, and by former House Speaker Newt Gingrich's for-college-credit television course in the 1990s are all evidence of the linkage between religious symbols and political programs through an ideology. Its purpose is to mobilize the *right* sector of the population to appropriate behavior by drawing boundaries around outgroups. In its efforts to mobilize for national goals, ideology typically makes use of negative symbols for outgroups, scapegoats, national enemies, or those who are not of us. In that sense, ideologies are similar to religious belief systems: they incorporate notions of a state of nature, of the source of sin, of redemption, and of the program to reinstate the proper moral order. Ideologies are most likely to be used initially by those who do not have access to the full range of sanctioning mechanisms available to governments—law, courts, police, jails—and must rely on the pristine power of an idea to gain control. Ideologies become connected with movements, in turn led by a vanguard that seeks control of state power to create or re-create the proper moral order.

Thus, a wide variety of social control and ideological mobilization instruments is available to political elites. Which instrument or combination is selected will depend on: (1) the context of the problem, (2) the script for interpreting history, (3) the effectiveness of the instrument, and (4) the advantage to political leaders.

A wide range of values is available for allocation by any political system. Lasswell and Kaplan (1950) enumerate four deference values—power, respect, rectitude, and affection—and four welfare values—well-being, wealth, skill, and enlightenment. Political parties are coalitions of groups that emphasize one or another of these values. Whichever sets of values predominate at a given time are seen as the "core values" or "owned issues" of the party. In turn, political actors ascend to leadership positions based on cultural priorities among these values and the relevant public's sense that political actors either possess these values or can further them.

In that respect the American parties have become reference groups with somewhat different perspectives about moral order. For Republicans, moral order includes economic progress and expansion, personal responsibility for the family, social constraint on cultural values, but the maximization of economic freedom; the principal active role of the government is to maintain order and protect citizens from external threats. For Democrats, moral order includes economic progress but always with an eye to the distribution of wealth and security, personal responsibility for the family but with assists from the government, personal freedom on cultural values but economic constraint, all because the principal role of government is to provide for social justice.

Struggles for party leadership often involve the interplay of these core values. For example, in the struggle to succeed President Reagan in 1988, George Bush had clearly shown both his merit in the economic marketplace and his devotion to entrepreneurial values. Many of his appearances from 1985 on, then, were at meetings convened by the religious and cultural right; he had to convince moralists of his righteousness. Televangelist Pat Robertson had already displayed his virtue and capacity for moralization; his task was to convince Main Street Republicans that he was an astute businessman, had met payrolls, and was driven by the entrepreneurial spirit. And so he highlighted his Christian broadcasting network and other profit-making spinoffs. It was one of the rare instances in public life when a preacher called attention to how well he had done by doing good.

Candidate Clinton perceived that both the health and economic well-being of the average middle-class American had taken a beating in the 1980s, while a lot of yuppie millionaires were created. Greed was a useful negative symbol for a party concerned with social justice. Thus he stressed those concerns as well as his skill and enlightenment—a successful governor of an underdeveloped state, a Rhodes scholar, a policy wonk, and a Christian who believed that wars could be immoral. Regardless of the battery of values available for symbolic manipulation by politicians, presidents cannot escape being cultural icons.

Again we offer summary generalizations about political systems, social control, and competition among values:

1. The function of politics is to make collectively binding allocations of values for a whole society. Politics presumes competition among values.
    A. Domination of the political system is likely to reflect social hierarchies.
    B. Those who dominate the political system have special access to the means of coercion, that is, the formal sanctioning mechanisms in a society.

2. Political systems rely on a combination of sanctions, compensations, and ideology to legitimize both the system and its outputs.
    A. Because of constraints on public resources, political leaders often prefer that the consequences of social change be addressed through informal sanctions.

3. Compensations such as religion, sports and heroic entertainment, and recreational uses of drugs provide safety valves that cushion perceived injustices in social hierarchies.
    A. While religion, with its alternative identity and hopes for a

future life, may initially mute the swiftness and severity of reaction to injustice, its transformationist impulses, transcendent standards, and group cohesiveness make it an eventual and persistent opponent of the political system.

4. Ideology is a vision of an alternate social order used by outgroups who lack legitimate access to the means of coercion and is evident particularly in periods of breakdown in the moral order.

5. Political parties and presidential candidates encapsulate certain core values but reflect priorities among those values.
   A. Political parties maintain core values but are also moving value coalitions, reflecting conflicts over value priorities among adherents and the value priorities needed to win a series of elections.
   B. Presidential candidates must encapsulate the values of a sufficient coalition of party adherents as well as the expectations of the general public.

Groups, Social Identity, and Salience

Marx and the Marxists firmly believed that the mode of production and distribution known as capitalism would lead to the formation of two classes—bourgeoisie and proletariat—each with respective interests and outlooks. By 1905, despairing of class consciousness among workers in England, however, Friedrich Engels wrote: "What capitalism did was to bring into close physical and symbolic proximity workers who imbibed radically different cultures with their mothers' milk" (cited in Benson 1979, 205). Irish and English workers could not develop a common consciousness because they were first Irish and English, Catholics and Methodists, competing "camps" facing a cultural divide larger than the economic interests that might unite them as factory workers or miners. Even when factory hands shared a common English identity, they often were riven by cleavages between church and chapel. What troubled Engels and has intrigued latter-day social scientists is both the persistence of and the continuing political relevance of what are sometimes called "primordial" bonds—ethnicity and race, religion, nationality, region, gender, or others. Political scientists from Bentley (1908) to Truman (1951) to Baumgartner and Leech (1998) have argued for the group basis of American politics. In the context of this project, we conceive of groups as primary carriers of cultural values and targets for cultural appeals.

Groups form the basis of cleavage in a larger society for a variety of cultural and political reasons: (1) whether based on voluntary affiliation or generational replacement, groups socialize members into their values;

(2) through processes of *social identification*, groups develop consciousness of kind so that it is possible for members to say "we . . . they"; (3) through the interaction of members, a sense of *social cohesion* develops that provides reinforcement for group identity and norms; and (4) through an advantageous political shorthand, political elites think of society in terms of groups.

Group socialization is a fundamental building block of moral order. *Meaning* in the words of Wuthnow (1987, 37) is "an attribute of symbolism" and is "a function of the context in which a symbol, or the individual himself, was located." Human reality is symbolically constructed; therefore its context in smaller groups is central to more overarching symbolic universes. According to Berger and Luckmann (1966), experience does not have meaning unless we have symbols to interpret it.

Berger and Luckmann divide the symbol world, first, into "everyday reality," a pragmatic world of "waking consciousness" that is divided into "spheres of relevance" for doing each task. A substantial share of daily tasks is located within primary or near primary groups—family and close friends, work groups, or some voluntary associations such as churches that elicit consummatory loyalties. Through such contexts, individuals can not only interact efficiently but share notions of what is real.

Berger and Luckmann also speak of higher orders of symbolism. These include: (1) "explanations," that is, common vocabulary words that transmit intuitive meanings, such as "wife," "preacher," "jock," and "politician"; (2) "rudimentary theoretical propositions" usually taking the form of simple moral maxims or proverbs, for example, "haste makes waste," "get what you can and tolerate what you must," "it is better to stick together than to hang alone"; (3) "explicit theories" that describe regularities in institutional sectors, such as, increased demand and limited supply will drive up price; in conditions of uncertainty about the electorate's wishes, a political party will edge toward the issue space occupied by the winning party in the most recent election; a nation lacking external enemies will divide into factional squabbles; and (4) "symbolic universes" that integrate theories or ideas from several institutional sectors, as often found in elaborate philosophies, worldviews, religious doctrine, or even something as simple as common religion and superstition, for example, military battles should not be fought on days under a certain constellation of the stars; nations that tolerate a specified type of "abomination to the Lord" such as abortion or widespread homosexuality will be destroyed by God; the disintegration of the family in a society that embraces liberal individualism will foreshadow both anomie at the level of the individual and generalized lawlessness at the level of society, with greater reliance on outlaw economic transactions and coercive actions by the state.

Each of these higher levels of symbolism, according to Berger and Luckmann, constitutes a "machinery for legitimation." We argue that individuals experience difficulty with meaning if they try to compartmentalize "knowledge" from a wider context that may conflict with "knowledge" from everyday reality. In fact, most of the group contexts that serve as the arena for everyday reality try to link together components of other contexts into a *plausible* picture of the world. While this picture may not meet a *consistency* standard of truth as one would expect from carefully integrated philosophies, doctrinal systems, or worldviews, it nevertheless meets a *coherence* standard (these terms were first suggested by Wuthnow 1987, 45–47).

Much of the linkages in politics done through media campaigns or publicists like Rush Limbaugh meet the plausibility test. They knit together symbols of common sense from everyday reality with simplified notions of more general symbolic universes so that the listener/viewer comes away saying, "I'll just bet that's true. It just stands to reason." So, if Tricky Dick Nixon used selective roll-call data to label earlier congressional opponents as pinks (note, not quite red), surely with all the powers of the presidential office he must have used dirty tricks to destroy honorable opponents for the presidency in 1972. Or, if Slick Willie Clinton, a Southern good-old-boy governor married to a tough feminist like Hillary Rodham, had a long-time extramarital affair with Gennifer Flowers, surely he used his state police guard to set up liaisons with female state employees who gave "come hither" looks. It just fits the pattern. And goodness knows what he would do, and did do, with women in the White House.

The point is that the symbols of meaning for everyday life into which we are socialized by close group affiliations become the frame of reference for more elaborate symbols that explain how the world works beyond everyday reality. Even the most powerful overarching symbols such as texts from sacred scriptures need homilies by which they become intelligible to us "where we are." And since the purpose of meaning is often to stimulate and legitimate action, those plausibility structures that involve the human will or are driven by emotions have far more power or efficacy than those worldviews and doctrinal systems that are heavily rational.

Secondly, groups are a basis for cleavage in society because they promote *consciousness* of kind through the process of *social identification*. In the language of Turner (1982, 16), "individuals who share a common identification of themselves . . . often . . . share no more than a collective perception of their own social unity, and yet this seems to be sufficient for them to act as a group." Through social identification with a group, we become aware of who we are and who we are not, of how we ought to behave and what we ought not do. We build personal identity from social identity, rather than vice versa. Becoming part of a collective permits social comparison as a way of nurturing self-esteem or of contributing to a sense of unjust deprivation, both of which are important political mechanisms. And fundamentally, Turner claims, "social identity monitors and construes social stimuli and provides a basis for regulating behavior" (21). Some social situations will switch an identity on or off. Group salience is a vital phenomenon in cultural theories of politics.

The power and cumulative effects of social identification are amply illustrated in Converse's study of the 1960 elections (1966). Analyzing NES data from the Kennedy-Nixon contest, Converse notes substantial crossovers of Protestant Democrats to Nixon, and Catholic Republicans to Kennedy. Thus, although Kennedy had tried to put his Catholicism to rest as a *campaign issue* at the Houston Ministerial Alliance meeting, it still had efficacy as a *social identification* that attracted or repelled voters. Even more interesting is the differential attraction among Catholics. Frequency of mass attendance—an *interaction* measure—had less effect in enhancing a Catholic vote for Kennedy than did *communal identification*, an item that measured how closely the Catholic respondent felt toward Catholics. Further, Irish Catholics who had voted for Eisenhower in 1956 felt an even stronger pull toward *Irish Catholic* Kennedy than Polish or Italian Catholics who had supported Eisenhower earlier. Similar communal affinities have been measured between evangelicals and Carter in 1976 and Episcopalians and Bush in 1988. The point is evident: it is not issues or group interactions alone, but social identification that can develop or disturb normal electoral patterns.

Cognitive psychology has generated a substantial body of knowledge about the contribution of social identity to intergroup relationships. Social heuristics, schema theory, stereotyping, and explanations for outgroup antagonisms all derive in one way or another from Turner's *categorization law* (28, 30). Social deduction "refers to the process by which a person is assigned some attribute on the basis of category membership." Stereotyping itself "creates or enhances perceived intragroup similarity." We will discuss these psychological mechanisms in more detail in chapter 5, which is devoted to the psychological mechanisms behind campaign strategies.

The third contributor to the group basis of cultural politics is *social cohesion*. The recurrent interaction of group members not only socializes specific cultural values but, more importantly, reinforces them; they become the basis for both crystallization of viewpoints and mobilization of behavior. People who interact regularly around shared values influence each other. The resulting social cohesion provides an affective basis for the group. It goes beyond the cognitive basis of social identification alone. In a sense, group interaction is the context for individuals to receive their marching orders about culture and politics. Normally, we would expect members who interact more regularly to hold onto more of the central values of the group and to be more likely to behave consistently with those values (see, for example, Homans 1950).

Analyses of the 1988 NES data and the 1989 Pilot Study demonstrate that even with other dimensions of religiosity (doctrine, denomination, devotion, and salience) controlled, the degree of religious involvement has a substantial independent effect on moral traditionalism and conservative stances on social issues (Wald, Kellstedt, and Leege 1993). That is, those who interact more with fellow members through church membership, attendance, and participation in other church activities are considerably more likely to display political attitudes consistent with church teachings. Social cohesion reinforces group values. A carefully controlled study of Protestant congregations in Florida also reveals the effects of behavioral contagion among frequently interacting co-religionists in conservative churches (Wald, Owen, and Hill 1988; 1990).

Finally, politicians act as though groups count and, in so doing, switch *group salience* off and on. In preparation for the casting of campaign themes, political handlers conduct research on "the white Southern vote," "the Catholic vote," "the union vote," "the Hispanic vote," "the women's vote," ad infinitum. Politicians do not necessarily think of these as bloc votes. Rather, they see tendencies in groups. By singling out groups for special kinds of treatment—a form of market segmentation—they attempt either to enhance or to depress the effects of these tendencies. If the context of politics is structured through such group symbols, one should anticipate that the individual voter will respond, at least partially, through a group hermeneutic.

Gerald Ford's celebrated gaffe in the 1976 debates and George Bush's deft handling of the pledge of allegiance in 1988 provide an interesting contrast between the positive and negative effects of group symbols. Richard Nixon had driven a wedge between the Democratic party and its group base among Southern and Eastern European ethnic, blue-collar Catholics on the Vietnam issue. Their sons and daughters, in good patriotic fashion, had fought the war against the spread of communism. Catholic ethnics resented the educated elites who had taken over the Democratic party and denigrated the war effort. Ethnics were still there for Republican beckoning in 1976, even after Watergate. But in the debate, President Ford got confused on his response to a question about communist domination of Eastern Europe, particularly Poland, and appeared to be soft in his understanding of how communism had swallowed up the relatives of these ethnics. Social identity with the country of origin became inadvertently salient, and these ethnic Catholic voters walked back to the Democratic column, even though its presidential candidate was a Baptist who spoke with a Southern accent. Some forms of social identification are more salient than others at certain times.

In 1988 George Bush, who had not established a pedigree in flag waving, flew Old Glory to victory. Again an immediate predecessor, Ronald Reagan, had reminded these ethnic Democrats of the importance of military vigilance against communism. Bush, a decorated aviator from World War II, could overcome his silk-stocking, old-wealth, prep school appearance by using a symbol that had special meaning to the ethnics who had lived by all the American rules. The pledge of allegiance, recited as a litany at every campaign liturgy, reminded ethnics not only that a fellow ethnic, Michael Dukakis, was suspect on communism because he was a "card-carrying member of the ACLU," a group who supported the "right" to burn the flag (shades of Senator Joseph McCarthy's earlier xenophobic appeals), but that the new leadership of the Democratic party was drawn from those who had *not* fought communism in Vietnam, who protested or resisted their country's call (Blumenthal 1990). Although very distant by birth and cultural affinities, Bush reminded ethnics that he was closer to them in values than the wayward ethnic sons and daughters now leading their party. This cultural appeal was duly rewarded at the polls, as many European ethnics continued to feel comfortable pulling the Republican lever.

The following generalizations and propositions can be drawn from this discussion:

1. Groups, as the primary context for cultural differences, form the basis for political cleavage.
    A. Groups socialize new members, whether voluntary affiliates or generational replacements, into their values.
    B. The more primary the group, in terms of its members' primal bonds, intensity of emotional commitment, or proportion of life space consumed, the more likely that "everyday reality" is defined through the group's symbols.
    C. Meaning and the machinery for legitimation from higher-order symbol systems are often integrated with primary group symbols, not through rationality and consistency tests, but through plausibility and coherence appeals.
2. Social identification, anchored simply in categoric membership rather than face-to-face interaction, is a powerful basis for structuring political choice.
    A. Social heuristics and stereotyping derive from social identification, and they allow individuals to complete the picture of

"our kind" and "their kind" on the basis of simple group categorization.

   B. Both outgroup differences and within-group similarities are enhanced by social identification processes.

3. Social cohesion, deriving from regular interaction among a group's members, reinforces and crystallizes the group's values and mobilizes members to act in appropriate ways.

4. Politicians use various means to make group membership salient and in so doing contribute to the structuring of society along cultural differences.

SUMMARY

This chapter has examined the raw materials of cultural theory in the realm of electoral politics. We understand culture primarily in terms of Wuthnow's *moral order*, a concept with strong affinity to religious worldviews or the symbolic construction of social reality. Culture becomes grist for political action in many ways and is largely articulated in terms of concrete appeals to the values of distinctive groups. Cultural appeals in politics are latent forces rather than inevitable aspects of public life. For the latent power of culture to be made manifest in elections, it requires the conscious efforts of political elites to reach specific groups. In the next chapter, we discuss the manner in which political activists attempt to draw on the power of concerns about moral order to politicize social differences.

CHAPTER FOUR

Election Rituals, Ideological Movements, and Group Politics

THE STAPLES OF cultural politics are ambitious politicians, as well as groups who need the resources of the state to promulgate or realize their values and interests. The variables are long-term social change, episodic events, and the latent and manifest identities and stereotypes of citizens. The products are political strategies, as well as ideological mobilization, both based on cultural differences. This chapter explores the process by which cultural appeals, which we understand as mobilizing tools that are "available" to those who seek them, are actually created and deployed in the electoral process.

We start with ambitious politicians, an essential component of cultural politics. Ambition—to be at the top, to control the personnel and policy of government, to have a place in the sun, the limelight—is principally what drives politicians (Downs 1957; Ranney and Kendall 1956; Schlesinger 1966). While politicians speak of public service and their programs for the nation, state, or city, *the program* is to gain public office and to stay there. Voters, parties, and election campaigns are the essential instruments to effect the program.

Elections are significant cultural rituals in and of themselves. But ambitious politicians will also use a variety of cultural appeals to gain mastery over their opponent and to legitimate their ascent to center stage in the political system.

RITUAL, CAMPAIGNS, AND ELECTIONS

Wuthnow (1987, 109) has defined *ritual* as "a symbolic-expressive aspect of behavior that communicates something about social relations, often in a relatively dramatic or formal manner." Ritual is a symbolic action that is embellished and repetitive. Properly done, ritual bestows legitimacy. By rehearsing appropriate social relationships over and over and over again, ritual reinforces meaning.

Elections, in a democratic order, are rituals. Repetitively, to call into being, simple procedures are used to legitimate someone's assuming enormous political powers. Following campaign appeals of months and years, those defined as duly registered citizens go to ordinary places in their neighborhoods—schools, firehouses, church parlors, township halls, recreational centers—stand in lines, sign poll books, pull levers on a machine or punch holes in cards or scratch boxes on a piece of paper or press a keyboard that flashes a computer menu—all quite ordinary. Their choices are tallied and aggregated within political units across the country. Conventions are followed in the awarding of their aggregated votes among the candidates. And suddenly the social hierarchy between president and citizen, Congress and citizen, is legitimated. The outcome may not be satisfactory to everyone, but if the ritual was done properly, the disgruntled citizen usually has to wait until the next election ritual to get even.[3]

In its simplest structure, the political system we call democracy has three components: (1) *ambitious politicians*; (2) a variety of *institutional actors* desiring either control or influence over the personnel and policies of government; these range from political parties to economic firms and culture-maintaining organizations, all of whom need the state for resources that will promulgate their values or further their interests; and (3)

---

[3] Well, not quite. Election is the dominant ritual for legitimation in the American democracy, but we are developing other rituals for delegitimation. Ginsberg and Shefter (1990) have described one of these as RIP—revelation, investigation, and prosecution. In instances where the election ritual has produced a suspect winner—whether by landslide or squeaker—another set of rituals can make it very difficult for that leader to govern. Charges of inappropriate behavior reveal that the winner has not performed properly within the ritual. Special investigators or prosecutors use painstaking search procedures followed by the klieg lights of congressional hearings or the hallowed sanctums of courtrooms to establish the legitimacy of those revelations. Then follows a determination regarding the legitimacy of the leader's remaining in control of the reins of government.

Examples of RIP are abundant: Nixon's landslide election in 1972 was followed by the Watergate investigations and his eventual resignation. Reagan's landslide victory in 1984 was followed by the Iran-Contra hearings. Speaker of the House James Wright, Democratic leader Tony Coehlo, and House Ways and Means chair Dan Rostenkowski were powerfully legitimated by successive election rituals but were felled by RIP in the early 1990s. Bill Clinton won by a squeaker in 1992 but was never given much opportunity to govern, as charges of scandal after scandal occupied his White House. House Speaker Newt Gingrich no sooner celebrated his "hundred days of revolution" in reordering the government in 1995 than he was derailed by charges of personal and ethical impropriety. In 1996 Clinton won more handily but was dogged by the charges of reckless sexual misconduct in the White House; eventually he was impeached but not convicted of the charges. Yet much of the time otherwise spent on governing was devoted to his denial and defense strategies. Following the failure of the 1998 Republican strategy to expand their control of the Congress, Speaker Gingrich felt compelled to resign as a party liability. His successor-designate, Representative Robert Livingston, never assumed the speakership because of his own admissions of sexual misconduct. And Representative Henry Hyde, the august chair of the House Judiciary Committee, which conducted the impeachment hearings, was tarnished by his own admission to "youthful indiscretions" (like Clinton, in his forties). All were exposed by political enemies and the press, although all had been duly legitimated by elections.

the *electorate*, composed in varying degrees of political isolates and group members. The first two sets of actors compete for the resources of the third—their vote, that is, their conferral or withdrawal of legitimacy—to accomplish their objectives. The instruments for this competition are the symbol systems used in campaigns and elections.

Campaigning or electioneering has the four characteristics of rituals: (1) it defines and regulates social relationships; (2) it provides a social message through dominant cultural values; (3) it conforms to known realities; and (4) it reduces uncertainty by conveying the actor's intentions (see Wuthnow 1987 for an extended discussion of these functions). For the most part, the lengthy campaign process culminating in the election meets these functions. However, campaigns, like markets, are somewhat imperfect. The actor's (campaigner's) personal meaning and strategic calculations may differ from the social meaning of the campaign and thus confound the other actors in the relationship (the electorate). Through promises, the campaigner may convey one set of intentions about policy that allows him to be viewed as acceptable to strategically important mainstream groups, but the actor may have neither the intent nor the capability to follow through on the promises, once elected. Yet in the emotional rationality of the campaign, such behavior "makes sense."

The campaign and election define and regulate social relations primarily through legitimating the ruler-ruled social hierarchy. It communicates that other mechanisms—elite circulation through ordination, resolution of group conflict through violence, etc.—are inappropriate. Competition for leadership and competition among values is permitted, but primarily within the constraints of the election ritual. It is always difficult to determine whether (1) failure of the electorate to participate in large numbers undermines the legitimacy of the ritual, (2) low turnout symbolizes high levels of consensus over values or contentment with policy, or (3) the continued involvement of elites from rival groups is what really matters in a democracy. Turnout remains a problematique for scholars.

In another respect, the campaign/election ritual defines and regulates social relationships. It specifies which groups are embraced by the political system and which values can lay legitimate claim to a place on the agenda. These fluctuate through time in any political system. Many African Americans had been systematically disenfranchised from post-Reconstruction on, until the civil right legislation of the mid-1960s guaranteed the vote. As the civil rights movement gained momentum in the 1950s and 1960s, a consensus developed among both blacks and whites that blacks "belonged," that is, should be treated as citizens, as full members of the community. For a time this consensus fueled policies of implementation that expanded opportunities for blacks in education, employment, and housing. But by the late 1970s, the consensus disintegrated as other values, particularly the concern about government growth, the role of the unelected judiciary, and the value of limited government, grew dominant once again. Ronald Reagan could call forgetting "the government off our backs and out of our pocketbooks." Not only was this a statement of principle about deregulation and taxation, but it was also a symbol of the perception that the federal government had gone too far in ensuring opportunity for African Americans; its programs taxed suburbanites, while redistributing revenues to the cities and the rural poor, both symbols for blacks (Edsall and Edsall 1991). Along with limited government, symbols of inequality ("quotas") were used to reverse the direction of policy, as legitimated previously at elections.

Similar reactive symbols about the *proper* place of women, minorities, and intellectuals were invoked in 1980 and 1994, as both the Carter and Clinton administrations responded to the legitimating claims of each for a place at the policy table. The profusion of high-level appointments for women, blacks, Hispanics, and Jews, and more recently gays and lesbians, left other groups who felt they had a corner on the dominant posts feeling symbolically disenfranchised. Agitators who play on the latter groups' feelings may use strong symbols during the course of campaigns to call attention to the displacement in social relationships—for example, "pointy-headed intellectuals" (a particularly virulent form of anti-Semitism), "effete snobs," "radicals," "feminazis" (equally virulent sexism), or a variety of terms for gays and lesbians too offensive to repeat.

Secondly, the campaign/election ritual provides a social message through dominant cultural values. The ritual reaffirms collective values. Few campaigners have the temerity to move outside the symbols that dominate at any given time. Their "issue images" provide a guide to what matters collectively. At the height of the Cold War and shortly after the McCarthy hearings (themselves considered a ritualistic witch hunt), for example, the footage of Richard Nixon's kitchen confrontation with Nikita Khrushchev at a trade fair in Moscow became a centerpiece of the campaign. Its social meaning was clear: though inexperienced Democrats could only talk UN diplomacy, Dick Nixon would get tough on those crude communists! Later, when Americans wallowed in collective guilt about Watergate (*we* had legitimated the Nixon reelection by a landslide), Jimmy Carter, a born-again Baptist Sunday school teacher who wore sweaters instead of suitcoats (one of us) could appeal to the American people—"trust me"—and call "for a government as good as its people." The social message was that this honest outsider could reclaim Washington from the scoundrels for us honest folk! After the first Reagan term, when the malaise of long lines at the gas pumps and staggering inflation was over, when the collective embarrassment of the Iran hostage crisis was concluded, when the rearmament against the Evil Empire of

Soviet communism flourished, then the passionate optimist, Ronald Reagan, could come to the American people in the grandeur of a sunrise (not sunset), and we all understood the message, "It's morning in America!" By 1984 the long night of Democratic misrule was over; the Reagan revolution had reinstated the proper values and restored our collective national pride. Still later, in the continued anti-Washington climate of 1996, Senate majority leader Bob Dole, the consummate Washington insider who had lived and led in the capital city since about the time that President Clinton was a Hot Springs, Arkansas, teenager, would choose to present himself to the American people simply as *citizen* Dole from Russell, Kansas. The message must always fit dominant cultural values.

Successful reaffirmations of collective values generally suggest who is to blame without implicating all of us. For example, diagnoses of the disintegration of the American family implicate illegitimacy for the rise in welfare, crime, generalized lawlessness, drugs, cheapening of human life, and so forth. And illegitimacy generally connotes *women* who have erred, usually those who are weakest on the social hierarchy, rather than men, who are more dominant on the social hierarchy. It is the women who have sex, fail to contracept, and make babies—not the men. Dan Quayle moved a step further than illegitimacy by fingering the cultural elites who control primetime television and throw up inappropriate role models. However, a lot of the public had watched Murphy Brown and thought she was funny. The Quayle appeal found supportive ears among the cultural populists of the religious Right, a growing base for the Republican party (and Dan Quayle), but was ridiculed by the press and the cultural elites, who were confident that Nielsen ratings also represented mainstream cultural values. Bill Clinton learned from the Quayle experience, shared the sense that illegitimacy did not bode well for Americans' traditional sense of appropriate social relationships (moral order), and confined the blame to illegitimacy itself. His campaign for welfare reform never strayed far from the illegitimacy symbol. In so doing, it carried the social message reaffirming a moral order but not implicating the rest of us, particularly men, in undermining that order.

The campaign/election ritual conforms to known social realities. This aspect of ritual is seen in two ways: (1) certain sequences of behavior must be followed for the principal practitioner of the ritual (the campaigner) to be seen as legitimate, and (2) the symbols employed in the campaigner's ritual must cohere into a plausible story, a script, for the electorate. There is generally a calculus of candidacy that makes the candidate viable (Abramson, Aldrich, and Rohde 1994)—prominence and experience, money, media mentions, elite and rank-and-file support, and a sense of electability. The campaigner builds momentum as he or she passes certain caucus, primary, and convention hurdles. But often cultural tests of character and personality challenge the candidate.

These tests are modified at different times in the life of the country. For example, the generation that went off to World War II centered on the dominant, gallant male in the context of fleeting relationships. Eternity may be tomorrow but ecstasy is tonight, the male claimed. The storied infidelities of John F. Kennedy were not only *not* problematic to his election but a badge of merit to which his generation of males deferred. The press, still a male bastion, could fantasize admiringly but see the behavior as irrelevant to the office. Females, in the social relations of that culture still lived as reflections of their male partners. Thus Kennedy could accept the office, look forward to his term, look forward to a new baby, and quietly continue the liaisons, even in the White House—a complete family man, no questions asked!

By 1992, however, even *rumors* of infidelity became high hurdles in the course of the campaign. The moral order that had developed in the interim saw women as persons in their own right, with their own aspirations and their own claims to autonomy. Neither charm nor power was a legitimate rationale for men to use women as playthings. The new sexual morality required informed consent by both parties. Candidate Gary Hart had tried to flaunt his prowess by the old reality in 1988 and was quickly discarded. Candidate Clinton passed some of the early hurdles toward being taken seriously as a ritual performer, but the womanizing charge involving Gennifer Flowers soon blocked his progress. He was able to slip through the horns of a dilemma by symbolizing another reality of contemporary male-female relations. Marriages are rocky roads. Wife and husband may love each other but have different goals. They pull apart and one or the other partner strays a bit. But instead of a divorce, they tough it out and may even develop greater mutual respect. A candid television appearance by the reunited Clinton couple on Super Bowl Sunday 1992 stressed such cultural realities. Implicit in that confrontation with the country was the moral maxim—"let he who is without sin among you cast the first stone." The Clintons merged higher-order symbolism with everyday reality to sidetrack the charges.

At the same time, the later allegations by Paula Jones and the conservative cultural groups who encouraged her to bring charges posed ever so much more explosive a challenge. The allegations conformed to another reality of contemporary social relations—lack of consent by the woman employee is what defines sexual harassment by the male superior. Particularly, the women's groups who had supported the Clintons were faced with a dilemma. Thus, even an incumbent president can be involved in a continuing campaign ritual where his relationships must conform to the current moral order. A president may be legally immune to charges but is never culturally exempt. A story that is coherent and plausible under one set of rules (moral order) may not "work" at another time or place.

Perhaps surprisingly, by late 1998, when the charges that Clinton had engaged in an illicit affair with a White House intern came to fruition, much of the public seems to have viewed itself as immune to the charges. For many, the accusers had become the equivalent of neighborhood busybodies, poking their nose inappropriately into other people's *private* behavior. While moral revulsion attached to Clinton following the release of the clinically detailed Starr Report, moral revulsion also attached to Special Prosecutor Starr and to the Republican majority for dragging the country through slime. The country seemed unable to judge itself—after all, we had elected him twice—and it seemed prepared to reserve harsher judgments for other types of nonsexual infractions by his designated successor.

Finally, the campaign/election ritual reduces uncertainty by conveying the actor's intentions. This is at one and the same time the very reason for the ritual and what makes the campaign/election imperfect as a ritual. Wuthnow (1987, 120) offers the profound observation: "ritual is most likely to occur in situations of social *uncertainty*. Other things being equal as far as the resources and freedom for engaging in ritual are concerned, the greater the uncertainty that exists about social positions, commitments to shared values, or behavioral options likely to influence other actions, the greater the likelihood that behavior will take on a ritual dimension of significance, that is, will involve important aspects of expressivity."

In Anthony Downs's influential economic model of democracy (1957), both parties and candidates interact rationally in a situation of uncertainty. Since they cannot gain all the information they need about each other, they participate in a cognitive miser's ritual: each relies on ideology. For Downs, ideology is a verbal picture of the good society and the principal means of achieving it. Ideology is indexed by the core values associated with each party. The respective candidates never stray too far from their party's core values, and the voters look for heuristic symbols that locate each candidate within the predictable range of his or her party's values. Much of campaign rhetoric involves the repetitive use of core values to praise one candidate or blame the other. This is done by attribution: "if X is a Democrat, no matter what he claims, he is just another tax-and-spend liberal"; "if Y is a Republican, she may claim to care about you but is out of touch with the good working families of this country." Events occur that trigger these attributions. In 1992 Clinton called for a spending program to jump-start the economy and for tax justice, that is, taxing the well-to-do, that made it easy for Republicans to categorize him. Also in 1992, a decade after their introduction, Bush marveled at the use of bar codes at a convenience store check-out counter, affirming precisely what the Democrats had been saying about this Republican leader's lack of contact with reality. The cognitive misers of the electorate needed little further information about each.

Honesty is sometimes a casualty of the use of campaign ritual to reduce uncertainty. In his 1984 acceptance speech, Walter Mondale offered a moment of unusual and politically stupid candor: "My opponent will promise never to raise your taxes. I just did (the opposite)." With sirens blaring and horns honking, he gave incumbent Reagan the "tax-and-spend liberal" issue to use against another Democrat! Candidate Clinton never gave his opponents such an opening, no matter how hard George Bush or Ross Perot pressed him on the balance sheet of his economic plan. Simply put, in this ritual the actor's (campaigner's) intention is to get elected, and the symbolic reduction of uncertainty is more relevant than the policy intent.

In a broader systemic sense well beyond the conduct of the campaign, the election ritual is essential in reducing qualms about the right of any person to the highest office in the land. Ours is a nation lacking an aristocracy, and no one has a divine right to any status. For a time, the men of learning and means governed, but the election of Andrew Jackson in 1828 legitimated a new myth that has democratized the nation: log cabin to White House. What makes a person honest is not the absence of political duplicity, but the evidence of humble origins or the ability to surmount adversity. "Honest Abe" becomes the model, a man of the people, "a man of sorrow and acquainted with grief," as Deutero-Isaiah has it. Others have followed the example. When faced with a slush fund scandal, vice presidential candidate Richard Nixon called the public's attention to his humble roots—raised in a bungalow in Whittier, California, loyal in wartime and persistent in completing Duke Law School, hand-picked by that paragon of honesty, Dwight David Eisenhower, struggling to make ends meet for his young family and their dog, Checkers. How else was a humble man to get somewhere in politics without the support of backers? Bill Clinton used the same kind of legitimating material. Never to know his biological father, standing up for his mother victimized by a violent, alcoholic second husband, finding solace in his saxophone and church choir, discovering a role model in JFK, fashioning a political career out of a Georgetown degree, a Rhodes Scholarship, Yale Law School, and J. William Fulbright as a sponsor, Clinton plunged into policy solutions to the problems of a backward state with his savvy wife. This became the 1992 version of the log-cabin-to-White-House myth. Citizen Dole from Russell, Kansas repeated the symbolic-roots material in 1996.

Even the well-to-do air their human stories of overcoming adversity in the campaign ritual. Herbert Hoover, a brilliant engineer, was a self-made millionaire from little Branch, Iowa. Patrician FDR surmounted polio and showed his grit. JFK survived a debilitating war injury. And George Herbert Walker Bush gained his own fortune on the roughneck Texas oil fields, where he learned to love pork rinds and detest broccoli. Even Dan Quayle became not the scion of a publishing empire but a newspaperman out of Hoosier hometown, USA, Huntington, Indiana. And although he had long ago moved to the affluent golf courses of Arizona, in 2000 Quayle used Huntington, Indiana again to declare his candidacy. No matter what their family station in the social hierarchy, democracy generates and legitimates its leaders through core egalitarian and perseverance symbols. If they are of us and have shown their mettle, if they convince us in the great election ritual, they have the right to be our leaders.

We conclude with several generalizations and propositions:

1. Ritual is a dramatic, repetitive symbolization of proper social relationships. It is a particularly expressive way to legitimate a moral order.
    A. Elections are the primary ritual of American democracy, legitimating leadership in a social hierarchy necessary for collective decision-making.
    B. Done properly, the election outcome satisfies the need for a legitimated order until the next election.
    C. Disgruntled losers, whether persons, parties, or groups, may use the RIP ritual—revelation, investigation, prosecution—to delegitimate an election outcome, but they will have to show how either the election process or a candidate's credentials were inappropriate for establishing a legitimate order.
2. The election not only selects leaders but also specifies which groups can be involved in the system and which values can be placed competitively on the public agenda.
    A. A new value consensus may lead to rapid policy advances for a group historically excluded from recognition.
    B. When the value consensus begins to disintegrate, opponents of the newly advantaged group will recall other values of the moral order as a means of halting or rolling back the advantages realized by the new group.
3. Campaigns revolve around the symbols of collective values dominant at that particular time, often involving the stuff of everyday reality to build plausible themes about higher order symbol systems.

A. Campaigners generally avoid symbols of collective blame. They demonize target groups that symbolize what is wrong in the social order and how the rest of us, through reaffirmation of values, can solve that problem.

4. Tests of candidate character must conform to social realities known at a given time. Those candidates who fail to conform to the dominant norms at that time are often dismissed.

5. Under conditions of uncertainty, parties and the electorate engage in cognitive misering through the use of ideology. They employ negative and positive attributions to characterize candidates through the historically dominant core values of their respective parties.

　　A. It is sometimes disadvantageous for the campaigner to reveal his or her full intentions and capabilities. He or she will instead reduce the electorate's uncertainty through symbols of collective values during the campaign ritual.

　　B. Given that American democracy is egalitarian, those candidates who symbolize humble roots, persistent effort, and/or ability to transcend extraordinary adversity are adjudged as legitimately qualified for the presidential office.

Political Strategies, Ideological Mobilization, and Cultural Mechanisms

We have repeatedly described cultural politics as a variable rather than a constant. By this, we mean that both the choice of cultural appeals and the suitability of the political environment work better under some circumstances than others. As a rule, we expect to find the cultural style most potent when long-term social change has produced strong challenges to the moral order. In the following section, we consider the time frames for election rituals.

Long-Term Social Change

Long-term social change disturbs the moral order. The established social hierarchies are no longer legitimated through consensus, and competing value systems gain credibility. Long-term social change may derive from a variety of sources: international conflicts requiring national mobilization; transnational economic forces demanding restructuring of domestic economic sectors; scientific and technological advances raising new moral questions; heavy immigration of new ethnic groups that places stress on the economy, housing, and educational systems aimed at those lower on the social hierarchy; middle-class assimilation of heretofore nondominant ethnic groups that also places stress on the economy, housing, and educational systems of the middle class; or, finally, baby-boom and bust cycles that lead to generations differing widely in size and life experience. Any can leave people with puzzles over how to behave. Any of these factors can lead to challenges on the group boundaries that define a nation. Any can lead to the scapegoating of less dominant groups or the targeting of external enemies. And all lead to displacements in the rank and social approval awarded the dominant groups.

As described in chapter 2, the country underwent massive changes in the social order during and following World War II. Traditional norms and social obligations were cast aside in the face of new situations. Even the reassertion of old norms had something of a facade to it, as the eventual social disintegrations attested. New types of people emerged as economic and political leaders and culture creators. In time, those feeling most displaced by new rules or no rules held the new elites accountable. They created a "parallel culture," employing the same technologies as the elites, to raise consciousness, gain converts, and mobilize opposition. By the 1970s and 1980s it was evident that not only was there a struggle for cultural dominance, but it was politically advantageous for parties or ambitious candidates to enjoin one side or the other. The struggle to fashion and legitimate a new moral order took on many forms. Some were developed by younger members of traditional elites seeking to shore up their rank in the social hierarchy. Most of the other forms, however, involved those "ordinary people" feeling displaced, or ambitious political leaders who saw advantage in their feeling displaced.

According to Wuthnow (1987, 156ff. and 233–47), groups feeling threatened by an emerging moral order will use ideology to symbolize their political efforts. He has elaborated six forms of ideological development that confront the risk, ambiguity, and unpredictability of uncertain social relationships: revitalization movements, ideological revolution, militant ideologies, counterreform movements, accommodationist efforts, and sectarianism. We will examine three of these types of movements that were prevalent in the post–New Deal era of American politics.

Revitalization movements, according to Wuthnow (1988, 233–34) "are attempts involving some form of religious, quasi-religious, or political ideology to collectively restore or reconstruct patterns of moral order that have been radically disrupted or threatened." While Wuthnow identifies five varieties of revitalization movements ranging from nativism to messianism, and all of which we argue have occurred in the United States, we think the form of revitalization that has had the most lasting impact on American politics of the era is the urban reform movement. It led the establishment elites of mainline Protestantism and progressive Republicanism to try to revitalize cities through community development programs, metropolitan government and other structural reforms, support for the civil rights movement, and empowerment of neighborhood groups of new ethnics through community action committees.

The old local elites of this country faced serious displacement problems in the 1950s and 1960s. While they competed for urban political leadership in the middle of the twentieth century with ethnic Catholics and Jews, they still controlled a goodly share of the economic structures, civic life, and cultural life. But the heavy black migrations north and the more recent Latino and Asian immigrations meant the loss of local control. The civil rights movement and the Great Society programs of the 1960s allowed local elites to link hands with government and neighborhood to revitalize their churches and restore their neighborhood bases. They sought cultural pluralism less than they wanted to socialize the new residents into economic and civic virtues. Through federal programs they shared positions of leadership on planning boards, a form of co-optation of the new peoples. Their public-regardingness (cf. Banfield and Wilson 1963) could be mimicked, and they would not have to give up essential values to accommodate the interests of the new arrivals.

There were three important political consequences of this reform or revitalization movement: (1) the progressive moralist wing of the Republican party, which had its roots in the party of Lincoln, found new purpose and vitality; (2) disapproving middle-class laity who felt threatened by the embrace of new groups loosened their ties to local churches, withheld funds, and attributed less moral authority to the clergy (Hadden 1969); and (3) some of the established leadership, strongly committed to this revitalization movement, were drawn into regular contact with Democrats who had similar commitments, relied on funding programs of the federal government based on their common values, and eventually traversed the divide into the Democratic party. But the numbers found in the third and first categories were substantially smaller than the numbers in the second. In a series of showdowns for leadership of the Republican party, the progressive wing that was allied with the revitalization movement lost to the conservative wing of the party—Nixon (Rockefeller 1960), Goldwater (Rockefeller 1964), and Reagan (Bush 1980). The Goldwater and Reagan ideals of limited government captured the value vision of the disapproving laity, particularly when government action meant that new groups would occupy positions on the social hierarchy equivalent to theirs. Thus, ambitious politicians outside the traditional Eastern Republican leadership could give representation to the those who rejected this revitalization effort and build their coalitions.

Counterreform movements are aimed primarily at those in the middle or lower ranks of the social hierarchy. They draw their leadership not so much from the traditional dominant elites who are attracted to revitalization or accommodation, but from displaced or aspiring elites. Revulsion over the values of ascendant elites becomes their mobilizing symbol. Typically their appeals resemble classic populism—the good, ordinary people taking their country back from the new elites. Counterreforms seek not so much to dominate the political system as to reinstate the predictability of the *traditional* values of the old moral order. The rejection of the Equal Rights Amendment and the re-emergence of evangelicals as a political force late in the post–New Deal period are prime illustrations of counterreform ideological movements.

In a political era that witnessed great successes for the feminist movement, Phylis Schlafly might be held up as the movement's example of a woman who did it all. Mother of a large family, active leader in a church body not noted for encouraging women in such roles, attorney, well-to-do, accomplished organizer and platform speaker for her Eagle Forum, Schlafly appeared to symbolize the contemporary values about women. The problem for the women's movement was that she spoke passionately on behalf of *traditional* values. A Catholic with a pre–Vatican II outlook sharpened by disgust with her church leadership's recent statements on war and peace and the economy, and an ardent free-enterpriser and anti-Communist, Schlafly favored audiences composed not of equally accomplished women, but of middle-class and working-class mothers, faithful within their respective religious traditions. Studies by Mansbridge (1986) and others show these women to value the role of homemaking and to be upset that feminists would seek personal fulfillment outside of spousal and maternal roles.

Traditional male politicians elected to state legislatures, especially from nonurban areas, saw in Schlafly a great ally for the status quo. If her counterreforms succeeded, legislators would not have to share a place in the sun with "pushy" women. They gave her all the public platforms she needed, and, although both Republican and Democratic traditionalists benefited from her counterreform efforts, she became a fixture on the Republican dais.

An even more important component of the counterfeminist movement has employed both status displacement and evangelical values to mobilize women foot-soldiers. The largest of the groups in this category appears to be Concerned Women for America (CWA), organized by Beverly LaHaye in 1979. Its local, even neighborhood, base is Prayer Action Chapters, but it also makes heavy use of Christian broadcasting. According to a study of evangelical political activists by Guth, Green, Kellstedt, and Smidt (1994), CWA best fits the populist model of middle- to lower-middle class women, over half of whom are fulltime housewives, spread across the country, born again through a sudden conversion experience, religion at the center of everyday reality, and surrounded by friendship networks of those with identical religious values, their own children in Christian schools or home schools rather than public schools, and determined to root out the evil that rules the land (Ephesians 5:11). Two-thirds of them feel there is only one correct Christian view on most political issues, three quarters call themselves not only conservative but part of the Christian right, all but a handful identify the three most important problems facing the county as "moral problems" (rather than economic justice, environment, etc.), 90 percent are on the Republican side of the aisle, 99 percent voted for George Bush in 1988, and about 40 percent feel the United States needs an explicitly Christian political party.

There are many other such interest groups, perhaps not so pristine in values and populist in orientation, who have been drawn into the Rev. Pat Robertson's Christian Coalition and mobilized within the current Republican party. Robertson is also a classic illustration of a counterreform leader, especially when contrasted with Al Gore, an accommodationist. Son of a conservative Democratic U.S. senator from Virginia, Robertson had a bumptious boyhood and avoided combat in Korea, serving by his own admission as a liquor supply officer. But he had a conversion experience, discovered a charism for preaching, produced and performed in a popular televangelism program, displayed considerable business acumen in developing a Christian communications empire and university, and entered politics as a populist Republican candidate. He designated his enemies as the cultural elites that "control" the mainstream media and the Democratic party. They became symbolized in a tarnished version of the lifestyle of Bill and Hillary Clinton. His following, largely pentecostals, is mobilized through classic negative outgroup appeals. His ability to generate a vote was seen in the 1994 congressional elections, particularly open-seat contests in the South. These elections completed at all levels of the ticket an evangelical religious realignment aborning since 1972 (Green et al. 1996, 291–99).

An *accommodationist* ideological movement is difficult to isolate from the normal processes of segmentation and agglomeration. Accommodationism adapts ideology to new forms of social relationships, not at the time of maximum disruption and intense value competition, but when things settle and the system is reintegrated. It is usually directed by ascendant groups and their leaders who replace the old leadership. Such leaders straddle both the old and new camps and are often subject to virulent charges of value pandering by those compatriots of their generation who go in counterreform directions. For example, Vice President Al Gore, the son of a populist senator from Tennessee, prepped in Washington and matriculated at Harvard. A Southern Baptist, he married Tipper, who railed at the satanism embedded in rock lyrics. Yet he appeared on

MTV in 1992, courting young voters. A centrist, he had the support of both blacks and whites in the "new South" and was respected for his economic program by business leaders. Yet he reached out to environmentalists through a book that made tough indictments of capitalism's systematic destruction of the natural environment. As a bundle, the symbols do not jibe. Yet as politics, the symbols make good electoral sense.

Accommodationism is primarily a movement of newer elites to assume the reins of leadership. Its appeals are pragmatic and its value syncretism is tolerant. It precipitates both schism by counterreformers and grudging acceptance by older elites sent to pasture by the value cleavages of the social disruption stage. The old elites and the accommodationists share one common perspective: a moral order in a pluralistic society is not easy to achieve without bargaining and compromise over the scope of coercive sanctions. Accommodationist movements often gain the eventual support of revitalizing movements.

Episodic Events

These types of ideological movements and their corresponding political strategies derive from the disruptions of long-term social change. Ambitious politicians and concerned groups also respond to *sudden* or *episodic events*. An event may come to symbolize a disruption in social relationships that makes group identification salient. During the post–New Deal period, several such events have had substantial electoral impact.

The civil rights movement, followed by the urban riots, presented unique opportunities for the politics of cultural differences. During this period the public symbols of the Democratic coalition had shifted from a party primarily concerned with social welfare to a party primarily concerned with civil rights and social justice. Already in 1948 the Dixiecrats bolted the convention after the adoption of young Minneapolis Mayor Hubert Humphrey's civil rights plank; Governor Strom Thurmond (D-SC) became the Southern Democrats' leader on that occasion, but the Democratic voting habit had been broken regardless of leader in successive elections. Then, in 1958, moderate and progressive Republicans were replaced in the senatorial landslide by liberal Democrats (Carmines and Stimson 1989). The last vestige of leadership symbolism furthering opportunity for black Americans through government action was slipping away from the Republicans. Democrats took on those symbols, particularly with Lyndon Johnson's strong advocacy of the civil rights legislation of the mid-1960s. Newly enfranchised or newly mobilized blacks became Democrats. Nevertheless, outside the traditional segregationist leadership in the South, there was still willingness to use government to encourage equal opportunity for all regardless of race.

However, two events upset the time series. Barry Goldwater offered a public philosophy of limited government that sanctified opposition to federal intervention on behalf of civil rights—as a matter of principle. The only states that Goldwater carried in 1964 were the five Deep South centers of segregation, but his campaign paved the way for successors who could find other approaches to representing racial resentment. The second event was the urban riots. The devastation of inner city after inner city reinstated segregationist stereotypes of blacks as lawless, at best, uncivilized, at worst, unworthy of the benefits of U.S. citizenship. The concentration of black voters on the Democratic side now became a negative symbol to many whites (Edsall and Edsall 1991).

The "tax-and-spend liberal" label came to symbolize the policy responses the Democratic party took to urban disorder. Democrats offered even more of the Great Society programs, arguing that unrest was the predictable response of an oppressed people. Republicans, on the other hand, co-opted George Wallace's "law'n order" symbol; the best solution to disruptions of a moral order that formerly had told people their place, how to behave, was strong law enforcement and severe penalties. They would tolerate no coddling of criminals; the argument that criminals were products of the lack of opportunity was phony. Until the opportunity presented itself in the 1994 Crime Bill championed by Pres. Clinton, Democrats watched haplessly as Republicans deployed these three negative outgroup symbols with strong racial overtones—tax-and-spend liberal, law'n order, soft on crime. Events at critical times, followed by different policy responses, made one form of cultural politics—that based on race—highly salient throughout much of the period.

Another event worked, for a time, to the Republican party's disadvantage. Deep in U.S. cultural roots is the notion that religion is evidenced in rectitude, in pious behavior (Weber 1946). The anti-Catholicism frenzies, following heavy Irish Catholic immigration in the 1830s, eventually got institutionalized in the core symbolism of the two parties. The austere, pious Yankees and their upper-Midwestern descendants gave the Republican party a claim to piety, which they often contrasted with the drunken, brawling Irishmen who were minions of big-city Democratic bosses. Well into the twentieth century, it was easier for corruption charges to taint the unholy Democrats than the pious Republicans, although the actual incidence of misdeeds was probably evenly balanced.

Added to this negative symbolism in the post–New Deal period was the fact that the militant advocates of changing social relationships centered their attention on the Democratic party. The drunken Irish worker of the nineteenth century was replaced as a symbol of licentiousness by feminists, gays, hedonists, and other disturbers of the moral order who seemed to call the shots at the boisterous Democratic conventions of

1968 and 1972. The first major attempt by a party to accommodate groups representative of major social changes occurred with the Democrats' selection of George McGovern in 1972. By contrast, Nixon and the Republicans could be seen as the symbols of decency. The Democrats began to lose more of their group base among Catholics and evangelicals.

Then came Watergate. This critical event unfolded a sequence of electoral conflict where piety and pride were the symbols for making cultural differences salient. What made Nixon's impropriety so harmful was that it violated a core Republican symbol, our expectation of how a Republican would act. Gerald Ford's response of pardoning Nixon only heaped coals of fire on the transgression; it was plausible to believe he had been named vice president through a deal, a plea bargain. Republicans now were not only impious but coddled criminals. The situation almost commanded the emergence of Jimmy Carter; the one-term governor but Southern evangelical could offer the country piety. He was an outsider who could restore symbolic integrity to that tainted city on the Potomac. Evangelicals, frightened by McGovern in 1972, could mobilize for one of their own in 1976. Again, in-group symbols served better than actual policy stances to reduce citizens' uncertainty.

Piety, appealing during periods of moral uncertainty, seems to wear rather less well in the long run. Lacking national policy experience and relying on close associates from Georgia who were political neophytes, Carter offered little competence on policy matters, and the country slipped, by his own admission, into a period of malaise. Worse yet, Carter was held responsible for a continuing insult to our national piety: an ayatollah in Iran, an infidel, made mirth of American honor by holding scores of countrymen captive over an extended period of time. The opposition party had to do little to make the event salient; news moralist Walter Cronkite reminded the country nightly how long it had been. Much as Nixon's moral transgressions were tailor-made for Carter's campaign of moral regeneration, Carter's failure to defend American honor virtually demanded a restorationist campaign. As if on cue, Ronald Reagan emerged in 1980 with a clarion call to bring America back to its rightful standing in the world and to its senses domestically. Appeals to national pride are typically rooted in a symbolic return to a sense of moral order. In Reagan's case, the famous "morning in America" ad in 1984 communicated a reelection campaign based on cultural fidelity.

A decade after the hostage crisis, another sudden event soon showed the transitory nature of once certain cultural appeals. In 1989 and 1990, as communist countries fell like dominoes, the Republican party was left without its salient anti-Communist anchor and the electorate was left confused. The Cold War had constituted a moral order; it had shaped national purpose and policy. The interstate highway system could otherwise have been labeled "pork," but it was, symbolically argued, essential for national defense. Fellowships for graduate school and the study of exotic languages, not normally a high public priority, were justified by the National Defense Education Act. Like any bureaucracies, the National Aeronautics and Space Administration and the National Science Foundation grew, but their growth was rationalized because we were in scientific and technological competition with the Soviets. The largest welfare/workfare spending program in the country, national defense, ate up the largest single share of the budget because we needed both military production capacity and defense preparedness. A whole way of life was validated by contrasting it with the communists.

Faced with the breakup of the communist empire, what was the electorate to do? What was to become of George Bush and Republican presidential fortunes? Bush's demise was about what could be expected when a given of the moral order was no longer available. For a time, Bush demonized as a Hitler the leader of a third-rate power who had recently been our ally against an Islamic fundamentalist country. But not enough people were living for whom Hitler was a demonic symbol, and in fact, St. George did not slay the dragon—he stopped short of taking Saddam out. There was talk of "a new world order," but few knew what it meant. Other problems, suppressed so long by the negative Soviet symbol, began to bother us more: the economy, lacking showy governmental action, was on an uninterrupted decline; jobs were exported; Japanese products were imported and foreign corporations took ownership of some of America's best-known trademarks; middle-class wages had remained flat or shrunk for a decade; the deficit grew and national debt management ate up more revenue than defense spending; entitlements seemed an important symbolic problem until we realized they went mainly to the dominant middle class; and so it went. And so George Bush went—in an election where Republicans and those who were previously attracted to Republican cultural symbols split up among Bush, Perot, and even Clinton, and not voting. An event can withdraw central symbols of a moral order so dramatically that political leaders cannot recover.

A final type of episodic event is one so dramatic that it captures the imagination of a group and becomes a basis for mobilization. The illustration is the hearings on Judge Clarence Thomas's nomination to the Supreme Court. The retirement of Associate Justice Thurgood Marshall from the high court presented a dilemma and an opportunity for Republicans. The dilemma was that the seat was viewed as a black seat by the symbolic representational rules of American politics, but few prominent blacks with the qualifications for the high court were not both Democratic and liberal. Judge Thomas, however, had served as President Reagan's director of the Equal Employment Opportunity Commission during its rollback in the favorable handling of complaints and was a recent appointee to the bench. Up from poverty, Baptist-reared, Catholic-educated, and now Episcopalian, Thomas fit the pattern of a man who had moved beyond the boost any government program might provide for a minority. Further, he had once served on the staff of Senator John Danforth; mainline Protestant revitalizers like Danforth, an Episcopal priest, and Senator Richard Lugar, a former Methodist lay minister, were insistent that the Republican party not jettison its historic commitment to equality of opportunity for blacks. On occasion, George Bush, an Episcopal layman, had also espoused those values. A nonevent of Thomas's confirmation was in the making.

But Anita Hill, formerly a close staff associate of Thomas and by then a law professor at the University of Oklahoma, confirmed rumors of sexual harassment by her boss. The fifteen white males on the Senate Judiciary Committee alternately assumed roles of judge and prosecutor, apparently depending on partisan needs. The White House, in a plan carefully crafted by David Gergen, systematically primed the public in positive symbols of fair play and negative symbols of aggressive feminism. It also cautioned Southern and border state Democrats on the committee who were up for reelection that they would commit political suicide if they supported Hill's claims. Judge Thomas fashioned his case through the symbols of a black male who faced a lynch mob. The White House was able to show progression in the polls toward its symbols—Hill was perceived as a liar—and it prevailed in the vote. Judge Thomas became Justice Thomas.

Yet the event crystallized the inadvertent mobilization of another group, women. Having tasted bitter defeat in the failures of states to ratify the ERA, and the gender gap having narrowed substantially by 1988, the women's movement had languished for nearly a decade without organizing symbols. The women's movement found its mobilizing event in several images: in the charges of sexual harassment committed by a male superior; in the passiveness of fifteen white males who "just didn't get it," and especially not the Democrats who were violating the expectation of sensitivity to social justice and civil rights; in the aggressive prosecutorial style of Senator Arlen Specter and the "hypocritical disbelief" of Senator Orrin Hatch, a respectable Mormon. In state after state, women entered and won primaries for the House and Senate; EMILY'S List and other political action committees (PACs) raised and disbursed record sums of money for women candidates.

It is too early to assess the consequences of this inadvertent mobilizing event. While record numbers of women were indeed elected to the House and Senate, as many women's movement leaders have pointed out, record numbers of women were *defeated* in these contests in 1992 and successive elections or reelections. Generally, the more limited the previous elective experience of the female candidate, and the more the reliance on this symbolic event to mobilize the vote, the less was the likelihood of success. While indeed more women carried symbolic cultural appeals under the Democratic banner, a substantial number of women ran successfully as Republicans. Thus, women's issues do not necessarily carry advantage for one party over another.

TACTICS OF GROUP POLITICS

Many of the cultural mechanisms are evident in the political strategies that respond to long-term change and episodic events. Let us make some of them even more explicit.

Strategic politicians appeal to "us versus them" feelings by manipulating symbols of *relative deprivation*. This concept refers to the tendency of people to judge their condition not by some absolute standards but by making comparisons between their situation and that of other groups. They ask who is benefiting from government policies, and whether that group deserves to benefit as much as "we" do. In cultural politics involving race, the Rainbow Coalition under Jesse Jackson's direction presumably linked people across racial boundaries; yet primarily it mobilized populist antagonisms against big business elites who, every member of the Rainbow Coalition perceived, were wealthy white males. The "tax-and-spend liberal" symbol used so successfully by Republicans conjures pictures for suburbanites of their tax monies being redistributed to benefit the urban underclass, most of whom are blacks "who deserve their plight." Further, revenues are redistributed by distant social planners who are electorally accountable to no one. Crime, plea-bargaining, and lenient sentencing call to mind images especially of blacks who live outside the laws that everyone else must obey, and who pay a price inappropriately small for their misdeeds. Even in a period where the curve depicting rates of illegitimate births to white women far outstrips the curve for black women, illegitimacy continues to be associated with black "welfare queens" who will get every penny they can out of the welfare system by having babies instead of working (cf. Katz 1989 and Gilens 1999 for evidence that these policy symbols are heavily racially charged). Each of these involves a calculus of relative deprivation brought on by a perceived imbalance in a white-dominated moral order.

Many of the uses of relative deprivation to manipulate religious beliefs for political advantage also involve revulsion over an unworthy group's being recognized by the state. Those faithful to a pietistic religious discipline may resent that gays and lesbians would be permitted in the military, because homosexuals should be precluded from the honor of representing their country; they are too sinful, "an abomination to the Lord." They may resent feminists in high-level Washington appointments because these women are not properly oriented toward marital and family responsibilities. Finally, they may resent secular humanists teaching in the schools because not all values are equally truthful, and those who advocate morally inferior values should not be allowed access to children's minds. In each case, the sense of relative deprivation comes from the recognition that someone who is "judged unworthy by God's law" is allowed equal access by the state. There are, of course, other stereotypical social heuristics operating in these cases: for example, gays are promiscuous and will use close quarters to force their advance on others who are not gay; feminists are secretly lesbian; or secular humanists are part of an international communist conspiracy to undermine the moral fiber of America.

Particularly on economic matters, relative deprivation is a useful political tool for politicians. For example, baby boomers and seniors are two groups pitted against each other in many policy areas. Boomers may fear that the generous payout policies on pensions and healthcare at the current time will deprive them of benefits when they grow older. Such economic differences are not of themselves cultural politics, but they become so when the groups attack the values and lifestyles of each other. Younger people question whether the lives of older people should be prolonged at great expense. Older people claim that boomers want everything right now, rather than waiting their turn for the good life.

Strategic politicians often *structure the group consciousness of in-groups*. Ted Sorenson's memo on behalf of John F. Kennedy at the 1956 convention indicated that simply the presence of a Catholic on the ticket could guarantee Democrats victory in the large states necessary for an electoral majority. Converse's analyses (1966) confirm that in-group perception matters to voters. Dan Quayle was selected over many highly qualified senators as George Bush's running mate in 1988 because of the political generation—baby boomers—that he represented. Bill Clinton and Al Gore were the first all-boomer ticket, and they brought different styles of campaigning to illustrate the fresh approaches of a new generation.

Strategic politicians also *heighten the perception of threat* to a dominant but vulnerable group's way of life. In 1990 Jesse Helms broke open a close but losing campaign with an ad that showed a quivering white hand holding a job rejection notice. The voice said, "You wanted that job but it went to someone else through affirmative action." The viewer could readily make the negative transfer to Helms's black opponent, Harvey Gantt. Race was the negative cultural appeal. Lee Atwater's revolving turnstile ad in 1988 featuring Willie Horton was of a similar cultural genre. Many prisoners passed through to the outside, but the close-up focused on the black male.

At times a party, White House, or campaign may *co-opt a "moral" activist*. For example, Richard Nixon's staff lost no opportunity to tout his friendship with the Rev. Billy Graham. The social meaning is that Nixon must not be morally suspect if Billy Graham associates with him. In 1960 Robert Kennedy convinced his brother that a call supporting the jailed Rev. Dr. Martin Luther King would tell a story that black voters would never forget. In both 1984 and 1980 Democratic nominees felt they could not emerge from the convention without the public support of the Rev. Jesse Jackson. In 1992 Bill Clinton saw greater political advantage in the reverse—in denouncing the radicalism of Sister Souljah's rap lyrics—and, in so doing, neutralizing any visible role Jackson could have at the convention; Clinton's ratings among white males leapt eight points following the incident. Yet in the darkest days of his impeachment, Clinton kept the Rev. Jackson visible at the White House. And he kept his link to the boomer generation's mega-chuches in the Rev. Bill Hybels.

Strategic politicians will *symbolically award the benefits of distributive or redistributive policies to groups*. For example, when a major bill is signed, not only its sponsors and party leaders are present for the White House photo-op, but the recognized leader of the group that most wanted the policy beams over the president's shoulder. Often when redistributive legislation benefiting a group languishes, it is relabeled with more positive symbols aimed at general support. Thus, parochial school aid faltered for over a century. When sanctified under the pluralistic symbol "school choice," the policy found more support. It is no coincidence that Republicans embraced the issue at a point where they had a special opportunity to attract Catholic voters. "School choice," as a policy symbol for subsidizing nonpublic schools through the children who attend them, also coincided with the rapid growth of evangelical Christian schools.

Ideological movements will also seek to *agglomerate a majority coalition within a party by adding on and integrating issues*. For example, conservatives under the Goldwater banner in 1964 staked out clear and (for the time) "extreme" positions on a number of issues. Their objective was to crystallize the vision of conservatives, to show them that they could take over a party. They were soundly trounced in the election. But instead of folding their tents and leaving the party to others who were more centrist, they remained friendly with the Wallace forces in 1968 and allowed Wallace to mobilize normally Democratic voters by negative outgroup appeals against war protesters, radical students, intellectuals, and government bureaucrats.

Once elected, the Nixon White House made use of the Wallace language, especially through speech writer Patrick Buchanan and Vice President Spiro Agnew. Kevin Phillips (1969) showed that cultural populism could pay handsome dividends. The cerebral conservatives of the original Goldwater movement then joined hands with the Wallace voters and the emerging religious right. The McGovern candidacy in 1972 came to symbolize to Catholics and evangelicals how far their party had strayed. And, although Watergate created Carter, and Carter was helpful in mobilizing even more evangelical voters, conservatives were able to put the grand coalition together by 1980 with the Reagan candidacy (Blumenthal 1986; cf. Crawford 1980; for insightful interpretations of this lengthy effort, see also F. Clifton White for the original design, as quoted in Freedman 1996). By the 1980s the public interest had been redefined in symbols that captured all of these conservative ideological and cultural groups.

At times, however, a *coalition* includes so many disparate groups and values that it *becomes unwieldy and must be purified*. Otherwise it spins with explosive centrifugal force. Luce and Rogow (1956) have demonstrated that a minimax strategy is safer for a party if it has policy objectives. The breakup of the New Deal coalition and the resulting Kennedy strategy illustrate both the problem and one solution. The Democratic party of the 1950s was an unwieldy coalition—urban ethnic Catholics, organized labor, intellectual liberals and Jews, southern Bourbon traditionalists, the Jeffersonian Democrats at the core of the party's Midwestern small-town base, and a growing number of blacks. The 1948 Dixiecrat bolt foretold the impossibility of this coalition. What was needed was something more culturally compatible.

Kennedy presented a unique opportunity. As a Catholic he had an affinal following in the large electoral college states of Northeast, Midwest, and Pacific Coast. He entered a marriage of convenience with Lyndon Johnson aimed at some Southern states but knew it could not last. He needed to mobilize new, more reliable support, if the loss of traditional Democrats in the South was inevitable because of racial differences. First, the creation of the "war on poverty" (recall that it was in the planning stages before Johnson assumed the presidency) and then a full embrace, however reluctant, of the civil rights movement would mobilize the new voters of a purified minimal majority. Blacks could and would vote. Poor whites in Appalachia or their migrant capitals like Flint, Michigan, or Akron, Ohio, would find benefits in Democratic programs. Intellectual liberals were dazzled by the Kennedy wit and Camelot. Catholics would stay with a Catholic. And labor had nowhere else to go. The strategy might have worked, were it not for assassins' bullets in 1963 and 1968 and a tragic accident at Chappaquiddick in 1969.

Republicans faced a similar problem going into 1996. The party of Main Street, country club, enterprisers, anticommunists, and mainstream

Protestants is increasingly the party of the lower middle class, evangelical Protestants, and young Wall Street flashes. The Christian Coalition has little in common with the coke-snorting arbitrageur and yuppie. The disaffected middle-aged couple who has lived by the rules all along asks why the greedy who scoffed at the rules got so rich in the 1980s, the very era of Reagan's cultural restorationism (see Phillips 1990; 1993, for a discussion of this Republican paradox). The question that made early and widespread endorsements so important moving into the 2000 primaries was whether the unwieldy coalition would blow apart or whether the party could find a soul that accommodates enough people.

Strategic politicians will also *forestall a nascent coalition* when emerging groups threaten their continued leadership. Schattschneider (1956, 201) showed how Southern Bourbons reacted to populism by reviving the tensions of Reconstruction. They produced a one-party system that disenfranchised blacks and poor whites alike. Race-baiting became a staple of this Democratic party system. Similarly, the Reagan forces used symbols of stiff resistance to abortion and support for school prayer at election time but did not follow through with stiff constitutional amendments or legislation. They needed the support of Catholics and evangelicals but feared what would happen to conservative leadership if the "too-religious" groups ever came to dominate the party (Leege 1992). Thus, traditional Republican leaders feel comfortable themselves using the specter of theocratic control as a way of driving a wedge between the moralistic forces now starting to dominate the party.

Another cultural strategy of politicians is to *exploit the negative effects of modernity*. Technology, particularly instantaneous telecommunication, the geographic mobility required of modern labor forces, and social disruptions resulting from rising expectations and status displacements all throw very different people into symbolic if not physical contact. People not like us are now in our town, are shown on our televisions, are acting up in parades. These people may have existed before, but at least we did not know about them. Now their behavior threatens us, and we worry that it will influence our children. They are at our hospitals and malls, their kids are in our schools, their images are on TVs in our kitchens and bedrooms, and their sexual innuendoes are online on our children's computers. An increasing share of public communications programming is devoted to negative contacts with such people—talk shows on TV, call-in shows on radio. It is the cultural politician's dream, all that uneasiness needing symbolic recognition and sound-bite solutions. It can be given timeworn respectability with the "town meeting" format, as Bill Clinton demonstrated in 1992. It can be given technological dazzle as the Ross Perot model of tele-democracy promises. Or it can remain in its more crass forms as the immense audiences for Rush Limbaugh or Howard Stern demonstrate.

Multiple points of access in the American political system also condition the possibility of cultural politics. Ideological movements, parties, or candidates can aim at legislative, executive, or judicial branches or at any level—international, national, state, local, special district such as school, or neighborhood. There is a parallel to the old political adage, "if you can't beat'em at the game, change the rules." It is, "if you can't beat'em at the game, change the arena of combat." Thus, ambitious political actors and institutions needing the resources of the state to promulgate their values will search for the most appropriate venue for success. That is evident in the antiabortion movement. Groups thought they could get a constitutional amendment from the Reagan administration to outlaw abortion but instead got a litmus test for Supreme Court appointees. Once the new majority was assembled on the Court, the *Webster* decision (*Webster v. Reproductive Health Services* 1989) shifted the arena of combat to state legislatures. There the availability of abortion is increasingly circumscribed, and many appellate courts are upholding restrictive legislation under norms of health or public safety. At the same time, various forms of "moral presence" or even more intimidating tactics are used at the level of the provider. In turn, those who want to assure readily available access to abortion have gained extension of provisions from the Racketeer Influenced and Corrupt Organizations Act (RICO) to make intimidation techniques very costly and have sought legislation to put *Roe v. Wade* into statute. Much of the politics of cultural differences is indexed by presidents using various symbols to acknowledge "the problem," but the actual combatants seek the most favorable venue for policy satisfaction.

Finally, the *scope of the modern state* pushes more and more of our pluralistic cultural differences into public decision-making arenas. Just as the technology of modernity removes the privacy of our respective folkways, so the philosophy of liberal individualism dominant in the modern state inexorably moves us toward national norms, either to protect us from others' values or to extend coverage—whether of benefits, opportunity, or respect—equally. That means the politicization of what was once the private sector. And that translates into many more topics for ambitious politicians to manipulate and for resource-seeking groups to defend. It also means that, in the face of the increasing number of issues, coalition cohesion becomes increasingly difficult. It is hardly a surprise, then, that such a large share of the post–New Deal political agenda addresses what are at root cultural differences about our conduct and social obligations.

The following generalizations may be drawn from this discussion of political strategies, ideological mobilization, and cultural mechanisms:

1. Long-term social change disturbs the social order so profoundly that it precipitates several kinds of ideological movements.

A. Revitalization movements involve the efforts of established elites, particularly religious, to co-opt newly recognized groups in civic restoration, but through the elites' values. However, elites may run the risk of losing moral authority over their traditional middle-class followers, and their political allies may lose control over political institutions to rival ideological movements.

B. Counterreform movements led by aspiring elites capitalize on the sense of displacement felt by rule-abiders in the lower and middle ranks of the social hierarchy. Through populist appeals they seek restoration of the old moral order.

C. Accommodationist movements are led by younger aspiring elites who straddle both social change and old values. Their new moral orders may have inconsistent elements, but they are driven more by the need to bargain than by the need to win on fine ideological points.

2. Sudden or episodic events offer fortuitous situations for ambitious politicians to create cultural symbols that dramatize group differences.

    A. Unexpected events—e.g., urban riots—can turn a positive, consensual symbol—e.g., equal opportunity—into a negative symbol of racial inferiority.

    B. Political elites face particularly great risks when they fail to live up to the conduct of symbols they own and regularly manipulate—e.g., piety and Watergate for Republicans.

    C. A sudden event that withdraws the salience of a symbol may cut adrift voters anchored in a party by that symbol—e.g., the unexpected demise of communism and the reliance on appeals to anticommunism and patriotism.

    D. An event that dramatizes lack of concern for a core value may countermobilize a group that perceives it has been taken for granted—e.g., the Thomas hearings before the fifteen white males of the Senate Judiciary Committee and the electoral mobilization of women.

3. Strategic politicians will turn long-term change and episodic events into opportunities to use cultural appeals.

    A. Strategic politicians will employ "us versus them" language to manipulate feelings of relative deprivation over group benefits, group worthiness, or group recognition.

    B. Strategic politicians will make group consciousness more salient through appeals to affinal ties.

C. Strategic politicians will make group consciousness more salient through heightening the perception of threat.

D. Strategic politicians will build bridges to social groups by co-opting their "moral" leaders.

E. Strategic politicians will devise policies that promise benefits to specific groups but justify them through consensual cultural symbols.

F. Strategic politicians will expand their coalition by symbolic appeals to groups formerly in the orbit of third candidates or the opposition party, usually by the creation of anxiety about another group.

G. Strategic politicians will divest some groups from their coalition when the coalition becomes unwieldy with culturally warring groups.

H. Strategic politicians can exploit the proximity of different groups created by geographic mobility and instantaneous communication to stoke fears about their values.

I. Strategic politicians can use multiple points of access to select the most accommodating level or branch of government to satisfy a group's aspirations for an appropriate moral order.

Summary

Social change provides the raw material of cultural politics—challenges to a moral order that threaten established standards of conduct. Unless these grievances are politicized—given shape and partisan coloration—they will not produce electoral change. In this chapter, we have considered the role of elections as legitimating rituals, the kinds of symbols deployed, and information provided to voters. Further we discussed the process and mechanisms whereby the challenges of social change can be shaped by elites into weapons of political construction or destruction. The scenarios may vary enormously as social change offers opportunities but identifies no sure-fire strategy for moving voters from their accustomed roles. This chapter has examined the tools that are available to elites who wish to politicize group differences rooted in cultural values. Their use will be conditioned by long-term change, as well as episodic events. In the next chapter, we move from the realm of possibilities to examine some of the specific mechanisms at work in recent electoral history. Where the focus in this chapter has been on elites and political actors, we turn in chapter 5 to the political parties that are the collective embodiment of the cultural impulses we have analyzed thus far.

CHAPTER FIVE

Psychological Mechanisms and Campaign Strategies

THE POLITICIZATION OF group differences is at the heart of post–New Deal political campaigns. A very large proportion of the active electorate remains identified with one or the other of the two political parties (Miller and Shanks 1996), and the membership of many groups is predisposed out of long-term group loyalties to remain within its traditional party affiliation. Yet American parties are catchall parties. Each party is a coalition of many groups. Not all aspects of group loyalty, group values, or group interests can be captured by the core values of a party or made salient in the party's efforts to win any given election. Thus, a party that maintains a plurality of identifiers may still lose an election if part of its coalition either hives off to the opposition or fails to vote. The minority party may achieve victory by strategic attraction of blocs from the majority party or by depressing turnout among certain groups, coupled with the maximization of turnout among its faithful.

We contend that that is precisely what has happened in American politics since the late 1960s. Though it was the majority party among the general population, Democratic presidential candidates lost repeatedly due to depressed turnout and defections to the Republican candidate.[4] In the midst of a general turnout decline during the period, the no-shows were more likely to be Democrats than Republicans; with a handful of exceptions, Republican turnout remained high. Further, when Democrats did vote, they were substantially less loyal to their party's presidential choice than were Republicans. We argue that these "political facts" were not chance occurrences but the product of conscious Republican strategies well founded in psychological mechanisms. Republicans throughout the era were very adept at the practice of cultural politics. As we have argued in the preceding chapters, cultural politics builds on ambition and coalition theories, social identification, and strategic politics. Its campaign tools are social heuristics, emotional appeals, particularly ones that generate enthusiasm in some and anxiety in others, symbolic argumentation based on plausibility rather than consistency, and heavy utilization of

---

[4] Independents who lean to a party are very likely to vote in that direction. Thus, most analysts treat leaners not as true independents but as partisans (Miller and Shanks 1996).

presentational forms in the visual media like TV to make plausible the sometimes subliminal connections among symbols.

We are not arguing that voters are irrational. Given the components of American politics at a time of great social change and cultural dissensus, the electorate made reasonable if not reasoned judgments (Popkin 1991). Nor are we about to accuse the Republican campaigners of making irrational appeals. Politics always involves preferences for one kind of moral order over alternatives, and what matters to groups of voters is often held passionately. The writers of the *Federalist* did not expect citizens and parties to act like altruistic saints. That is why they fashioned a constitutional democracy, a limited government. In so doing, they gave us a recipe for electoral conflict whenever one set of groups felt another set had appropriated the powers of government to diminish the place of the first set. If democracy in time of consensus is often trivial, democracy at times of dissensus is often rancorous. Republicans fashioned presidential victories among those who feared the government had "gone too far"; their strategists visually pointed us toward the groups who, at the core of the Democratic party, were undermining our way of recognizing moral and material standing, our way of doing things. And when Democrats saw opportunity and necessity in making cultural appeals, they did so as well. Let us examine the psychological mechanisms that undergirded this era of cultural politics.

Party Cores and Issue Ownership

Voters perceive each party as the preserve of different groups. During the height of the New Deal, voters considered the Democrats the party of Southerners, labor, small farmers, Catholics, intellectual liberals, and Jews. Voters considered the Republicans the party of big business and Wall Street, merchants, bankers, and small-town entrepreneurs, mainline Protestants, and traditional elites. Blacks were not central to either party. Certain issues are "owned" by one party (Petrocik 1994). Ideological labels—liberal for Democrats and conservative for Republicans—come to summarize a constellation of groups and issues (Conover and Feldman 1981). Our use of a theory of emotions and symbols when related to groups is fundamentally different from other emerging theories of political action under conditions of limited political knowledge (e.g., Lupia and McCubbins 1998). Lupia and McCubbins suggest that campaigns require politicians and their surrogates to provide new information. Individuals then pick and choose which information they assimilate into their pool of political knowledge by drawing a link to existing knowledge (the basic premise of connectionist activity). We suggest that politicians offer known symbols—typically symbols that generate strong emotive responses—to the electorate and directly connect them to groups within the electorate. For members of the politicians' core constituency, this acts to reinforce partisan loyalty. For individuals of the opposition coalition, the hope is that these symbols will weaken ties to previous partisan loyalties and at best encourage voters to defect from their partisan predisposition or at least to encourage them to stay at home.

This process of symbolic manipulation becomes troublesome when new groups grow in size, are granted the franchise, and exercise their bargaining power over policy. Or when new historical events thrust up issues along divides different from the old fault lines, the party core becomes unsettled. Certainly the parties' agendas were changed by World War II and its aftermath, particularly by the upward mobility of Catholics, new opportunities and problems for women, the industrialization and urbanization of the South, the emergence of Blacks, and the large recent migrations of Spanish-speaking people and Asians who were becoming potential voters. To use all of the tools of cultural politics, politicians must be able to find new symbols or update old symbols to capture the current political reality and draw linkages between group and symbol for the electorate.

For a time, partisan stances on issues remain defined as before, but in time the party's leadership redefines its core and calls attention to (and in turn shapes) a new coalitional configuration. For example, the 1964 Civil Rights Act passed the Senate with substantial Republican support. While Hubert Horatio Humphrey (D-MN) led the majority forces, Everett McKinley Dirksen (R-IL) produced the Republican votes to override Southern Democratic opposition. A core component of the Republican coalition, mainline Protestants from the Midwest, lobbied the party's electoral representatives relentlessly on behalf of this epochal bill (Hadden 1969). Then the 1964 presidential campaign saw a Republican opponent of the act go down in defeat while showing extensive, perhaps eventually majoritarian, support for the Republican party in the South. Still, Senator Dirksen joined with President Johnson and Democratic leaders to shepherd through the Voting Rights Act of 1965. In 1966, when Johnson's civil rights proposal included an "open housing" title, Senator Dirksen refused to support it, and Republicans refused to join Northern Democrats in a cloture vote to halt a Southern-led filibuster (Sobel 1967). From that point forward, the Republican party came to be viewed as the party that would apply the brakes to government action to enhance opportunities for minorities. (We discuss the phenomenon more in chapter 9.) In any event, the ideological basis of the two parties shifted (Conover and Feldman 1981), and the groups perceived to be at the core of each party began to change (Miller and Wlezien 1993).

The dominant groups of each party fluctuate as a function of historical events, party elites' definitions of the importance of a group to a winning coalition, and the rival candidates' labeling of the parties. Whatever "owned" issues become salient in a given campaign fluctuate as a result of the same factors. Voters will process campaign information both with the residue of past perceptions and with the recent activation of memory. For example, late in the post–New Deal period, Bill Clinton presented himself as a centrist Democrat, as a throwback to the days before "tax-and-spend liberals" came to dominate Democratic party imagery. Yet his health-care reform proposal became an easy target for a Republican symbolic appeal—just more big government that will transfer tax dollars from self-sufficient Americans to those undeserving social deadbeats "who don't live right."

A Theory of Emotions in the Campaign

Our approach to the political psychology of cultural politics both deviates from and draws on the predominant scholarly approaches to the understanding of voter decision-making. To place our approach in the context of existing scholarship, we briefly review the major approaches to voting.

Over the last quarter century, much of the literature on campaigns and voting has addressed the rationality of the American voter. In part, this line of inquiry was a reaction to the earliest sociological studies of voting that saw the vote choice as a product not of careful information searches and the weighing of alternatives, but of group memberships (Lazarsfeld, Berelson, and Gaudet 1948) and social contexts that reinforced predispositions (Berelson, Lazarsfeld, and McPhee 1954). It also flowed from V. O. Key's posthumously published (1966) critique of *The American Voter* and its psychological theory, viz., that vote choice is a product of a force field involving parties, candidates, and issues, but that party identification predisposes one's assessments of the other forces. Finally, the exploration of voter rationality reflected the attraction of parsimonious economic theories (Downs 1957) and advances in positive theory (Riker and Ordeshook 1973).

Yet seldom could rational-choice theorists characterize the voter as exercising more than *bounded rationality*. Even Downs pointed out that the costs of information seeking were too high for the individual voter, so the voter relied on party ideology as a shortcut. Party elites, in turn, shaped a reasonably predictable picture of party ideology for the voter. Fiorina (1981) argued that the voter acts as a cognitive miser by doing *retrospective voting*, that is, evaluating the performance of the incumbent president and his party before deciding whether to seek information about the opponent's prospective promise. Research since then has often shown that party identification heavily influences retrospective and prospective assessments (Abramson, Aldrich, and Rohde 1998).

Operating from different orienting theories drawn from cognitive psychology, political psychologists addressed rationality by focusing on how voters process information. *Schema theory* (Conover and Feldman 1984; Lau and Sears 1986; Lodge and Hamill 1986, and many others) argued that candidate and party perception "fit" preexisting expectations based on the social and political identifications/locations of the voter. In a sense the stimulus-organism-response model suggested by Berelson et al. in the 1948 voting study found an elaborated formulation. Further, cognitive psychology was used to demonstrate that voters applied *social heuristics* to their judgments about candidates and parties (Brady and Sniderman 1985; Sniderman, Brody, and Tetlock 1991); they knew each by the company it kept. Voters only needed fragments of information in order to fill out the picture of the political object; inferring them from group labels could simplify attributions of the issue positions of candidates or parties, or of attitudes within groups. For example, if Walter Mondale appeared regularly on the platform with the Rev. Jesse Jackson, it meant that Mondale would embrace racial preference policies as president. The phenomenon is as common in social stereotyping (Taylor, Peplau, and Sears 1994) as it is in political judgments such as candidate choice and referendum voting (Kinder and Sears 1985). We argue that *social heuristics constitute the central mechanism in political choice behavior in cultural politics.* It is the mass populace's way of *satisficing* in the information search (Simon 1957; Tversky and Kahneman 1974).

The power of social heuristics as a tool for understanding what has happened in recent campaigns and voting is that it merges the cognitive, affective, and evaluative functions of choice behavior. It is easy for voters to link seemingly disparate policies, issues, or stories of reality when affective shorthand can bridge limited information to judgments. We will argue that emotions or feelings are the central target of the campaigner because emotional arousal leads to characteristic behavioral states of activity or inactivity (Marcus et al. 1996).

Marcus and his associates point out that, in the human species, conscious awareness makes use of a wide variety of sensory gathering, interpretive, and control systems, including those of which the individual is hardly aware. We argue that presentational forms—for example, images or segments on TV or videotape—do not require the logic of discursive reasoning. The viewer fashions a plausible story from the images; the story often becomes laden with positive or negative affect. But presentational forms are seldom limited to the visual; voice-overs and music are used to create a mood. Jarring noises, raspy voices, or agitated music can stoke an affect of threat, fear, or nervousness; distant orderly sounds of nature, mellow voices, and flowing harmonies can evoke a sense of calm and relaxation (Boynton and Nelson 1995; Johnson-Cartee and Copeland 1997). The content of a spoken message is often less important than the mood the entire set of presentational forms creates; the primary function of the spoken message is to plant words useful in the linking of information, mood, and judgment.

Drawing on Marcus and associates, our theory of campaign dynamics pays close attention to the manner in which campaigns stimulate enthusiasm, generate anxiety, or stoke disappointment. According to psychological theory, individuals who feel a sense of confidence and efficaciousness approach tasks with enthusiasm and mastery. Individuals who sense that their meaning world is shifting at a time they would still like to exercise control will feel anxious and threatened. They will take the actions, whether it be information search or behavioral change, necessary to reinstate an orderly world. When self-confidence wanes or when the individual loses confidence in the responsiveness of the external world to his or her actions, disappointment, loss of enthusiasm, and withdrawal follow.

When the citizen is integrated into a political system, a similar set of psychological states is common. When political leaders on whom we depend perform effectively, we become enthusiastic. In the campaign setting, the confidence that a campaigner will go to bat for our values *and can win* will generate high turnout among the enthusiasts. Doubt about either the candidate's ability to win or his or her commitment to our values, once elected, will dampen enthusiasm and depress turnout. Fear or anxiety about a takeover by forces alien to our party's historic values or core groups will stimulate a search for information about the opposition party or its candidate and will often lead to defection.

How does this apply to campaign strategy? Politicians play these moods either through majority coalition or minority coalition strategies. Previous research (Miller 1990) demonstrates that despite the heralded rise of independents in the post–New Deal period, the overwhelming majority of voters still perceived politics through partisan schema. Since much of the post–New Deal period was characterized by a normal Democratic majority in identifiers, Republicans' best prospects of winning involved stimulating enthusiasm (and suppressing anxiety) among the party faithful, furthering depression among the Democratic faithful, and creating anxiety among Democratic doubters. Faithfulness to core party values and the appearance of being a winner would stimulate the former. But because the number of Republicans was not in itself sufficient to win, Republican leaders would have to do all they could to stimulate anxiety and depression among Democrats and independents who leaned Democratic. The latter could often be accomplished most effectively by using presentational media to link negative group symbols to the Democrats. Using the givens of social identification, perception of the group basis of the party, and social heuristics, Republicans portrayed the ways in which Democratic candidates exemplified disappointing or anxiety-producing behavior. They successfully chipped away at the old New Deal coalition along several cultural dimensions: race in the 1960s, both religion and gender in the 1970s and thereafter, patriotism in the 1960s (addressed to working-class ethnics), and then generationally thereafter by cumulating the symbols of the 1960s counterculture (drugs, sexual permissiveness, lack of respect for traditional ways, etc.).

Such a strategy appears well within the range of democratic campaign appeals. For, what is viewed as a negative campaign by the opposition is considered a positive campaign by the enthusiasts. It is telling it like it is. For example, throughout the middle of the twentieth century, moral restorationists showed little desire to imbibe in politics; conversion and prayer were the only hope for society. But as Republican campaigners gave increasing voice to their fears about moral degradation in America, evangelical Protestants mobilized heavily and entered the party's core by the 1990s. They became enthusiastic about the restoration of a moral order through political action; no longer would their group enemies dominate American public life. In like manner, in the late 1960s, quiescent African Americans came to political life as they sensed the Democratic party would champion their cause. The Democrats could point to a string of legislative, court, and administrative actions that were undermining historic domination by white segregationists. To blacks, these were positive uses of cultural campaigning; to white segregationists, whether of southern states or northern cities, Democrats were guilty of negative cultural campaigning. Heavy mobilization of heretofore passive groups was the result in each of these illustrations.

Campaigners used mood and social heuristics in both a *conversion strategy* and a *mobilization/countermobilization strategy*. The mobilization strategy was aimed at the party faithful: when in office, it made retrospective appeals to the successful performance of the incumbent president or vice president; when out of office it showed the rectitude, commitment to core party values, and competence of the candidate, and exuberance over the likelihood of the candidate's winning. All were designed to generate enthusiasm and turnout among loyalists.

As the perpetual minority party, Republican campaigners aimed their countermobilization and conversion strategies at segments of the Democrats and independents who leaned Democratic. Imagery of incompetence and inability to measure up to the job were used to depress turnout and loyalty among Democratic faithful. Carter, a peanut farmer, could not stand up to the Soviets or the ayatollahs. Dukakis looked like comic strip character, Snoopy, when he tried on the symbol of strength in a military tank. Concern over what unworthy groups would be advantaged by government stimulated anxiety. In Republican symbolism, McGovern and Clinton would turn the government over to the counterculture. Jesse

Jackson would trump every Mondale policy on behalf of African Americans. Because anxiety stimulates both learning and uncertainty about what to do, the negative campaign had the effect of converting some Democrats, suppressing turnout among other Democrats, and increasing enthusiasm and satisfaction among Republicans. A voting electorate of the right size and composition could be created regardless of its initial partisan loyalties.

Often during the period, Democrats failed to understand that presidential elections are about values, not just experience with governing. When the Democratic breakthroughs came, they resulted from the majority party taking over the agenda early and fighting the campaign on its issues. In 1976 outsider Carter's themes of trust and good government capitalized on the grievous failure of the Nixon administration to display rectitude in the presidential office. We could be proud of ourselves again by ousting those who broke trust. James Carville's definition of the 1992 campaign—"It's the economy, stupid"—reminded the organization not to try to play the election on the Republican's symbolic turf, but to stress what had happened economically to the middle class and working class while Republicans had talked patriotism, tough treatment of criminals, no favoritism of blacks and women, and so forth. Clinton exemplified just enough centrist cultural symbols, and there was sufficient confusion following the end of the Cold War, to neutralize the Republican party's cultural advantages. In other campaigns, however, Democrats never could define the agenda—for example, the retrospective voting judgments of 1972 and 1984 (positive toward incumbent) and 1980 (negative toward incumbent)—or they lost control of the agenda through indolence following the 1988 convention.

When the majority party reclaims the Oval Office, the minority party must forestall the development of a nascent coalition. Republicans chose to do so by creating anxiety and depression among the ruling party. As Congress opened its 1993 session, divided government had given way to unified Democratic leadership. Many people appeared optimistic that gridlock was over. But younger Republicans in the House, in particular Representative Newt Gingrich, were able to occupy Clinton by raising culturally salient issues like gays in the military or loss of choice in health care that hurt Democrats; when the action shifted to the Senate, Minority Leader Robert Dole was able to use the filibuster or threat of filibuster to frustrate all but a couple of key Democratic policy initiatives. With Clinton weakened and on the ropes, a bevy of RIP charges followed. Democrats were depressed over their president's inability to act. Republicans, still a minority party, were enthused over the bright prospects for the future.

In the 1994 elections, turnout told the story. Many normally Democratic voting groups—African Americans, women, urban residents—failed to show. Those Republicans who were attracted by rectitude symbols were mobilized in increasing numbers. Those independents and Democrats who were most anxious about their future—such as white males—often defected. The outcome was that slightly over 20 percent of the total eligible electorate swept in Republican majorities in the House and Senate, the first instance of total control of the Congress by Republicans in forty-four years. The emerging cultural issues of the decade—affirmative action, civil rights for gays in the military and in our communities, pressures on women to measure their success outside of domestic roles, welfare and illegitimacy—all lent themselves to management of moods.

As the balance of party identification changes, the strategic behavior of the respective parties' leaders will change. Thus, the post-1994 election polls showed a boost in Republican identifiers that put Democrats slightly in the minority for the first time since the New Deal. Democrats fought back in the same manner that Republicans had when they were the permanent minority. No sooner was the House preparing to organize than Speaker-to-be Gingrich was exposed as a flawed human being whose moral peccadilloes rivaled Clinton's. Senators Helms, Packwood, and Thurmond were all characterized as morally or mentally unfit to assume high leadership posts in the Senate. The specter of domination by the Religious Right was held over the Republican party; the forecast of only religiously intolerant persons being able to win the 1996 Republican presidential nomination was trumpeted. The object of Democrats was to unsettle moderate Republicans, to create sufficient anxiety about their party that they would be less enthused about its successes and more concerned about where the center of gravity in American politics now lay. Democrats had suspected this strategy might be successful with one targeted group—seculars. That their instincts were correct is carefully documented in analyses by Krueger (1998); Democratic seculars increased their turnout in 1992, but Republican and independent secular turnout declined. As our case studies will later indicate, these cultural appeals also cut into normal Republican advantages among highly educated, business and professional women. Democrats exploited the Republican party's symbolic bow to the Religious Right with negative outgroup appeals.

Cultural Theory vs. Other Theories of Campaigns

Our cultural theory of American political campaigns grafts a theory of emotions onto group affiliations. It draws elements from each of the three dominant theoretical approaches to American voting behavior. At the same time as it synthesizes these elements, it expands the scope of voting and participation phenomena that can be explained.

Early studies grounded in Lazarsfeld's research group at Columbia University emphasized the role of the campaign in cueing dormant preferences among partisan loyalists. This research framework drew the basic conclusion that a minimal amount of conversion occurs as a result of consuming campaign information. Instead, candidates seek to (1) trigger partisan behavior among their loyalists and (2) attract undecided or "independent" voters. Partisanship is seen as structured within groups.

Later work within this tradition by Huckfeldt and Sprague (1995) suggested that voters are strongly influenced by friendship networks. While partisanship still plays an important role in the contextual effects model, its placement is not as dominant. Instead, friendship groups play the essential role in shaping individuals' attitudes and behaviors, activation, and vote choice. Unlike antecedent studies, the campaign itself produces little *direct* effect in activation of loyalists, persuasion of "independents," or conversion of the opposition. Campaign themes filter through social networks, thus *indirectly* triggering political behavior.

The "Michigan model" approached voters as elements in a force field. Recognizable elements in the field were parties, candidates, and issues. Research showed the dominant position of party as a reference group. Often lost from research later inspired by the Michigan model was a chapter in the *American Voter* that showed that other primary and secondary group attachments shaped party identification. Although this model is fundamental to much of what we do, our cultural theory is more cognizant of the values group members share, and the symbols campaigners can utilize to activate or deactivate these voters.

Our cultural theory of party loyalty, abstention, and defection also parallels economic models of party identification (Rochester School), but seeks to overcome their limitations. Fiorina (1981) argued that historical and socialization factors created early choices regarding party identification. Party identification is then increasingly shaped over the life cycle by a running tally of retrospective evaluations of the president's performance and comparative evaluations of the parties' platforms. Party identification could vary continuously over a lifetime as new evaluations form about issues and performance.

Our model posits that social factors such as religion or race shape enduring *affective* bonds toward one of the political parties. Individuals identify with parties because they contain "people like me." Our view of party change uses the traditional Michigan model of party identification as a strong affective attachment but also allows for greater transformation based on updated cultural evaluations regarding the party image. Yet, unlike the Fiorina model, which that views changing party identification as psychologically unproblematic when updated evaluations of issues positions and performance call for a switch, we argue that a defection from the party comes only after much anxiety. Because these links to party are more deeply felt than in the economic model, individuals could remain identified with one of the parties but abstain or vote for the opposite party's candidate if they get convinced, often by cultural campaign appeals packaged in the form of efficient symbols, that the leader of their party is not acting like one of us (see Southern white Democrats). Over time, if the other party can consistently and effectively use these cultural appeals, the individual may actually change party identification. Thus, when considering social groups' attachment to a party, we would normally expect party coalition evolution (secular realignment) rather than oscillation.

The Machinery of Contemporary Campaigns

Scholars have long lamented the demise of precinct-level party organizations. They have also taken note that workplace organizations such as labor unions have lost both their memberships and their ability to mobilize disproportionately for one party. The nearest things to precinct-level organizations and solidary incentives in American politics nowadays are churches (Hertzke 1992; Kellstedt et al. 1994).

What has replaced the old campaign organizations and social networks is the modern campaign industry. Polling, focus groups, market segmentation, and talk shows help identify what is salient to the electorate in any given election. Salience, in such arenas, is usually a concern expressed with considerable emotion and negative valence. The modern campaign industry looks for the "hot buttons," the issues or concerns that reflect the greatest anxiety within key blocs of the electorate. The industry seeks to isolate what disappoints people most about their leaders. The television and newspaper news industries focus considerable attention on these negative stories, and in so doing they stoke disappointment, discontent, and anger. Because of the strategies of cultural politics, disproportionate attention focuses on both disappointment and potential defection from the majority party's coalition.

The campaign response to disappointment is a straightforward countermobilization strategy: he let you down. He does not deserve your support. Don't vote for him again (translated, don't vote at all).

The campaign response to anxiety and potential defection is more complex. Sometimes it involves the manipulation of symbols of cultural threat: a harmful group is becoming culturally dominant because of what government has done or failed to do. Sometimes it involves manipulation of symbols of relative deprivation: a group is receiving recognition it does not deserve or material benefits it did not earn—at your expense. Sometimes it involves labeling and manipulation of the free-rider argument, as, for example, draft resisters who retain the benefits of freedom based on others' sacrifices, or mothers who receive welfare benefits for successive illegitimate babies without working to support themselves. Such appeals are components of conversion strategies: your party always respected people who lived by the rules, but now it has left you in favor of people who are culturally very different from you.

The campaign response to anxiety also may couple negative outgroup symbolism to positive rewards for defectors. Group benefits will come to those who mobilize in support of the new (to them) party. For example, a voucher permitting choice of schools will assure parents that their children will not have contact with unionized teachers who have degenerate or relativistic values. Tax cuts will assure that there is insufficient money to be reallocated to welfare free-riders. Reducing the size of welfare checks and placing children in orphanages will reduce exposure to inappropriate role models. Constricting access to abortion services will minimize the presence of an industry that is thought to degrade cultural standards. Removing immigrants from eligibility for public benefits will protect the benefits for "our own" citizens in need.

Issue positions and policy stances are carefully developed to respond to "hot buttons" (see Edsall 1999 for a discussion of wedge issues in campaign 2000). Politicians interacting with pollsters crafted the celebrated Contract with America. Its selling to the public during the first one hundred days of the 1995 Congress was scripted to use codewords for negative group symbols; unfortunately for Republican leaders, the script of what symbols to use and what symbols to avoid inadvertently fell into the hands of the press. Newspaper articles made educated elites aware of how we were being manipulated by scripted code words, but it made little difference to the mass of Democratic voters who were, at that moment, more preoccupied with the O. J. Simpson trial than with the massive changes unfolding on Capitol Hill (Times-Mirror 2000).

Politicians also pay close attention to the salience of an issue to a coalition partner. In a report remarkable for its open references to the instruments of cultural politics, Edsall (2000, A04) argued that the National Rifle Association (NRA) was spending its entire political treasury on mobilizing fearful gun owners against candidate Al Gore. Turnout was the key, not what the polls say about support for gun control laws. Said one NRA board member: "What is important is who will vote? Gun owners will vote when they are mad or fearful and they are both this time." The NRA was expanding membership drives in 2000 because President Clinton was the only major politician since the mid-1960s, when gun control became an issue, not to pay a price for advocacy of gun control; further,

GOP candidate Bob Dole dropped the gun rights issue from his 1996 campaign. This time, according to Edsall, the NRA wanted to make sure Republicans noticed the group's ability to mobilize voters. Another board member argued that proponents of gun control would not vote primarily on that issue; gun owners will. The group symbols and American patriotic imagery the NRA used were vivid: "They are coming after our guns. Gun owners know that if Gore is elected, they will face the day of the long sad march to the government office. They will face the tearful line with their grandfather's priceless old relic cradled in their arms, forced to hand it over to a greedy, disrespectful bureaucrat." The lengthy television advertisement used to recruit members for the 2000 combat showed NRA President Charlton Heston clutching a Kentucky long-rifle, not a pistol or assault weapon. In the voice that he used when playing Moses parting the Red Sea, he disdainfully warned Al Gore, "I am coming after you with the rifle clutched in my cold hand." Despite the climate created by school killings in the 1990s and political assassinations or attempts even on fellow Republican Ronald Reagan, no coalition partner throughout the campaign publicly disowned the Heston imagery. Normally for cultural politics, the disclaimer follows the full play of the mobilization effort. For his part, Gore portrayed "Bush and the NRA as 'anti-family' advocates of allowing people to carry concealed weapons in shopping centers, churches, events and in their cars, and that the sheer number of guns in circulation makes them accessible to dangerous people."

What these illustrations make clear is that contemporary campaigning is a continuous process. The public moods political elites wish to stimulate are shaped as often by policy debates as by campaign-season advertisements. That is, of course, not new. What is new is the great care and expense that goes into market segmentation, that is, finding the target groups at which to aim emotion-inducing appeals. What is also new is the sophistication with which symbols are created and presented, symbols that drive wedges between groups without acknowledging "prejudicial" or "bigoted" feelings toward those not like us.

The following generalizations are drawn from the discussion of psychological mechanisms and campaign strategies:

1. Because political parties consist of core groups and are known by different sets of "owned" issues, voters enter any given election with partially developed schema of expectations about the party's candidate.
    A. With fragments of information, the voter can heuristically decide where this year's candidate fits in the partisan scheme and which groups will likely dominate the party or a future administration.

96 • Chapter Five

   B. Based in such judgments, the voter can decide whether or not to vote, whether to stay loyal to a partisan predisposition or to defect.

   C. Satisficing in the information search allows the voter to integrate the cognitive, affective, and evaluative dimensions of choice. Reason and emotion become indistinguishable.

2. A theory of emotions in political campaigns argues that voters can become enthusiastic, along one dimension, and anxious, along another.

   A. If voters become enthusiastic, they are more likely to turn out. If they become depressed by their typical option, they are less likely to turn out.

   B. If voters become anxious about their typical option, they are more likely to seek additional information and possibly to defect to another option.

3. Parties and campaign organizers build on existing levels of partisanship and manage the emotional appeals of campaigns to control not only the direction of the vote, but also the size and composition of the electorate.

   A. The minority party seeks both to discredit the majority party's candidate and to create anxiety among his potential followers, at the same time that it creates confidence that its own candidate can win. Often the former is done through cultural appeals to vulnerable groups in the majority party's coalition.

   B. The majority party seeks to generate confidence and enthusiasm among its potential followers so that they will turn out and not defect.

4. The machinery of modern campaigns is directed to segmenting vulnerable groups and making negative appeals to them on salient cultural issues. It also seeks to heat up the salience of issues or fears that will increase the turnout of coalition members.

5. The outcomes of presidential elections during the post–New Deal era are a function of both turnout and defection, over the short term, and gradual realignment of vulnerable groups, over the long term. Thus party cores and owned issues may gradually change.

Summary

Culture is connected to the electoral process through the party images and cognitive associations that voters develop. These images and associations are not random or happenstance. They result from the mobilizing efforts of elites who seek to manage the emotional reactions of voters. In this process during the latter stages of the New Deal and the post–New Deal party system, cultural themes and issues have become potent means by which the Republican minority has effectively demoralized the numerically dominant Democratic majority. But Democrats have taken advantage of the potential of cultural politics when their majority is threatened.

To this point, our argument has developed largely in an inferential manner with illustrations and anecdotes. Although we have offered explicit propositions derived from our observations, the analysis has been unsystematic. Following a historical narrative and a methodological description, we will offer an explicit framework for assessing cultural influences among the electorate and apply it to four lines of electoral cleavage.

PART TWO

Case Studies of the Political Mobilization of Cultural Differences

This section presents a historical narrative detailing the cultural strains in the New Deal coalition, a methodology for assessing cultural politics, and case studies of the components and mechanisms of cultural politics during the post–New Deal era. For analytical purposes, we have arranged the case studies under the topics of patriotism and nationalism, race, and the collision of gender and religion.

The primary historical narrative tells the story of how the struggle to define who we are, and are not, pervaded and influenced American politics in the post–New Deal period. Woven into this narrative is material based on content analyses of issue imagery and campaign themes targeted at specific groups. Then, following a methodological chapter, we present three substantive chapters that focus specifically on how voters responded to social change, episodic events, and campaign themes throughout the period. In each chapter we will examine the American National Election Studies time-series from 1960 to 1996 and, in a few instances, from 1952 to 1996. The purpose of this exercise is to map when fragmentation in existing party coalitions occurred. This will be done through measures of party loyalty, turnout, and defection. These outcome measures direct us to where we can anticipate successful strategies of mobilization, demobilization, and defection in a given campaign or a sequence of campaigns. The final part of each chapter examines the central issue and group clusters to which groups in the electorate seem to be responding in any given election. In particular, we hope to show how a set of issue and group feelings is unsettling to a target group so that it departs from its customary partisan loyalty; that is, the group has a high proportion of no-shows or defectors. Where the data exist on the National Election Studies, we will assess whether certain groups are responding differentially to the stimuli of a given election. No organization, even one as competent as the Principal Investigators and the Board of Overseers of NES, is sufficiently prescient to know exactly what to measure in any given election. Thus, we will not always have the hard test that we want. But given the cumulative and self-correcting nature of science, we hope we can stimulate other investigators to address these questions more cleverly and with better datasets than characterizes our initial foray.

The eleventh and concluding chapter reviews our theory of cultural politics and the dynamic model of campaign strategies, sorts through the central empirical findings to summarize the groups and the cultural appeals that destabilized the partisan coalitions, and analyzes the search for efficient symbols, namely, cultural symbols employed in the campaigns that provide a shorthand for multiple groups and behaviors that the targeted voters are known to dislike. The chapter then reviews how political elites manipulate efficient symbols to shape the size and composition of the electorate. Finally, the book concludes with a brief discussion of some normative concerns about efficient symbols and cultural politics, and an agenda for future research.

CHAPTER SIX

Cultural Strains in the New Deal Coalition

IN THE BROAD and chaotic sweep of American political development, scholars have isolated several lengthy periods of electoral stability. These eras, known variously as *party systems, electoral systems,* and *electoral orders,* have been characterized by a common political agenda, a dominant political party, and stable party alignments in the mass electorate. Each such period emerged from short but intense outbursts of political activity stimulated by social traumas like war, economic collapse, and major social changes. The same forces eventually overwhelmed the electoral coalitions that sustained these party systems. Most scholars agree that this pattern—concentrated bursts of political upheaval followed by long waves of political consolidation—has been repeated at least five times since the adoption of the Constitution (Clubb, Flanigan, and Zingale 1980).

In that manner, the Depression of the 1930s eventually produced an electoral period known as the New Deal party system. Marked by commitment to the welfare state, vigorous response to threats from totalitarian forces on the international stage, and the dominance of the Democratic party, this system rested at base on "the emotional bond tying millions of voters—especially Catholic and Jewish voters climbing out of their big-city ghettos in the North—to Franklin Delano Roosevelt and the New Deal" (Gerstle and Fraser 1989, xi). From 1932 through the mid-1960s, this system produced Democratic victories in seven of nine presidential elections, routine Democratic dominance of Congress and of the largest states, and what some scholars describe as a political culture with fixed pillars that limited debate to marginal issues (Beck 1979).

In its fourth decade, the 1960s, the system that had seemed so stable began to come apart at the seams—a word chosen for very specific purposes. The New Deal alignment was challenged by the emergence of new issues that entered the political agenda. Under these pressures, stable party coalitions began to appear unwieldy, as dealignment and some realignment ensued. As we have argued at some length in earlier chapters, the pressures that undermined that system were effectively shaped and wielded by political elites in search of power. Taking up issues produced by social and economic change, party leaders worked to frame these debates in terms that would either widen (Republicans) or narrow (Democrats) the seams that ran through the heterogeneous party coalitions.

This chapter narrates a story of American electoral politics in the post–

New Deal period. We begin with the immediate post–World War II period, when signs of fatigue and hopes for a new beginning were already evident, focus intensely on the critical 1960s, and follow the breakup of the Democratic electoral coalition from the 1970s into the 1990s. This is electoral history as the perceptive journalists, historians, and social commentators of the late twentieth century have reported it. In reviewing elections chronologically, we will emphasize the three large cleavages that together tell the story of post–New Deal cultural politics: patriotism, race, and gender/religion.

In their narrative history of the "long 1960s," Maurice Isserman and Michael Kazin (2000) refer not to a span of ten years but to the "movements and issues" that arose following World War II and continued to define the political agenda well into the 1970s. For these historians, the 1960s are "a story about the intertwined conflicts—over ideology and race, gender and war, popular culture and faith—that transformed the U.S. in irrevocable ways" (ix). Using different words and phrases, other observers have identified essentially the same mix of volatile cultural conflicts as the fault line in the post–New Deal party system. Gary Wills (1998) reports on the redefinition of the "political" in the 1960s. Once considered an arena to resolve foreign and economic policy disputes, the realm of politics was broadened to admit women, blacks, religious outsiders, and others who raised concerns about identity and rights. The fundamental question animating politics since the 1960s, he contends, is "What is America as a social entity going to make of itself?" Giving more attention to the impact of the Cold War on post-1945 political life, John Kenneth White (1997) nonetheless finds the period defined by attempts to answer the same animating question, "Who are we?" This concern was crystallized by Scammon and Wattenberg's "social issue," a phrase from 1970 that denoted a set of political issues that raised questions about central values within American public and private life. James Hunter's *Culture Wars* (1991) bore a similar subtitle—*The Struggle to Define America*.

We begin the story with the issue that first became the bearer of cultural politics in the postwar period, patriotism and nationalism. From the end of World War II until the middle 1960s, the Cold War provided politicians fertile opportunities to engage in the routines of cultural politics; the mode of discourse was repeated many times over in the 1970s and 1980s. In the next section, we introduce the question of race. Although it burst upon the national political scene most dramatically in the mid-1960s, racial politics had roots already at the founding. We tell the story from the 1940s until the mid-1960s. The subplots of nationalism and race fused electorally in the late 1960s, the subject of an interlude that takes us through the next decade. In the final act of this story, beginning around 1980, gender issues enter the electoral calculus in a significant way and provoke a countermobilization characterized by religious conflict. Here too race, gender, and religion are overlain in the 1980s and 1990s.

NATIONALISM AND PATRIOTISM

The war-weary Allies had returned home. Lives in suspension for a half-decade, they were now eager to get a real life—spouse, family, education, good job, safe home. After a total war against totally evil enemies, it was time to step back and recover the good life, seemingly lost since the stock market crash of 1929, even before the tyrants had threatened the world. Americans had protected democracy, Christianity, freedom, our way of life—and were all united in that sacred cause, that "Good War."

The message Sir Winston Churchill delivered in Fulton, Missouri, on March 4, 1946, however, was hardly the one Americans wanted to hear. Troubled by the way Stalin had implemented the Yalta and Potsdam agreements, Churchill saw a new threat to democracy, Christianity, and freedom in the aggressive communism of the post–World War II Soviet Union. "A shadow has fallen upon the scenes so lately lighted by allied victory," he intoned, "Nobody knows what Soviet Russia and its Communist international organization intends to do in the immediate future, or what are the limits, if any, to their expansive and proselytizing tendencies." Moreover, at a time when Moscow should also have been returning to normalcy, the Russian bear was creating an Eastern European buffer by placing in power "puppets," often from small minority communist parties. An "iron curtain" had descended, enveloping "all the capitals of the ancient states of Central and Eastern Europe . . . Warsaw, Berlin, Prague, Vienna, Budapest, Belgrade, Bucharest, and Sofia" (Churchill 1974, 7290). At that moment, Greece, the cradle of Western civilization, was threatened.

During the next two years, as country after country "fell" to Communist parties allied with Moscow, as the atrocities of Stalin were compared to Hitler, the "Cold War" became a fixture in our vocabularies and a point of orientation for national policy. The external threat was fused with internal subversion. When the Soviets successfully detonated first an atomic bomb and then a hydrogen bomb, conspiracy theorists asserted that only spies could have passed them the secret. Then China fell to Communists—something that could only have happened, they charged, because our State Department was filled with naïve leftists who thought the Chinese communists were simply agrarian reformers. They asked, why hadn't the U.S. military dropped the bomb on Moscow before all this had happened?

The country was beset with enemies from without and within. As if to disprove charges that they too had been infected with the virus of leftism, the major religious communities joined in what was invariably called a crusade—preparing the United States for the Armageddon against godless communism. Protestant fundamentalist groups that had their roots in the 1930s were reincarnated as the Christian Crusade, the Christian Anti-Communist Crusade, and the Church League of America (Wilcox 1996, 35–36). Their training schools and seminars developed a small but fervent popular base that helped fuel the rise, and survived the demise, of Senator Joseph McCarthy. Conservative Catholics claimed that the century of social encyclicals beginning with *Laborem Exercens* in 1891 was targeted at the rise of Marxism. Democracies had to destroy communism. Popes devoted Marian years to prayers for the overthrow of communism. Southern and Eastern European ethnic Catholics, only a generation removed from the immigrant experience, renewed their historic distrust of the Russian empire and its messianic religion.

The Cold War linked a complex set of ideas about external enemies and internal conspirators into something resembling a *worldview*. The coherence of this worldview rested on deep myths about American national purpose. What became known as the Cold War consensus was "internationalist, financially generous, global thinking, UN supportive and institution-building, deterrence-minded, at least verbally, democracy-preferring, anti-Communist, and above all, committed to oppose isolationism" (Bloomfield 1974). Rooted in America's moralistic attitude toward foreign affairs, this worldview tapped deeply into American Puritan thinking—that we were a people called by God, as Ralph Waldo Emerson argued, to "be a beacon lighting for all the world the paths of human destiny" (quoted in ibid., 62). Although altruism was undoubtedly involved, postwar programs to rebuild the economies of Germany and Japan were also motivated by a desire to keep them free of Soviet designs. The same motives drove foreign aid and, later, third-world development programs. Because Americans perceived that Soviet-based Communists did not share this ideology, the United States came to oppose not only Soviet initiatives around the globe but often indigenous efforts to throw off control by imperial Western powers or dictatorial regimes.

The language of American foreign policy was piously moralistic and used techniques well known to cultural politics, as discussed in earlier chapters. Our policies were divinely inspired; our enemy's policies came from the devil. Our accomplishments reflected a superior intelligence and structure for society; if our enemy accomplished the same thing, it was only because they stole our technology. The familiar positive within-group attributions and negative outgroup stereotyping were evident.

The perception of threat, the fit with America's self-image, the lack of intimate familiarity with Russia—all these conditions provided politicians a wonderful opportunity to own an issue. At first Democrats defined the problem as rebuilding Europe and halting the spread of communism. One prong of this strategy, embodied in the Marshall Plan and other postwar relief efforts, attempted to create more humane and just conditions for workers under capitalism. This would reduce the appeal of communism. To implement the other prong, the Democrats advocated the policy of *containment*. Democrats also trusted in *collective security* and *multilateral diplomacy*. NATO and SEATO assured the United States of collective strength. In time, the United Nations became a principal actor in the cause of peace and security. Whatever the wisdom of the Democratic strategy, it stopped well short of aiming for a rollback of communism. The first test of containment in Korea, under a Democratic administration, was unsatisfactory to much of the public precisely because a strategy of limited war precluded total victory.

As the Cold War wore on, it united both the isolationist and the internationalist wings of the Republican Party. Opposition to Soviet-based communism gave common purpose to the Republican design for American foreign policy and the GOP's domestic efforts. For Republicans who had chafed under the growth of the federal government in the 1930s and 40s, this national purpose could provide a template for whittling down the state while protecting us from the external enemy and maintaining order in the face of internal threats to national unity. The latter two became intertwined: a rash of strikes was taken as evidence that communist agitators had infiltrated organized labor.[5]

While Senator McCarthy grabbed the headlines, Richard Nixon took the lead role in framing the Cold War as a cultural issue, creating a style of electoral politics that came to characterize the era. It was not simply the practice of negative campaigning, something that dated to the time of Adams and Jefferson. It was negative campaigning in the context of the Cold War: the *patriotism* of the domestic political enemy was suspect. If he or she is not a communist then surely he or she is a fellow traveler, an ideological compatriot of the Kremlin. It was also negative campaigning in the context of a perceived permanent majority of people inclined to favor the opposition party. Thus, to quote journalist Sidney Blumenthal (1990, 256), the strategy was designed "to cripple the Democratic coalition." Consistent with our argument in chapter 5, this negative

---

[5] Two decades later, in similar fashion, student protest movements were to become proof of communist infiltration of U.S. universities. Later still, when the protestors grew up and joined the faculties as "tenured radicals," the worry was that "communists and godless atheists" had found their ultimate control in the centers of higher learning. This was an even greater threat than external communism (Kristol, quoted in White 1997).

strategy sought issues where there were deep cultural divides in the majority Democratic coalition, created anxiety through the use of fear and animosity, and either immobilized segments of the majority or caused them to defect.

Nixon came to this strategy informed by political success. In 1946 he likened incumbent Congressman Jerry Voorhis's voting record to that of Vito Marcantonio, a socialist member of Congress from New York City, and charged that "his voting record in Congress is more Socialistic and Communistic than Democratic." Building on this experience, Nixon subsequently defeated Helen Gahagan Douglas for the U.S. Senate in part by circulating a "pink sheet" describing her "socialistic and communistic votes" and charging her with being a fellow traveler with "Hollywood" people in the communications industry known to be "card-carrying communists." California political consultant Murray Chotiner worked with Nixon on marketing methods to find what people fear and on media methods to spread innuendo and create anxiety. This campaign design became so prominent in California politics that Eugene Burdick's (1956) fictional political handler in *The Ninth Wave* built all campaigns around two emotions—fear and hate.

In Washington, Nixon added another component to the design of modern campaigning in the context of the Cold War: the use of investigative techniques and news leaks to focus the media on negative features of opponents, all within ongoing public policy deliberations. In this instance, the enemy was the Eastern establishment "present at the creation" of the Cold War system. It was personified in Alger Hiss, a deputy to Dean Acheson and a policy planner at the Yalta Conference where, it was charged, postwar Europe was carved up into spheres of influence. The hearings made Nixon the central political hope for the anticommunist groups that had been trying to gain entree to Washington since the 1930s.

Out of the White House so long by 1952, Republicans convinced a popular war hero to head the ticket. Though a candidate of the Eastern establishment, Dwight Eisenhower was essentially nonpartisan. If they could not nominate Senator Robert Taft, Midwestern conservatives, drawn out of their isolationism by the Cold War, demanded a spot on the ticket for a nominee who represented what they felt was the faithful core of the party. Popular California Governor Earl Warren was "too liberal," but young Senator Nixon fit the bill nicely. A native of the second most populous state and a member of the generation that fought World War II, Nixon had already gained a national reputation for talking tough about external enemies and routing out internal enemies.

The ticket fashioned the first Cold War campaign slogan of "Korea, corruption, and communism," reminding voters that Democrats had recently "lost China." In a nation frustrated with labor strife and a Korean War we seemed unable or even unwilling "to win," Ike carried a landslide and cut deeply into the Democratic popular coalition. Particularly noteworthy were his vote totals among Catholics; he had established a Nationalities Division of the Republican National Committee that targeted campaign appeals on Eastern European, ethnic Catholics. Nixon drew two lessons: (1) segments of the Democratic coalition could be hived off through the right appeals, and (2) the most potent appeals involved Cold War symbols of military strength and anticommunism.

When Nixon's turn came in 1960, he had the misfortune to face a Democratic opponent with no less impressive Cold War credentials than his own. Senator John F. Kennedy had served on the Senate's permanent investigating committee that looked into corruption and Communist influence in organized labor. He had been injured in combat while commander of a PT boat in the Pacific theater. No Red scare would work here for the Republicans. Instead of cultural appeals and scapegoating, Nixon had to rely on his vice presidential credentials, contrasting his proven ability to stand up to communist leaders with Kennedy's inexperience. He used footage of his "kitchen debate" with Soviet leader Nikita Khrushchev throughout the campaign. Nevertheless, in the mind of the press and eventually the public, he lost the first debate and eventually the election.

President Kennedy's first Cold War crisis was an invasion plan, inherited from the Eisenhower administration, to depose Cuban Communist leader Fidel Castro. Poorly conceived and executed, the invasion never got farther than the beach. Once again a military effort by Democrats had failed to roll back communism. This one was a national embarrassment that seemed to showcase Kennedy's inexperience.

Never again would a Communist beat a Kennedy. When the Berlin Wall came to symbolize the Iron Curtain, Kennedy delivered his famous "Ich bin ein Berliner" address, telling Europe that it would never be abandoned to the spread of Communist regimes. The Soviets, seeing that the Wall did not bring retaliation beyond symbols, decided to locate nuclear warheads in client-state Cuba, thus clearly upsetting the balance of power. The Kennedy government steeled itself for a showdown, eyeball to eyeball with nuclear warfare; it threatened nuclear retaliation on Moscow, not Cuba, if the warheads were not removed. It set a deadline. The Kremlin blinked. The Kennedy brothers now showed the toughness the Cold War required. But the Cuba issue festered, a Communist regime ninety miles offshore making a mockery of the Monroe Doctrine. There were several consequences for Cold War politics: (1) It reinforced that Democrats should never cede the anti-communist advantage to the Republicans, and it probably prodded both Kennedy and Lyndon Johnson to mire the U.S. military more deeply in Vietnam than hindsight would have argued was desirable. (2) It changed the rhetoric surrounding foreign aid, particularly in the Western hemisphere, from economic to military rationales. (3) It changed the perception of Catholic missioners in Latin America from religious leaders committed to social justice, to agents of revolutionary change who would benefit the Communists. In its wake, the Catholic Church became a prime target for cultural politics and a venue for cultural and political conflict between Republican leaders and those Catholics who maintained a social justice platform. And (4) it made Cuban refugees solidly Republican, a small but strategically important bloc in Florida politics, with its substantial electoral college yield.

After Kennedy fell to an assassin's bullets, Lyndon Johnson and the hawkish entourage of foreign policy leaders JFK had assembled began to measure progress in Vietnam by body counts rather than political stability. In its early stages, the American presence in Vietnam was still justifiable in terms of the Cold War consensus and did not yet divide the Democrats internally during the 1964 election. In the GOP, the anti-Communist far Right had grown in influence and moved into the leadership vacuum in the 1964 nominating process in support of Senator Barry Goldwater. Yet the bloody primaries with Governor Nelson Rockefeller left Goldwater with an extremist label. It was Lyndon Johnson who played the Nixon Cold War negative card with the "Daisy Girl" ad. The ad showed a little girl happily picking petals off a daisy until the picture dissolved into a mushroom cloud; it raised fear of Goldwater's suitability for commanding the nuclear arsenal. For his part, Goldwater linked fears of communism, xenophobia, and the need for patriotism in an ad that had children reciting the Pledge of Allegiance, while Goldwater implied that Democrats would not stand up to Soviet Communists. He was also the first to introduce a staple of contemporary cultural politics, direct-mail appeals for funds, based on negative attribution to outgroups who were perceived to be at the core of the opposition party (Levine 1995, 137).

RACE

If there had been a party of civil rights in the nineteenth and twentieth centuries, it most assuredly had been the GOP. Even during the New Deal, the Democrats had been the party of social welfare, not necessarily social justice. Yet Democrats were an odd congeries of traditional Jefferson-Jackson agrarians, Southern Bourbons, and classic outsiders—racial, ethnic, religious, and intellectual minorities. With the championship of the little guy and with all of these minorities, sooner or later pressures would build to transform the party of social welfare also into the party of social justice.

At the 1948 Democratic convention, the delicate balance among factions was undone by Hubert Humphrey's proposed civil rights plank to the party platform. The plank upset the long-standing compromise that allowed the party's Southern wing a veto on racial policy. While he drew on lofty ideals and pointed to the executive orders on desegregation issued by Democrats Franklin Delano Roosevelt and Harry S Truman, Humphrey's greatest weapon was a change in political geography. The northward migration of African Americans during the Depression, World War II, and its aftermath had provided big-city Democrats an opportunity to mobilize a new group of voters. Perhaps the mobilization of blacks in Northern swing states would compensate for the likely loss of white Southerners. Those who felt most threatened, symbolically and politically, bolted to Strom Thurmond's Dixiecrats, who carried the states of Alabama, Mississippi, Louisiana, and South Carolina. From that small beginning there was both danger and opportunity for the parties and politicians in the cultural divide over race.

The reorientation of the parties proceeded in fits and starts over the next two decades. The 1952 and 1956 Democratic platforms retained the 1948 plank, but the 1956 statement included recognition of the importance of state and local prerogatives. Candidate Adlai Stevenson, a social welfare Democrat, offered cautions about moving too swiftly on civil rights and voiced respect for the principles embedded in the Confederacy (cf. Carmines and Stimson 1989, 36). All four Dixiecrat states returned to the Democratic column.

Throughout the period, Republican platforms retained strong civil rights planks. Further, Republicans followed their words with actions, using the presidency (albeit reluctantly) to enforce court orders on desegregation of schools and using the Congress in 1957 to pass the first civil rights act since Reconstruction. The court-ordered integration of Little Rock Central High School was particularly gripping. The new medium of television brought vivid images to the nation from Arkansas as Governor Faubus verbally sparred with the commander-in-chief, and troops cordoned a path through jeering white mobs. Jim Crow was going, and Southern Democrats did not lose the fact that *Republicans* used the federal government to upset the traditional moral order on race.

The two parties might have converged on racial policy had not the recession of 1958 begun to change the base of the Republican party. Much of its progressive Northeastern and Midwestern senatorial leadership lost to liberal Democratic candidates. At the same time some new conservative Republicans were being elected out of the fringe South.

Many remaining Republicans still supported the Civil Rights Act of 1960, but the public focus had shifted to Humphrey's social justice wing of the Democratic party (cf. Foley 1980 for a discussion of the takeover of the Senate by liberal Democrats). Over the objection of Southern delegates, this group carried strong civil rights planks into the party's 1960 platform.

Although the Republicans explored the idea of weakening the GOP commitment to civil rights in the 1960 platform, Nixon's desire for party unity prompted him to strike a deal with Northern progressives. Against the opposition of the growing Southern wing of the party, the platform mirrored the Democratic commitment to use the federal government to assure civil rights to racial minorities. Nixon got the nomination and his platform, but the losers on the civil rights issue found a new star—Senator Barry Goldwater of Arizona, who offered a principled defense of states' rights and liberty that side-stepped direct racial discourse. In effect, Goldwater rearranged the priorities so that liberty symbols preceded (and preempted) rights symbols.

Early in the 1960 campaign, both candidates zigged and zagged in their overtures on race. Southern Democrats used blatant appeals to negative outgroup affect by distributing fliers picturing Nixon standing next to two African American men and charging him with membership in the NAACP (Jamieson 1992, 80). UN Ambassador and progressive former Massachusetts Senator Henry Cabot Lodge, Nixon's running mate, said there would be a black man appointed to the Cabinet and reiterated the promise even after Nixon demurred (ibid., 243). In a major address in Atlanta, Nixon tried to link himself to Southern culture through his college roommate, a "Georgia boy," and strongly endorsed the states' rights theme. He charged that the Democratic party had deserted the South by abandoning the principle that differences should be settled locally, not in Washington (White 1962, 269–72). Still, he remained confused about whether and how he should appeal to blacks or Southern whites; he thought he could win Texas, South Carolina, and Louisiana with appeals to states' rights, but he was not ready to abandon his party's historic commitment to civil rights.

Earlier in the campaign, John F. Kennedy preferred to ignore the matter. He had his picture taken with Mudcat Grant, a "popular Negro pitcher with the Cleveland Indians," in the words of the flier distributed by the Democrats' Civil Rights Division (White 1962, 252). But apart from the antiblack cultural campaigning done by Southern Democrats, Kennedy had no racially motivated strategy. He had never been an ardent spokesman for civil rights in the Senate. Then in the waning days of the campaign, he made a strategically important telephone call to Coretta Scott King, inquiring after her jailed husband. For African Americans the call was perhaps the signal needed to decide between two candidates, both of whom seemed to embrace quiet progress on civil rights. The next day, Kennedy's brother and campaign manager, Robert, called a Georgia judge and asked for King's release. The word spread like wildfire in black communities. King's father, who had earlier endorsed Nixon, publicly changed his endorsement to Kennedy. A million fliers describing the sequence of events were printed and distributed at African American churches the Sunday before the election, and radio ads were also disseminated through black stations (Jamieson 1996, 142–43).

Only the analysis of data can help to resolve whether Kennedy's symbolic gesture on race or his Catholicism led to widespread Protestant Democratic defection and the loss of several Southern states. With the Republican center of gravity shifting in a southwesterly direction, Nixon was done (for now), Goldwater was emerging, and Nelson Rockefeller was the symbol of an older GOP that did not understand how people felt about expanded federal control over the racial order or anything else. The traditional culture was poised for a *counterreform movement.*

By instinct a cautious but exceedingly ambitious politician, President Kennedy was rather deeply planted in that traditional culture himself. As president, he first tried an accommodationist approach to racial change, giving civil rights a lower priority than his other domestic programs. Accommodationism, however, is not an effective strategy when value conflict becomes intense and sometimes violent. Hundreds of cities, North and South, had witnessed black demonstrations and boycotts, and intimidation by the white power structure. Clergy led the black protesters, and the black church became the staging ground for transforming the moral order (McAdam 1982). White religious leaders were joining their black brothers and sisters, and the civil rights movement successfully appropriated the symbols of morality. The defenders of the status quo were seen as violent, desperate men—whether blocking schoolhouse doors, aiming fire hoses at peacefully assembled church folk, bloodying the heads of dispersing youths, or committing or conniving in the murder of black children and white civil rights workers.

By midsummer 1963 Kennedy himself came to define the civil rights issue in terms that clearly called for an end to the old moral order of apartheid: "We are confronted primarily with a moral issue. It is as old as the scriptures and is as clear as the American Constitution. . . . If an American, because his skin is dark . . . cannot enjoy the full and free life which all of us want, then who among us would be content to have the color of his skin changed and stand in his place? Who among us would then be content with the counsels of patience and delay?" (Kennedy 1964, 469). Scriptures, the Constitution, standing inside another person's skin—this was the kind of cultural politics that moved beyond racial differences to the common culture of Americans' deepest beliefs and experiences (for a discussion of the common culture, see McClosky and Zaller 1984). While still disagreeing with the cross-racial coalition of civil rights leaders on details and strategy, Kennedy put the full weight of his administration, particularly the Justice Department under his brother's leadership, behind comprehensive civil rights legislation.

The tortuous legislative process heated up about the time shots rang out of the Texas Book Depository in Dallas. Lyndon Johnson led the effort through to success as Congress passed the Civil Rights Act of 1964, the first civil rights act with teeth since Reconstruction. And it was not lost on Republicans and Southern Democrats that those teeth belonged to the *government in Washington* headed by a white Southern Democrat. The vote in both houses of Congress told the story of the future: in the House of Representatives, Northern Democrats voted 141 to 4 in favor, but Southern Democrats voted 92 to 11 against. Republicans voted 138 for, 34 against, but included in the latter were 12 Southerners. The key vote in the Senate was for cloture on the filibuster. Here 44 Democrats and 27 Republicans favored cloture, while 23 Democrats and 6 Republicans opposed it.

The principal Republican opponent, Senator Barry Goldwater, viewed the solution as a local matter, not something to be mandated by the Supreme Court and enforced by the federal government. He rode this philosophy and his opposition to the 1964 Civil Rights Act to victory in the 1964 primaries. Though the early stages of the general election campaign of 1964 downplayed racial themes, they grew more prominent over the course of the campaign. While Goldwater's staff urged him to exploit a white backlash, he would approach the issue only by stressing state autonomy on matters of race, employing symbols of small government and local problem-solving. Johnson's forces were less restrained. In a five-minute, nationally aired television ad that focused mainly on foreign affairs and national defense, "Republicans for Johnson" mentioned the Ku Klux Klan's endorsement of Goldwater (Jamieson 1996, 194–95). The segment showed white-sheeted Klansmen burning a cross and focused on the Alabama KKK leader who professed hatred for "niggerism, Catholicism, and Judaism." He concluded: "I like Barry Goldwater. He needs our help" (Diamond and Bates 1992, 132).

Goldwater himself began to use cultural code words for racial differences. At the Republican convention, retired President Dwight D. Eisenhower had set the stage by warning against "maudlin sympathy" for vicious criminals who were raised poor and underprivileged (White 1965, 241–42). Later in the campaign, Goldwater turned to this crime theme many times. One nationally aired TV ad staged a riotous confrontation between young men and police (Jamieson 1996, 209); another telecast on "moral issues" focused heavily on rioting, juvenile delinquency, and lenient treatment of criminals, with the pictures carrying the social content (ibid., 209–11). A Goldwater-funded organization, "Mothers for a Moral America," ran a film with negative symbols of pornography, alcohol use, sexual promiscuity, and rioters—again featuring black youths—and contrasted it with pictures of clean-cut white youths, the flag, patriotic symbols, and, oddly, positive symbols of blacks in cotton fields (ibid., 209–15). Thus, already in 1964, Republican campaigners stressed the racial codewords implicated in crime, morality, and welfare, and the "offenders" pictured on television were primarily blacks.

Goldwater lost in 1964 due to fear of nuclear escalation in Southeast Asia, loyalty to the fantasy of Camelot, youthful idealism, and a national consensus on the need to change racial apartheid. Johnson won virtually everywhere except the Deep South. Goldwater carried five states by massive to solid margins—87 percent in Mississippi, 70 percent in Alabama, 59 percent in South Carolina, 57 percent in Louisiana, and 54 percent in Georgia. Ambitious young Southern politicians who by the 1990s had come to lead the Republicans in the House and Senate caught the first glimpse of the party of their future.

Blacks also found a home for the rest of the post–New Deal period. Although over half had supported Eisenhower in 1956 and one-third supported Nixon in 1960, only 10 percent supported Goldwater in 1964 (Carmines and Stimson 1989). Black registration and turnout increased in succeeding elections with the help of federal registrars and church-based voter mobilization drives. In the states of the rim South it nearly doubled. Contrasted with the old moral order on race, Southern voters could now look to the Republican party as the white party and the Democratic party as an increasingly black party.

1968: The Great Divide

By 1968 the prolonged agony of the Vietnam War had reduced the Cold War consensus to shambles. The racial consensus, the confidence in gradualism as a means of ending apartheid, was also in disarray by the late 1960s. The intersection of these two dimensions reached a fever pitch in the late 1960s and early 1970s, dominating the nominating process and elections of 1968 and 1972.

By 1968 fear was the order of the day. For five years, television had conveyed a seemingly unending stream of images chronicling urban unrest, skyrocketing crime, the antiwar, antidraft revolt among college students, and public exhibitions of drugs and sex that scandalized moral traditionalists and disgusted most middle Americans. Then "the whole world watched" as police encountered student protesters outside the Democratic convention hotels in Chicago. The convention became a metaphor for the violent struggles over the content of American culture.

These circumstances were well suited to Richard Nixon, who had withdrawn from politics following his gubernatorial defeat in 1962. He knew how to deal with the politics of resentment. "The secret of politics," he once opined, "is knowing who hates who" (Wills 1979). From earlier campaigns he had learned to identify the vulnerable points in the Democratic coalition and to craft a campaign around them by the adroit use of marketing and media tools. Easily disposing of primary rivals, Nixon had already prepared for the general election.

The object was to remake the Nixon image that went before the voters (McGinniss 1969). But no positive image exists in a vacuum. The Nixon style was always to contrast it with what was resented, what was feared. For example, Nixon's chief image creator, Roger Ailes, presented Nixon as a "fresh, spontaneous, open politician" in his "Man in the Arena" panel shows (Blumenthal 1990, 256–57). But then Ailes would make sure that the audience included people who expressed a "visceral politics of resentment" toward outgroups. Voters would identify with the members of the audience but be reassured by Nixon's statesmanlike handling of their grievance. Ailes and, later, Lee Atwater played the same role for Republican presidential nominees over the next quarter century.

Nixon also assembled a public opinion polling apparatus with an almost unlimited budget and extraordinary capacity to trace the unfolding effects of a sequence of images or ads (Kessel 1984, 126–27). Very early, the polling team discovered that views on military strength correlated highly with feelings about crime, violence, and domestic disorder. These, in turn, were linked to dissident and disorderly groups in society. Thus, the Nixon ads could be of a whole cloth. A Vietnam War ad could show wounded servicemen with perplexed faces and question why incumbent (Democratic) leadership could not bring the war to an "honorable (winning?) end." Then other ads showed scenes of rioting, violent crime, or a woman walking down a dark city street in terror, and the voice-over would say, "This time vote like your whole world depended on it. Nixon" (cf. Levine 1995, 144–49, for a compendium of the Nixon ads). The ads make it abundantly clear what emotion was to be tapped. One said, "Freedom from fear is the basic right of every American. We must restore it." No longer are the Cold War enemies outside our borders or confined to the Eastern establishment; they are found in a Democratic government that coddles Communists and criminals alike, that tolerates extremist forms of dissent by people who fail to live by the rules of the moral order.

Apart from Nixon's formidable enterprise, the Democrats had to cope with defections on the right and left. Former Democrat George Wallace campaigned on visceral racial and "law 'n' order" appeals aimed at Southern Democrats and white ethnics. On the left, the antiwar leader, Senator Eugene McCarthy, withheld his endorsement of nominee Hubert H.

Humphrey until the last week of the campaign. The surprising closeness of the general election, however, taught Nixon still more lessons about cultural politics: (1) Campaigning must be a permanent enterprise in the White House; (a) it required the staging of negative pseudo-events so that the media would keep negative attributions about opponents alive, even in their search for the truth, and (b) it required control of the press, by whatever measure, so that the president maintained control over his political agenda. (2) Since Wallace took several Southern states that should have been in the Republican column, Nixon's appeals must be even more vigorous in their stereotyping of outgroups and their use of negative social attribution. And (3) more blue-collar Democrats must be convinced that economic security is not more important than personal security, living by the rules, and patriotism in the face of the Cold War. By 1970 Charles Colson, special assistant to the president, urged Nixon to polarize the electorate on social issues. Wallace's phrase "law 'n' order" could be deployed to make "the public believe that Democrat, Liberal permissiveness was the cause of violence and crime" (quoted in Blumenthal 1990, 60). As social disorder grew so rapidly over Nixon's first term, with chaos on the campuses and demonstrations by the antiwar movement, it was easy for Vice President Spiro Agnew's wordsmiths to call intellectuals and antiwar opponents "effete snobs" and to disdain the Democrats as the party of "acid, amnesty, and abortion." Again one's stance in the fight over communism was the centerpiece for all other disorders. But increasingly the label "liberal" incorporated additional negative attributions.

If the intervening four years had not created a hospitable enough climate for the evolving versions of the Cold War campaign, the Democratic party again did its best to provide cannon fodder. After Nixon's special assistants had undermined front-running Democratic candidates in the early primaries, Senator George McGovern, a prairie state progressive in the tradition of Norris and LaFollette, had become the Democratic front-runner. But his assets to the reformed Democratic party were precisely what made him vulnerable to a cultural campaign. McGovern's strongest supporters—antiwar youth, feminists, "militant" blacks, and educated, well-off converts from the Republican side (a.k.a. "limousine liberals")—were particularly unsympathetic to the old Democratic core, including Catholics represented by big-city bosses and blue-collar workers represented by union leaders. The McGovern reform rules had so changed the party that old-line leaders felt they had been disowned and their party hijacked. Finally, McGovern's call for sizable defense cuts and the psychiatric treatments of his first vice presidential nominee raised doubts about the Democrat's suitability to lead the United States in dealings with the Soviet Union.

The Cold War style of cultural politics perfected by Nixon reached its zenith in 1972. While many ads aimed at working-class and middle-class Americans subtly played on fears of outgroups or on the economic effects of McGovern's defense cuts, perhaps one ad epitomized the advantage Nixon had with the Cold War/patriotism dimension. On screen, a hand swept away toy soldiers, ships, planes, and carriers. A voice quoted Senator Humphrey, saying that these (McGovern) "cuts are cutting into the security of this country." Then a drum roll played "Hail to the Chief" as a stately Nixon reviewed the fleet. A voice assured the viewer, "President Nixon doesn't believe we should play games with our national security. He believes in a strong America to negotiate for people from strength" (Levine 1995, 155–56).

Watergate Aftermath

The story of 1976, however, was Republican failure. With the Vietnam War ended and Nixon's presidency over, due to Watergate, the election became a retrospective morality play between a born-again Southern Baptist and a life-long politician who had pardoned Nixon. Moreover, a critical Cold War politics gaffe squandered the Republican advantage among blue-collar Catholic ethnics and the restless old core of the Democratic party. While President Gerald Ford's ads stressed his military and congressional service (over the inexperienced Georgia Governor Jimmy Carter), Ford got tongue-tied in the first debate and listed a number of Eastern European countries that he did not think were "under the domination of the Soviet Union." The earnest Carter, who had already done well among Catholic ethnics in the Pennsylvania primary, responded simply, "I would like to see Mr. Ford convince the Polish Americans and the Czech Americans and the Hungarian Americans in this country that these countries don't live under the domination and the supervision of the Soviet Union behind the Iron Curtain" (Levine 1995, 169). Carter was an Annapolis graduate who, while not serving in combat, had worked with Admiral Hyman Rickover in creating the nuclear submarine. Ford was perceived as an amiable bumbler, a man who had "played football too long without a helmet." The opportunity for a Republican advantage out of Cold War cultural politics simply did not present itself in 1976. Carter was an outsider to the national Democratic party, an outsider to Washington, an evangelical, and a patriot. The "liberal" summary label was attached to him only later during his term in the White House.

As president, Carter faced daunting foreign policy problems. Despite détente and although internal corruption had taken much of the steam out of the Politburo, the Brezhnev Doctrine—asserting the right to Soviet control over its satellites—remained. Nevertheless, Carter hoped to enter a new era of negotiations with the Soviets, convinced that their goals were changing. Just as he was building support for the Salt II Treaty, the Soviets invaded Afghanistan and Carter was forced to conclude that Soviet Communist goals remained the same as they had throughout the Cold War.

The Middle East also presented Carter with three serious electoral problems. Concerned that the U.S. commitment to Israel isolated America from the surrounding Arab countries, Carter tried to bring "balance" to the country's pro-Israel tilt with a series of friendly overtures to Arab states and to the Palestinians. Predictably enough, this unnerved American Jewish organizations. But it also was thought naive by anti-Communist organizations and an emerging group of "neoconservatives," a term for former Democrats, largely Jewish and Catholic publicists, who had become alienated by the social forces represented in the Democratic party and by the antiwar stances it had embraced beginning around 1972. Ironically, Carter's attempt at evenhandedness also upset "dispensationalists" of the emerging evangelical Right who thought peace in the Middle East would delay their prophesied time tables for the Armageddon and the second coming of Christ (on prophesies by Pat Robertson, a leading televangelist of the religious right, see Blumenthal 1990, 102–3; on dispensationalism, see Wilcox 1996).

The second Middle Eastern problem came from the oil embargoes. The oil-producing nations first collectively flexed their muscles under Gerald Ford's watch. Americans faced modest shortages of gasoline and higher pump prices. Early in his administration, hoping to prod Detroit to produce more energy-efficient cars, Carter had adopted policies that deliberately tightened supplies. When the nations that comprised the Organization of Petroleum Exporting Countries (OPEC) voted a limited embargo on oil supplies in 1979, prices skyrocketed, creating lengthy lines at the pump and fueling astronomical inflation rates.

The third Middle Eastern problem registered deeply with the American public. A fundamentalist Islamic regime had toppled the shah of Iran. In November 1979 Islamic militants took hostage more than fifty people connected with the American diplomatic mission. Carter announced their release as his top priority and refused to pay ransom for them in any form. It was a matter of American national honor. But the hostage crisis trailed on and on. A poorly planned rescue mission failed in the desert sands, reminding an older generation of the Bay of Pigs fiasco, also under Democrats. Carter seemed cursed by the fates in his inability to rebuff this insult to U.S. national pride. Once again it seemed that Democrats had led the country to a Cold War foreign policy failure.

In 1980 Ronald Reagan had inherited much of the campaign marketing apparatus that had run Nixon's permanent campaign. He brought a new pollster, Richard Wirthlin, and, in time, added a crafty cultural politician from recent Southern campaigns, Lee Atwater. Ailes especially liked his new charge because he was easy to script and knew how to take cues. Even back in the 1950s when General Electric chose Hollywood actor Reagan to present its political philosophy as host of *Death Valley Days*, he had test-marketed as remarkably capable of convincing viewers of the truth of his message. He was an optimist with a passionate belief in American exceptionalism. He was a veteran of the effort to oust Communists from the leadership of the entertainers' unions in the 1940s. Further, Reagan had gone well beyond the Cold War consensus found in the containment policy. He wanted the vestiges of communism gone—everywhere. He was the delight of what had once been the far-right fringe of the Republican party but what was now becoming its core. Finally, Carter's appointments of Jews and women to high domestic and federal court posts and his willingness to work with visible "liberals" in the party had alienated many of the evangelicals he had energized in 1976, and they now provided foot soldiers for Reagan.

Not a great deal of cultural campaigning was needed on the issues that symbolized patriotism. Everybody knew where Reagan stood and where Carter had failed. Instead, most of the campaign appeals centered on failed domestic promises, racial or gender matters. Even a Reagan ad tracing Carter's foreign policy failures to his appointments pictured U.N. Ambassador Andrew Young, a black man. One ad, run widely, charged that Carter let Russians move far ahead in the arms race, but it did not make negative cultural appeals to lack of patriotism by Democrats. By now perhaps, lack of patriotism was sufficiently integrated with the term "liberal" that a reference to the "failure of liberal Democratic administrations" connoted it. The 1980 election was largely a retrospective campaign on issues involving patriotism, American pride, and the rampant economic crisis. Reagan needed only the free media to make his point. Nightly, CBS news anchor Walter Cronkite posted the number of days the hostage crisis had brought insult to national pride.

Gender/Religion

The 1980 campaign also witnessed the expression of another important cultural conflict in American electoral politics, discord over gender roles. The question of how men and women should live as men and women and as citizens with equal opportunities eventually became intertwined with broader questions about social tradition and moral order. The principal antagonists in this conflict were feminists on the one side against religious traditionalists on the other.

Even before the granting of suffrage in 1920, the political parties anticipated that women could constitute a new electoral resource to be mined for votes. At the same time, the interests of women were seldom defined beyond the hearth. Harvey (1998) argues that the parties appointed mobilizers of the drive for suffrage to staff newly created women's divisions. In the process, women's unique policy interests were co-opted, independent women's organizations were diminished, and few policy concessions were granted. Where office seeking through party organization advantaged men, the concomitant argument that women's party loyalty should take precedence over their loyalty to women's interests reduced women's status in party policy circles until the 1960s.

Ironically, the drive for equality for women in the 1960s and 1970s gained momentum from the drive for civil rights for minorities in the 1950s and 1960s. Consistent with its heritage, the Republican party had a long history of involvement with the women's suffrage movement and extended that approach to women's rights. As early as 1940 it had placed a plank in its platform that called for an equal rights amendment and mandated "equal positions on the party's national and executive committees" for women (Melich 1996, 10). Democrats, the leadership of whose coalition included Southern traditionalists and evangelicals, Northern ethnic Catholics, and organized labor, were much slower to embrace the principle of equality for minorities and women. But equality is an abstract political concept. The real political struggle began as the nation sorted out the meaning of equality in everyday life, in the family, on the job, around the town, and in the chambers of the courts and legislatures.

Following the post–World War II demobilization, the baby boom and vastly expanded educational and employment opportunities for men had returned mothers in large numbers to the home and had made "good providers" of their husbands. Yet, more and more women were acquiring higher education, many women had remained in or entered the labor force, and the first heavy wave of divorces began to hit a war generation that had coupled under different rules. For the less educated and less skilled woman, divorce was a ticket to poverty. For the more educated, married or not, there was an increasingly guilty conscience about the failure to use acquired skills in productive and meaningful ways outside the home or volunteer organizations. This was, after all, a nation that valued self-reliance, entrepreneurship, and personal responsibility. Given the social composition of the Republican party, the pressures for getting serious about equality between the sexes were first felt there. When Betty Friedan's *The Feminine Mystique* was published in 1963, it was as though the veil had been lifted for educated women: meaningful work inside and outside the home was central to women's identity (Fox-Genovese 1996, 111).

Another factor also accounts for the early Republican embrace of the drive for women's equality, as well as its later distancing itself from the feminist movement—votes. The Republicans "sorely needed sources of support for a party that had been badly crippled by its disastrous electoral defeats of 1932, 1934, and 1936" (Melich 1996, 10). Republicans sensed they would have to compete for the votes of women. The prevailing political wisdom was that women, if they voted, would vote the same way as their husband, if they had a husband. Yet in the 1950s President Eisenhower vocally supported opportunities for women, especially "equal pay for equal work." He reinforced his words with the appointments of Oveta Culp Hobby, Ivy Baker Priest, and Clare Booth Luce to what were then considered prominent positions—for women. The first measured gender gap since the advent of survey research appeared in the two Eisenhower elections. In 1952 Republican Eisenhower gained the support of 58 percent of the women but only 53 percent of the men, and in 1956 his support grew to 61 percent of the women and 55 percent of the men (Costain 1992, 33).

As the New Deal coalition splintered into Dixiecrats, Progressives, and sundry other groups, Democratic party leaders also realized that visible efforts aimed at women were desirable. New coalition partners were needed to replace those lost on race or patriotism. John Kennedy created a prominent Presidential Commission on the Status of Women. Kennedy signed the first equal pay bill in 1963. And in 1964, after Kennedy's assassination, congressional Democrats amended Title VII of the Civil Right Act of 1964 to add sex to race, creed, color, and national origin as categories where employment discrimination was prohibited (ibid., 37). Many Democrats and many Republicans by now had introduced equal rights amendments to the U.S. Constitution. Democrats contested the traditional Republican ownership of the gender equality issue.

In 1964 Republicans began a retrenchment from the gender equality banner. It probably happened as a by-product of the evolving GOP position on civil rights for minorities. Having opposed the Civil Rights Act of 1964 on the grounds that it infringed on states' rights, presidential candidate Barry Goldwater could hardly support equivalent legislation for women. As the Republican party increasingly built its appeal around cultural traditionalism, aiming at white Southerners and blue-collar Northern Democrats, its new coalition was held together by a common opposition to the federal government's role in changing the old moral order on race and, by implication, gender.

The inclusion of gender in the 1964 Civil Rights Act was treated as somewhat of a lark on the pages of the influential *New York Times*, the *Wall Street Journal*, and the *New Republic* (Harrison 1988). On a scale of deprivation, some argued, middle-class and professional white women could hardly be considered in the same class as blacks. But to the developing women's organizations, this dismissal was precisely the treatment that could rally mobilization. By election year 1968, a vigorous, independent, policy results-oriented movement had taken shape and held candidates from both political parties to its litmus tests (ibid.; Harvey 1998). Henceforth the women's movement as a potential voting bloc could be neither ridiculed nor ignored.

But now a forceful countermovement developed, one that was to crystallize party images by the late 1980s and 1990s. It is difficult to isolate gender from race, because the arguments both for and against the drive for racial equality were transferred to gender equality. And it is especially difficult to isolate gender from religion because the arguments for traditional gender roles and reproductive norms have become deeply embedded in religious rationales for the moral order. The most vocal defenders of these traditional roles and norms—Catholics and evangelical Protestants—became the target groups, first, for cultural appeals about gender and, eventually, for intraparty struggles for control of nominations, platforms, and public policy.

Gender issues had a lot to do with the realignment of evangelical Protestants, had something to do with perturbations in Catholic voting patterns, and contributed heavily to the budding realignment—in opposite directions—of housewives and of professional and managerial women. The respective parties' handling of gender issues opened a new gender gap between men and women, and especially between women with different values and locations in the social structure. The principal tools are well known to symbolic politics: social attribution, stereotyping, and relative deprivation. There seem to be three central dimensions around which gender conflict swirls: reproductive ethics, women in the economy, and norms about women as nurturers and men as providers. These issues have loomed large in every election since 1980.

The Religious Reaction

From the 1950s through the 1970s, American religion experienced what some scholars have described as the "Third Disestablishment" (Hammond 1992). Unlike the first such episode, which eliminated legal recognition of Christianity, or the second, which effectively reduced Protestant hegemony, this third episode reduced the social privilege that "Judeo-Christian" religions had long enjoyed. What some see as a shift in church-state regimes can also be interpreted as a change in the moral order governing religion. In time, as politicians recognized the mobilizing opportunities presented by this development, the Third Disestablishment would become grist for cultural politics. It would also increasingly intersect the women's movement.

The major religious effect of the Third Disestablishment was to displace the Protestant ethic as the authoritative model of personal conduct. Religion was no longer recognized as the sole arbiter of morality, and the rise of moral relativism challenged the very possibility of transcendent, authoritative standards of human behavior. As the embodiment of the displaced norms, organized religion was redefined as simply one more voluntary institution, respected, perhaps, but not granted much legitimacy outside its own sector.

The transformation of religion was both caused by and symbolized by changing patterns of religious affiliation. Through immigration and conversion, new, non-Christian religions claimed an increasing share of the public and demanded recognition previously reserved for Protestants, Catholics, and Jews. With their emphasis on personal autonomy and self-fulfillment, many baby boomers left the mainline and Catholic churches, as well as the synagogues of their parents, explored the alternative new religions, or developed their own faiths and forms of spirituality outside of organized religion (Roof 1993; Wuthnow 1998). These changes were reinforced by transformations in legal norms. The Supreme Court prohibited state-supported prayer or Bible reading in public schools, ritualistic acts that had reinforced the semi-official status of Christianity. Nontraditional, nontheistic, and marginal faiths gained a measure of legal equality with the more established religious traditions as the Court broadened the meaning of conscientious objection and gave more protection to unconventional religious expression (Hammond 1998). Similarly, the rights of the nonreligious were given parity with believers as the Court expanded the meaning of the Establishment clause of the First Amendment through the *Lemon* decision.

These sudden and seemingly radical changes created fertile grounds for countermobilization and cultural politics. While the changes can be understood to have "liberated" religion and promoted religious diversity, traditionalists saw them as antireligious measures that trampled on the religious preferences of the majority. In poll after poll, Americans reported their perception that religion was losing its influence on society. Conservative intellectuals perceived a secularist bias that sought to confine people of belief to a narrow sphere and to erect barriers to keep them out of the public square (Neuhaus 1984). The real danger was to morality, which, the traditionalists believed, could not be sustained absent a transcendent source for moral norms. Accordingly, political mobilization by religious conservatives has attempted to frame debates over issues like prayer in schools and holiday religious observance as conflicts between "people of faith" and "militant atheists" or as efforts to "drive God out of the schools." In the rhetoric of religious liberals, by contrast, the operative division is between those who respect America's constitutional heritage of church-state separation and the "radicals" and "ayatollahs" who would submit America to theocracy.

Despite their differences, each side uses appeals that transcend the traditional denominational conflicts from the niche era of American religion. In the earlier period, for example, efforts to obtain state funding for religious schools elicited unwavering opposition from most Protestants, particularly evangelicals, who saw them as schemes to fund Catholic religious education, and from Jews who rejected the use of public money to subsidize Christianity. Under the new alignment, these proposals have been relabeled as vouchers and tuition tax credits, repackaged as means to effect the generic goal of "religious freedom," and marketed directly to the more observant members of all religious communities. They are even sold as the best hope for minorities to break out of terrible public schools, an interesting twist on desegregation. They continue to draw opposition from seculars, religious centrists, and religious liberals, regardless of denomination.

The earliest efforts to politicize these differences date from the 1964 campaign. In that effort, Goldwater was urged to run strongly on cultural issues: "The big issue . . . is the moral crisis in American today. It is made up of several components: crime, violence, riots (the backlash), juvenile delinquency, the breakdown of law and order, immorality and corruption in high places, the lack of moral leadership in government, narcotics, pornography—it all adds up to the picture of a society in decay. . . . This issue—morality—can be the 'missile gap' of 1960" (Freedman 1996, 254).[6] Although this appeal did not bear fruit in 1964, it became an undercurrent in subsequent Republican campaigns. Commentators invoked "the social issue" or variants such as "old values," "traditionalism," or "family values" to describe the cultural tensions that divided the Democrats and offered an opportunity for Republicans to mobilize disaffected members of the opposition.

In the effort by Republican elites to diminish the Democratic hold on Catholics and evangelical Protestants, several issues proved particularly effective. In time, however, the traditionalist movement increasingly focused on the emerging moral order about gender.

The feminists' call for equality between the sexes clashed sharply with the notion of gender complementarity prevailing among traditionalists. In the moral order embraced by the conservative wing of American religious communities, men are best suited to the task of earning a living

---

[6] The author of the memo, F. Clifton White, was too modest in his assessment of the staying power of the social issue. Rather than serving as a one-election issue like the missile gap, the concern over public morality worked in the post-Vietnam era something like the "bloody shirt" served Republicans in the post–Civil War period.

and providing standards of discipline, while women are more appropriately equipped to play the roles of helpmate, homemaker, and child rearer. This gender complementarity was both "natural"—something suited to the different endowments of the two sexes—and divinely ordained. Enforcing gender equality in the face of such glaring differences would, religious traditionalists believed, unleash dangerous social trends and undermine an important prop of the common culture.

Feminism also intersected with another dimension of cultural change in the domain of public education. Although women continued to dominate the teaching profession, educational politics took on a new urgency as the character of public school teachers changed. Moral traditionalists portrayed the National Education Association (NEA), the largest teachers' union, as the property of blacks, Jews, and single parents. The NEA became a strong force in Democratic politics and replaced industrial unions as the most reliable voting strength of the party. Parents were warned about the damage inflicted when they gave up their children to these social engineers and radicals. The NEA became a target for those who regarded cultural change as threatening. The public schools were held liable for a host of social problems afflicting contemporary society.

Feminism would have been challenging enough to people with such a worldview but became even more so when it became allied to the cause of liberalized abortion. Feminists seized on the 1973 Supreme Court decision in *Roe v. Wade* because they believed that control over reproduction was essential to making women equal to men (Mansbridge 1986). Women should be able to decide when they would interrupt their work or educational program to have a baby. Traditional Christian theology had argued that God created a human life at conception, and it could not be subjected to a later human choice. Religious traditionalists reacted so strongly against the decision because it seemed to threaten and devalue the unique quality that set women, as bearers of children, apart from men. *Roe v. Wade* and the abortion issue, increasingly the defining issue of feminism, became an important "wedge issue" that Republicans wielded in the attempt to detach Roman Catholics from their traditional Democratic allegiance, an allegiance that was already fraying by the 1970s.

The Catholic leadership had been the primary opponent of liberalized abortion laws before *Roe*, and the bishops soon emerged as the national leaders of the attempt to roll back the tide of reproductive rights swept in by the decision. By 1980 the issue had clearly crystallized as a source of partisan differences. The Republican platform gave support to a constitutional amendment prohibiting abortion while Democrats were defined as the prochoice party. As these positions emerged, the bishops pronounced themselves more satisfied with the position of the Republican nominee and came close to endorsing the GOP ticket in 1980, 1984, and 1988

(Byrnes 1991). The Republicans took advantage of their growing ties to the Catholic hierarchy. The Reagan campaign film included a shot of Catholic Cardinal Terence Cooke of New York at Reagan's bedside as the candidate recounted Cooke's words that "God must have been on my side" when he survived an assassination attempt (Jamieson 1996, 454). Reagan also continued to tie his positions to the emerging political movement known as the "New Christian Right," a group of organizations led by clergy from the evangelical Protestant tradition. Even if his actions did not often correspond with his words, Reagan made clear that he shared this constituency's aversion to the apparent decline of traditional morality on all fronts.

1988 and Beyond

In the last three elections of the era, cultural politics fused around the themes of patriotism, race, and gender/religion. The Republican handlers who had run the permanent campaign for nearly two decades had discovered a central tenet of their case in 1988: by building up the negatives of their Democratic opponent, putting the enemy on trial, they could successfully divert attention from their nominee's own weaknesses. It was a strategy of mobilizing the committed and demobilizing the vulnerable segments of the opposition so that the electorate was the right size. The practitioner of this exercise in 1988 was George Bush, who easily defeated Senator Bob Dole for the nomination.

When Governor Michael Dukakis of Massachusetts won the Democratic nomination against lackluster opposition once characterized as "the seven dwarfs," he still ranked far ahead of Bush: On the all-important negative rating, he was only minus fifteen while Bush was at a very high minus forty-one. Unfortunately for Dukakis, his negatives were so modest because voters knew little, positive or negative, about him. Instead of aggressively campaigning to fill out that picture, Dukakis stayed put in Massachusetts until the traditional Labor Day opening of the campaign.

The permanent campaigners on the Republican side set out to educate the electorate about Michael Dukakis. Lee Atwater, by now the leading strategist, isolated three negatives around which the campaign would be built: "(1) High tax, high spending . . . (2) To the left of Carter-Mondale in opposing every defense program . . . (3) Social issues. McGovern, [Ted] Kennedy, [Jesse] Jackson liberal: prison furloughs . . . 'card-carrying member of the ACLU' . . . vetoed the Pledge of Allegiance" (Blumenthal 1990, 259).

Atwater, Ailes, and Robert Teeter test-marketed these ideas on "about a dozen white Catholic Democrats [in New Jersey] who had voted for Reagan but were leaning to Dukakis" (ibid.). After noting that over half shifted to favoring Bush, they were ready to go with ads, speaking scripts, photo ops, and schedules. Knowing the magnitude of his negatives, Bush consented.

The psychological stuff of Atwater's summary is a social attribution theorist's dream: (1) taxing and spending have been shown through multivariate analyses to be code words for race; so are the prison furlough and fear of crime (Hurwitz and Peffley 1997; Jacoby 2000; Peffley, Hurwitz, and Sniderman 1997); (2) national defense cut, Pledge of Allegiance, and "card-carrying member" all tap into the rhetoric of Cold War patriotism; (3) McGovern/Kennedy/Jackson had become negative symbols of racial and social change brought on by the 1960s generation; and (4) fear of crime and fear of the Soviets tapped a common dimension. The campaign was based in some of the strongest basic research of our day, research that scholars aimed at understanding stereotyping, so that we might devise prosocial interventions to overcome it. Ironically, in the hands of the permanent campaigners, this knowledge became the equivalent of Hiroshima to the nuclear physicist.

The rest is history. The Willie Horton ad featured, as one Bush campaign staffer said, "a big black rapist" (Blumenthal 1990, 265). Atwater publicly made reference to the "Dukakis-Horton ticket." Candidate Bush always invoked the Pledge of Allegiance and literally wrapped himself in the American flag. In one of his more clever negatives he said, "I wouldn't be surprised if he [Dukakis] thinks a naval exercise is something you find in Jane Fonda's workout book"[7] (ibid.). The inept Dukakis had been photographed donning a helmet and battle fatigues and riding in the turret of a tank; he had swung the cannon toward the camera. It was supposed to symbolize that *he* was the one who was tough on defense. Instead, the Republican handlers made the edited tank-ride footage into an object of ridicule in the campaign. In an ad run over and over again, the announcer chronicled Dukakis's defense-cut positions, the camera zeroed in on the Snoopy-like Dukakis who appeared to be bemused at his own silliness behind the cannon, and the announcer pronounced, "And now he wants to be our commander-in-chief. America can't afford that risk" (Levine 1995, 233–34). Hawkish vice presidential nominee Dan Quayle's subterfuges to escape the draft during the Vietnam War seemed irrelevant. Bush's numbers turned around, and the Dukakis negatives skyrocketed; Americans expressed fear about that kind of a weak and misguided man in the White House. After a strong first debate, Dukakis, given to dispassionate rational discourse on constitutional issues, failed to show any emotion in response to the opening question of the second

---

[7] Fonda, a movie star and peace activist, had visited Hanoi, married students for a Democratic Society founder Tom Hayden, and become a favorite symbol of fellow-traveling.

debate—a hypothetical about the death penalty for a man who had raped Dukakis's wife. Seeing his opportunity, Bush called Dukakis "the ice man" (Germond and Witcover 1989, chap. 1). Some argue that his failure to grasp the importance of this question in the life of women caused him to lose a natural advantage with this sector of the electorate. Interestingly, Dukakis showed growing strength on the coasts and in suburbs, but Bush carried the South and the heartland in a stunning campaign turnabout.

In 1992, however, the Republican cultural campaign could never gather steam. The opportunities were certainly there. Bush had become one of the most popular presidents on record after he stood up to Saddam Hussein in the Desert Storm war against Iraq. But he did not get rid of this tyrant whom he demonized as "a Hitler," stopping the war short after achieving immediate military objectives. This Cold Warrior had forgotten the Republican charge that only Democrats leave wars unfinished. Now the Democrats in Congress who had voted against the operation could not be painted as unpatriotic. But the fundamental change for Bush in 1992 was that the Cold War really was over. The fall of the Berlin Wall on November 9, 1989, signaled the end of Soviet dominance in Eastern Europe; the demise of aggressive and totalitarian communism in the Soviet Union was soon to follow. The patriotism issue that had anchored Republican campaign strategy from the early Nixon years onward was gone.

The end of the Cold War generated a new problem for Bush. The huge investments in weapons systems that were part of the anti-communist offensive by Reagan and Bush—expenses incurred with reduced taxes but without offsetting deep cuts in social spending—had sent the budget to the verge of bankruptcy. In the ensuing era of deficit politics, Bush got maneuvered into reneging on his "read my lips, no new taxes" pledge. The Democrats in Congress had trapped him. Where was the strength of this erstwhile Clint Eastwood?

Ironically, most of the Democratic party's heavy hitters decided to sit out 1992 in view of Bush's Gulf War popularity. When his ratings plummeted they could not crank up their funding machines fast enough for the front-loaded primaries. Bill Clinton, a young many-term governor of Arkansas, emerged with the nomination. He appeared to be an easy target for negative campaigning, with apparent moral flaws on adultery and sexual harassment, draft-dodging, sellouts to corporations in Arkansas, campaign finance violations, an inability to extract himself from a stream of half-truths, and on and on. *But cultural politics is not simply negative campaigning on predefined moral issues. It requires pinning the candidate to negative outgroups, and generating fear and anxiety about the influence of such groups.*

The Bush permanent campaign organization tried many initiatives, but none ever caught on with a significant sector of the Democratic coalition. Clinton was a centrist who appeared to bridge group differences. A bundle of contradictions, he could legitimately claim to occupy issue positions Republicans had heretofore exploited in presidential campaigns. An eventually fatal illness deprived Bush of the services of Lee Atwater, and Bush's own victory over Patrick Buchanan eliminated his use of the far-right journalist who had created so many of the effective cultural appeals used earlier by Agnew, Nixon, and Reagan. Bush himself seemed to back off of visceral group appeals, running honesty ads and economic policy appeals, but only touching on patriotism issues later in the campaign.

If Bush was reticent about cultural appeals, some of his supporters were much less reluctant to maintain the goals and rhetoric of the Cold War. Lacking the external enemy, the Cold War style transfers attention to the internal threat. In cultural conservatives' perception, cultural liberals took the place of Communists. Not long after the fall of the Berlin Wall, Irving Kristol, one of the first and perhaps paramount neoconservative intellectuals, observed:

> There is no "after the Cold War" for me. So far from having ended, my cold war has increased intensity, as sector after sector of American life has been ruthlessly corrupted by the liberal ethos. It is an ethos that aims simultaneously at political and social collectivism on the one hand, and moral anarchy at the other. . . . Now that the "Cold War" is over, the real cold war has begun. We are far less prepared for this cold war, far more vulnerable to our enemy, than was the case with our victorious war over the global communist threat. We are, I sometimes feel, starting from ground zero and it is a conflict I shall be passing on to my children and grandchildren. (quoted in White 1997, 278)

The Democrats entered the 1992 campaign very much aware that they could capitalize on poor economic conditions only by preventing Republicans from effectively using cultural issues against them. By solidifying Clinton's image as the product of modest circumstances, a sunny small-town boy who sang in the church choir and regularly attended Baptist Sunday school, the Democrats could then move against the Republicans by raising concerns about the vitriolic denunciations of diversity throughout the GOP nominating convention. The electorate could focus on the economy because the Democrats had largely insulated their campaign from the damaging cultural appeals that hurt previous nominees.

The problem persisted for the Republicans in 1996. Ever the crafty politician, Clinton had outmaneuvered "intransigent Republican leadership" into taking the blame for the late-1995 shutdown of the federal government over budget differences. The Contract with America, trumpeted by the Congressional class of 1994, only a year later looked like an extremist manifesto directed by a Lenin-like leadership. Clinton's State of the Union address in January 1996 occupied many of the cultural positions that moderately conservative Republicans espoused. At a patriotic high point of the address, he primed the public to think of his likely opponent, Senator Robert Dole, as old; he heaped praise on the World War II generation who gave their lives for freedom *fifty years ago* and singled out Dole as an exemplar of that generation.

Apart from his age, Dole was not well suited to energize the evangelical Protestants who had become the core of the Republican electoral movement. Dole was not born again and seldom wore his religion on his sleeve. Anxious not to repeat the strident culture war rhetoric of the 1992 convention, Republican leaders staged a tame convention featuring smiling young mothers, darling babies, and a prochoice, divorced and remarried Italian Catholic congresswoman as its keynote speaker. Dole seemed to invigorate no one, least of all his own age cohort, who doubted that he would have the stamina to be an effective president.

Patriotism was no longer an issue. Even the transfer of patriotism to the culture lacked spark. Dole, whose divorce from his first wife had been hastily arranged when a reporter got wind of Dole's affair with another woman, was not a culture-war patriot. There was little to spark evangelical foot soldiers as their leaders looked ahead to the election at the millennium. Whenever cultural conservatives did become visible with more Clinton sex-lies allegations during the campaign, allies of the president, particularly from women's groups, held up the specter of undivided theocratic control at both ends of Pennsylvania Avenue. In this calculus, the cultural politicians of the left seemed to argue for a cultural balance of power.

SUMMARY

This extended story of culturally based political campaigning, based heavily on the accounts of leading journalists and observers, has emphasized the paramount role of cleavages based on patriotism, race, gender, and religion. We now move from journalism to social science, exploring how the electorate responded to these value-laden appeals.

CHAPTER SEVEN

A Methodology for Assessing Cultural Politics

THE POST–NEW DEAL period has witnessed partisan realignment along two cultural dimensions: race and religion. Both were *secular realignments*, if one may use that deliciously ironic concept to describe a religious realignment. That is, each involved a change in the partisan predispositions of groups that developed over several successive elections. The consequence was that many Southern whites and evangelical Protestants, both mainstays of the New Deal coalition, came to vote with some regularity for Republican presidential candidates; gradually both they and new voters entering the electorate also came to embrace Republican party identification and voted increasingly for Republican senatorial and congressional candidates. The net effect is that Republican presidential candidates now start the contest with a substantial electoral college advantage—similar to that enjoyed by Democrats from the settlement of Reconstruction through the New Deal. Further, the concluding days of the post–New Deal see the Republican party on the threshold of controlling national representative institutions with regularity.

Much of this movement can be attributed to societal changes that have had dramatic effects on sequences of election outcomes. Yet no cataclysmic event could be isolated. For example, in the period since the Korean War, Republicans have exercised three periods of dominance—Eisenhower, Nixon-Ford, and Reagan-Bush—yet scholars could not decide whether this was a longer than usual dealignment or when the realignment had actually occurred. There was no dramatic event to focus attention on a critical election. Everett Ladd (1991) likened the effort to fix the realigning election to "Waiting for Godot."

The notion of secular realignment is essential to interpreting the post–New Deal period's emphasis on cultural politics. There was no cataclysmic racial war. But there were some very important events that changed both the nature of political discourse and group loyalties. There was no religious war, and certainly nothing to compare with the persecution of Catholics in the mid-1800s. Yet there were skirmishes over the reach of government, values apparently embedded in government policies, and values lived by or symbolically embraced by political leaders that made partisan foes of former friends; it mobilized millions of people for whom politics was formerly a tainted and corrupt business to be avoided in the hope of eternal life. If there was cataclysm it was in the impending threat of divine retribution, not in the past event that occurred, like a war or depression. The life-and-death exception, of course, was abortion—and that messed up a whole party system for some.

Of course, fundamental to the concept of secular realignment is an acceptance that groups move in different patterns relative to one another. In assessing the shifting nature of support bases for political parties, it becomes imperative that we can map shifts in party loyalty over time. The remainder of this chapter provides preliminary considerations about (1) the measures we have devised for mapping stability and change in the electorate; (2) the procedures for isolating issue imagery and campaign themes; (3) efforts to detect the central issues and group feelings that affected each election outcome; and finally, (4) attempts to detect how issue clusters and group feelings perturbed substantial segments of specific groups away from party loyalty.

Measures of Party Loyalty, Turnout, Defection, and Partisan Yield

Three of the most venerable measures on the American National Election Studies address party identification, turnout, and choice among presidential candidates. When the much-heralded rise of independents came in the 1960s, the utility of party identification was called into question, but several scholars have shown that independent leaners act quite like strong partisans and that party identification is a durable measure of partisan predisposition (Keith et al. 1992; Miller and Shanks 1996; Weisberg 1980). Some questions have also been raised about respondents' propensity to overreport turnout. The National Election Studies, however, have conducted a variety of vote validation studies to estimate the amount of overreporting of turnout; when all is said and done, the self-reports on surveys are hardly less reliable than precinct and county records of the incidence of voting (Abramson and Aldrich 1982; Belli, Traugott, and Rosenstone 1984; Traugott, Traugott, and Presser 1992). Finally, although overreporting of voting for the winner in congressional elections remains a problem, self-reported candidate choice for president is quite accurate (Wright 1993). Thus, the three measures that form the backbone of our case studies have withstood close scrutiny and can be used with as much confidence as can be attributed to survey data.

Scholars have combined party identification and presidential candidate choice to generate a measure of party loyalty (Abramson, Aldrich, and Rohde 1994; Flanigan and Zingale 1994). Generally, such a measure has shown greater party loyalty, that is, voting for the candidate of the party with which one identifies, within the minority (Republican) party than the majority (Democratic) party. The assumption has been that, since the coalition that composes the majority party is larger, it is harder to hold it together; intraparty factionalism leads to the loss of some partisans in any given election. Further, the majority party is more likely to attract people with weaker interests in politics, and they are more susceptible to media appeals from the minority candidate. Both assumptions are suspect. Both, but particularly the latter, require the inclusion of turnout data in a measure of party loyalty. Those with less interest in politics are at least as likely not to vote as to defect. And intraparty faction members who are dissatisfied with the candidate are at least as likely to skip voting in the presidential contest as to cross over to the opposition candidate.

For these reasons, we develop a measure of *party loyalty* that includes all three pieces of information—party identification, turnout, and presidential candidate choice. We use it as our dependent variable in the multivariate analyses of each of the *empirical case study* chapters. Further, our measure of party loyalty generates a more detailed picture of the payoff from partisanship. We produce a party loyalty score for each group by multiplying the percentage identifying with a particular party by the percent of partisans who turn out and support their respective candidates. Simply put, what we term *partisan yield* is the percent of the total group that support their party's candidate for president. This is a politician's calculus of the vote. It matters not a great deal to the campaigner what proportion of the population or of a given group identifies as a Democrat or Republican. The campaigner needs to know through time what proportion identifies with the party, goes to the polls, and actually votes for that party's candidate.

Furthermore, with partisan yield measures for both Democrats and Republicans, we can calculate a measure of *partisan advantage*, by subtracting one from the other. This measure allows us to see at what point in time the relative measures of partisan yield shift to the advantage of one or another party. It is not uncommon for a group—for example, white Southern Democrats—to shift their basic party identification through time to the Republican side. Assuming high party loyalty to the new party, the partisan advantage measure will now favor the Republicans. Also not uncommon is that a group—again white Southern Democrats— may maintain Democratic identification but either fail to vote or to vote but defect to the Republican candidate. The measure of partisan advantage may show a similar outcome in each case, but the underlying causes are fundamentally different. From our perspective as political scientists, the ebb and flow of partisan advantage affords us a view of secular dealignment, alignment, and realignment.

By combining party identification, turnout, and presidential vote choice, our measure of party loyalty allows us to present group-by-group information on advantage as well as to diagnose what is happening to non-loyalists. In the mapping section of each case-study chapter, we include figures such as figure 7.1 for the entire population of each designated group. Each figure consists of three panels, each panel telling a unique part of the story for the group in question. Combining each set of panels, the figure provides a map through time of the group's size, its partisanship, participation rates, degree of loyalty, and size of partisan advantage. The reader can also easily infer the proportion of the group that has remained independent or unaffiliated by adding the two partisanship percentages and subtracting the sum from 100 percent. Since independents are disproportionately younger people entering the electorate, information about fluctuations in their size may at times become important in our discussions of partisan alignment. In totality, the figures provide a mosaic of change and continuity in the American presidential electorate—our dependent variable.

The top and bottom panels of each figure graph loyalty information about Democrats and Republicans, respectively. We break down partisans into three categories: (1) those loyal to the party, (2) those who stay at home on Election Day, and (3) those who vote for the opposition candidate. Party identification then is the sum of this decomposition. Formally, the top line in the first panel of each figure represents *Democratic party identification*—the proportion of the group reporting their partisanship as strong Democrat, not so strong Democrat, or independent-leaning Democrat. Similarly, the top line of the figure in the bottom panel represents *Republican party identification*.

The decomposition of party identification in the aggregate produces three strata in each figure. From bottom to top:

Loyal Partisans—the percentage of the entire group (Catholics, Southern whites, homemakers, etc.) that is both partisan and loyal to their partisan preference, for example, a Catholic Democrat who turns out and votes her party for president (shaded black)

Stay-at-Home Partisans—the percentage of the group that is partisan but does not turn out (shaded white)

Defecting Partisans—the percentage of the group that is partisan, turns out, but votes counter to party preferences, for example, a Catholic Democrat who turns out but votes for Nixon, the Republican presidential candidate in 1972 (shaded gray)

The middle panel of the figure presents *partisan advantage*—the percentage difference between loyal Democrats and loyal Republicans. (A positive number favors Democrats; negative, Republicans.) To provide an indication of group magnitude, we also provide the number of cases used in the analysis along the horizontal axis of this panel.

The utility of this set of measures is that it allows us to take any desig-

134 • Chapter Seven

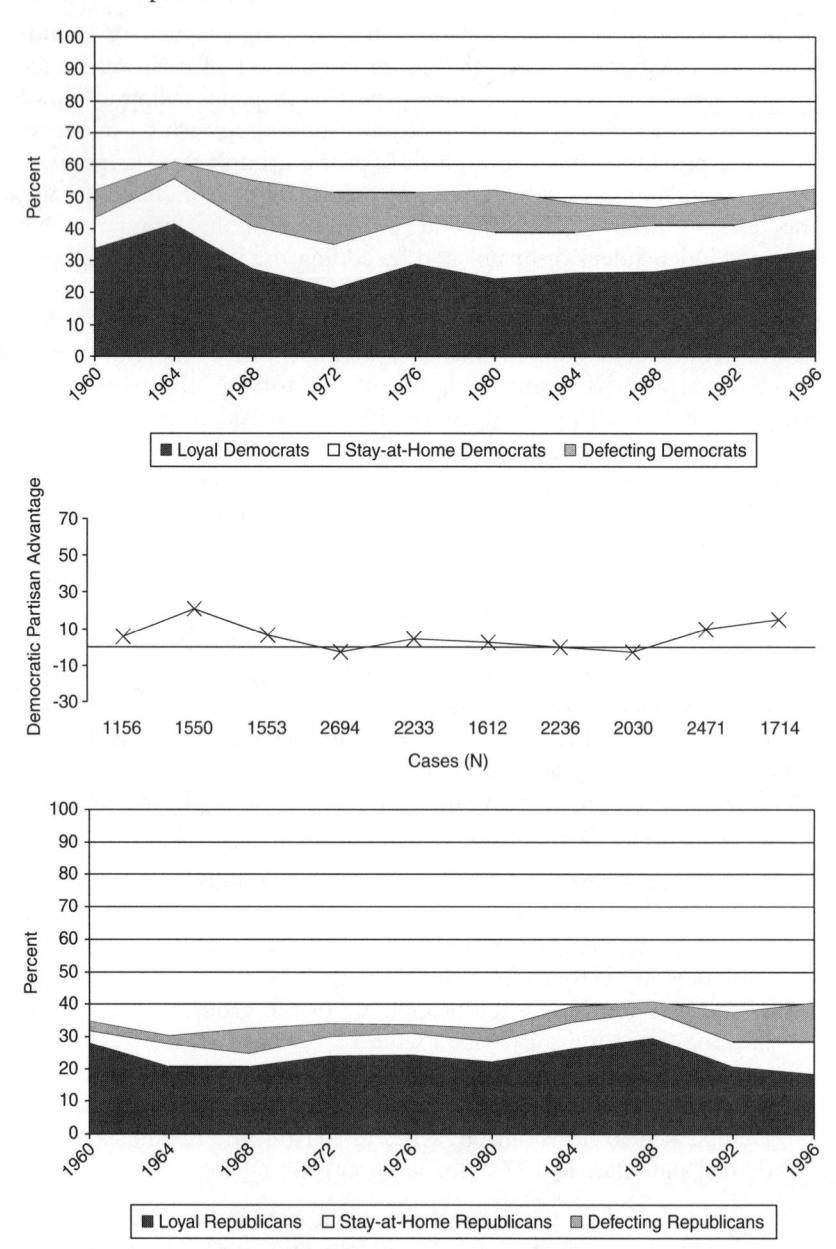

Figure 7.1. Partisan Patterns of Entire Population, 1960–1996

nated group in the electorate and (1) see its basic patterns of partisanship and loyalty, (2) measure precisely when it stays stable and when it shifts, and (3) diagnose whether the shift is the result of low turnout, defection, or a change in the group's party loyalties. This information is all summarized in the group figures and provides clues as to when a campaign appeal is operating on the group.

Figure 7.1 illustrates how these measures operate among samples of the entire adult population from 1960 to 1996. The Democratic party remained the party of choice for the electorate throughout the time-series. There was, however, steady erosion in Democratic party identification from about twice as many Democrats as Republicans in 1964 until only 6 or 7 percentage points separated Democrats from Republicans during presidential elections in 1984 and 1988. After 1988 the Democratic edge widened again during the Clinton elections of 1992 and 1996.

Politically, the real story for this period was in the partisan vote yield (shaded black). In all elections except 1964, Republicans were more likely to turn out than Democrats (turnout failure is left white). Furthermore, with the exceptions of 1964, 1992, and 1996, Republicans were far less likely to defect to the opposition than were Democrats (shaded grey). In the turbulent years of 1968, 1972, and 1980, one-fourth to one-third of self-identified Democrats actually voted for the Republican or third-party candidate. Only in Johnson's landslide of 1964 and Clinton elections of 1992 and 1996 did Republican defections reach the magnitude of Democratic defections. In any given year, the effects of defections can be devastating to party fortunes. For example, in 1972 although Democratic identifiers represented just over 50 percent of the electorate compared to the Republicans' just over 30 percent, Democrats suffered nearly four times as many defections.

The true magnitude of these acts of partisan disloyalty among the electorate can be seen when we combine the turnout and defection figures. For example, in Nixon's successful election of 1968, a quarter of the Democrats did not vote and another quarter defected from Humphrey; yet only 18 percent of Republicans failed to vote, and only 12 percent defected to Wallace or Humphrey. The net result was that the Democratic party identification advantage of 22 points was reduced to 4 points in comparative vote yield. In 1972, it got even worse: more than 60 percent of self-identified Democrats either stayed home or defected. Republicans, however, had higher turnout and miniscule defections. The result was that an initial 18-point Democratic advantage in party identification was transformed into a 4-point Republican advantage in vote yield. Only later in the time series did Democrats begin to show partisan yield advantages that start to approach their initial advantages in party identification. And then it was not because Democrats suddenly turned out in a show of loyalty but because Republicans were uncharacteristically disloyal. Something obviously was changing again in the electorate.

The true independents rose in number as the baby boomers entered the electorate in the late 1960s and 1970s but declined as they started connecting with party institutions in the Reagan-Bush years. From figures developed later for substantive chapters, we can conclude that independence was not a halfway house between the parties but was the way this particular cohort entered the political, or perhaps apolitical, arena.

We employ this type of mapping for each of our target groups, namely, groups a political party targets for destabilizing appeals. When either abrupt or gradual change occurs, our eyes will be drawn to the elections where perturbations in partisanship first appear. Then, in other ways, we must isolate the nature of the campaign themes addressed to this group and must estimate the extent to which such issue or group appeals have altered party loyalty within that group.

INFORMATION ABOUT CAMPAIGN THEMES AND TARGET GROUPS

In an effort to gain deeper understanding of campaign themes aimed at various target groups, we have used a modified form of content analysis. Our sources are the principal political scientists and communications specialists who have addressed campaign themes, speeches, and advertisements during this period (Diamond and Bates 1992; Jamieson 1996; Johnson-Cartee and Copeland 1991; 1997; Levine 1995; West 1997), the leading journalists who have written either historical series or in-depth analyses (Blumenthal 1990; Edsall and Edsall 1991; Germond and Witcover 1981; 1985; 1989; 1993; White 1962; 1965; 1969; 1973; Witcover 1970; 1977), and finally the campaign managers (Matalin and Carville 1995; May and Fraser 1973; Runkel 1989).

With each expert source we have classified the theme, speech, or advertisement by the *cultural topic* or *mechanism* embedded in it (e.g., race, gender, religion, patriotism), *year* of use, *party* or *candidate* employing it, *target group* (e.g., Southern whites, African Americans, women/mothers, Catholics, evangelical Protestants, working class), *frequency/extensiveness* of use (e.g., national TV for four weeks, radio stations in four Southern states for ten days, religious broadcasting networks throughout the campaign, black churches), and *content* (e.g., a KKK endorsement of Goldwater; a montage of black urban rioters, the war in Vietnam, pictures of abject poverty, and Hubert Humphrey smiling; "get out of jail free" cards; a bear frightened by a hunter carrying a gun).

Because these secondary sources did not lend themselves to systematic analysis, no quantitative analysis is done and no term for campaign themes or advertisements enters equations. Further, not until 1992 did NES ask respondents to recall a campaign ad, and then it did so with little success. Thus, we can only treat this indirect content analysis as suggestive; it tells what analysts, journalists, and the campaigners themselves claim was operating in the environment of voters and, more particularly, targeted groups. This information entered the narrative in chapter 6 and is seen in each case study chapter.

COGNITIVE STRUCTURES OF ISSUES AND GROUPS

Ambitious politicians and their handlers have many tools to control the size and composition of the electorate. With insinuative imagery, politicians are able to create a sense of unease with whom the opponent represents. Alternatively, like incumbent Reagan's "Morning in America" ads, politicians are able to galvanize the loyalties of those already in their camp while saying to others, "why vote the party when you can vote for good feelings?" Campaigns are often about issues, but fundamentally, campaigns are about conflict. Cultural campaigning is the conflict between "us" and "them." The strategic politician has tools available not only to manipulate issue frames, but also to manipulate perceptions of who is "us" and who is "them." Social psychology suggests that neither issues nor groups exist in a vacuum. Instead, issues overlap, interlock, and intermesh. Similarly, groups also overlap with other groups. And issues are connected to groups. This fundamental interlocking provides politicians with efficient campaign tools. While addressing certain taboo issues (or even groups) directly may be political suicide, by appealing to other issues politicians can still stoke latent group concerns. This is the basic fodder of cultural politics.

In this section, we detail how we identify deep cognitive structures and how they have shifted in the electorate. We perform independent factor analyses to examine how people structure issues and how they structure groups. These factors, provide us with impressions of the fundamental political landscape. Finally, we perform a second-order factor analysis to determine how issues interplay with groups. Efficient campaign strategies tap into these deepest cognitive structures (Sniderman, Brody, and Tetlock 1991).

Central Issue Clusters, 1960–1996

Historical eras are often characterized by enduring issue conflicts. Sometimes episodic events thrust up concerns that cry for attention; long-dormant differences between groups are once again exposed. There is often a symbiotic relationship between ambitious political actors and the positions important sectors of the public take on these issues (Shafer and Claggett 1995). Acting through democratic electoral structures, elites will take positions on issues so that they will mobilize some segments of the public and demobilize others. Thus, issues wax and wane in importance.

The post–New Deal period has been characterized by several sets of issues. The rise and decline of the Cold War stimulated fears of enemies external and internal; the role of the United States in the world could be shaped by responses to these enemies. The enduring American dilemma—equality of opportunity for racial minorities—came to a head again a century after the Civil War. Changes in family structure, education, and employment raised a host of questions about the roles and opportunities of women, often against the backdrop of enduring religious rationales for the prewar social order. How active or limited the federal government should be was often debated in the context of these changes in racial and gender relations; the uses of tax dollars could become an index for social attitudes. And, as always, upward and downward turns in the economy raised concerns about economic policy.

Scholars have found the American National Election Studies time-series of issue items to be a helpful resource for interpreting the flow of issues during the post–New Deal period. For example, Carmines and Layman (1997) utilized factor analysis with an orthogonal rotation to isolate three enduring issue clusters labeled "racial," "social and cultural," and "economic and social welfare." They mapped the importance of each issue throughout the period and showed how various groups differed in their positions.

Shafer and Claggett (1995) did not use NES data, but they did perform factor analyses on various items and beliefs found in the Times-Mirror polls pooled from the late 1980s. They found six factors labeled—cultural values, civil liberties, and foreign affairs; and social welfare, civil rights, and social insurance. They performed a second factor analysis using the factor scores from the first data reduction and found that the first three loaded well on a "cultural-national" deep factor and the second three described an "economic/welfare" deep factor. They found that the political parties and various component groups of each party took differing positions on these issues. The resulting conflicts set the boundaries for coalition formation by ambitious elites. However, Shafer and Claggett could only speculate about differences through time because, using a pooled dataset derived from a short time frame, they lacked sufficient measures through time.

We use NES data from 1960 to 1996 to isolate the issue clusters that structured public thinking in these elections. From the range of issue items that appeared in given election studies and sometimes recurred through much or all of the time-series, we have abstracted the issues that account for most of the variance in the electorate's issue thinking. However, we have proceeded a bit differently from Carmines and Layman. We have done factor analysis using a principal components extraction technique. We retain all factors with eigenvalues greater than one and drop any item whose correlation does not reach 0.4 with at least one factor. A minimum of two issues defined a factor, but often it was as high as five or six issues. Since positions on various political issues load not only on a central factor but sometimes on a related factor, an *oblique* method rather than Carmines and Layman's orthogonal method is the preferred rotation. Civil rights, for example, can hardly be isolated from the role of government; policy on crime, as a public order concern, is not attitudinally isolated from stance toward Communists. Neither should the measurement model treat these issues as though they were intended to be independent of each other. In fact, the most efficient cultural symbols used by campaigners are those that tap into several factors.

Since we examine the partisan behavior of specific groups targeted for "disabling," legitimate questions concern whether the factor analysis on issue positions should be based on the general electorate or should be done separately for each group. Like both Shafer and Claggett (1995) and Carmines and Layman (1997), we have opted for the former. While campaigners target specific groups to reduce turnout or arouse defection and perhaps eventual realignment, these groups exist within the larger electorate. We assume they are subject to much the same general media and imbibe in larger public moods. They gauge appropriate positions in part by what friends and conversation partners from their own group do, but also in part by what the public seems to be thinking about a president, a contender, a party, an issue, a rival group. The later multivariate analyses that seek to explain unsettled partisan behavior, however, are based on the assumption that targeted groups will deviate from the general moods of the public precisely because they are the subject of special attention by political elites; their failure to vote, their defection, or their realignment will be an understandable response to the way certain issue clusters or group perceptions affect them. Our factor analyses for each year, then, include the total NES sample. We substitute the mean value to approximate positions for missing data.

These factor analyses readily show that racial concerns endured throughout the post–New Deal electoral period but were particularly evident from 1964 until 1980, when Republicans made their greatest electoral gains. They surged again both in 1988, when the Bush campaign inserted, in their words, "a big black rapist" into the campaign, and in 1992. The role of government and the appropriateness of social spending were also on people's minds in most of the elections but were especially evident at the takeoff of the civil rights era in 1960 (but that could be because of the dearth of civil rights items on the instrument) and again in the later Reagan-Bush era. Typically, when the direct concern for race policy wanes, concern about the role of government and what it spends money for waxes (see, for example, 1984 and 1996). There are many instances where race-related concerns and government role overlap. There is little question that these were tapping similar parts of attitude structures, or, to put it more directly, that the domestic policy conservatism of Goldwater, Reagan, and Dole was a codeword for negative feelings about governmental action to improve the lot of racial minorities. Furthermore, by the 1980s, often items included on a race factor begin to load noticeably (but not above the 0.4 threshold) on a cultural/moral factor. Increasingly, policies related to blacks become lumped with changing policies related to women and homosexuals. The moral order being disrupted, in short, needs to be perceived not solely along a black-white dimension, but along generic "outsider" terms. Perhaps that is more palatable to a public feeling badgered by charges of prejudicial attitudes.

Cynical and distrustful feelings toward government are also a staple of the post–New Deal period, surfacing typically as the second strongest factor in every presidential election. When citizens are highly distrustful of government, it is easy for political elites in the Republican party to transfer that distrust to the contemporary "party of government," namely, the Democrats. In particular, the more that citizens feel the government is ignoring their wishes anyway, the easier it is to sit out an election or to get sufficiently angry to vote for the "outs" who promise to make government responsive again. Once again, some items from the race factor appear at subthreshold levels on distrust of government. There may be a racial frame of reference to the sense that government ignores popular opinion or that government serves the few.

Foreign policy and issues of national defense also appeared in each election. These, however, are more transitory, focusing on a current foreign policy problem; even the more enduring orientations such as isolationism/internationalism and wariness of Communists are typically referenced by a specific hot spot in the world. By 1972, when the items first appeared regularly on NES, the morally traditionalistic concerns over gender roles, abortion, and other components of social change structure the thinking of the electorate, sometimes in ways that parallel race. Initially, women's rights and, later, homosexual rights often show a loading of greater than 0.2 on the racial factor; treatment of criminals also loads on the racial factor. Finally, concerns about economic policy surface sufficiently in 1976 and 1980 to appear among the factors. It is interesting that, for the most part, when economic issues surface, they are included on the role of government or the racial factors.

Group Clusters, 1964–1996

We performed a parallel factor analysis of group feeling thermometers on NES, using similar procedures to isolate underlying structure. If certain groups occupy a common mental space, it becomes quite efficient for campaigners to rely on *social attributions*. That is, a symbol for one of the groups can fill in negative or positive information about other groups. For example, if the Supreme Court is a negative symbol associated in the same space with blacks, and if blacks occupy a negative space alongside the women's movement or feminists, it may be easy for strategic politicians to link up the negative feelings about both black activists and feminists with symbols of the Supreme Court. In fact, this is precisely what anti-ERA forces did with the codeword "desexegration." They transferred negative feelings about African Americans and court-ordered integration into a specter of Supreme Court decisions about the moral orders of the family, gender roles, "women warriors," unisex bathrooms, and so forth (Mansbridge 1986; Matthews and De Hart 1990).

The sample of groups from 1964 to 1996 changed from year to year as the principal investigators and the NES Board perceived that certain groups were becoming more or less salient to the election.[8] Thus, we should not anticipate a fixed structure of groups within each factor. At the same time, campaigners actively seek to alter discussion. We noted, for example, that the Clinton organization had concluded there was too much visibility for black activists in the Democratic core and put distance between the party and black activists by attacking Sister Souljah's militant rap lyrics. In turn, the Rev. Jesse Jackson had nowhere near the visibility in the party conventions of the 1990s that he had in the 1980s. We should expect the party factor of 1984 and 1988 to link Democrats and black groups but to find that linkage weakening by 1992 and 1996.

Some striking changes in group structure occurred as a result of both substantive change and group sampling. Most important is the factor defining who is at the core of the party. In the early years, that is, the 1960s, the space occupied by party includes only the two parties at polar opposites, and conservatives loading in the same direction as Republicans. Not meeting the 0.4 threshold but still loading in varying degrees on the Democratic direction for the factor in 1964 are the military at −0.351, liberals at −0.267, and labor at −0.221. Loadings below 0.2

---

[8] Because individual respondents approach the feeling thermometer differently, some routinely giving warm (positive) ratings to all groups, others clustering their ratings toward the middle or at the chilly (negative) end, we have followed the standardization procedure of Wilcox, Sigelman, and Cook (1989). A respondent's score for each group is calculated as a deviation from the mean of that respondent's scores across all groups.

are considered too unreliable to indicate much substantively; Southerners are close at 0.194 on the conservative and Republican direction. By 1968 conservatives load at 0.233 on the regional cultural divide between labor and Southerners, but the latter do not yet load on a party dimension. The military, ironically, and liberals, not so ironically, are still loading but at subthreshold levels with the Democratic side of the party factor; perhaps this is the lingering effect of the cold warriors leading the White House during the escalation of the Vietnam War. Note that blacks are still not perceived in partisan terms, even after their massive realignment in the 1964 election (see chapter 9). By 1972 labor is added to the party core solidly on the Democratic side. The military is dropping off the party radar and is now appearing modestly on a social change/law and order factor, and it appears at the core of that factor four years later. By 1976 big business is in the party core on the Republican side, but labor is perturbed by blue-collar cultural conservatism and weakens ties to the Democratic party symbol, while poor people and people on welfare are now seen as closer to that space. The year 1980 rolls back closer to the original sparse party symbol, but 1984, the year of Ronald Reagan's landslide reelection, is an important celebration of much broader partisan coalitions at odds with each other. Liberals, labor, the Democratic party, and the women's movement are now seen in the same camp, with black militants not that far away; conservatives and Republicans are linked, and now the military, a symbol of order, is seen in their orbit. A somewhat similar coalition appears in 1988, although blacks are considerably less central and women drop out. In 1992 and 1996 the party coalitions first emerging in 1984 are fully crystallized. By 1996 in the Clinton reelection, the Democrats are in tight with liberals, labor, and the women's movement. Republicans and conservatives have now added Christian fundamentalists to their perceived party core. Blacks by now are relegated to a distinct minorities factor and simply are not a central component of the "new" Democratic party.

Other group clusters have shorter lives or they start humbly and become more central to the affective feelings of the public. In 1964, for example, a factor links whites and the military against blacks and liberals. Another factor, perhaps of residual nativist or Ku Klux Klan sentiment, pits Southerners against Catholics and Jews. Blacks and whites remain polarized throughout much of the period, and Southerners and labor are uncomfortable with what each symbolizes. The struggle for order in the face of social change appears in 1968 and picks up steam in the factors of the 1970s. There are separable racial and gender dimensions to it in 1972, but often these are merged. Blacks as a symbol shift about, sometimes linked to poor people and welfare recipients, sometimes to disorder, sometimes to racial antagonism with whites, sometimes to antiestablishment symbols, sometimes to Chicanos. Once evangelical political activists or Christian fundamentalists enter the sample of group objects, they appear in antagonistic combat with the women's movement, the Supreme Court, civil rights leaders, and liberals. By 1996, as women's groups evolve into the Democratic core, Christian fundamentalists are anchored in the Republican core.

There is no question as we move through the 1980s and 1990s that the cleavage between these religious groups and the women's movement has nudged the racial cleavage off of the center stage of group political differences. The party systems of 1960 and mid-1990 are somewhat different. The question yet to be explored is whether issue clusters and group clusters occupy overlapping mental space. That is, can the discourse about issues and the conflict between groups be part of the same mental processes?

Second-Order Factors, 1964–1996

To find out whether issue positions and group feelings occupy the same space, we have conducted second-order factor analyses using the familiar principal components extraction with an oblique rotation. Factor scores have been entered into equations for each presidential election year. Although it is always risky to label factors, particularly the deep mental structures inferred from second-order factor analyses, both the enduring and the transitory factors tell much about the structure of political thinking throughout the post–New Deal period. Furthermore, it is these second-order factors that most closely tap into how people actually think about and cognitively cluster parties, issues, and groups.

The central theme of American cultural politics was race. Its subtheme was the role of government. Later on, concern for cultural change in primary units of society became dominant. All three merged in varying degrees with pictures of the political parties. Cynicism or lack of trust in government was also present throughout, and it often was linked with isolationist perspectives on America's international involvement. Cruder forms of regional antagonism, age-old religious conflicts, and labor versus Southern Protestant whites are also evident, but the enduring story is the way party images link not only to ideological but to cultural differences.

When the combined time-series begins in 1964, party has a more modest definition, including only the two parties and conservatives linked to the Republicans; there are hints that people connect liberals and labor with the Democrats. But party ideology is also defined by conservative opposition to an activist governmental role and resentment over government spending. Feelings toward Catholics and Jews, on the one hand, and Southerners, on the other, are also caught up in differences between the parties.

By 1968, however, party ideology takes on a much fuller meaning that is clearly anchored in differences on civil rights policy, and age-old antagonisms between Northerners and Southerners concerning what government should be doing. The objectionable actions often have racial overtones. This race-based party ideology carries throughout the entire post–New Deal period, following the protest led by George Wallace. In the 1970s it adds components with negative feelings toward groups that symbolize threats to law and order or groups that are thought to perpetrate crime or social unrest. The white middle-class establishment is seen positively, while blacks, civil rights leaders, and liberals become the enemy. In fact, by 1972 the conservative reaction to social change loads with over half of all the issue and group factors. There is clear crystallization of the moral and political order, and it is encapsulated in the party images. This race-based party ideology continues through the Reagan-Bush years. By 1992, however, partisan differences become interlarded with race and class dimensions. And by 1996 a newer imagery of party emerges that links religious groups' positions on cultural issues such as gender roles, abortion, and homosexuality to the older notions of government role and social spending. During the Clinton years, race is omnipresent, but it becomes separated as a group phenomenon from party; nevertheless, it continues to manifest itself in a racial frame of reference for what government should do. Activist government remains associated with things that benefit blacks and disadvantage whites.

So, despite all of the advances in equality of opportunity since the system of apartheid was abolished in the United States in the 1960s, and despite the fact that the crude and often violent confrontations between white and black have given way to more civil relations, and despite the move from the visceral language of a George Wallace to the benign and "principled" language of a Ronald Reagan—the politics of racial differences still lie latent in the minds of the American body politic. They are deeply insinuated in the way we think about political parties and the way we apply our operative political philosophies. Frames of reference developed in this struggle have been carried over to the perceptions of opportunities for women, how they should behave in home and outside, and what rights other groups challenging the moral order should have. Popular perceptions of cultural restorationists, particularly the evangelical Protestants and Christian fundamentalists who would use government to reinstate the "family values" from an earlier time, do not separate them from racial thinking. And even in years like 1980 when economic policy is so central to public discourse, the economy is but a powerful current mingling in the river of what the government should do on race.

As one would expect, the older forms of nativism and antinativism were evident early in the post–New Deal period, stimulated by the Kennedy candidacy in 1960 and its aftermath for the decade. The kinds of antagonism toward the federal government that grew from the Civil War and especially Reconstruction manifested themselves forcefully again in 1968 and had a strong resurgence with Ronald Reagan in 1980.

In a worldview so interwoven as the Cold War, one should anticipate a higher-order factor dealing with international involvements and the Communist enemy. Indeed it is there throughout much of the post–New Deal but in a curious way. The early isolationist position is linked consistently with cynicism and distrust of government. As time goes on, the same distrustful position is manifested in both an external dimension—unwillingness to negotiate with communists, hawkish positions on military involvement—and an internal dimension—dislike of blacks, opposition to civil rights legislation, opposition to cultural change based on gender roles, and so on. In 1980, perhaps given the discourse of that election year, it becomes fairly tightly integrated around cultural and racial differences and aggressive anticommunism. Isolationism has given way to a militarily aggressive internationalism. In 1984 cynicism and distrustfulness focus entirely on domestic matters—race and poverty—but later in the decade and in the 1990s they are associated with dovish international stances toward external enemies.

The emergence of evangelical politics gives focus to wariness about groups committed to cultural change and policies that further change. The moral traditionalism policy factor attaches itself to a variety of other factors after it first emerges in the McGovern debacle of 1972, but it is firmly anchored with evangelical groups from 1988 on, perhaps reflecting the prominence of Pat Robertson and Jerry Falwell in that year, and becomes central to the differences between the parties in 1996. As an aside, it is interesting that big business passes off the scene as a negative symbol of the Republican party later on in the period. As a nation we have grown closer together on capitalist economic policy, and farther apart on racial and other cultural policies. Rival groups and ideologies come to convey these differences.

ACCOUNTING FOR CHANGES IN PARTISANSHIP

However intrinsically interesting the history of these issue and group clusters may be, they are only a stage in the development of our evidence. Their central purpose is to help us understand the sources of party loyalty and defection within target groups. Therefore, in the empirical case studies, we will use the second-order factor scores to model loyalty, demobilization, and defection, primarily among Democratic groups—because our theory of campaign dynamics calls for that—but occasionally among Republican groups when they are thought to respond negatively to their own party's appeals. By grouping issue positions and group feelings in the same cognitive space, the second-order factor scores most closely approximate the schema used by satisficing voters. They combine social heuristics with partisan-owned issues. Candidates then need only remind voters of portions of the package to transmit a much larger message and create either enthusiasm or anxiety in target groups (e.g., the use of law-and-order themes to speak indirectly about race). The levels of enthusiasm or anxiety will lead to three choices by partisans: loyalty to the party, staying home, or defection to the other party.

In choosing a statistical technique to estimate the effect of these second-order factors on the dependent variable, we need to consider the specific nature of the data. First, the partisans' choices of loyalty, staying home, or defection are bounded, because the probability of falling into each of these categories must always sum to one and range between zero and one. Second, the three categories on the dependent variable are just that, categories. We cannot assume that they range equidistant on a scale from loyalty to disloyalty, thus approximating an interval-level variable. Furthermore, some independent variables, such as cynicism, should influence the relative probability of falling in the stay-at-home category more strongly than the defection category; this negates the possibility of the categories being ordered.

Addressing the first concern, the bounded nature of the choices implies that the relationship between our independent and dependent variable is nonlinear. That is, we would expect that the influence of an independent variable would decrease as the probability of falling into a particular category approaches near certainty—either zero or one. Even if our dependent variable were ordered, ordinary least squares models would at best be inefficient because of heteroskedasticity but more likely lead to incorrect inferences. Having a nonordered, three-category dependent variable such as ours suggests that we move to a maximum likelihood estimator such as multinomial probit or logit. We opted for *multinomial logit*.[9]

---

[9] While multinomial probit may be more acceptable statistically, this technique is very computationally intensive and is not found in most major statistical packages. Compared to multinomial probit, multinomial logit uses vastly less computing resources, is found in many of the major statistical packages, and conforms nicely with the structure of our data. One potential problem with multinomial logit is the assumption of the Independence of Irrelevant Alternatives. Simply stated, this assumption claims that the ratio of the probability between the first two choices is unchanged by the addition of a third or more choices. To determine if this assumption holds in our data, we used Hausman and McFadden's

To identify the implied structural model, one category of the dependent variable is arbitrarily selected as the baseline and standardized to zero. This standardization produces one less set of parameters than categories of the dependent variable. We chose the "loyal to party" category as the baseline. This has the effect of producing two sets of parameter estimates that, if positive, indicate that an increase in the independent variable results in an increase in the relative probability of being in that category compared to the baseline category. Likewise a negative coefficient indicates that an increase in the independent variable results in a decrease in the probability of being in that category relative to the baseline category. In practice, our two sets of parameter estimates tell us how increases in the second-order factor scores change the relative probability of (1) remaining loyal compared to not voting, and (2) remaining loyal compared to defecting, respectively. Although this technique allows us to compute the change in relative probability of falling into one category based on a unit change in our second-order factor scores, we chose to use a *sign and significance* standard of interpretation. We chose this approach with three underlying principles in mind: (1) differing levels of measurement error across variables always plague social science data, rendering any discussion of point estimates risky (especially when not using a latent variable approach); (2) statistical models, as well as theories, are to be used, not believed; and (3) greater parsimony and readability could be achieved using a sign and significance approach.

To aid the reader when interpreting the multinomial logit tables, we include a direction code key for Democratic groups and Republican groups (see table 7.1). This key notes the expected signs of the second-order factor scores for both stay-at-home and defect. Four classes of variables exist, with higher scores indicating (1) more conservative opinions, (2) more cynical opinions, (3) more conservative and more cynical opinions, or (4) more conservative and less cynical opinions. We expect increasingly conservative scores to positively influence Democratic turnout failure and defection, while increasingly conservative scores should promote Republi-

---

(1984) test for this property. Results from the Hausman test indicate that we can generally be confident that the assumption of the Independence of Irrelevant Alternatives holds across our models, and that we can make valid statistical inferences from parameters generated by the multinomial logit model. As a further test for the robustness of our findings, we utilized the multinomial probit routine in LIMDEP 6.0 to analyze White Democrats and Republicans as well as Catholic Democrats. Of significant variables in the multinomial logit models, we never see sign flipping, and only occasionally when a variable is borderline statistically significant in the logit equations do we see factors become insignificant in the probit models. Because of the computational intensity, the findings of the Hausman test for IIA, and the apparent general robustness of multinomial logit parameters, we base our findings on models generated by multinomial logit.

TABLE 7.1
Direction Codes for Second-Order Factors: Democrats/Republicans, 1960–1996

	Democrats		Republicans	
Factors	Stay at Home	Defect	Stay at Home	Defect
Govt Role/Social Spending[a]	Positive	Positive	Negative	Negative
Cynicism/Trust in Govt[b]	Positive	Positive	Positive	Positive
Strength of U.S.[a]	Positive	Positive	Negative	Negative
Isolationism/Internationalism[a]	Positive	Positive	Negative	Negative
Race/Civil Rights[a]	Positive	Positive	Negative	Negative
1964				
Old Social Cleavages[a]	Positive	Positive	Negative	Negative
Party Ideology[a]	Positive	Positive	Negative	Negative
Cynical American First/ Anticommunism[c]	Positive	Positive	Positive	Negative
1968				
Race Based Party Ideology[a]	Positive	Positive	Negative	Negative
Cynicism/Trust in Govt[b]	Positive	Positive	Positive	Positive
Anticommunism/Law & Order[a]	Positive	Positive	Negative	Negative
Antinativism/Prominorities[a]	Positive	Positive	Negative	Negative
1972				
Conservative Reaction to Social Change[a]	Positive	Positive	Negative	Negative
Cultural Populism[c]	Positive	Positive	Positive	Negative
Elite Religious Liberals[a]	Positive	Positive	Negative	Negative
1976				
Opposition to Racial/Social Change[a]	Positive	Positive	Negative	Negative
Cynical Isolationism/Moral Restorationism[c]	Positive	Positive	Positive	Negative
Cultural Populism[a]	Positive	Positive	Negative	Negative
Race-Based Party Ideology[a]	Positive	Positive	Negative	Negative
1980				
Race-Based Party Ideology[a]	Positive	Positive	Negative	Negative
Retreatist Racial Populism[a]	Positive	Positive	Negative	Negative
Moral Restorationism[a]	Positive	Positive	Negative	Negative
1984				
Race-Based Party Ideology[a]	Positive	Positive	Negative	Negative
Race, Rights, Taxes[d]	Negative	Positive	Negative	Negative
Moral Restorationism[a]	Positive	Positive	Negative	Negative

TABLE 7.1
Continued

	Democrats		Republicans	
Factors	Stay at Home	Defect	Stay at Home	Defect
1988				
Race-Based Party Ideology[a]	Positive	Positive	Negative	Negative
Cynical Isolationism[d]	Negative	Positive	Negative	Negative
Moral Restorationism[a]	Positive	Positive	Negative	Negative
Racial Interests[a]	Positive	Positive	Negative	Negative
1992				
Race/Class/International Order-Based Party[a]	Positive	Positive	Negative	Negative
Cynicism/Trust in Govt[b]	Positive	Positive	Positive	Positive
Black Nationalism[a]	Positive	Positive	Negative	Negative
Morally Restorationist-Based Party[a]	Positive	Positive	Negative	Negative
1996				
Morally Restorationist-Based Party[a]	Positive	Positive	Negative	Negative
Embrace of Internationalism[d]	Negative	Positive	Negative	Negative
Outgroup Antagonism[a]	Positive	Positive	Negative	Negative

[a] Higher scores more conservative.
[b] Higher scores more cynical.
[c] Higher scores more conservative and more cynical.
[d] Higher scores more conservative and less cynical.

can loyalty compared with staying at home and defection. Increasing cynicism should positively predict failure to turn out and defection for both Democrats and Republicans. For the two classes of variables that combine cynicism with a liberal-conservative component, we treat cynicism as the dominant component when predicting turnout. Regardless of the liberal-conservative direction of the second-order factor score, higher cynicism always positively predicts stay-at-home. Alternatively, the liberal-conservative component of the factor always predicts defection, such that higher conservative scores predict Democratic disloyalty while higher conservative scores negatively predict Republican disloyalty regardless of cynicism.

To illustrate our use of the parameters, we interpret the coefficients of two groups: white, non-Latino Democrats and white, non-Latino Republicans (tables 7.2 and 7.3). We chose four variables that represent the four classes of variables found in the models.

150 • Chapter Seven

TABLE 7.2
White, Non-Latino Democrats, 1960–1996

Factors	Stay at Home	Defect	Controls	Stay at Home	Defect
1960					
Govt Role/Social Spending	0.228	0.607****	Education	−0.753***	−0.082
Cynicism/Trust in Govt	0.337****	−0.213	Gender	0.726****	0.387
Strength of U.S.	0.438****	0.525****	Income	−0.194	−0.004
Isolationism/Internationalism	0.309***	0.246**	Cohort	0.263	−0.366
Race/Civil Rights	−0.082	0.083	South	0.834****	0.831****
			Constant	−1.781***	−1.362**
N	519		LR χ^2 [20]	132.77	
1964					
Old Social Cleavages	0.257**	0.311*	Education	0.048	0.270
Party Ideology	0.230	1.716****	Gender	0.169	0.115
Cynical American First/Anticommunism	0.366****	0.704****	Income	−0.268****	0.130
			Cohort	0.460*	−0.284
			South	0.397*	0.748**
			Constant	−1.613****	−2.835****
N	733		LR χ^2 [16]	183.78	
1968					
Race-Based Party Ideology	0.408****	0.851****	Education	−0.466**	0.098
Cynicism/Trust in Govt	0.526****	0.473****	Gender	−0.343	−0.385*
Anticommunism/Law & Order	0.141	0.048	Income	−0.580****	−0.240**
Antinativism/Prominorities	0.092	−0.016	Cohort	1.167****	0.594****
			South	1.191****	0.762****
			Constant	−0.433	−0.588
N	608		LR χ^2 [18]	174.90	
1972					
Conservative Reaction to Social Change	0.300***	0.798****	Education	−0.572****	−0.160
Cultural Populism	0.186	−0.043	Gender	0.159	−0.212
Elite Religious Liberals	−0.018	0.418****	Income	−0.253****	0.106
			Cohort	0.291*	−0.265*
			South	0.842***	0.674****
			Constant	0.075	0.615
N	936		LR χ^2 [16]	272.44	

Table 7.2
Continued

Factors	Stay at Home	Defect	Controls	Stay at Home	Defect
1976					
Opposition to Racial/ Social Change	−0.112	0.069	Education	−0.481****	0.119
Cynical Isolationism/ Moral Restorationism	0.282****	−0.156	Gender	0.539****	0.319
Cultural Populism	−0.042	−0.036	Income	−0.323****	0.129
Race-Based Party Ideology	0.024	0.799****	Cohort	0.505****	−0.006
			South	0.592****	0.120
			Constant	−1.383***	−2.167****
N	724		LR χ^2 [16]	145.18	
1980					
Race-Based Party Ideology	0.411***	0.804****	Education	−0.580****	0.441***
Retreatist Racial Populism	−0.138	0.096	Gender	0.160	0.065
Moral Restorationism	0.038	0.022	Income	−0.306****	−0.116
			Cohort	0.966****	0.461***
			South	−0.022	−0.300
			Constant	−1.087	−1.739****
N	493		LR χ^2 [16]	94.58	
1984					
Race-Based Party Ideology	0.418****	1.353****	Education	−0.636****	0.016
Race, Rights, Taxes	−0.060	−0.090	Gender	−0.217	0.332
Moral Restorationism	0.295***	0.234*	Income	−0.386****	0.042
			Cohort	0.888****	0.182
			South	0.461*	0.360
			Constant	−0.437	−1.704***
N	617		LR χ^2 [16]	193.98	
1988					
Race-Based Party Ideology	0.602****	1.501****	Education	−0.765****	0.138
Cynical Isolationism	0.203*	0.440****	Gender	0.037	0.664**
Moral Restorationism	−0.023	0.338**	Income	−0.476****	−0.056
Racial Interests	−0.070	0.137	Cohort	0.671****	0.808****
			South	0.755****	0.428
			Constant	0.138	−4.226****
N	478		LR χ^2 [18]	170.50	

TABLE 7.2
Continued

Factors	Stay at Home	Defect	Controls	Stay at Home	Defect
1992					
Race/Class/International Order-Based Party	−0.105	0.541****	Education	−0.617****	0.083
Cynicism/Trust in Govt	0.038	0.228**	Gender	−0.098	−0.049
Black Nationalism	0.024	0.119	Income	−0.523****	0.072
Morally Restorationist-Based Party	0.752****	0.817****	Cohort	1.221****	0.999****
			South	0.368	−0.125
			Constant	−1.665***	−3.477****
N	703		LR χ² [18]	211.43	
1996					
Morally Restorationist-Based Party	0.705****	1.419****	Education	−0.779****	0.080
Embrace of Internationalism	0.117	0.260*	Gender	0.385	0.023
Outgroup Antagonism	−0.119	−0.265	Income	−0.644****	−0.181
			Cohort	1.440****	0.834****
			South	0.194	0.088
			Constant	−2.112****	−2.816****
N	527		LR χ² [16]	147.55	

Source: American National Election Studies (1960–1996)
Note: Multinomial-Logit Regression estimated via maximum likelihood, with voting Democratic as the base category. *Indicates $p < .1$ (two-tail) **Indicates $p < .05$ (two-tail) ***Indicates $p < .025$ (two-tail) ****Indicates $p < .01$ (two-tail) The LR χ² [*df*] statistic is the difference between likelihood ratios of a model estimated simply with a constant and the models reported above. This is similar to the joint F test of OLS regression.

A type 1 factor like the Morally Restorationist-Based Party variable from 1996 ranges from liberal to conservative. For Democrats, we expect positive coefficients for both the stay-at-home and defecting categories relative to remaining loyal. For Republicans, we expect this relationship to be reversed (table 7.1, notes). The coefficients substantiate our expectations for both Democrats and Republicans. Democrats who are uncomfortable with their party's image are more likely both to stay home (0.705) and to defect to the other party (1.419) rather than remain loyal (table 7.2). Republicans who score highly on this factor are less likely to stay home (−1.256) and to defect (−1.409) rather than remain loyal.

A type 2 factor such as the 1968 Cynicism/Trust in Government variable indicates higher levels of cynicism with higher scores on the factor.

TABLE 7.3
White, Non-Latino Republicans, 1960–1996

Factors	Stay at Home	Defect	Controls	Stay at Home	Defect
1960					
Govt Role/Social Spending	−0.317	−1.128****	Education	−0.730	−0.368
Cynicism/Trust in Govt	0.881****	0.041	Gender	0.314	−0.311
Strength of U.S.	0.096	−0.239	Income	−0.036	−0.109
Isolationism/Internationalism	0.178	−0.140	Cohort	0.752	0.313
Race/Civil Rights	−0.091	−0.184	South	1.036***	−0.974
			Constant	−3.216****	−1.228
N	367		LR χ^2 [20]	76.65	
1964					
Old Social Cleavages	0.052	−0.392**	Education	−0.254	−0.069
Party Ideology	−1.189****	−1.435****	Gender	0.268	0.603**
Cynical American First/ Anticommunism	−0.000	−0.227	Income	0.062	0.100
			Cohort	0.179	0.320
			South	0.865**	−0.732
			Constant	−1.585*	−1.678**
N	402		LR χ^2 [16]	124.90	
1968					
Race Based Party Ideology	−0.462***	−0.464**	Education	−0.235	0.141
Cynicism/Trust in Govt	0.716****	0.613****	Gender	−0.406	−0.464
Anticommunism/Law & Order	0.106	−0.172	Income	−0.505****	0.126
Antinativism/ Prominorities	−0.085	−0.219	Cohort	0.755****	−0.129
			South	0.901****	0.400
			Constant	−0.442	−1.357
N	451		LR χ^2 [18]	92.21	
1972					
Conservative Reaction to Social Change	−0.363***	−1.143****	Education	−0.627****	0.044
Cultural Populism	0.230*	0.030	Gender	0.015	0.539*
Elite Religious Liberals	−0.098	−0.233	Income	−0.518****	−0.031
			Cohort	0.546****	−0.248
			South	0.910****	−0.441
			Constant	−0.258	−2.384****
N	759		LR χ^2 [16]	156.61	

TABLE 7.3
Continued

Factors	Stay at Home	Defect	Controls	Stay at Home	Defect
1976					
Opposition to Racial/ Social Change	−0.197	0.051	Education	−0.357**	0.030
Cynical Isolationism/ Moral Restorationism	0.549****	0.438****	Gender	−0.145	−0.220
Cultural Populism	0.033	0.016	Income	−0.336****	−0.100
Race-Based Party Ideology	−0.579****	−0.758****	Cohort	0.677****	0.097
			South	0.010	−0.491
			Constant	−0.528	−0.817
N	600		LR χ^2 [18]	114.37	
1980					
Race-Based Party Ideology	−0.372*	−0.715****	Education	−1.041****	−0.149
Retreatist Racial Populism	0.158	0.237	Gender	−0.270	0.021
Moral Restorationism	−0.373*	−0.693****	Income	−0.392****	0.057
			Cohort	0.719****	0.481*
			South	0.033	−1.420****
			Constant	0.641	−2.132**
N	414		LR χ^2 [16]	107.31	
1984					
Race-Based Party Ideology	−0.841****	−1.238****	Education	−0.796****	−0.198
Race, Rights, Taxes	0.109	0.326	Gender	−0.122	−0.213
Moral Restorationism	−0.200	−0.626****	Income	−0.331****	−0.381**
			Cohort	0.704****	−0.187
			South	0.569***	−0.746
			Constant	−0.223	0.319
N	656		LR χ^2 [16]	157.45	
1988					
Race-Based Party Ideology	−0.996****	−1.365****	Education	−0.877****	−0.401*
Cynical Isolationism	−0.322****	−0.745****	Gender	−0.485**	0.127
Moral Restorationism	−0.096	−0.456****	Income	−0.412****	0.085
Racial Interests	0.323***	0.396*	Cohort	0.868****	−0.382
			South	0.790****	−0.946*
			Constant	0.298	−0.308
N	604		LR χ^2 [18]	219.88	

TABLE 7.3
Continued

Factors	Stay at Home	Defect	Controls	Stay at Home	Defect
1992					
Race/Class/International Order-Based Party	−0.809****	−0.612****	Education	−0.787****	−0.174
Cynicism/Trust in Govt	0.097	0.184*	Gender	−0.674****	−0.427**
Black Nationalism	−0.012	−0.362****	Income	−0.363****	0.206*
Morally Restorationist-Based Party	−0.531****	−0.774****	Cohort	0.620***	0.417**
			South	0.794****	−0.426*
			Constant	−0.531****	−0.621
N	676		LR χ^2 [18]	239.71	
1996					
Morally Restorationist-Based Party	−1.256****	−1.409****	Education	−0.795****	−0.233
Embrace of Internationalism	0.375***	−0.176	Gender	−0.482	−0.135
Outgroup Antagonism	0.365**	0.078	Income	−0.448****	−0.283**
			Cohort	1.374****	0.622**
			South	0.294	−0.018
			Constant	−1.127	−0.584
N	488		LR χ^2 [18]	175.58	

Source: American National Election Studies (1960–1996)
Note: Multinomial-Logit Regression estimated via maximum likelihood, with voting Democratic as the base category. *Indicates $p < .1$ (two-tail) **Indicates $p < .05$ (two-tail) ***Indicates $p < .025$ (two-tail) ****Indicates $p < .01$ (two-tail) The LR χ^2 [*df*] statistic is the difference between likelihood ratios of a model estimated simply with a constant and the models reported above. This is similar to the joint F test of OLS regression.

This variable has no liberal-conservative component. We expect all positive coefficients, indicating that both Democrats and Republicans who score highly on this variable increasingly stay at home and defect to the other party relative to remaining loyal (table 7.1, notes). The results from the model confirm our hypotheses: Democrats are more likely to stay at home (0.526) and defect (0.473) when they score highly on this variable. As expected, Republicans who score highly on this variable are more likely to stay at home (0.716) and defect (0.613) rather than remain loyal.

The third and fourth classes of variables contain both a cynicism component and a liberal-conservative component. A type 3 variable such as the 1964 Cynical American First/Anti-Communism factor increasingly becomes conservative and cynical as values become higher. We expect higher scores on this factor to increase the likelihood that both Democrats and Republicans will stay at home rather than remain loyal (table 7.1, notes). Our expectations are confirmed for Democrats (.366): higher scores increase the probability of staying at home rather than remaining loyal. For Republicans, this factor does not meet standard levels of statistical significance ($p < 0.1$); higher scores on this factor appear to neither increase nor decrease Republicans' likelihood of staying home rather than remaining loyal. In regard to defection, we expect that higher scores for Democrats would increase the probability of defection, while higher scores for Republicans would decrease the chance for defection (table 7.1, notes). Again, the model indicates that Democrats who score highly on this factor are more likely to defect (0.704) than to remain loyal. This factor fails to reach statistical significance for Republicans, indicating that higher scores neither promote nor discourage defection.

A type 4 variable combines cynicism with a liberal-conservative component such that higher scores on the factor indicate that an individual becomes more conservative while less cynical. An example of this type is the 1988 Cynical Isolationism factor. Because higher scores indicate less cynicism, Democrats and Republicans with high values on this factor should be less likely to stay at home relative to remaining loyal (table 7.1, notes). While Republicans who score highly on this factor do decrease their chances of staying at home (-0.322) rather than remaining loyal, Democrats who score highly on this factor diverge from our expectations and actually increase their chances of staying at home rather than remaining loyal (0.203). We expect higher scores on this factor to increase the probability of defection relative to remaining loyal for Democrats, while higher scores for Republicans should decrease the likelihood of defection relative to remaining loyal (table 7.1, notes). Democrats who score highly on this factor are more likely to defect (0.440) rather than remain loyal, just as Republicans who score highly on this factor decrease their likelihood of defection (-0.745) rather than remain loyal—confirming expectations for both groups.

The target groups selected in each substantive chapter have been based on historical analysis and content analysis of campaign themes. Perhaps this sampling procedure does not have the rigor some would like. We feel it is a substantial improvement over the group-selection algorithm in Shafer and Claggett (1995), where groups at each iteration are selected because they are unlike the remaining population. The consequence of Shafer and Claggett's approach is that large *swing groups* like Catholics (25 percent of the population) who are routinely the target of cultural appeals by campaigners were omitted from their analysis. Some other groups are not "groups" at all but only strata in a demographic classification. Our strategy seeks to be informed by expert-observer judgments about the groups the campaigners are approaching with their cultural appeals.

Finally, we note that with the number of parameters estimated in this analysis, we would expect, given a $p = 0.1$ threshold, that we would find as many as 10 percent of the individual coefficients to show anomalous findings (although half of those should be spurious results that conform to our theory). In total, 524 second-order factor coefficients are significant across the multinomial regression models. Of these, only 32 do not conform to our "expected" signs. This represents approximately 6 percent of the total significant second-order factors. Rather than trim the models and give an artificial sense of tight structure, we have retained the full models and acknowledge findings that are contrary to our expectations.[10] Few analysts are sufficiently clever to figure out every finding in social research.

---

[10] One second-order factor (Racial) was removed from the multinomial regressions analysis for 1996 in order to obtain unbiased parameter estimates. This factor has a high intercorrelation with the other independent variables in the model (multiple $R = 0.818$) and a high correlation with the Outgroup Antagonism factor individually ($R = 0.689$), thus introducing unreasonable levels of multicollinearity. Further, three of the four components of the Racial factor are also included in other second-order factors, and it was the last second-order factor extracted, with a borderline eigenvalue (1.1).

CHAPTER EIGHT

Keeping America Purposeful, Powerful, and Pure

WORLD WAR II and the Cold War incubated the permanent campaign. They created a national political style of mobilization against enemies, external and internal. They nurtured lingering fear that those with whom we differed politically would undermine the national purpose. They suggested that negotiation could lead to appeasement. For many groups, presidential politics had an urgency far exceeding economic gain. As the bearer of Western civilization against barbarian tyrants, America must never for a moment lose its resolve. In their view, God made the United States the stewards of the earth, the one best hope for mankind. Since the dominant American cultural values celebrated American exceptionalism, it should come as no surprise that presidential campaign themes and imagery would tap into such symbols.

THE APPEALS OF COLD WAR PATRIOTISM

The historical narrative of chapter 7 found patriotic cultural appeals against external communist enemies and their internal sympathizers evident from the late New Deal period to the fall of the Berlin Wall. The first schism in the bipartisan Cold War consensus confronted the containment policy and its limited war in Korea. The Eisenhower-Nixon campaign theme was "Korea, Corruption, and Communism," all negative attributions to the Democratic leadership. The Republican National Committee created a Nationalities Division aimed at dislodging Catholics from their New Deal loyalties. This group of the Democratic electorate remained a prime target for patriotic and nationalistic appeals throughout the post–New Deal era. Because both Nixon, on his own in 1960, and Kennedy, a Roman Catholic, shared a common Cold War perspective, it was difficult for Nixon to make cultural appeals along this dimension, so he emphasized instead his experience. Another cultural dimension, religious affinity, was far more salient, and Republicans lost ground among Democratic Catholics for a decade. In 1964 candidate Goldwater developed major new initiatives on patriotism themes, broadening them to the enemies of America's moral fiber; he tried to reach beyond Catholics to the "silent Americans" of all religious traditions and the law-abiding middle and working classes. Here again, the appeal was less salient than the memory of a slain president, threats to the racial consensus, and fears over Goldwater's political style. Yet many of the instruments for later cultural politics came into use in this campaign.

In 1968 and 1972 patriotic cultural appeals reached their zenith. Despite escalation in Vietnam, the United States appeared unable to secure its objectives. Domestically, protest against the military draft had thrown campuses and cities into chaos. The educated and the well-off appeared least willing to carry on the American crusade. Recognizing enormous discord in the Democratic coalition and some modest losses in his own, Nixon refined the Goldwater appeals to reach beyond the cerebral dimension to the emotions of law-abiders. He candidly admitted his use of fear in the ads; to many Americans, the forces at work in the streets and on the campuses, challenging U.S. policy and perhaps the government itself, were indeed scary. His objective was to attach them to the Democrats, either as Democrats or as the legacy of Democratic lack of resolve. The language of "hippies," "pointy-headed intellectuals" (borrowed from the Wallace campaign), "effete snobs," and "limousine liberals" was intended to (1) increase discontent and damp turnout in the traditional Democratic base, (2) attract defectors, or, better yet, (3) align as Republicans the sectors of the younger generation who did not imbibe in such countercultural or lawless behavior. More broadly, as we have argued throughout the book, this language was part of an effort by Republicans permanently to overcome their minority status by promoting the conversion of loosely attached Democrats to the GOP. These themes, particularly in the context of racial codewords, proved highly salient with target groups, as succeeding chapters will show. By 1976, however, Watergate drove the election; Governor Carter's persona muted the effectiveness of continued patriotic appeals—a born-again Baptist, Southerner, Naval Academy graduate who helped Admiral Rickover develop the nuclear submarine for our arsenal against the Soviets. But during his term, the word "liberal" became an efficient symbol that loaded up all of the negative codewords for race, crime, weakness against our foreign enemies, women who would overthrow their appropriate roles and sacrifice family values, and the public expression of religion. Evangelicals, now mobilized, had become disaffected with the Carter administration.

In 1980 and 1984 the Reagan themes were not as diverse as were Nixon's. "Liberal" seemed to capture it all, telling us whom we did not want making policy in Washington. The language of "desexegration," the "welfare queen" from the South Side of Chicago, the picturing of a black U.S. ambassador to the United Nations, and the pillorying of those who advocated energy conservation instead of producing oil all suggested who was undermining American strength toward external enemies. Accordingly, the 1984 themes stressed national restoration. Fifty years of liberalism had been stanched, and the country was on the right course. The long night was over—it was "morning in America."

By 1988 the Republican cultural appeals were hardly subtle. Dukakis would be as deft at fighting Communists as the comic strip character Snoopy. His approach to crime was to send on furlough "a big black rapist" and then to argue academic points of constitutional law. He was a Bostonian, not Middle American; Greek Orthodox, not Western Christian; married to a Jewish woman who had been treated for psychological disorders. For good measure, Bush pledged allegiance to the flag at every stop. The target groups remained the same—Catholics, evangelicals, Southerners, working-class men, housewives, and, curiously, successful professional women put off by a weak man better suited for the academy than the real world.

By 1992 Republicans could no longer stress patriotic themes in reference to an *external* enemy, communism. They did claim credit for winning the Cold War and the Gulf War, but there was no external menace threatening Western civilization. In both 1992 and 1996, thus, the party could only call credit to heroes. But heroes celebrate the past, instead of concentrating on clear and present dangers. When the new themes of *internal* threat to "family values" were emphasized, Democrats retaliated with charges of theocracy and religious extremism. Their target groups were historic Republican coalition members—the better educated, young business and professional women, and mainline Protestants. The transfer of patriotic themes to moral restorationist themes, however, lacked the salience provided by an external menace.

Analysis of Target Groups

We now trace the possible effects of patriotic/nationalist themes on various target groups: Catholics, Southern whites, and groups of various educational attainment.

White Catholics

One of the earliest and most sustained target groups was Catholics. In the 1930s the pope had urged the flock toward a vigorous anticommunism, and many Catholics had emigrated from the countries that were now behind the Iron Curtain. If Democrats could be shown to be weak on communism, the issue might be of sufficient salience to disrupt normal Catholic affinities for the Democratic party. Figure 8.1 maps the partisan patterns of white, non-Latino Catholics from 1952 to 1996.

Evident immediately is the impact that John F. Kennedy had on Catholics in both parties, but particularly on Catholic Democrats. Democratic

Keeping America Powerful and Pure • 161

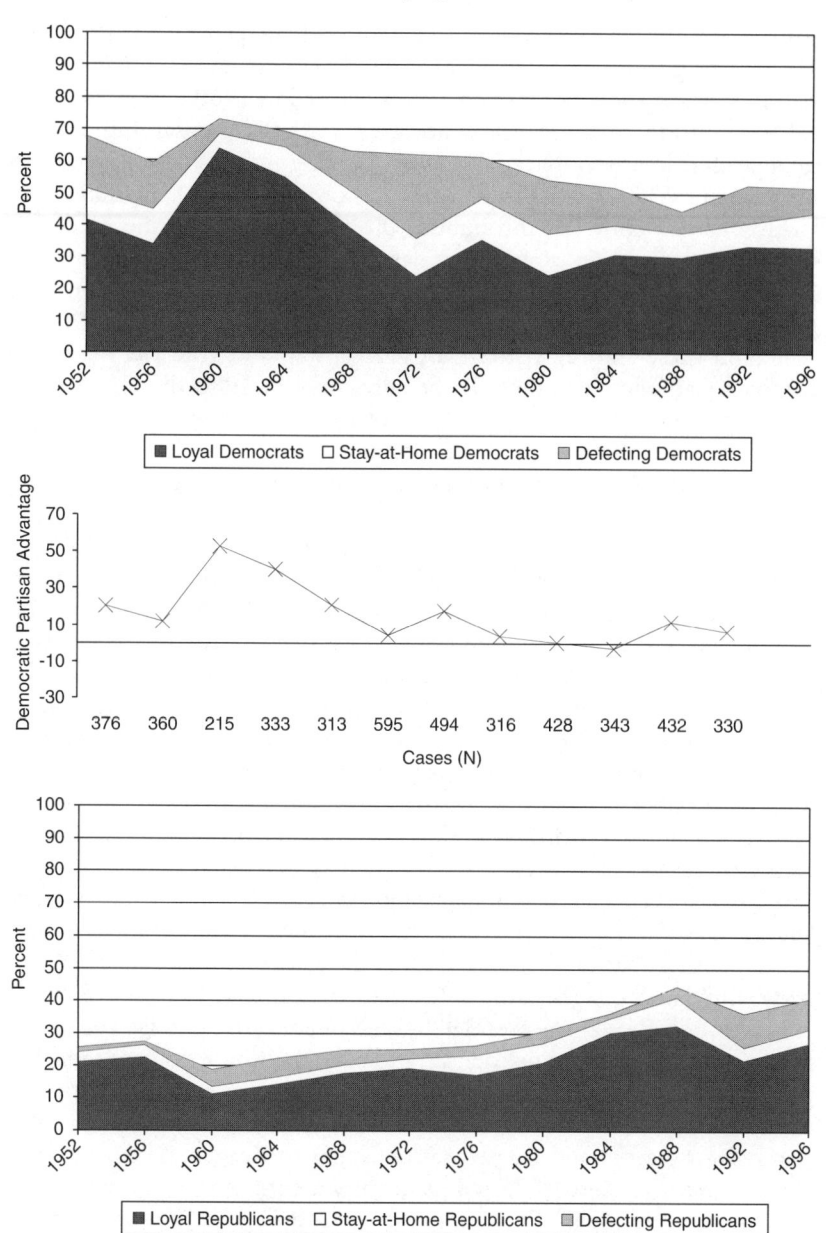

Figure 8.1. Partisan Patterns of White, Non-Latino Catholics, 1952–1996

party identification spiked at 73 percent and 69 percent in 1960 and 1964. The greatest proportion of loyal Democrats among white, non-Latino Catholics for the time-series was reached in 1960 (64%) and 1964 (55%). Outside of those years, however, Catholic partisanship made a gradual shift in a Republican direction, peaking in 1988 after eight years of Reagan. While partisanship shifted, however, the Democratic vote yield remained fairly flat throughout the time-series, with the exception of the Kennedy bump. Republican partisan yields finally caught up to the Eisenhower years in the first Reagan run, jumped quickly by ten or more points in the 1980s, and then moved downward swiftly in the 1990s.

Behind these shifting patterns of partisanship and vote yield is a very complex Catholic electorate. To be sure, only in 1988 did the partisan advantage shift to Republicans. Most of the time, if we compare white, non-Latino Catholics with the electorate generally (see figure 7.1) we find that Catholics yield about 6 percent more Democratic votes than the electorate as a whole.

From the perspective of cultural campaigning, 1968 and especially 1972 were dramatic elections. Although Democratic identification shifted downward only a few points from the Kennedy bump, Democratic yields plummeted. Election year 1968 signaled trouble ahead for Democrats as 19 percent failed to vote and 20 percent defected, mainly to Wallace; still, 18 percent of Republicans also defected, mainly to Wallace. With Wallace out of the picture in 1972, however, the bottom dropped among Catholic Democrats. Faced with the opportunity to embrace the McGovern antiwar, socially liberal party—the party that had thrown out the delegations of big-city Catholics and union leaders—42 percent of all Catholic Democrats crossed over and voted for Nixon, and 19 percent again did not vote. The gap between Democratic party identification (62%) and Democratic vote yield (24%) was the greatest in the entire time-series. Although Carter was to cut these backdoor losses of "Nixon Democrats" in half in 1976, the party would never be the same in Catholic circles.

In the first Reagan race of 1980, realignment of Catholic voters was finally evident. Democratic identification dropped by 7 percent, and Republican identification grew by 5 percent. But now it continued to be accompanied by low turnout among Catholic Democrats, 24 percent reporting not voting, and 31 percent defecting to Reagan. Thus, an initial Democratic advantage of 23 points in party identification was reduced to 4 points in vote yield. The realignment—and alignment—of Catholics continued throughout the Reagan-Bush era. By 1988 Democratic identification dropped to a new low of 45 percent, and Republican identification grew another 14 points since 1980 to reach 45 percent, virtually even in a group that had begun the era heavily Democratic. Alignment of younger generations with the Republican party is suggested by the decline in the percent of independents.

This latter point suggests that the real story among Catholics is in the generations. Figure 8.2 maps the changing partisanship of New Deal–generation Catholics and post–New Deal generation Catholics; the former entered the electorate from 1932 to 1964, and the latter came of political age after 1964. After three elections (1968, 1972, and 1976) of fairly similar partisanship, the generations diverge vastly, beginning with the first Reagan election. The New Deal generation dropped 9 points in Democratic partisanship from 1964 to 1972 and gained 7 points in Republican partisanship. In 1980 it dropped another 5 points in Democratic identification and gained 3 points in Republican identification. From 1980 to 1992 the older generation remained stable in Democratic partisanship but gained only 4 more points in Republican identification. Then, after four years of the Clinton administration and with a Republican candidate of their age cohort, the New Deal Catholic Democrats plummeted 10 percent in Democratic identification and surged 10 percent in Republican identification by 1996.

Younger Catholics, however, followed quite different paths. Starting nearly as Democratic but with far more independents than their elders, these baby boomers actually were attracted to the McGovern party, aligning or slightly realigning Democratic. From there on, however, they moved in a Republican direction. The gradient in Republican alignment and realignment was steep during the Reagan-Bush years. From 1976 to 1988 Republican identification climbed from 24 percent to 52 percent of boomer Catholics, independents dropped from 20 percent (in 1980) to 12 percent in 1988, and Democratic identification plummeted from 60 percent to 35 percent. Then, just at the point where the stork and the grim reaper were foretelling a rosy future for Republicans among younger Catholics, the demise of Bush and the onset of the Clinton years coincided with a steep resurgence in Democratic identification. It grew from 35 percent in 1988 to 54 percent in 1996, while Republican identification abruptly declined from 52 percent in 1988 to 40 percent in both 1992 and 1996. Furthermore, by 1984 the younger generation had replaced its elders as the majority of Catholic voters. The modest 1-point Democratic advantage in 1984 and the 3-point Republican advantage in vote yield in 1988 shown in figure 8.1 was entirely the work of younger Catholics. They gave the Republicans 8- and 17-point vote-yield advantages in those years. And, just as fickle, they gave the Democrats a larger vote-yield advantage in 1996 (8 points) than did their elders (4 points).

These figures cast entirely new light on the so-called Reagan Democrats. Most of the action by Catholic Democrats toward the Republican

164 • Chapter Eight

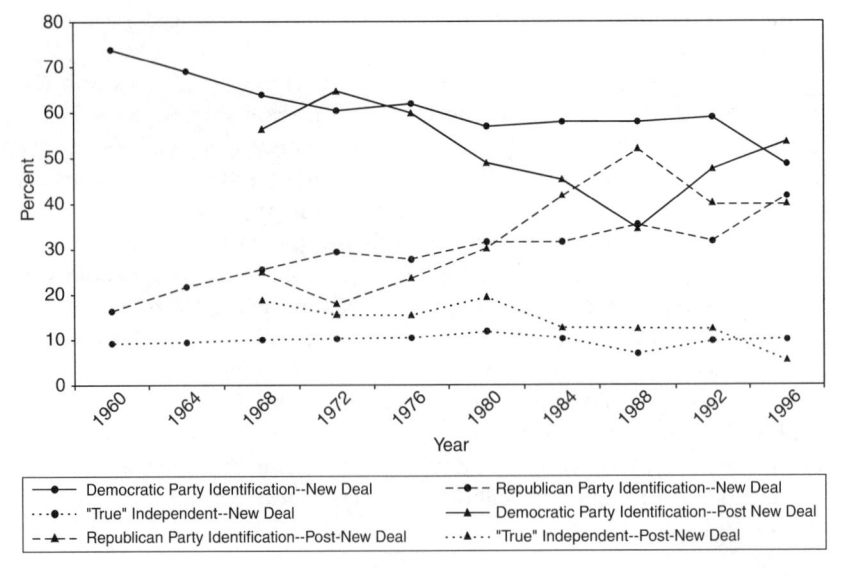

Figure 8.2. Partisan Preferences of New Deal and Post–New Deal White, Non-Latino Catholics, 1960–1996

party was in the massive defections and realignments of New Dealers during the Nixon years (49% of New Dealers defected in 1972). The "Reagan Democrats" among Catholics were misnamed all along; they were the "Nixon Democrats." Nixon Democrats outnumbered Reagan Democrats by a ratio of 5 to 3. Reagan did attract substantial defections in this generation in 1980 (35%), but he could not hold them in 1984 (23%). Most importantly, Reagan and his party attracted massive realignments and alignments (24% Republican in 1976 to 52% Republican in 1988) *among Catholic baby boomers.* But here again, the party could not hold these younger Catholics into the Clinton years.

Was it patriotic themes that dissembled Catholics from the Democratic party in the Nixon and Reagan years? Certainly that was the initial strategy from the Eisenhower period, and both Nixon and Reagan were staunchly anti-Communist in their public rhetoric. But table 8.1 tells a rather different story. The reader will recall from the discussion in chapter 7 that the table presents merged issue and group factors that might dislodge a target group from its traditional party loyalties. Since it was important for the minority Republican party to reduce the size of the Democratic coalition, it offered themes that would stimulate disillusionment, reducing turnout, or heighten anxiety, increasing defection. Presumably these themes, repeated over time, would enhance long-term alignment with the Republican party. Certainly the figures have suggested that something

TABLE 8.1
White, Non-Latino, Catholic Democrats, 1960–1996

Factors	Stay at Home	Defect	Controls	Stay at Home	Defect
1960					
Govt Role/Social Spending	−0.034	0.625*	Education	−19.432****	0.312
Cynicism/Trust in Govt	0.334	0.299	Gender	0.881	−1.697**
Strength of U.S.	0.701	0.372	Income	0.074	−0.234
Isolationism/Internationalism	0.153	0.247	Cohort	0.364	0.041
Race/Civil Rights	0.564	−0.142	South	0.491	1.866*
			Constant	14.677	0.129
N	155		LR χ^2 [20]	24.87 (n.s)	
1964					
Old Social Cleavages	−0.177	0.642	Education	0.430	0.096
Party Ideology	0.170	1.843****	Gender	−0.267	0.285
Cynical American First/Anticommunism	0.602***	0.831***			
			Income	−0.235	−0.213
			Cohort	0.386	0.759
			South	1.413***	1.005
			Constant	−2.006	−3.802
N	213		LR χ^2 [16]	44.24	
1968					
Race Based Party Ideology	0.214	0.900****	Education	−0.503	−0.234
Cynicism/Trust in Govt	0.832****	0.436*	Gender	−0.779*	−0.340
Anti-Communism/Law & Order	0.094	0.085	Income	−0.377*	−0.257
Antinativism/Prominorities	0.359	0.193	Cohort	0.967**	0.231
			South	0.607	0.446
			Constant	−0.227	0.192
N	174		LR χ^2 [18]	36.38	
1972					
Conservative Reaction to Social Change	0.593***	0.641****	Education	−0.499*	−0.286
Cultural Populism	−0.118	−0.193	Gender	0.004	−0.096
Elite Religious Liberals	0.030	0.410****	Income	−0.406***	0.061
			Cohort	0.882****	−0.144
			South	0.567	0.765**
			Constant	−0.809	0.629
N	304		LR χ^2 [16]	64.64	

TABLE 8.1
Continued

Factors	Stay at Home	Defect	Controls	Stay at Home	Defect
1976					
Opposition to Racial/ Social Change	−0.296	−0.042	Education	−0.858***	−0.020
Cynical Isolationism/ Moral Restorationism	0.089	−0.216	Gender	0.708*	0.288
Cultural Populism	0.166	−0.021	Income	−0.423**	0.097
Race-Based Party Ideology	0.452*	0.951****	Cohort	1.056****	0.371
			South	0.685	−0.724
			Constant	−2.227**	−2.430***
N	240		LR χ^2 [18]	61.14	
1980					
Race-Based Party Ideology	0.858**	1.491****	Education	−0.317	0.908**
Retreatist Racial Populism	0.196	0.299	Gender	0.219	0.690
Moral Restorationism	−0.051	−0.023	Income	−0.248	−0.547***
			Cohort	1.113***	0.244
			South	0.272	−0.011
			Constant	−2.030	−1.653
N	133		LR χ^2 [16]	47.36	
1984					
Race-Based Party Ideology	0.772*	1.644****	Education	−0.357	0.789*
Race, Rights, Taxes	0.044	−0.163	Gender	−0.676	−0.057
Moral Restorationism	0.210	0.220	Income	−0.320	−0.205
			Cohort	0.554	0.094
			Constant	−0.021	−0.715
			South	0.188	−1.436
N	177		LR χ^2 [16]	47.43	
1988					
Race-Based Party Ideology	0.059	1.883****	Education	−0.298	−0.296
Cynical Isolationism	−0.099	0.496	Gender	0.111	0.971
Moral Restorationism	−0.155	0.157	Income	−0.747***	0.275
Racial Interests	0.162	−0.122	Cohort	0.841	1.065*
			South	0.795	0.404
			Constant	−1.121	−5.481**
N	120		LR χ^2 [18]	44.47	

TABLE 8.1
Continued

Factors	Stay at Home	Defect	Controls	Stay at Home	Defect
1992					
Race/Class/International Order-Based Party	−0.072	0.738***	Education	−0.685*	−0.038
Cynicism/Trust in Govt	0.098	0.374*	Gender	−0.121	−0.326
Millennial Hopes	0.290	0.383*	Income	−0.362	0.271
Morally Restorationist-Based Party	0.515	0.421	Cohort	1.138**	0.652
			South	1.160*	0.497
			Constant	−2.141	−2.929
N	189		LR χ^2 [18]	45.84	
1996					
Morally Restorationist-Based Party	0.291	1.562****	Education	−0.454	0.786*
Embrace of Internationalism	−0.062	0.150	Gender	−0.196	0.480
Outgroup Antagonism	0.125	−0.303	Income	−0.681****	−0.746*
			Cohort	2.711****	−0.135
			South	0.223	0.997
			Constant	−5.374****	−0.910
N	147		LR χ^2 [16]	52.19	

Source: American National Election Studies (1960–1996)
Note: Multinomial-Logit Regression estimated via maximum likelihood, with voting Democratic as the base category. *Indicates $p < .1$ (two-tail) **Indicates $p < .05$ (two-tail) ***Indicates $p < .025$ (two-tail) ****Indicates $p < .01$ (two-tail) The LR χ^2 [*df*] statistic is the difference between likelihood ratios of a model estimated simply with a constant and the models reported above. This is similar to the joint F test of OLS regression.

was paying handsome dividends among Catholics. Within various levels of statistical confidence and within the limitations of NES variables, the table isolates what it was.

Although factors that tap into patriotic themes appear in several election years, for the most part these are not the themes that worked great change among Catholic members of the Democratic coalition; only infrequently do they reach statistical significance. In 1964 the anticommunist theme was significant, both in reducing turnout among Catholic Democrats and in encouraging defectors. By 1968 patriotism had been superseded by the most dominant factor of the entire period—racial issues and group feelings that had become packaged together with negative feelings about the Democratic party and positive feelings about the Republican party. The other important factors moving Catholics away from their party were cultural change and moral restorationism. We will reserve treatment of these dominant factors until chapter 9 (race) and chapter 10 (gender and religion). Distrust of government rose in both 1964 and 1968 and was implicated in the disillusionment with party that precipitated declining turnout in both elections. Part of this factor was the escalation in Vietnam and lack of confidence that Democrats had a policy to stop communism. But part of the distrust concerned Democrats' use of government to change the moral order on race. The dominant cultural story among white Catholics, then, was not patriotism and nationalism; it was race and moral disorder.

Southern Whites

The South has long military traditions peppered with patriotic rhetoric. Even at the time of the Civil War, it was Southern leaders who argued they were true to the founding principles of the Republic. The American military buildup at the time of the two great wars brought federal funds disproportionately to the states of the Old Confederacy, as both military bases and defense contracts developed this "Third World" section of the country. By tradition and economic interest, one should expect Southerners, most of whom were Democrats, to be responsive to Cold War appeals to anticommunism and patriotism.

Yet race had become an even more prominent issue in the South. The moral order on race established around apartheid principles was unraveling, and with it the basis of Southern Democracy. The Dixiecrats had bolted from the 1948 Democratic convention, formed the States' Rights party, and carried four Southern states. Absent a Democratic splinter group in 1952, the Eisenhower-Nixon ticket saw opportunity in the South. Some of its attraction would indeed be through appeals to anticommunism, but a large part would be based on the perception that the national Democratic party had shifted from a social welfare/social insurance New Deal party to a social justice post–New Deal party. Northern liberal senators were supplanting Southern conservative senators in the party leadership by the time post–New Deal politics came to full bloom in 1960. Southern politics was affected by religion in 1960 and driven by race in the decade thereafter. Yet it would be a mistake to claim that everything happening to the Democratic party in the South was the result of race.

Indeed the Southern branch of the party was undergoing a sea-change during the post–New Deal period. Figure 8.3 attests first to the huge amount of instability in partisan Democratic voting patterns; calling oneself a Democrat predicted nothing about vote yield. The near-equality of

Keeping America Powerful and Pure • 169

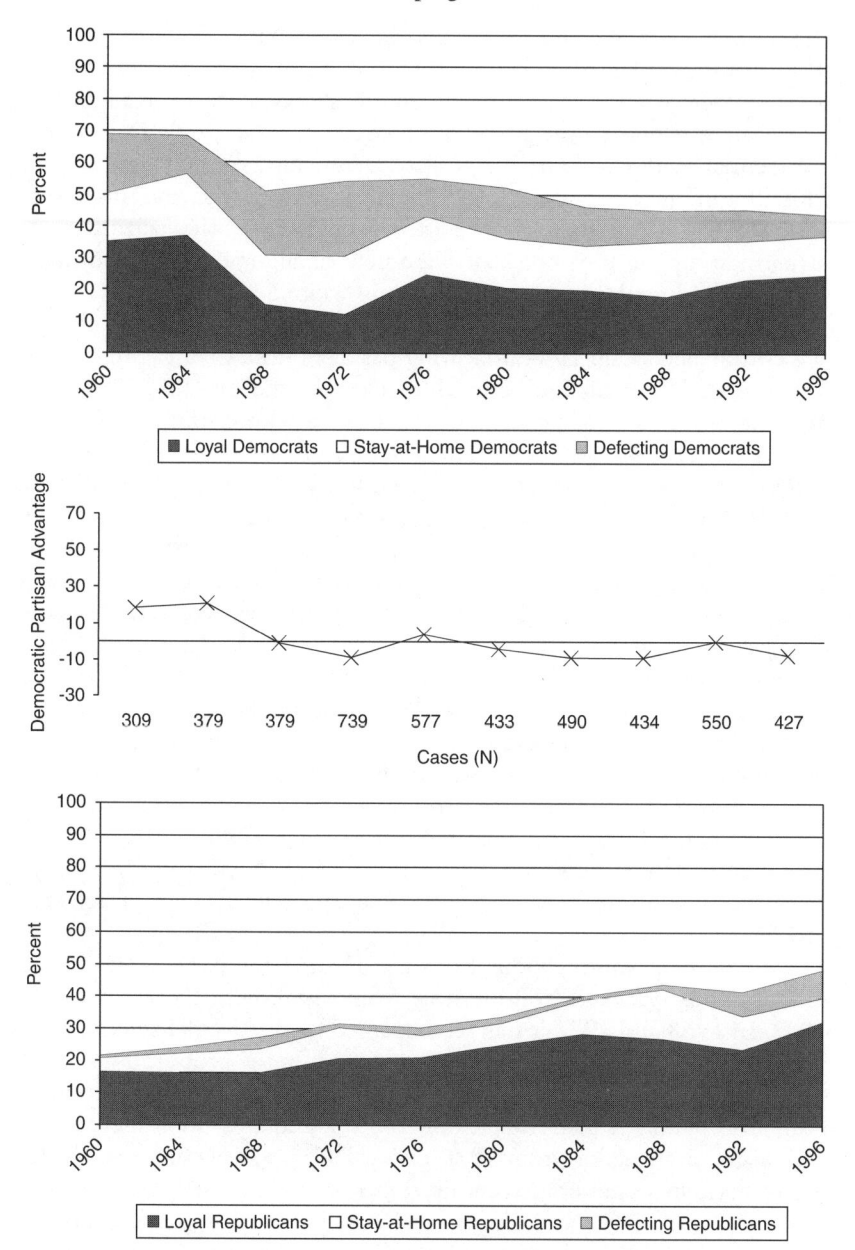

Figure 8.3. Partisan Patterns of Non-Latino, Southern Whites, 1960–1996

170 • Chapter Eight

size among the three ribbons across the Democratic figure is evidence that a Southern Democrat was as likely to defect or sit out the election as to vote Democratic. Secondly, the figure shows a steady realignment of Southern whites to the Republican side. After the 1960s Democratic presidential candidates carried a positive Democratic partisan yield among white Southerners only once, in 1976. Another way of saying this is that we have had more than a generation where either the perturbations in partisanship or the forces of alignment/realignment have normally yielded solid Republican majorities among white Southerners.

The time-series describes a secular realignment, not an abrupt change at a critical election in 1964, following passage of the Civil Rights Act. In fact, the defection of Southern white Democrats from LBJ (18%) was more modest than it had been four years earlier with Catholic JFK (27%) and *set a record for the lowest Southern white Democratic defection until 1996, when white Democrats were in a minority.* But by 1968 the Wallace candidacy and Nixon's new Republican party lured over a third of the Southern white Democratic vote away, and another 27 percent did not vote. In 1972, 44 percent defected and 34 percent did not vote, leaving a Democratic yield of only 12 points. This was an even worse Democratic vote yield than among white Catholics. Then, when Carter, a Southern governor, first ran in 1976 and when Clinton ran in 1992, defections shrank to only one in five. But by 1992 the proportion of white Southerners identifying as Democrats had declined to 45 percent, a faithful remnant only two-thirds of its size at the beginning of the period. Failures to turn out accounted for around one-third of all Southern white Democrats throughout the Reagan-Bush years. In 1996 for the first time ever, white Republicans outnumbered white Democrats in the South. Nevertheless, turnout improved in the 90s, and only 15 percent defected in 1996.

The Southern white exodus from the Democratic party came in two spurts, 1968–1972 and continuously from 1980, with the exception of 1992. In 1968 and 1972 it was accompanied by massive defections, some decline in turnout in 1972, and some increases in the proportion of independents. But it was also matched in two spurts of Republican identification, an 8-point increase from 1964 to 1972 and 4–6-point increases in each successive election from 1980 onward. Temporarily halted in 1992, the increase in Republican identification resumed in 1996, pushing Republicans to plurality and almost majority status among white Southerners. Overall, Republican party identification among Southern, non-Latino whites more than doubled over the post–New Deal period. Only the first Carter and Clinton contests stopped the momentum of the secular realignment.

Contrasted with figure 7.1, figure 8.3 shows that Southern whites launched their realignment earlier than electoral movements elsewhere in the nation. It followed swiftly on the heels of the civil rights advances of the 1960s and picked up further momentum during the Reagan years. It would appear, then, that both Nixon and Reagan were able to convince Southern Democrats that the party so deeply inscribed in their cultural history was under the control of hostile forces. For four generations, Southern Democrats had found political themes that had kept their people in the fold. But by 1968 Democratic partisan yields plummeted so far downward that, from there on, only a moderate Southern Democrat could restore faith in the party; even that faith could not be sustained into a second term. Otherwise the Democratic advantage in partisanship was left a hollow shell, first by defection and then by massive alignment/ realignment.

Patriotic cultural appeals did play some role in this movement away from the Democrats, as can be seen from table 8.2. In fact, *white Southern Democrats were very responsive to the entire battery of cultural appeals*, far more so than other vulnerable groups in the Democratic coalition.

In 1960 already they either failed to turn out or defected from their party in the battle against communism. In 1964 they sat it out or defected out of distrust of the Democratic administration because it did not seem to be making decisions that benefited U.S. interests in this fight. The Goldwater themes, then, were perceived as patriotic appeals as much as racial appeals. By 1968, however, Republican themes on race prevailed. Though distrust of the government accounted for both turnout failure and defection, the racial content dominated the patriotic content. And the race-based partisan ideology itself came to dominate the entire period of defection and realignment through 1988. In Bush's 1988 campaign, however, both turnout and defection are responsive to cynical feelings that Democrats would weaken our resolve against communism; some of this lingered into 1992 when Bush ran for reelection. Most of the movement as a result of cultural appeals by now, however, was caught up in moral restorationism.

Thus, although race and moral restorationism were the major factors in the dissolution and realignment of Southern whites, patriotism and anticommunism constituted important contributory themes.

Level of Education

Whenever one analyzes strata in a demographic classification, it is difficult to argue that these are "groups." Although initial placement in one level may be an ascribed status, and movement to another level may be an achieved status, demographic categories are not typically highly organized "groups" with systematic opportunities for interaction, norm so-

TABLE 8.2
White, Non-Latino, Southern Democrats, 1960–1996

Factors	Stay at Home	Defect	Controls	Stay at Home	Defect
1960					
Govt Role/Social Spending	0.811****	1.002****	Education	−1.312****	−0.836***
Cynicism/Trust in Govt	0.471***	−0.182	Gender	2.035****	1.164****
Strength of U.S.	0.502**	0.576****	Income	−0.111	−0.001
Isolationism/Internationalism	0.147	0.085	Cohort	−0.118	−0.599
Race/Civil Rights	0.247	0.416*	Constant	−2.069	−0.509
N	198		$LR\ \chi^2\ [18]$	82.83	
1964					
Old Social Cleavages	0.224	0.204	Education	−0.091	0.356
Party Ideology	0.572***	1.563****	Gender	0.598*	0.409
Cynical American First/ Anticommunism	0.411**	0.631****	Income	−0.083	0.012
			Cohort	0.092	−0.342
			Constant	−1.433	−2.031*
N	237		$LR\ \chi^2\ [14]$	67.85	
1968					
Race Based Party Ideology	0.655****	1.010****	Education	0.003	0.363
Cynicism/Trust in Govt	0.886****	0.787****	Gender	0.250	−0.340
Anticommunism/Law & Order	0.281	−0.007	Income	−0.559***	−0.356
Antinativism/Prominorities	0.098	0.012	Cohort	1.217****	0.987**
			Constant	−0.942	−0.626
N	197		$LR\ \chi^2\ [16]$	68.89	
1972					
Conservative Reaction to Social Change	0.553****	1.192****	Education	−0.497*	−0.096
Cultural Populism	−0.094	−0.159	Gender	0.236	−0.246
Elite Religious Liberals	−0.010	0.331**	Income	−0.123	−0.009
			Cohort	−0.030	−0.405
			Constant	1.157	1.766*
N	332		$LR\ \chi^2\ [14]$	78.47	
1976					
Opposition to Racial/ Social Change	−0.047	0.390*	Education	0.002	0.446

TABLE 8.2
Continued

Factors	Stay at Home	Defect	Controls	Stay at Home	Defect
Cynical Isolationism/ Moral Restorationism	0.451****	−0.007	Gender	0.280	0.113
Cultural Populism	0.085	0.114	Income	−0.356**	0.047
Race-Based Party Ideology	−0.233	0.572***	Cohort	0.277	−0.620**
			Constant	−0.528	−0.779
N	247		LR χ² [16]	53.88	
1980					
Race-Based Party Ideology	0.204	0.349	Education	−0.572*	0.212
Retreatist Racial Populism	−0.212	0.115	Gender	0.366	0.437
Moral Restorationism	0.087	0.207	Income	0.095	0.232
			Cohort	0.522	0.354
			Constant	−1.419	−2.912****
N	172		LR χ² [14]	21.66	
1984					
Race-Based Party Ideology	0.658**	1.911****	Education	−0.604*	0.327
Race, Rights, Taxes	−0.248	−0.233	Gender	−0.218	0.789*
Moral Restorationism	−0.023	−0.297	Income	−0.452**	−0.285
			Cohort	1.003****	0.340
			Constant	−0.023	−1.960
N	771		LR χ² [14]	64.86	
1988					
Race-Based Party Ideology	0.644*	1.730****	Education	−1.196****	−0.079
Cynical Isolationism	0.560****	0.647****	Gender	0.095	0.814
Moral Restorationism	0.219	0.562***	Income	−0.440**	0.004
Racial Interests	−0.123	−0.200	Cohort	0.500	0.143
			Constant	1.847	−2.020
N	169		LR χ² [16]	79.95	
1992					
Race/Class/International Order-Based Party	−0.148	0.714**	Education	−0.188	0.238
Cynicism/Trust in Govt	−0.157	0.319	Gender	0.233	0.318
Millennial Hopes	0.202	0.046	Income	−0.553****	0.247
Morally Restorationist-Based Party	0.693***	1.004****	Cohort	1.074****	1.080***

TABLE 8.2
Continued

Factors	Stay at Home	Defect	Controls	Stay at Home	Defect
			Constant	−2.014	−5.234****
N	202		LR χ² [16]	72.88	
1996					
Morally Restorationist-Based Party	1.289****	1.816****	Education	−0.897****	−0.270
Embrace of Internationalism	−0.051	0.158	Gender	0.807	0.630
Outgroup Antagonism	−0.462*	−0.246	Income	−0.610****	0.138
			Cohort	1.353****	0.107
			Constant	−2.105	−1.974
N	161		LR χ² [14]	67.42	

Source: American National Election Studies (1960–1996)

Note: Multinomial-Logit Regression estimated via maximum likelihood, with voting Democratic as the base category. *Indicates $p < .1$ (two-tail) **Indicates $p < .05$ (two-tail) ***Indicates $p < .025$ (two-tail) ****Indicates $p < .01$ (two-tail) The LR χ² [*df*] statistic is the difference between likelihood ratios of a model estimated simply with a constant and the models reported above. This is similar to the joint F test of OLS regression.

cialization, goal-setting, and mobilization. Yet politically, it may make sense to include these as groups. Occupants of the same strata may share a common identity (e.g., poor folks, highly educated), be socialized into common outlooks (uneducated Southern farmers perceived as "rednecks"), and be the target of campaign appeals (the good common people of this country have to take this country back from rich Wall Street bankers, larcenous trial lawyers, or pointy-headed intellectuals).

In that spirit, we analyze partisan perturbations of various educational categories. Earlier, we noted how the Republican party sought to transform its base from well-off, educated people to the medium-educated middle class and the less-educated working class; many traditional Republicans may have "understood" this was a strategy necessary for victory (Melich 1996; Phillips 1969). Initially thought to be isolationistic, such Democratic groups had been well socialized into a common patriotism and could be repelled or unsettled by a Democratic party that was not sufficiently anti-Communist or respectful of America's greatness. At the same time educated elites, who might have naturally been based in the Republican party during the early Cold War consensus, might eventually be put off by continued heavy attention to armaments, given the demise of aggressive international communism.

Generally one would expect the less educated to be more responsive to appeals based on xenophobia and fears surrounding strategies for dealing with communism. Those less educated had historically been in the New Deal Democratic coalition. Thus, the Nixon and Reagan Cold War campaign appeals and the Democratic move to the left in 1972 should be expected to have more impact on the less educated than the more educated. At the same time, as the far-right strategy—beyond containment to dissolution of communism—gained influence in the Republican party with Reagan, we should anticipate some growth in the Democratic party indicators among the more educated.

Figure 8.4 summarizes the Democratic partisan advantage—the politician's calculus of the vote—from tables for highly educated whites (baccalaureate or higher) and less educated whites (completed high school or less) throughout the post–New Deal time-series. It is clear that less-educated white citizens were more Democratic, and more-educated whites were more Republican. It is also clear that the less educated reacted in more volatile ways to given elections—for example, Johnson-Goldwater, Nixon-Humphrey-Wallace, Nixon-McGovern, Carter-Ford, Clinton-Bush-Perot, and Clinton-Dole-Perot. What is also hinted is that the even more strident anticommunist/propatriotic campaigns of Reagan in 1984 and Bush in 1988 were enough to pull less-educated whites to the Republican side of the ledger, a feat accomplished previously only in the contrast between Nixon and the McGovern peacenik Democrats. Finally, in data not shown in the figure, there was a slight increase in Democratic identification among educated whites in the 1980s, accompanied by a sharp increase in the Democratic partisan yield in 1984 and thereafter. Educated Democrats defected to Reagan in 1980 after the failed Carter foreign policy (44%), but hardly at all to the Republicans thereafter. Less-educated whites, however, sharply increased their Republican identification in the Reagan years and seldom defected until the 1992 race. The gradual but growing convergence of the two curves fits the Republican strategy to make elections more competitive; the party's candidates have increased their vote yield in the more numerous group of the electorate, namely, the less educated. But there was a compensatory price among the more educated.

Patriotic themes and anti-Communist fears played some role in these compensating movements. We have run multinomial logit regressions for four groups: less-educated Democrats (high school diploma or less), mid-educated Democrats (some college or completion of college), mid-educated Republican (same), and highly educated Republicans (postbaccalaureate work or advanced degree). Since the comparative tables are too lengthy to reproduce here and can be accessed at our website, we will simply summarize them. Clearly, race dominated the concerns of the less- to mid-educated partisan groups. Later in the time-series, moral restora-

176 • Chapter Eight

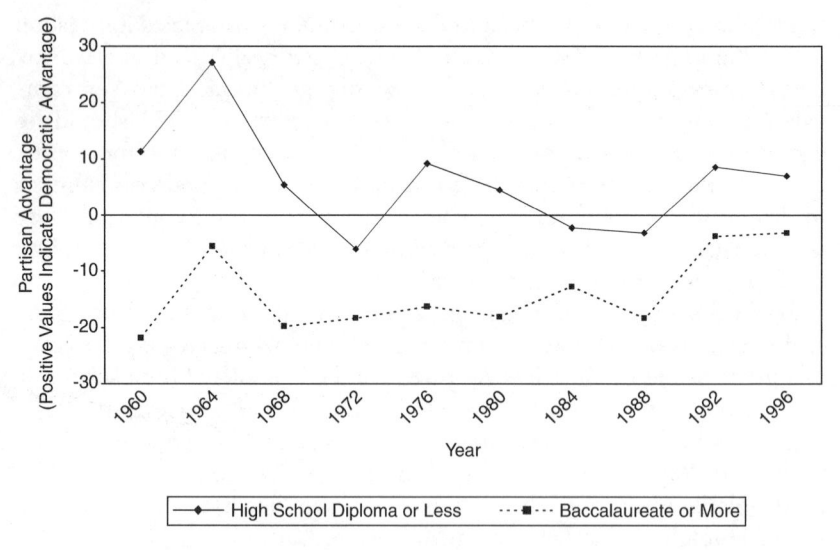

Figure 8.4. Partisan Advantage of Non-Latino Whites by Level of Education, 1960–1996

tionism replaced race-based party ideology as the central factor for these groups. Generally, the more the Nixon and Reagan-Bush campaigns stressed race or racial codewords or moral disarray to attract Democratic defectors and mobilize mid-educated Republicans, the more well-educated Republicans defected to the Democrats after 1976. Each of these points will be developed in its appropriate chapter.

Patriotic and anticommunist themes, however, were important both in the early 1960s and the late 1980s. The strength of U.S. defenses led both to turnout failures and to defections among less-educated Democrats already in the first Nixon run in 1960. In 1964 these themes, refocused as strong America-first, anti-Communist appeals were again a major cause of turnout failure or defection within this group. This, of course, was well before the Phillips strategy, but it gave Republicans a foretaste of electoral benefits within the Democratic core. Once the patriotism strategy was in full play, however, it was less important among less-educated, white Democrats than were negative attributions about race. In 1976 and 1980, following the end of the Vietnam War, ironically, isolationism was associated with turnout failure. But in 1988 Bush's ridicule of Dukakis's defense postures was accompanied by both turnout failure and defection among less-educated white Democrats. In 1992 concern for the leadership role of the United States in the world led this same group to defect, primarily to incumbent Bush. Thus, patriotic themes coupled with anxiety about Democratic nominees did dissemble this less-educated group from the Democratic coalition.

The same themes had more muted effects among both white Democrats and Republicans of middle educational attainment. Race and, later, moral restorationism were so paramount in their minds that only in 1988 did fear for American leadership against communism nurture substantial defections among the Democrats. The strident way in which these themes were developed in 1988, however, nudged mid-educated Republicans into the Democratic camp. In 1992 the Bush patriotism and leadership themes actually depressed turnout among mid-educated Republicans.

The more-educated Republicans experienced a modest backlash to their party's patriotism and anticommunism themes in the 1960s and even depressed turnout in Ford's reelection race in 1976. By 1988 and 1992, disgust with Bush's patriotism themes generated high defection rates among highly educated Republicans and even suppressed turnout within this highly participatory group in 1996. The original bearers of the Cold War consensus, then, drifted away from their party as it utilized unpatriotic attributions toward educated elites. Unwelcome, for the most part they continued to vote, but for the opposition party. Further, as the party utilized Irving Kristol's advice after the fall of communism to continue the Cold War style against our *internal* enemies—the agents of cultural change, the morally reprobate new class—educated Republicans seemed to be driven farther into the Democratic voting habit. As we will see in chapter 10, moral restorationists became the new enemy of educated Republicans.

The data suggest that groups of various educational levels, and particularly the extremes, were responsive to Cold War cultural themes. While Republicans registered gains among one core group of the Democratic coalition, Democrats registered gains among a stable anchor of the Republican coalition, as each responded differently to appeals concerning external and internal enemies.

Summary

In this chapter we analyzed how nationalistic and patriotic campaign appeals impact the political behavior of specific target groups during presidential elections. The aftermath of World War II solidified the notion that foreign political ideas and actions could threaten Western civilization as we knew it. More crucially, negotiation and appeasement of foreign enemies could actually destroy our once isolated nation, our city on the hill. Taking this concern to its logical extreme, foreign states and ideas were not the only threat to our cultural values, but instead, diligence also was needed to keep our internal enemies under control.

Early in the period Kennedy and Johnson fought the good Cold War fight; later the Republicans solidified their role as champions of American exceptionalism and unflinching anticommunism. Reformulating Goldwater's nationalist appeals, Nixon found it easy to label the Democrats as heretics to our nationalist civil religion. Publicly, the Democratic party became the haven for peaceniks, draft-dodgers, and pinkos. Those who followed the rules and actually fought in the wars (the working class, the less educated, Southerners, Catholics), Nixon claimed, no longer were represented by their traditional national party, much less the Democratic nominee. By 1980 Reagan needed only to stress themes of national restoration to remind citizens of the failed Carter foreign policy and national shame. We needed to rerealize the strong America. Liberals could not be trusted with our national interests. A cerebral Dukakis riding in a tank did little to dispel the notion that Democrats were weak on a host of pressing issues, including both relations with foreign enemies and handling of domestic criminals. By 1992, with the collapse of communism, Republicans could now only claim victory. America lay safe, but Republicans lost a core political resource; the long threat of communism vanished.

Various groups were targeted with patriotic campaign appeals. As our analysis demonstrates, these appeals were used with mixed effects among target groups. After all, targets are sometimes missed. Catholics moved from a dominant Democratic group at the beginning of the times-series to a nearly evenly divided swing group by the end. Yet despite the patriotic campaign strategy, nationalistic themes did little to move Catholics. The real story of Catholic movement lies somewhere else. Southerners also started the time-series overwhelmingly Democratic and ended with nearly half identifying as Republicans. Moreover, defection rates often equaled loyalty rates among Southern Democrats. Though not the dominant cause, patriotic and anti-Communist appeals did significantly contribute to Southern disloyalty throughout the period.

Republicans also targeted the middle- and less-educated Democratic groups with patriotic appeals. These groups might be disaffected with a Democratic party controlled by intellectuals and college radicals. Though the middle-educated Democratic strata moved little, based on these appeals, less-educated Democrats responded consistently throughout the time-series. Not surprisingly, because the Republican appeals demonized foreign policy intellectuals and elite campus radicals, higher-educated Republicans reacted to these appeals by sometimes staying at home on Election Day and more often defecting to the Democratic nominee.

While the impact of patriotic cultural appeals was overshadowed by the importance of moral restoration and racial concerns throughout the time-series, the campaign style developed after World War II and refined during the Cold War presages most of the more successful attempts at cultural politics. A campaign appeal focusing on domestic threats to cultural norms often overshadows individuals' anxiety about external enemies.

CHAPTER NINE

Race and the Transformation of the Contemporary Party System

THE MOST CAREFULLY studied effects of cultural politics in recent elections have addressed race, particularly the historic shift between the parties in the 1960s (Carmines and Stimson 1989; Edsall and Edsall 1991; Kinder and Sanders 1996; Sears and Citrin 1982; Sniderman and Piazza 1993). This chapter examines stability and change within black and white groups over the entire post–New Deal period. Some of the white groups thought to be in the vanguard of the change probably were not; others deserve more attention. Some groups responded to different types of campaign appeals than others. Finally, for African Americans the realignment was abrupt—a classic critical election in 1964. For many white groups the gradual pattern of change resembled secular realignment and was quite complex, first with declining turnout and/or defection, but eventually with altered partisanship. Political elites found the racial dimension of cultural politics fruitful but faced ever-present risks in alienating core groups within the party's coalition.

THE STRATEGIES AND DILEMMAS OF RACIAL APPEALS

Racial politics is a difficult terrain. On principle, Americans are deeply committed to equality for all citizens. The dominant issue is whether and how *government* should be an engine to assure equality. For some throughout American history, a prior issue is whether African Americans qualify for the privileges of citizenship. For them, any government action reassuring blacks is an insult. For most Americans in the latter half of the twentieth century, however, the question was to what extent taxing, spending, and regulation by the federal government were legitimate instruments for changing a culture of racial inequality. The consensus during the era of Civil Rights legislation was that government had to assure certain basic political rights; even then there was substantial opposition among Southern Democrats. As the movement to change the racial order came to Northern cities, however, the nation realized that similar sentiments about the "place" of African Americans abounded across the country. The pace of legislative remedies slowed as assurances of equality touched metropolitan-wide schooling, housing, public accommodations, and employment opportunities. All were matters many had privileged for market action in the private sector. Politicians knew there were votes to be had, and that party coalitions could change based on this constellation of racial/governmental concerns.

With the unfolding of the 1960s and 1970s, racial politics edged into other areas—particularly crime and welfare dependency. In each case empirical research has shown that the frame of reference for the other— "them," the perpetrators, the unworthy—was African Americans (Gilens 1999). Thus, both fear and relative deprivation were emotions waiting to be aroused by campaign appeals.

Campaigners could use principled appeals or opportunistic appeals. The difficulty is that the same language could mean different things to different sectors of the electorate. "States' rights" might mean democratic responsiveness from a unit of government closer to the people. But it might also mean that no federal court order would force my white children to go to school with black children. "Local control of schools" has similar meanings. Harsh penalties against lawbreakers might be an instrument for maintaining order in society; yet it might also mean great disparities in the sentencing of blacks because of the initial booking by a racially prejudiced officer of the law (cf. Eisenstein 1977). Prison furloughs may or may not be a wise strategy for rehabilitation, but to some it may suggest that more *black* criminals are on the loose. Forced birth control after the second child out of wedlock may be seen as an instrument to break the cycle of welfare dependency, but to some it is the means for keeping the black population in balance with the white population. Thus in some sectors of the electorate, arguably principled appeals have the net effect of playing to racial fears and stereotyping.

Often then in the post–New Deal period, campaign advertisements had a theme, but they also carried a subtheme. The theme avoided direct racial content because most Americans were committed to equality (Mendelberg 1997). The subtheme deployed one or another racial codeword implicated in the strategies of cultural politics. Such discourse is evident particularly after the reorientation of the political parties along the racial divide in the mid-1960s.

Chapter 6 described the thematic and subthematic content in both the Goldwater and Nixon campaigns. The subthemes would not have been salient without the episodic events of the 1960s. The climate for civil rights advances had changed drastically from pre-1965 to post-1965. In earlier civil rights forays, blacks were the victims. But in the long hot summer of 1965, chaos came not to the South but to the Northern cities. In a frenzy of behavioral contagion, one inner city after another was looted, burned, and devastated. Gone was the strategy of peaceful

Race and the Party System • 181

nonviolence, of passive resistance, of collecting empathic onlookers through courageous examples. Gone even was the "pushy black" who still sat at the negotiating table. Now the TV showed the flames, the smoke, the lawlessness, the carnival atmosphere of the looters. The symbolic terms of discourse for whites had been changed from empathy to fear, from common rights to unlawful taking. The imagery of sharing was replaced by the imagery of grabbing. Civil rights advocates, whether black or white, no longer monopolized the moral symbols as they had for the first half of the decade.

The responses of Democrats and Republicans to the urban disorders fixed in the public's mind two different philosophies of government. Democrats responded with shock and regret, to be sure, but also with reminders that that is the way people will explode after centuries of repression. Republicans responded with outrage and the desire to bring to justice the individuals who perpetrated the destruction. Democrats blamed the system and wanted to change it. Republicans blamed the individual criminal, and many also stereotyped the group. Democrats accused Republicans of blaming the victim. Republicans accused Democrats of coddling criminals. Since Democrats held control of the national institutions of government, their response was to direct more and more Great Society programs into impoverished neighborhoods. To whites in ethnic neighborhoods and suburbs, this simply meant that their tax dollars were being channeled by a bunch of distant planners to people who had created their own miserable plight.

The new partisan divide offered Republicans another opportunity to overcome their minority status by cutting away at the Democratic coalition. The Democratic response to urban violence held the party's base constituency in the African American community, but it threatened to detach the white ethnics who had long been another pillar of the party. For Republicans, there was no such dilemma. An emphasis on crime and punishment would appeal both to the party's suburban core and to the disaffected Democrats who, GOP leaders hoped, could be persuaded to join the GOP for the long haul.

Edsall and Edsall (1991) have described this as a "chain reaction" of race, rights, and taxes. A whole new set of political symbols was available for cultural politics. They were anchored, as we pointed out in chapter 3, in the everyday reality of citizens. Negative references to "give us our rights" suggested "grabbing" more than "what one had worked for." "Law 'n' order" was essential to bring these "savages" under control. "Taxes" and "tax-and-spend liberals" described big government solutions that took money from my pocket for giveaways to the undeserving. "Policy analysis" meant "pointy-headed intellectuals" out of touch with law-abiding, hard-working citizens; they proposed more and more schemes of taxing and spending, and urban development and roadways that destroyed white ethnic neighborhood institutions.

Compounding the problem was that some government solutions involving affirmative action in hiring and education and minority set-asides in contracting sounded to working stiffs like reparations for minorities. The white middle-class and working-class ethnics could not understand why they should be held accountable for something that had happened, in their perspective, a century or two ago. But why shouldn't each generation have to work its way up like every other immigrant group had? Although most of the actual programs of affirmative action and minority set-asides were to be developed later during the Nixon years, LBJ had introduced the idea to the public. They were perceived as part of a Democratic scheme to change the world through government action. If the reordering of the racial caste system were to be halted, it must be done by a political party that did not believe in activist government.

In the Democratic debacle of 1968, Governor George Wallace of Alabama spoke a language that attracted Southern white and Northern ethnic alike. It was not the cerebral philosophical discourse of liberty and states' rights used in the public Goldwater campaign. It was the visceral fears and anxieties of little people whose America no longer seemed in order. Many of these people, particularly Northern Catholic ethnics, remained loyal to mainstream Democrats when there was a Kennedy on the ticket (cf. Rieder 1985). But assassins' bullets and erratic driving had removed the Kennedy brothers from the viable Democratic options. While the Nixon organization barely squeaked through the 1968 election with a minority of the popular vote, it learned a new language of the common man for dealing symbolically with race more effectively than the cerebral language of the earlier 1960s. From then on, it was not necessary or even desirable to make direct racial appeals. Other symbols were socially acceptable surrogates.

Richard Nixon's 1968 acceptance speech at the Republican convention was filled with the central images: urban riots, Americans dying in Vietnam, domestic crime. His words called attention to the people who we are not, by affirming who we are: the "great majority . . . the forgotten Americans, the non-shouters, the non-demonstrators" who oppose all of these things (Jamieson 1996, 229). The Wallace campaign themes, carried first through thirty-minute broadcasts and then five-minute ads, set the agenda: an end to welfare abuses and to federal intervention on both civil rights and busing to achieve racial quotas, and an all-out assault on crime (ibid., 230–31). Each conjured images of lawless blacks or a federal government unresponsive to its (white) people. Wallace's two basic television ads were his statement against busing, and a visual of a street light being broken by a shady character (ibid., 231). As noted in chapter 6, Nixon's ads made direct references to crime and fear. He stressed repeatedly that the first "civil right" is to be "free of violence," a clear contrast with the meaning of "civil rights" for blacks (ibid., 249–50). His ads called for work, not welfare, and argued to Southern audiences that federal power is extended too far on school integration.

By contrast, Hubert Humphrey had far fewer ads, but his speeches stressed the essential equality of all human beings and the need for national "repentance and reconciliation" (ibid., 226; White 1969, 399–400). Later in the campaign, however, Humphrey turned strident against Wallace, calling a vote for Wallace a "vote for bloodshed, riot, and hate," and advised labor union members, "George Wallace's pitch is racism. If you want to feel damn mean and ornery, find some other way to do it, but don't sacrifice our country" (White 1969, 418, 424). His campaign manager, Joe Napolitan, later mused that even the few ads their agency suggested had two spots with "Negroes as narrators, an insane thing to do" (Diamond and Bates 1992, 156).

The "permanent campaign," as the Nixon White House organization came to be called, learned to merge principled language with suggestive social attribution. The wisdom of this strategy was vindicated in the tax revolts of the late 1970s. Sears and Citrin (1982) had analyzed the Proposition 13 campaign to limit property taxes in California. Two ballot initiatives put forward by Howard Jarvis and Paul Gann in 1978 carried, and a third by Jarvis in 1980 went down to defeat. Sears and Citrin found that voters responded to the initiatives through a *schema*, a more or less coherent set of predispositions linking attitudes toward the size and priorities of government, political ideology, party identification, self-interest, cynicism, and symbolic racism. Despite the absence of overt racial rhetoric, Sears and Citrin found that supporters of another proposition, 6, were heavily influenced by their perceptions about which race was advantaged by government programs. Racial attitudes linked party, ideology, and political philosophy and were stronger than most demographic or self-interest variables. As the 1960s moved into the 1970s and 1980s, then, we should anticipate that racial factors should coalesce with party images as a boundary line separating the two parties. And we should expect substantial partisan dissembling as a result of the subthemes.

The political handlers of presidents Reagan and Bush never lost these lessons. The reduction of *taxes* was the way to reduce government programs, and the reduction of *government programs* was the way to keep whites' hard-earned money from undeserving black hands. The reduction of *regulations* symbolized not only freedom from the long reach of the federal government, but less civil rights enforcement and a diminished role for liberal intellectuals. The *emphasis on returning government to the people through state and local government* meant that local majorities, not national standards, would control the policies surrounding the moral order on race. At times more overt racial symbols were used, for example, the Willie Horton ad in 1988 and the "quota" language leading up to the 1992 campaign, but normally it has not been necessary for Republicans to get that explicit about race. The symbols sufficed (Gilens 1999; Mendelberg 1997). In the 1990s the operative symbols for Democrats became "multiculturalism," and for Republicans, "politically correct (PC)."

Democrats, for their part, have also kept racial symbols alive, sometimes to their electoral disadvantage. Jimmy Carter, a symbol of the new Democratic party in the South where white racial moderates and blacks coalesced, sought to neutralize race in elections; yet his appointments symbolized to Southern whites that he shared national Democratic priorities. In the 1976 campaign, Carter made it very clear that he was the alternative to George Wallace—a Southern governor who embraced opportunity for white and black alike. He lost no opportunity to present an inclusive image: surrounding him in his opening speech of the campaign from the porch of FDR's summer home in Georgia were Roosevelt's sons and a famous black musician. In an early address at the Martin Luther King Hospital in Los Angeles, he argued that a Southerner could bring a deeper understanding of the civil rights movement to the White House. In his principal fund-raising letter to Northern liberals, he distanced himself from the popular images of white Southern politicians as racists. He carefully deployed radio ads to targeted audiences. One, limited to black radio stations and heard in black churches, included an endorsement by Martin Luther King, Sr., noted that daughter Amy attended a predominantly black public school, and offered many testimonials in the black "religious witnessing" style. But he did not leave the white front uncovered: his radio ad aired on country-and-western stations throughout the South condemned anti-Southern bigots and claimed, "On November 2, the South is being readmitted to the Union" (all illustrations drawn from Jamieson 1996, 352–56; also Diamond and Bates 1992, 237–40). Thus, ironically, he was treating Northerners as the "enemy" who stood in the way of Southern white pride.

Once elected, however, he brought more blacks and women to high-level managerial positions and to the bench than any previous president. In his reelection bid in 1980, he ran ads on black radio featuring those appointments; another set of ads to the same audience were built around the insinuation by the Rev. Jesse Jackson that Governor Reagan was a racist because of his strong advocacy of states' rights in his Southern addresses and ads. To white Southern audiences Carter presented endorsements by Southern governors telling how good it had been to have a Southerner in the White House, and how Carter, as the country's commander-in-chief, had been a worthy successor to Gen. Lee (Jamieson 1996, 411–13).

Both Walter Mondale and Michael Dukakis allowed major roles for the Rev. Jesse Jackson in the Democratic conventions of 1984 and 1988. Jackson's influence on the party platform and availability to the press symbolized what many whites took to be disproportionate attention to the black agenda in the Democratic party. Mondale handed the "tax-and-spend" code word to Reagan in his 1984 acceptance speech, and Dukakis's civil libertarian record was a setup for the "soft on crime" codeword for race. Governor Bill Clinton, however, took the race issue out of the contest early in 1992. He attacked the racially antagonistic and violent lyrics of Sister Souljah. Within the week he showed an 8 percent increase in support among white males. Jackson appeared hurt and confused and never played the dominant role in the 1992 convention that he had earlier.

In the late 1980s and 1990s, "welfare," "welfare cheats," "freeloaders," and "welfare queens" had become racial code words. When "welfare" was used, most people called to mind the program for Aid to Families with Dependent Children. Of all forms of welfare, AFDC was a modest but growing portion. The reality was that welfare had far more white recipients than black. But the white public tended to think of welfare as the direct result of illegitimacy among blacks. When the phrase "three or four generations of welfare without a job" was used, whites tended to think of black grandmothers, mothers, and daughters—all of whom had their first child without a husband early in the teen years. Republicans made reference throughout the post–New Deal period to "welfare reform" as a racially laden policy idea. In the 1990s Democrats joined them, with Clinton calling for "abolishing welfare as we know it" (with all the racial undertones). Further, Clinton supported the death penalty, a symbol of toughness on crime with subthemes of black criminals.

Republican campaigners from Reagan onward have generally confined their race-related appeals to these racial codewords. In 1980, in addition to his economic themes about soaring inflation and unemployment, Ronald Reagan repeated his philosophy of government in nearly every address and advertisement: cut social spending, restore states' rights and cut off the long reach of the federal government, and free the energies of the people from suppression by government. He did not need overtly racial content or fear of (black) crime in this contest. His philosophy of government was well understood as restoring "common sense" to racial advantages. The only overt appeal was a reminder in a national TV ad prepared by the National Conservative Political Action Committee that ostensibly questioned the wisdom of Carter appointments: its centerpiece was U.N. Ambassador Andrew Young, a black minister and former mayor of Atlanta (Jamieson 1996, 423). The "good feeling" surrounding Reagan's reelection campaign in 1984 had little need of overtly racial ads because the Democrats had already taken care of that at the convention; they had presented themselves as the party especially friendly to blacks and to the more aggressive spokespersons for racial change.

The 1988 Democratic convention was no different. But as we pointed out in chapter 6, the Bush campaign organization felt driven by his low ratings to hammer home many of the racial fears of the 1960s and 1970s. It whipped the many versions of the Willie Horton theme into a frenzy in voter-rich Democratic target states. At the very moment, the National Rifle Association also peppered the South and Southwest with billboards and radio ads claiming that Michael Dukakis has done everything he could to take guns away from "ordinary citizens" (ad material summarized from Jamieson 1996, 470–78; Levine 1995, 232–33; Diamond and Bates 1992, 277–81). In this context, gun control now had become a racial codeword; those who deprive citizens of guns take from whites their equalizer with the black street criminal.

It is difficult to assess the meaning of the "new racism" on which successful political appeals have been based. Careful work by Sniderman and Piazza (1993) shows that the appeal of racial politics for less-educated whites continues to be based on prejudice and bigotry. Stereotyping through code words is an effective appeal, both in mobilizing the faithful of one's party and in creating anxiety in the opposition party. But for the better-educated, according to Sniderman and Piazza, the appeal is less to stereotype than it is to an ideology about the appropriate role of government. Support for the principle of fairness remains, but it is linked also to individual initiative. It is not simply that the government should not be doing these things for blacks, but it should not be doing these things *at all.* If the policy—job training, child care, transportation allowance—can be argued in terms of its eventual contribution to self-sufficiency, Sniderman and Piazza show, better-educated Americans will at least hear out the arguments. In a sense, cultural appeals on race are now being transmitted through the screen of deep cultural values rooted in Calvinism and individual responsibility. Early in American history, Tocqueville predicted that this would be one of our most enduring values. The net political effect of the "new racism" is that raw appeals continue to attract the less educated but may be risky among the better educated unless the racial appeal can be framed against a "work ethic."

The Changing Racial Bases of the Parties

We now examine NES data for certain target groups: African Americans, Southern whites, working-class whites outside the South, white Catholics, and those exposed to different levels of education. Most were, in one way or another, thought susceptible to the notion that the Democratic party represented black interests while the Republican party would use constitutional principles or common sense to protect the existing moral order on race. At the same time, some were thought to be a potential source of backlash, if the Republican appeals to racial fears were too blatant.

African Americans

For African Americans, 1964 was a *critical election*, a sharp realignment and not the continuation of a gradual secular trend favoring the Democrats. The civil rights movement and the parties' responses to change in the moral order surrounding race stimulated an abrupt discontinuity in party identification, mobilization and turnout, and vote choice that persisted throughout the post–New Deal period. Blacks became and remained Democrats. The only problem has been sustaining turnout within a group that possesses fewer of the socioeconomic and psychological correlates of political participation.

Figure 9.1 offers composite evidence of the change among African Americans. The disjuncture in the time-series that drives all other figures in the table is the partisan shift and crystallization evident in Democratic identification in 1964. The black response to the Civil Rights Act of 1964 and presidential candidate Barry Goldwater's opposition to it yielded nearly a 30-point increase in Democratic identification, a 14-point drop in Republican identification, and (not shown) a combined 15-point drop in true independents and apoliticals. Nearly half of the Democratic gain came from the *realignment* of Republicans, while the other half resulted from the *alignment* of formerly nonaligned blacks. Many of the latter, it is to be assumed, could register for the first time, a product primarily of Democratic legislative leadership and Democratic presidential pressure.

The partisan shift reached its peak in the 1968 election. Another nearly 10 percent of all blacks embraced the Democratic party, leaving the Republicans with only 3 percent and the nonaligned at a combined 6 percent. This, of course, was a tumultuous racial election. It followed the urban riots, the congressional reorientation of the Republican party on racial issues, and the assassination of Dr. Martin Luther King. Long-time civil rights advocate Hubert H. Humphrey was the Democratic standard bearer. This time around, Republican Richard M. Nixon was calling for a rollback of the federal government and tough punishment for lawbreakers. And George C. Wallace issued the visceral siren call for segregationists and populists. If ever race were salient for blacks, this was the election. No wonder that the Democratic party never again peaked out above 90 percent of black identifications.

On the other hand, 1972 saw a large decline in Democratic identifica-

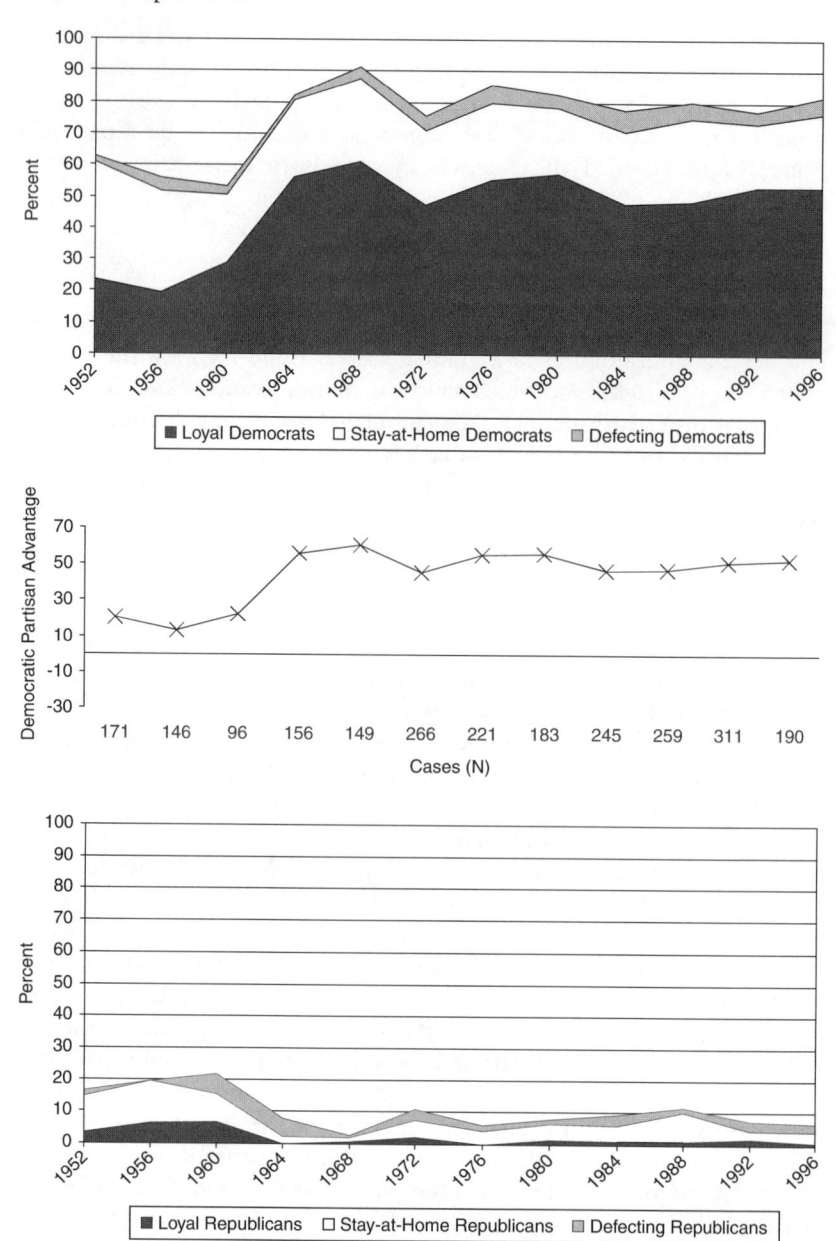

Figure 9.1. Partisan Patterns of African Americans, 1952–1996

tion among blacks and a large increase in independents and Republicans. As president, Nixon had turned out to be less an enemy of progressive policies for racial advancement than his 1968 rhetoric would have suggested. On the Democratic side, urban party organizations were rent by schisms, not only between black and white Democrats, but between "machine" blacks and "reform" blacks. In 1976, with the Carter racial reconciliation appeals, Democrats recovered their popularity among blacks. Thereafter, black identification with the Democratic party remained on a plateau at about the level achieved in the first blush of realignment/alignment.

Party identification, however, does not tell the whole story for African Americans. In cultural politics, nonvoting and defection are every bit as important to election outcomes as growth and decline in party identification. To be sure, studies of the social, psychological, and politico-legal correlates of the vote have effectively explained the historically low turnout of blacks. Yet these same studies also point to enhanced turnout from group consciousness and social connectedness, particularly through black church networks (Dawson 1994; Rosenstone and Hansen 1993; Tate 1993; Verba and Nie 1972; Verba, Schlozman, and Brady 1995). Thus, we should expect nonvoting to be a problem, but fluctuations in turnout may signal salient group factors operating in any given election. Furthermore, we should expect some defections from a party when its candidate fails to offer to a group either policies or symbols that match those offered by the opposition. In figure 9.1 the black ribbon, *proportion loyal to the party*, summarizes both; as discussed earlier, it consists of those with a designated party identification who actually report going to the polls and voting, and who report selecting their party's nominee. Of the two diagnostic ribbons, the white ribbon shows the proportion who failed to vote, and the grey ribbon the proportion who selected a candidate other than their party's nominee, that is, the defectors.

Low turnout plagued both the Democratic and Republican parties among African Americans. While defections were relatively modest among black Democrats, failure to vote reduced the partisan yield figures typically to two-thirds or less of their potential. On the other hand, defections have been more severe among the few blacks who identified as Republicans. At the critical juncture, 1964, three-fourths of all black Republicans who voted (if the small samples are reliable) reported defecting from Goldwater to Johnson. Defection rates remained relatively high among all black Republican voters throughout the post–New Deal period. Often when defection rates were lower, such as following the blatant racial themes in 1988, the failure to vote went extremely high. The net effect has been partisan yields barely above zero among black Republicans. Thus, in the post–New Deal period, blacks were Democratic when they voted. Otherwise, with modest exceptions they neither voted nor voted for the Republican presidential nominee, even when they identified as Republicans.

The *partisan advantage* measure is the balance sheet of the ledger. It tells operationally how partisanship has been translated into a voting advantage for one or the other party. Clearly Democrats have been advantaged within the black subpopulation. The advantage was greatest in the Humphrey (60 points) and Johnson (56 points) candidacies, the two Carter candidacies (55 and 56 points), and the two Clinton candidacies (51 and 53 points). The former two came during the peak of the civil rights era, when the strong Democratic push and the Republican recoil built Democratic identification and turnout. The second Carter candidacy generated both high loyalty and good turnout among black Democrats, turnout being the highest in the entire time series. In both of the Carter runs for the Oval Office, most black Republicans simply did not vote or defected. In the Clinton-Bush-Perot contests, black Democratic turnout recovered slightly from the low recorded in 1988, a low reminiscent of pre-1964 turnout. Democratic partisan loyalty matched levels of the civil rights era and the first Reagan election. Clinton perpetuated the pattern set by Johnson and Carter before him: the yield on Democratic identification among blacks is much higher when a Southern moderate runs.

The paradox of high Democratic identification and lower turnouts has prompted some scholars to argue that black partisan behavior is better described as *structural dependence* than as *group loyalty* (Pinderhughes 1987; Tate 1995; Walters 1988; Walton 1990). It is not so much that blacks are a loyal constituency in the Democratic party, but that blacks have no place else to go. The American two-party system offers few bargaining advantages to a third-party movement, certainly not one based on a relatively small proportion of the total population. Whites outnumber blacks in the eligible electorate about 7–1. Politically, the Republican party has little reason to respond to black concerns since it can mobilize whites with negative outgroup appeals. And Democrats often cannot win *with* black support, but they certainly cannot win *without* it. Thus, blacks remain identified with the Democratic party, but they are restive in that identification.

Democrats did continue to give African Americans some reason to mobilize. Particularly the "new Southern Democrats," Carter and Clinton, appeared at home in the black community. Their frequent appearances in black churches and particularly Clinton's speaking cadences suggested that they are "of us." Both appointed prominent African Americans to cabinet and subcabinet-level positions. All Democratic nominees supported affirmative action, targeted education, and job training programs. Since the turnout failures can be accounted for primarily by a resource theory of participation, coupled to an endemic skepticism that white political leaders would ever really understand black interests and values (Tate 1995), we have not run logistic regressions on the African American time-series.

Southern Whites

The reader is encouraged to review our discussion of Southern whites, especially figure 8.3. Next to blacks, this was the most mobile sector of the electorate during the post–New Deal period. At the beginning of the period, two-thirds of all white Southerners identified with the Democratic party; by the end of the period, nearly half of all white Southerners identified as Republicans. From 1972 to 1988 one-third or more of all Democrats failed to vote. Even worse, in 1968, 35 percent of white Southern Democrats defected to Wallace or Nixon, and in 1972 fully 44 percent crossed over to Nixon. Defections to Reagan were also very high in 1980 (44%) and 1984 (26%). Some alignment (about 6%) and realignment (about 8 or 9%), occurred from 1980 onward. With the exception of 1992, when Bill Clinton was leaning heavily on Southern themes, the Republican party gained 4 to 6 percent of new Southern white adherents in each presidential year. From 1972 onward, partisan yields favored the Republicans by 4 to 9 percent in every election except the first Carter run and the first Clinton run.

The country had grown accustomed to references to the "Solid South." The South, however, began the post–New Deal period as Democratic and quickly became Republican. Obviously something massive was at work here; as we discussed in chapter 8, either overt or codeword racial appeals are implicated. Referring to table 8.2, we see that Southern white Democrats were responsive to the entire battery of cultural appeals, but nothing matched race and the role of the government in assuring equality. From 1968 to 1988 the factor that included feelings toward blacks, government programs intended to improve the condition of minorities, political action by blacks, negative feelings toward the Democratic party, and positive feelings toward the Republican party consistently accounted for partisan defections. Even before that, in 1960 and 1964, race was implicated in the role of the federal government and revulsion to the direction the Democratic party had taken. After 1988 those Southern whites who had remained Democratic were primarily put off by concerns about moral degradation, but race remained a modest factor in 1992. Until 1972 and again in 1984 disapproval of the party on racial matters was an important factor in depressing turnout. Most of the time, however, race created sufficient anxiety to push Southern white Democrats into Republican arms.

Scholars have argued that any presidential election nowadays begins with a massive electoral college advantage for the Republican party, largely because of the Solid South. While that may be true, Clinton was able to pull away some Southern states in 1992 and 1996. The evidence suggests that the racial divide had declined in salience for the remaining Southern white Democrats in those campaigns. Both turnout failures and defections had narrowed by 1996, as the agenda shifted to moral concerns beyond race. Because of the ways majorities can be cobbled together in Southern states—either among whites alone for Republicans or among blacks and whites for Democrats—both political parties are likely to continue deployment of some forms of cultural politics.

White Catholics

The reader is also encouraged to review our discussion of white Catholics, particularly by reexamining figure 8.1. Kennedy's candidacy created a huge bump in Democratic identification and loyalty that diminished by 1968. Excluding that, vote yields remained predominantly Democratic with the exception of 1988, and party loyalty remained basically flat. The story was in defections to the Republican side, especially from 1968 to 1980, and then a steady Republican alignment of the newest generation of Catholics coupled to modest realignment of the older members of the post–New Deal generation. Curiously, the younger Catholic men and women separated dramatically in the 1990s, younger men becoming heavily Republican and younger women trending Democratic.

Catholics have generally been thought to be more compassionate toward the poor and the "other," and to have been more accepting (than other religious groups) of government action to assure equal opportunity for minorities (Gallup and Castelli 1987; Greeley 1989). Yet, the jeering and violent mobs of whites in Gage Park (Chicago) and Cicero during Martin Luther King's Northern marches suggest some Catholics were not immune to racial antagonisms. The fascinating study *Canarsie* (Rieder 1985) indicates a long history of Catholic racial ambivalence going back to the draft riots in New York City following the Emancipation Proclamation. Freedman's gripping intergenerational narrative of three Catholic families (1996) indicates that, while the first and second generations loved what the New Deal did to create economic opportunities and social acceptance for ethnic Catholics, the second and third generations resented Great Society programs and federal intervention to assure equal opportunities for African Americans. The second generation defected or stayed at home, but the third generation entered the local leadership of the Republican party. In particular Kevin Phillips's "Southern strategy" for Republican victory was also directed to urban and inner-rim suburban Catholic men who feared big government and resented tax transfers and racial/gender favoritism. Phillips (1969) thought the big issues—civil rights backlash, taxation, ERA and the women's movement—could dissemble Catholic men from the Democratic party.

That Phillips was right is evident from reinspection of table 8.1. Already in 1960, modest defection—even from Kennedy—occurred over the federal role and social spending. By 1964 defection was precipitated by negative reactions to the Democratic party as a civil rights party. In every election thereafter from 1968 to 1992, white Catholic Democrats defected to the Republican party primarily because of race-related matters. While Catholics as a group may be more compassionate toward the poor and blacks, those white Catholic Democrats who were mobilized to defect to the Republican party showed less warmth toward blacks and black political activity, disliked government programs that were intended to increase opportunity for blacks, reacted negatively to the directions their party had taken, and embraced the Republicans. In elections from 1972 to 1984, this constellation of racial factors also modestly depressed turnout but heavily depressed it in 1972. Generally, however, Catholic Democrats upset over race actually voted for the Republican candidate. While race receded in salience by 1996—moral restorationism replaced it—no other cultural factor had the same staying power throughout the post–New Deal period.

As with the Southern white Democrats, it is difficult to discern whether white Catholic Democrats were hearing principled appeals or were reacting from visceral dislikes or a sense of relative deprivation. Certainly those ethnic Catholics who were at the lower to middle rungs of the employment ladder were in competition with African Americans for some of the same jobs, homes, and neighborhoods. Whatever the reason, Republican campaigners were more successful among Catholics with the racial symbols and codewords than they were with the patriotic and moral restorationist packages.

Working-Class Whites outside the South

Outside the South, the secular realignment of working-class whites that Kevin Phillips predicted never really came. Examining figure 9.2, we note that in one late-Reagan year, 1988, there was a sudden dip in Democratic party identification and a corresponding increase in Republican identification. For most of the time-series, however, the identification curve was remarkably flat. The National Election Studies did not have a comparable measure of subjective social class for each year in the time-series; as a result we have treated respondents in the bottom two income quintiles as "working class."

Non-Southern, working-class whites followed somewhat different pat-

194 • Chapter Nine

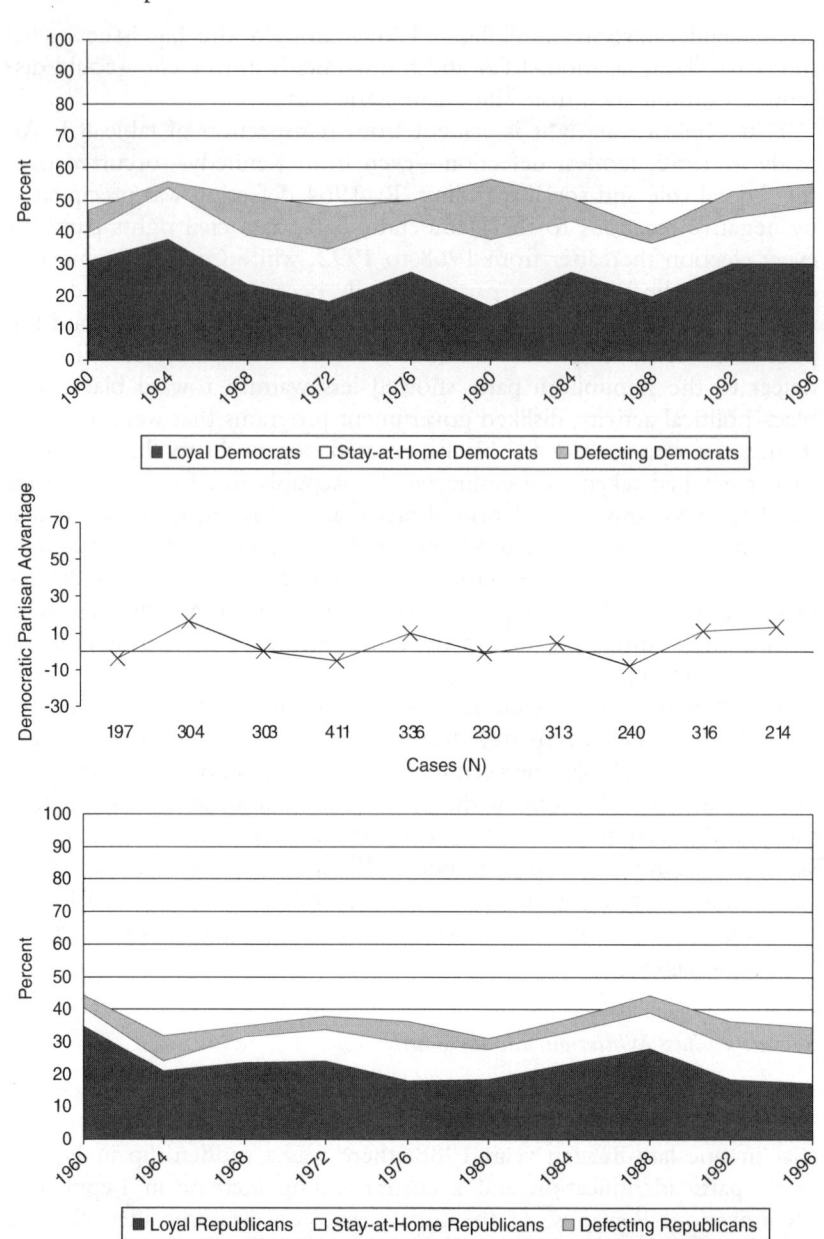

Figure 9.2. Partisan Patterns of Working-Class Whites Outside the South, 1960–1996

terns than whites in general (comparative figure not shown). They began in the 1960s as slightly less Democratic than whites in general, during the Reagan years moved 8 points more Democratic than whites in general, and have stayed at that comparative level ever since. At the time when others were realigning Republican, they became increasingly Democratic; only in 1988 were working-class whites outside the South more Republican than Democratic, following a sudden shift in party identification. Just as swiftly, they switched back to Democratic identification in the 1990s.

Yet their turnout figures were exceedingly low, not unlike those of African Americans. When combined with defections, the Democratic advantage among working-class, non-Southern whites was quickly dissipated. In 1968, for example, despite a 16-point advantage in party identification, 30 percent of the Democrats failed to vote and 25 percent defected, leaving the Democratic and Republican partisan advantage equal. In 1972 a 10-point Democratic party identification advantage was wiped out by 34 percent nonvoting and 28 percent defecting to Nixon, leaving a 6-point Republican advantage. In 1980 Democratic nonvoting was 37 percent and defections primarily to Reagan were 33 percent. In 1988 Democratic nonvoting was a whopping 41 percent but defections to Bush were only 11 percent.

Beyond simply socioeconomic factors, we suspect some powerful cultural forces were suppressing turnout or encouraging defections among working-class whites. These are evident in the entire period from 1968 to 1988. Inspection of table 9.1 suggests that working-class white Democrats outside the South were responding to some of the same appeals as white Southern Democrats and white Catholic Democrats, but not nearly with the same consistency.

Racial appeals were the most powerful cultural force. They appeared especially in the elections between 1968 and 1984 and were typically the sole cause for defections to the Republican candidates. In 1972 working-class white Democrats outside the South were particularly put off by elite religious liberals who joined or led the civil rights and antiwar protest movements. Note that earlier in 1960 they defected over worries about U.S. strength. Ironically, in 1988 the racial concerns made salient by the Bush campaign became the prime factor explaining failure to *turn out*, not crossover voting. When they failed to vote or defected in the 1990s, however, it was primarily for reasons of moral disgust. In 1996 also their dislike for outgroups—whether black or Hispanic—led to defection.

The patterns for working-class whites outside the South are slightly different from those for Southern whites and white Catholics. First, working-class whites are less likely to vote than all other target groups, except for African Americans. Yet with the exception of their lower education level,

TABLE 9.1
White, Non-Southern, Non-Latino, Working-Class Democrats, 1960–1996

Factors	Stay at Home	Defect	Controls	Stay at Home	Defect
1960					
Govt Role/Social Spending	0.140	0.463	Education	−18.778****	−0.670
Cynicism/Trust in Govt	0.348	0.018	Gender	0.249	−0.652
Strength of U.S.	0.725*	1.317****	Cohort	−0.337	0.714
Isolationism/Internationalism	0.706***	0.349	Constant	17.267	−0.640
Race/Civil Rights	−0.590	−0.119			
N	84		LR χ^2 [16]	29.15	
1964					
Old Social Cleavages	0.413*	0.219	Education	0.355	1.456
Party Ideology	−0.323	0.443	Gender	−0.034	19.032****
Cynical American First/Anticommunism	0.319	0.749	Cohort	0.782	1.028
			Constant	−2.679***	−44.218
N	155		LR χ^2 [12]	19.13	
1968					
Race Based Party Ideology	−0.141	0.996****	Education	−0.774	0.287
Cynicism/Trust in Govt	0.437**	0.471**	Gender	−0.758*	0.425
Anticommunism/Law & Order	0.374	−0.075	Cohort	0.817*	0.492
Antinativism/Prominorities	0.092	−0.170	Constant	0.182	−2.472**
N	137		LR χ^2 [14]	32.23	
1972					
Conservative Reaction to Social Change	0.275	0.068	Education	−1.052*	−0.549
Cultural Populism	0.098	−0.071	Gender	−0.448	−1.306****
Elite Religious Liberals	−0.054	0.994****	Cohort	0.435	−0.255
			Constant	1.193	2.876****
N	153		LR χ^2 [12]	40.66	
1976					
Opposition to Racial/Social Change	−0.373*	−0.394	Education	−1.005**	0.426

TABLE 9.1
Continued

Factors	Stay at Home	Defect	Controls	Stay at Home	Defect
Cynical Isolationism/ Moral Restorationism	−0.054	−0.191	Gender	0.578	0.362
Cultural Populism	−0.009	0.125	Cohort	0.309	−0.028
Race-Based Party Ideology	0.323	1.021****	Constant	−0.747	−2.432*
N	142		LR χ^2 [14]	21.07	
1980					
Race-Based Party Ideology	0.524	1.294****	Education	−0.762	0.145
Retreatist Racial Populism	−0.317	−0.058	Gender	−0.468	−0.787
Moral Restorationism	0.318	0.035	Cohort	1.381****	0.849**
			Constant	−0.692	−0.351
N	112		LR χ^2 [12]	31.55	
1984					
Race-Based Party Ideology	0.354	1.302***	Education	−1.018***	−0.092
Race, Rights, Taxes	0.027	0.013	Gender	0.106	0.161
Moral Restorationism	0.488*	0.292	Cohort	0.514	0.023
			Constant	−0.210	−0.831
N	129		LR χ^2 [12]	30.37	
1988					
Race-Based Party Ideology	1.675****	0.909	Education	0.464	1.209*
Cynical Isolationism	−0.065	0.497	Gender	−0.333	0.542
Moral Restorationism	0.091	0.987*	Cohort	0.528	1.648*
Racial Interests	−0.575*	1.002	Constant	−0.641	−8.361***
N	84		LR χ^2 [14]	28.92	
1992					
Race/Class/International Order-Based Party	−0.428	0.241	Education	−0.838*	−0.422
Cynicism/Trust in Govt	−0.031	0.921****	Gender	−0.757*	−0.064
Millennial Hopes	−0.235	0.374	Cohort	1.081***	1.496****

TABLE 9.1
Continued

Factors	Stay at Home	Defect	Controls	Stay at Home	Defect
Morally Restorationist-Based Party	1.311****	0.325	Constant	−0.762	−4.527****
N	148		LR χ^2 *[14]*	48.59	
1996					
Morally Restorationist-Based Party	0.781*	2.397****	Education	−0.678	0.577
Embrace of Internationalism	0.305	0.693**	Gender	0.150	0.962
Outgroup Antagonism	−0.284	−1.080****	Cohort	1.198***	2.368****
			Constant	−2.322*	−9.528****
N	108		LR χ^2 *[12]*		

Source: American National Election Studies (1960–1996)
Note: Multinomial-Logit Regression estimated via maximum likelihood, with voting Democratic as the base category. *Indicates $p < .1$ (two-tail) **Indicates $p < .05$ (two-tail) ***Indicates $p < .025$ (two-tail) ****Indicates $p < .01$ (two-tail) The LR χ^2 *[df]* statistic is the difference between likelihood ratios of a model estimated simply with a constant and the models reported above. This is similar to the joint F test of OLS regression.

their dearth of civic resources constitutes a less effective explanation for turnout failure than do their cultural concerns. Early in the time-series it was defense policy against external enemies, then it was cynicism about Democratic administrations, then it was race, and more recently it was the battery of gender/religious issues that reduced turnout. They took out much of their disgust and disillusionment by not voting. They were the classic *disabled* group that we discussed in our theory of campaign strategies.

Secondly, they do not seem to respond along *as many* cultural dimensions as, for example, Southern whites—with the notable exceptions of 1968 and 1996. Perhaps they have less resources for involvement in communication networks that personalize the full range of cultural appeals. Late in the time-series, age cohort is also an important factor diminishing turnout. Perhaps older workers who have toiled faithfully, lived by the rules, and not gotten ahead have become alienated from a campaign system that has failed to address their most central issue—economic security and advancement.

Perhaps, indeed, these are the lunch-bucket liberals who have seen the demise of a unionized economy and are poorly anchored in the current political system. Their stable partisan distributions may reflect an inertia that accompanies decreasing hopes for economic justice. Working-class whites outside the South have responded to some short-term factors in some elections, but they seem to have resisted the long-term trends that characterized other groups.

Level of Education

If level of education can condition responsiveness to both the Cold War consensus and patriotic anticommunist appeals when the Cold War was on the wane, then surely it can differentially affect reactions to overt or codeword racial appeals. That was precisely the point of the Sears and Citrin argument. Social class and education are highly correlated. Thus, consistent with our earlier arguments, we should expect that less-educated whites, particularly Democrats, would have their partisanship perturbed by racial appeals, while more-educated whites, particularly Republicans, would be embarrassed by racial appeals that were perceived as too blatant and would either sit out such elections or defect to the Democratic candidate.

We have already seen in chapter 8, and particularly in figure 8.4, that these expectations were sustained by the data in all nine elections from 1960 to 1992. The factor that summarized feelings toward blacks, black political activity, and government policy to assist blacks in their quest for equality proved highly significant in explaining defections by less-educated white Democrats. In only two of the elections was the racial factor important in suppressing turnout. In short, racial appeals created sufficient anxiety to mobilize less-educated white Democrats as Republican voters. Sometimes a second race-related factor was significant as well. While patriotic and anticommunistic themes appeared significant in two elections, and moral restorationism grew in importance, nothing else matched race. *Nearly all the successful Republican appeal to less-educated white Democrats during the post–New Deal period tapped into their racial feelings.*

Both overt racial appeals and the racial codewords were the primary factors accounting for turnout failures and especially defections by college-educated, white Democrats. Late in the time-series, concern for the preservation of traditional values pushed racial matters into a less prominent place, but even then they were not lost. In fact, white Democrats at this education level were the first to defect specifically because of their concerns over the civil rights drive already in 1960. Then, their racial concerns explained almost all defection until the 1990s when moral restorationism overshadowed race. But by this time, Republican candidates were more likely to deplore what had happened to family values then to deploy racial codewords.

Thus, Republicans found susceptible targets for their overt and codeword racial appeals not only among white Democrats with minimal education, but also with those who had some college or who had completed college. The critical time seems to have been from 1968 to 1972 when the appeal was quite overt, and the Wallace symbols took a slightly less offensive character on the lips of Republican leaders. After 1972 the emerging Reagan party was able to transfer most of the negativity to the Democratic party. The Democratic party provided wonderful assists as it came to symbolize more and more extreme positions in the struggle for racial equality. In a very real sense, the Democratic party itself was responsible for inadvertent demobilization and active defection by its middle-educated white core. All Republicans had to do by the Reagan years was to point to the people who were now highly visible in the opposition party, and it tapped into the enduring racial fears of many cognizant white Democrats.

Such an approach, however, was hardly risk-free for Republicans. It may be difficult at the turn of the millennium to remember that the Republican party was once the progressive party and the civil rights party—willing both to use the powers of the federal government to assure equality of opportunity and to use the federal budget to advance the economic fortunes of all groups in the country. The intraparty struggles between progressives and conservatives at midcentury had prophesied that the progressives were vulnerable. In the post–New Deal period, particularly after the 1958 decapitation of the progressives, the conservative ascendancy transformed the party. Yet it had retained the loyalties of a well-educated, professionally employed, civic-minded core group. That is where the risks would be evident over the next four decades. More and more, the Reagan and post-Reagan party's symbolic strategies to incorporate those opposed to progressive civil rights policies and those supportive of moral traditionalism would nudge middle- and highly educated Republicans into the arms of the Democrats.

We have already noted in chapter 8 that Republican leaders' uses of code words for race, as well as civil rights policy itself, drove highly educated Republicans increasingly in a Democratic direction. In 1964 already the most significant predictor of both turnout failure and defection by college-educated, white Republicans was deep disappointment with the racially conservative movement that had captured the party. These same concerns reappeared in all years except 1976 and 1980. They peaked with Bush's 1988 campaign. By the 1990s, however, disgust with their party's commitment to the agenda of the Religious Right was the principal factor that mobilized defection to the Democratic or independent candidates. In three of the elections, their sense that the Republican party had lost its historic purpose on racial equality precipitated turnout failures, as well, even among this highly participatory segment of the electorate.

Any issue, like race, so long on the American agenda, is bound to be the subject of political give-and-take. Ambitious politicians from either party will look for advantage among the dominant racial majority. The Emancipation Proclamation and Lincoln's later interpretation of the Civil War as a righteous war to end slavery had precipitated strong opposition even among his Republican supporters. Post-Reconstruction Southern Democratic politicians had built nearly a century of electoral invincibility on the race card. Thus, it should come as no surprise that post–New Deal Republicans, so long shut out of the White House and increasingly in the minority on Capitol Hill, should find a variety of ways to package issues surrounding racial equality, after the civil rights movement had pricked the national conscience. People construct many rationales to justify an existing moral order on race. There was ample material in the American cultural and political experience to limit further change. And the terrible instabilities of the 1960s generated sufficient fear of extremists of any stripe that there were receptive audiences to overt and codeword appeals. In the end, the national party system was transformed. Historic coalitions crumbled, and groups had to learn to live with new partners. Some found cohabitation untenable and switched loyalties.

SUMMARY

In this chapter we analyzed the dynamic party system through the lens of race. As the Democratic party shifted from its Jeffersonian-Jacksonian roots, first through the social welfare party of the Roosevelt coalition, then to the Humphrey party of social justice, the composition of its electoral coalition shifted dramatically. The critical election of 1958 purged the Republican congressional party of most of its moderate Northeastern and Midwestern leadership. Conservative Republicans from the fringe South and West filled this leadership vacuum with a renewed focus on individual responsibility and states' rights. In the other camp, Southern Democratic leadership was slowly overshadowed in the 1960s by the more racially tolerant party elites from the Midwest and Northeast. By the mid-1960s the parties' positions on race were solidified. The bipartisan coalition that once supported the 1960 and 1964 Civil Rights Acts collapsed by the 1966 vote, resulting in a party system bifurcated by race.

This fundamental shift in policy stances by congressional leadership led to the development of campaign themes by strategic politicians that embraced the dynamics of the new party system. From 1960 until 1988, each Democratic ticket placed emphasis on courting the African American vote. Conversely, the Republican party explicitly emphasized negative outgroup appeals in 1968 and 1972 to those individuals—once at the core of Roosevelt's New Deal coalition—who were most alienated by the Democrats' embrace of pro–civil rights postures and the African American voter. Later, with the exception of 1988, these explicit appeals were no longer needed for Republicans; other appeals such as crime, gun rights, welfare, and social spending now sufficiently carried negative racial symbols. As our analyses indicated, the general saliency and subsequent success of these campaign appeals to Democratic white Southerners, white Catholics, white working-class Democrats outside the South, and less-educated to moderately educated white Democrats were mediated by the specific context of each campaign and the basic level of racial tensions within society as a whole. Further, throughout the period these various racial appeals drove some Republicans, largely among the most educated, from the party's electoral coalition. Late in the time-series—partly because of Clinton's stands on the death penalty, welfare reform, and rap music, and partly because many disloyal or demobilized Democrats finally changed party affiliation—religion and gender surmounted race as the primary mechanisms for drawing Democrats from the majority partisan coalition.

CHAPTER TEN

Gender, Religion, and the Second Party Transformation

A THIRD FACTOR joined race and patriotism as an agent of culturally inspired political transformation in the post–New Deal era. The complexity of this third component is evident from the various names given to it—the social issue (Scammon and Wattenberg 1970), traditional values, family issues, social conservatism, moral traditionalism, and so forth. While we might have taken any number of specific political controversies as emblematic of the new political fault line, this account frames the cultural cleavage in terms of two major forces that collided—the women's movement and pietistic churches. Although other issues became part of the mix, emancipated women and morally traditionalist churches best represent the clash between emerging and settled moral orders that loomed so large in the 1980s and beyond.

THE GATHERING STORM

The story of how men and women should live together as men and women and as citizens with equal opportunities became politicized in the post–New Deal period in a very complex manner. Even before the drive for civil rights for minorities had convulsed the nation and upset partisan coalitions, both parties sought to enlarge reliable voting blocs. Ever since women won the suffrage, they had been an undermobilized sector of the electorate. To attract women, both parties offered symbolic inclusion and policy benefits.

In the 1950s, the Republican administration placed several women in highly visible but noncabinet roles. Democrats, who had already appointed a woman as secretary of labor in the 1930s under FDR, and had experienced the positives and negatives of an activist First Lady, followed with a host of favorable policies in the 1960s: the Equal Pay Act of 1963 (amending the Fair Labor Standards Act of 1938), Title VII as an addition to the Equal Employment Opportunities Act in 1964, and Executive Order 11375 of 1967, adding women to the coverage of the Office of Federal Contract Compliance created in 1965. Not to be left behind, the Nixon Administration joined a Democratic Congress in election year 1972 in a number of actions that placed jurisdictional teeth in the legislative actions of the 1960s and added Title IX to the Educational Equity Act of 1972 (Freeman 1975). Most importantly, the parties collaborated in the passage of the Equal Rights Amendment to the U.S. Constitution in 1972, and twenty-eight states immediately ratified it.

Women had experienced difficulty uniting into a large organization that would further their interests since the suffrage fight. In the 1920s a schism developed when younger women sought to use the franchise to change social conventions rather than reform society. The reformist impulse was narrowed to the employment market (ibid., 16). By the 1940s women's involvement in white-collar, mainly clerical, jobs had increased, but pay and advancement were poor. In the 1950s the proportion of women completing higher education soared while the birthrate declined. Yet, while women entered the employment market, business, and the professions (beyond teaching) in unprecedented numbers, their occupational rewards decreased relative to those of men in similar fields. College-educated white women in the professions most noticed the discrepancies between preparation and reward. Even within the student radical movement, women were treated as clerical support and sex objects; they were often hooted off the stage with demeaning sexual innuendoes if they chose to assert leadership (ibid., 30–39).

Several important consequences followed these experiences: (1) early organizational agendas—for example, of the Federation of Business and Professional Women's Clubs and the Women's Equity Action League— would focus on employment and education; (2) these would be *women's* organizations, since men continued to view women more as subordinates or playthings; and (3) the central perspective that would motivate policy and group mobilization would be *relative deprivation.* The early leadership was heavily white, educated, middle class, and mainline Protestant. They followed essentially egalitarian and achievement-oriented principles drawn from Reformed Protestant theology. The opportunities and achievements of middle-class men became their reference point for measuring whether action for change was necessary. Both their conscience and battle flag was Betty Friedan's *The Feminine Mystique,* published in 1963.

The styles of political activity changed as the 1960s moved into the 1970s. When the National Organization for Women was organized in 1966, it was basically a civil rights organization for women. It had a democratic structure, local chapters, and some leaders drawn from the federal bureaucratic structures that were extending opportunities for women. The "black consciousness" movement, however, had disinvited whites committed to social justice, and the draft resistance movement centered on male concerns. Therefore, younger women, fresh from campus organizing experiences, had movement energy to expend and were drawn into urban collectives (Freeman 1983). Confrontational styles now joined conventional interest group activity. Communication networks were well established along the Boston-Washington axis, and a few other cities and college towns. However, that was not where the action was centered in the fight to ratify the ERA. Many of the women were strangers to state capitols and to state politics, especially in the states that were slow to ratify. They were often easy to pillory as "outsiders."

As the women's movement was gaining strength and converts, American religious life was also developing in ways that would hasten the conflict. For much of American history when politics had a distinct confessional character, political conflicts took place among groups separated from one another geographically or largely sealed off from social interaction across denominational lines by powerful symbolic boundaries. These conflicts followed the fault line between Protestants and Catholics. The cleavage gained power as it drew on deep historical associations and stimulated voters by activating latent group loyalties and stereotypes. Protestants, for example, gained cohesion by associating Catholic proposals to obtain state funding for parochial schools with images dating back to the Reformation (Jorgenson 1987; Pratt 1967). In the period between the world wars, Protestant nationalists commonly sounded such themes to justify immigration restriction, mandatory school instruction in English, isolationism, and the maintenance of racial segregation (Higham 1970; Jackson 1967).

The election of 1960 was probably the last of the confessional era, the final great contest between Catholicism and Protestantism. A generation after the disastrous Smith nomination, the Democrats once again entrusted their presidential nomination to a Roman Catholic. John F. Kennedy was a very different type of Democrat from Smith. Whereas Smith evoked the Lower East Side, an immigrant constituency, and the rough-and-tumble world of working-class machine politics, Kennedy carried an air of patrician grace. For the generation of Catholics who had fought World War II, earned college degrees through the GI Bill, acquired jobs in corporations and the professions, and settled the suburbs, Kennedy represented the inclusion of Catholics in the American Dream.

Mindful of what befell his co-religionist in 1928, Kennedy took great pains to render the religious issue moot in 1960 (Jamieson 1996, 124). He drew a sharp line between his Catholicism and his political loyalties, respecting the historic American demarcation between church and state. Kennedy visited the Houston Ministerial Alliance, assuring them that he had no intentions of promoting papal interests in the United States.

These efforts did not prevent a recurrence of the sharp divisions in Catholic and Protestant voting patterns that had also emerged in 1928. Throughout the country, the Kennedy candidacy disrupted normal voting trends as Catholics supported Kennedy at record rates, and Protestants, particularly in the South, crossed over to vote for Richard Nixon (Dawidowicz and Goldstein 1963). Jews also showed strikingly high levels of support for a fellow religious outsider, and blacks, as noted earlier, were grateful for Kennedy's dramatic show of support for the imprisoned Martin Luther King, Jr. The confessional nature of this vote was revealed by the mink-clad woman in Bucks County, Pennsylvania, who attributed the Republican defeat to the KKK—the core Democratic constituencies of "the Kikes, the Koons, and the Kat'lics" (Michener 1961, 203). Even so, the level of confessional conflict and the electoral impact in 1960 were distinctly muted compared to the Smith contest.

Kennedy's success had largely removed the old religious issues from the national agenda. Both parties seemed eager to appeal to Catholics by including them as running mates on presidential tickets. The new religious cleavage that emerged after 1960 reflected the transformation of religion in the radically different social circumstances that developed after World War II. It stressed personal uprightness and public morality. It transcended denominational boundaries, rather than being anchored in ecclesiastical differences.

Catholicism ceased to be a political handicap in part because Catholicism became less exotic. Suburbanization undercut the tight linkages among community, ethnicity, and denomination, the ties that sustained niche-style religion and confessional politics. Under the impetus of the GI Bill, Catholics were part of the major population streams that moved from the city centers to the suburbs. In time, they also migrated in large numbers to the South and West. Many Catholic ethnic groups had earlier settled in rural areas and small towns. This dispersion has been associated with a substantial upward mobility as Catholics have caught up with and, in most cases, surpassed Protestant education and income levels.

The ethnic aspect of American Catholicism has also grown more complex. Catholicism was never an exclusively white phenomenon but has become increasingly multiracial with the growth of significant African American, Hispanic, and Asian subcommunities. Among white ethnic Catholics, on the other hand, historical distinctions among Irish, German, Polish, and Italian groups have lessened as "national" parishes rooted in urban neighborhoods gave way to suburban parishes that attracted migrants from elsewhere, and marriages crossed ethnic boundaries. The suburban parishes became beehives of ministries, psychological and social service activities, catering to the needs and family pathologies of successful suburbanites (Leege 1988).

While Catholicism was losing its outsider status, the Protestant sector of American religion was undergoing striking differentiation. The major denominations within mainline Protestantism—Episcopalianism, Methodism, Congregationalism, and Presbyterianism—had long been widely distributed geographically but still evinced a distinctive social character. Wherever they were found, these traditions were associated with wealth, status, power, and respectability. In his Iowa town, Randall Balmer (1996, 4) recollected, these "mainline" Protestants "belonged to the Rotary Club and sipped whiskey sours at the country club . . . ; they sat on the school board and city council." Such local notables often clashed with the "new breed" of activist clergy who redefined the mission of the mainline churches when they enlisted in boycotts on behalf of unionized agricultural workers, marched for open housing in the cities, and led demonstrations against American involvement in Vietnam. For reasons that still escape complete explanation, the mainline traditions suffered severe membership declines from the 1960s through the 1990s. By the end of the century, at least in numerical terms, the mainline had become the sideline.

By contrast, the postwar period brought dynamic growth and prosperity to the evangelical Protestant denominations. Once essentially a religious culture of the rural and small-town South and border states, evangelicalism exploded in the postwar era. Though evangelicalism retained this base, it increasingly became a presence in metropolitan areas and in the "unchurched" suburbs that developed around urban cores. Evangelicals quickly narrowed the educational and income gaps that had separated them from the high-status Protestant denominations. By moving into urban areas and achieving a measure of affluence, they also began to confront the social tensions and alternative moral perspectives that had been uncommon in their rural redoubts.

These changes in religious life complicated the task of converting religious sentiment into political action. The decline of niche religion reduced political cohesion *within* religious groups. With fewer reinforcing traits in common, members of a religious group are less likely to behave as a political unit. Unless appeals by political elites render group membership salient, as they did for Catholics in 1960, the simple fact of religious group membership should exert less impact on vote choice.

Greater differentiation within religious groups has also increased the opportunities to create transdenominational coalitions. Several scholars of postwar religion (Green and Guth 1991; Hunter 1991; Wuthnow 1988) have argued that existing denominations are increasingly fractured by a new cleavage dividing *religious liberals* (also called modernists and progressives) from *conservatives* (traditionalists, the orthodox).[11] Within each

---

[11] To a degree, the conflict between liberals and conservatives may also undercut traditional denominational lines by stimulating the emergence of nondenominational churches. The most explosive church growth in the recent period has been among the community and nondenominational churches that exist outside traditional denominational structures.

major religious tradition, it is argued, these factions have developed around conflicting notions of morality and the priorities of the church. The conflict may tap into different religious issues within each denomination—the ordination of women, styles of prayer and worship, lay authority, matrilineal descent—but they also bear a strong resemblance to one another because they incorporate political and social controversies over feminism, homosexuality, educational objectives, the foreign policy of the United States, and other such questions. In pursuing their agendas, the liberals and conservatives have developed special-purpose organizations expressly to link people who share social and political values, despite differences in religious tradition.

The rise of political and social conflicts that cross denominational lines may be abetted by the emerging cleavage between the *secular* and the *religious*. Religion has been such an important element in the definition of American respectability that surveys have habitually identified only a very small segment of people who deny any religious identity or embrace the "atheist" or "agnostic" label. Nonetheless, there has been a marked increase over time in the proportion of religious "nones" (Glenn 1987), an even larger increase when survey items are written to remove the assumption that religious affiliation is the normal state of adult Americans (Leege, Kellstedt, and Wald 1990). If the proportion of nones has increased, there also appears to have been a striking shift in their social character. Unlike the past when formal religious affiliation was usually highest among the most affluent strata, the ranks of the religiously *uninvolved* are now drawn disproportionately from the highest levels of the social pyramid. Some of this growth is an offshoot of the decline in mainline Protestantism and Judaism, but the "New Class" seems also to have been supplied disproportionately by the disaffiliation of young, upwardly mobile Catholics.

The religious significance of this development remains open for debate, but it has nonetheless proven useful fodder for political entrepreneurs.[12] Americans certainly *perceive* a decline in the influence of religion in society, and intellectuals on the right have nurtured this perception by attributing it to a growing antireligious bias in the public square.

To return to the developing storm between women committed to cultural change and the conservative church movements, tensions reached a boiling point over the proposed Equal Rights Amendment to the Constitution. In January 1973 lawyer and conservative Catholic activist Phyllis

---

Such megachurches are often designed with an ecumenical appeal in mind and may join conservative social issue positions to evangelical religious themes.

[12] For example, research on the attitudes of the nones has often suggested that they share in the broad religious consensus that permeates the United States (Reimer 1995).

Schlafly positioned her Eagle Forum as the fulcrum in the resistance to ratification. In state after state where the emerging women's liberation movement lacked local structure (cf. Mansbridge 1986 for the story about Illinois; Matthews and De Hart 1990 for the story about North Carolina), she built coalitions out of the Concerned Women for America, evangelical prayer chains, ecumenical parachurch organizations, and other groups who were upset with the new values and lifestyles (Hunter 1991; Wuthnow 1988). Schlafly and others convinced the Republican party to drop its historic platform support for governmental action that would increase opportunities for women, and eventually the ERA was defeated.

That such conflict between the women's movement and religious conservatives would develop, and that political parties would seek to capitalize on it, was probably inevitable. The women's movement is a *transformational movement* (Katzenstein and Mueller 1987, 5). It addresses both a broad range of policy issues and daily life experiences dealing with the economy, the military, language, the construction of history, family, and sexuality. Its object is to change society by transforming the culture. It seeks to modify consciousness, personal identities, and relationships. Because it is so difficult to change culture by law, gender conflict swiftly moves into the arena of symbolic politics. If they had not begun so, the women's movement quickly traversed the boundaries of the prevailing moral order on gender relations. Their collective consciousness would oppose traditional norms and the institutions that socialize people into such norms. As a result, adherents to the women's movement "will be treated not as political opponents, but as ridiculous, dangerous, heretical or crazy elements of society" (ibid., 93). In their vision, changes in primary group relations would foster equality and percolate upward through all economic, social, and political institutions. Lacking the historic institutional investments that had built organizations to preserve the status quo, they had to rely on women's consciousness, that is, *social identification*.

Churches, on the other hand, perform both prophetic and priestly functions for the society. They become prophetic in the face of grave social injustice, as they had in support of the civil rights movement. But then, that movement went sour as cities burned and parishioners withheld financial support and respect for leadership (Hadden 1969). At just this moment in history, the women's movement was asking the churches to sustain and extend their prophetic ministries to another source of injustice. By 1977 Nixon-establishment Protestant Jill Ruckelshaus was succeeded by Manhattan activist and Jewish Congresswoman Bela Abzug as chair of the International Women's Year (IWY) commission. The 1977 IWY convention in Houston sought to build alliances with "our lesbian sisters" and was characterized by Congressman Robert Dornan as "sick, anti-God, and unpatriotic," and by Republican leaders as "a gaggle of outcasts, misfits, and rejects" (Melich 1996, 86–88). Earlier in the 1970s, feminist leaders had set a commitment to the prochoice position on abortion as a defining article of the movement. Given the psychology of *social attributions*, it would have been difficult even for mainline Protestant and Catholic leaders to sustain a prophetic ministry on behalf of the movement. Opposition to the women's movement, as then defined, became part of the rhetoric of televangelists, political entertainers like Rush Limbaugh, and, most importantly, dedicated evangelical Protestant leaders and parishioners.

In the ensuing battle, churches held the organizational advantage. They were legitimizing the status quo in primary group and societal relations, had evolved as American society's natural agency for socializing cultural norms, could claim to speak with the force of divine law, and were anchored in massive communications networks with congregations in every locale of the country. Even when not unified in their opposition to the women's movement of that time, they were still organizationally larger than any other quasi-political organization, such as labor unions. If the women's movement came to rely primarily on *social identification*, their opponents in the churches could tap both social identification and *social cohesion*, that is, regular interaction among like-minded people. For these devout people, moral decay seemed everywhere, and women's libbers and their supporters in the media were to blame for the failures of the nation.

Their advantage was not lost on political elites. By 1978 the principal political operatives of the Reagan movement had established contacts with the traditionalist women's groups and evangelical clergy. The professionals taught the preachers how to infiltrate county political committees and conduct politics. In 1979 Paul Weyrich chose the name "Moral Majority" for the movement, and the Rev. Jerry Falwell became its leader. The preachers were given prominent prime-time exposure at the 1980 Republican convention, delivering prayers. In the platform, Republicans pulled back from their previous statements on gender equality, this time placing an emphasis on legislative protections for family values and respect for homemakers. Although the official Reagan campaign minimized social issues—who needed them when the country's honor had been spited by an Islamic holy man and when inflation had burgeoned to the 18–21 percent range—the traditionalist women's groups extended great effort in the campaign. Reagan used his likeable personality to convince moderate women, especially Republicans, that he was their friend. The Moral Majority, however, argued that its foot-soldiers accounted for Governor Reagan's victory.

After appointing the first woman to serve on the U.S. Supreme Court, in 1983, and strengthening the anti-abortion planks to the platform, in early 1984, the White House orchestrated a convention with much larger numbers of women delegates and speakers. The most prominent was Jeanne Kirkpatrick, U.S. ambassador to the United Nations, whose opening night address referred to the "San Francisco Democrats" and their selection of Congresswomen Geraldine Ferraro as the nominee for vice president. Ferraro's nomination had successfully culminated the single-minded efforts by women's organizations to place a prominent woman on a presidential ticket (Bonk 1988; Mueller 1988). It was a highly visible breakthrough not unlike the importance to Catholics of the Smith or Kennedy nominations. Even coining the term "gender gap" to describe "Reagan's female problem" was part of a long-term strategy to convince the Democrats that there were votes to be mined through social identification as women.

The innuendo to San Francisco, known by social attribution as the center of homosexuality, drugs, and alternate lifestyles, was not lost on target groups within the Democratic coalition. The speech signaled an intense attack on Ferraro throughout the campaign by "private" organizations with ties to the Reagan-Bush reelection committee. Archbishop O'Connor of New York City instructed the flock that they could not support for high office a Catholic whose position on abortion was contrary to Catholic teaching. She was either refused permission or embarrassed out of marching in the Columbus Day parades in New York and Philadelphia. She was called an apostate. She was charged with receiving Mafia money, and no male Italian American organization rose to her defense. Everywhere she appeared she was pursued by anti-abortion demonstrators, often numbering tens of thousands. Even New England blueblood George Bush chose to refer to his debate performance against Ms. Ferraro as trying to "kick a little butt." Reagan, a popular incumbent with an upturning economy, could stand above the fray that his local campaign organizations had orchestrated or his national organization had encouraged. He won by a landslide and claimed a mandate for his mix of economic and social conservatism.

Reagan's conservatism, often called *egalitarian individualism*, was particularly well suited to the conflict with these women. The feminist movement was based on an active role for government as a central agent in the transformation of the status quo. From its inception before the turn of the century, the women's movement was proreform, pro–social welfare, progovernment (Bashevkin 1998). It saw society through its constituent units of groups; through collective action, underprivileged groups would use government to redress their disadvantage. The sense of conservatism that Reagan (and Margaret Thatcher in the Great Britain) captured so well, however, was individualistic, was committed to rewards through markets, not government, and "elevated personal responsibility far above any notion of the state's role" (ibid., 5). Collective action was as much the enemy as was governmental action. Reagan ridiculed group identities or group consciousness—whether as women, blacks, or whatever—as shackles that impeded individual enterprise. Only individuals could "take charge of their lives" (ibid., 165). This philosophy resonated with the growth of libertarianism, but it threw up some difficult hurdles for the Protestant and Catholic religious traditions. Both liked "personal responsibility," but they did not want the poor or outcast to be forgotten. And Catholics, informed by centuries of Catholic social teaching, were unwilling to jettison collective identities as important building blocks of the moral order. Despite, or perhaps because of, the attacks, "feminist consciousness" continued to grow throughout the Reagan years (Klein 1987).

If nothing else, the Democratic party was coming to be seen as the opposite of the Republican party—prochoice, profeminist, prowelfare, the bastion of alternate life-styles. While some evangelical politicians felt they could challenge the old guard and libertarian Republicans for control of the party through the nomination of Pat Robertson in 1988, they failed in that mission. Yet they convinced leaders that the party could not win without its foot-soldiers. Although an even more restrictive plank on abortion was added in 1988, one implicitly favoring the life of the fetus over the life of the mother, the party recognized the growing employment of young women outside the home and the pressing need for adequate daycare. A plank called for federal assistance for local daycare providers. By the 1990s twenty to twenty-five of the state party organizations were thought to have been controlled by the Religious Right.

Just as parts of the agenda of the women's movement, particularly issues of education, employment, and legal rights, were much broader than those matters that brought them into conflict with traditionalist churches, so conservative religious groups also were activated by a wider agenda of social issues. At various times during the post–New Deal peroid, they included marijuana use, rebellious youth, the "godless" content of school textbooks, school prayer, school vouchers and other forms of tax support for Christian schools, a variety of contexts for gay rights, welfare support for successive children out of wedlock, the conditions that spawn crime, gambling, exemption of quasi-political religious organizations from taxes, and on. The concerns with race and patriotism were also refracted through the lens of cultural traditionalism. The politicization of these concerns becomes evident in the language and images of political advertisements. And as we have already seen in chapter 6, many cultural traditionalists came to link race, gender issues, and religious institutional concerns under the perception of rampant moral decay.

CULTURAL RESTORATIONISM IN CAMPAIGN APPEALS

Although he is often associated with states' rights and economic conservatism, Barry Goldwater has often been overlooked as the first candidate of the period to make heavy use of cultural restorationist themes. Chapter 6 reported on the memo from Goldwater's campaign manager, urging him to make "moral decay" the missile gap of the 1964 campaign. In a classic demonstration of symbolism aimed at housewives, a Goldwater organization developed an ad linking Goldwater to clean-cut youths, the flag, and patriotic marches, while associating the Democrats with black rioters (Jamieson 1996, 212–15). Asking plaintively, "What has happened to America?," another ad cited fear of crime, the availability of pornography, and political corruption in (Democratic) Washington as signs that the White House should be dedicated to improving national morality (Diamond and Bates 1992, 139–40).

The success of the 1968 George Wallace campaign in mobilizing discontented Northern Democrats on racial and social themes showed how the anxieties of cultural conservatism could be harnessed, and it provided an important model for Republican campaigns. As a small-town boy, raised in a family without much money but with hard-working parents who believed in sacrifice, the Nixon portrayed by the 1968 campaign had been the right instrument to return America to a simpler time of moral order (Jamieson 1996, 254). But the theme was given a harder edge in the postelection speeches of Nixon's vice president, Spiro Agnew. Agnew's writers created phrases that demonized the advocates of social change—"nattering nabobs of negativism," "effete intellectual snobs," "limousine liberals," "bra-burners"—in contrast with the virtuous "silent majority" of hard-working, law-abiding Americans.

That message was powerfully reinforced in 1972 when the Democrats appeared to give their convention and nomination over to the counterculture. The triumph of the "new class" seemed evident: college-educated professionals from the baby boom generation who favored affirmative action, liberalized abortion, gay rights, and the decriminalization of marijuana. The McGovernites attracted new Democratic votes from affluent havens of cultural liberalism like the Upper East Side of New York and West Los Angeles but severely weakened Democratic standing in traditional strongholds such as the declining neighborhoods of Queens and the "smudged-stucco working class" communities outside Los Angeles (Barone 1990, 509; Rieder 1985). The claim that their party represented "acid, amnesty and abortion" must have troubled faithful working-class Democrats who wondered what had happened to the party of Roosevelt. This sense of unease was fanned by Republican advertisements portraying the Democrats as hostile to such fundamental institutions as the military, the middle class, and the police, while associating the out-party with welfare recipients, marijuana, draft dodgers, and school busing (Jamieson 1996, 303–7).

Watergate had badly derailed the Republican majority project in 1974, and the Democratic choice of a nominee steeped in evangelical piety robbed the GOP of its major cultural thrust in the 1976 campaign. After that momentary disruption, the party returned to its cultural offensive. In both 1980 and 1984 Ronald Reagan was offered to voters as the incarnation of such traditional American values as hard work, military strength, patriotism, a sound economy, and economic freedom. The God-talk, the American exceptionalism, the classic affirmation of the spiritual purpose of the nation were extremely convincing in his delivery (Shannon 1982). Reflecting the underlying religious realignment making itself felt in their core constituencies in 1984, the Democrats tried to dissemble Republican seculars and mainline Protestants by tying Reagan to the Reverend Jerry Falwell, the head of Moral Majority and a symbol of evangelical extremism (Jamieson 1996, 453–54). Poaching on a traditional Democratic constituency, however, the Republicans took advantage of their growing ties to the Catholic hierarchy. The Bush campaign in 1988 sought to capitalize on the same images that worked so well for Reagan.

Scarred by the elections of the 1980s, Democrats entered the 1992 campaign very much aware that they could capitalize on the poor economic conditions only by preventing Republicans from effectively using cultural issues against them. By solidifying Clinton's image as the product of modest circumstances, a sunny small-town boy who sang in the church choir and regularly attended Baptist Sunday school, the Democrats could then move against the Republicans by raising concerns about the vitriolic denunciations of diversity throughout the GOP nominating convention.

As noted in chapter 2, the 1992 Republican convention was given over to the hard edge of social conservatism through featured platform speeches by Pat Buchanan, Pat Robertson, Marilyn Quayle, and others. In particular it modeled the *proper* role of women in a changing world. Having lost the Cold War as an issue and with an economy in serious trouble, the GOP saw few alternatives. Nonetheless, these speakers gave the Democrats plenty of ammunition to fashion a campaign that painted the Republicans as "a party of ideologues and zealots" (McWilliams 2000).

In attacking the Republicans on this dimension, Democrats had to walk a fine line. Criticism of the Christian Right could easily be taken as criticism of religion in general, never a wise strategy in a country where 85 to 90 percent of the population claims religious affiliation. Indeed, when Democrats attacked pro-Republican clergy as theocratic and intolerant, the GOP routinely deplored the "injection" of religious bigotry into the campaign. Clinton surrogates often cloaked their attacks by posing a threat to the women's movement—Republican control of both the Congress and the White House would strangle reproductive rights. In his acceptance speech, the candidate himself was even more circumspect (Smith 1994, 218-19). Clinton promised a "New Covenant" with the goal of "healing America" from the divisions that inflamed public life. While Republicans always blamed "them" for social problems, Clinton had a vision of America derived from civil religion in which there is no them; there is only us. One nation, under God, indivisible, with liberty, and justice, for all. That is *our* Pledge of Allegiance, and that's what the New Covenant is all about.

The contrast with the Republican message in Houston could not have been more striking. In offering such appeals, Clinton intended to reassure his party's base constituency of the Democrats' continuing support for minorities and women's rights. Beyond energizing the base, the discourse of inclusion was also intended to appeal to prochoice and feminist Republicans who were shaken by their party's embrace of social conservatism. Indeed, exit polls showed that 28 percent of women identifying as Republicans voted for Clinton. Further, the 1992 campaign gave the Democrats a golden opportunity to claim the moral center from the Republicans. The fear of extremism now worked to the Democrats' advantage. Record numbers of women, mostly Democrats, were elected to the House and Senate. More devastating for Republican fortunes, Ross Perot drew heavily from Republican and independent men.

As the post–New Deal period unfolded, the Republican strategy was not only to split the women and mobilize the evangelical foot-soldiers, but also to create a *backlash among men* over gender issues. Throughout the post–World War II moral order into the 1960s, men had a pretty good deal. Jobs expanded, incomes grew, educational opportunities were abundant, and wives took care of the kids. But then came the economic revolution.

Women were now competitors in the university and in the marketplace. Men's wages seemed to top out or decline, and job opportunities were constricted. In the Reagan-Bush years, when the politicians benefited from a male backlash, "women's average wages grew by 30% while the average income of men actually declined slightly" (Fox-Genovese 1996, 133). Class and gender differentials developed overlays: "Between 1973 and 1992 the average wages of the bottom 60 percent of male workers fell by 20%" (ibid., 135). For middle- and upper-middle-class males the problem was affirmative action. Educated women were filling jobs that men previously had locked up. By 1972 women held 47 percent of the most lucrative professional and managerial jobs (ibid., 114). The *comparable worth gap*, that is, the difference in earnings between women and men performing the same job, had narrowed. Instead of women earning 59¢ for each dollar a man earned, women were now earning 71¢. But for professional and managerial jobs, by 1992 women earned 90¢ on every man's dollar (ibid.).

The emerging moral order no longer overwhelmingly advantaged men. From the perspective of *relative deprivation*, the economic dominance of men was threatened. Meanwhile, in the home women were arguing that men should share domestic and child-rearing chores. When economically autonomous women could not take it any more, they were willing to walk out. The frustration and anger of men was a beckoning political resource for a minority party needing to assemble a winning coalition.

By the mid-1970s Republicans had blanketed white males with *quota* arguments. Affirmative action, in reality, set not quotas but targets. Once set, an employer would extend extraordinary efforts to find qualified women or minorities. The more demanding the job, white men reasoned, the less likely it was that a minority candidate would have the qualifications to fill it. But their experience told them that it was different with women: they would qualify. The political reality played on such fears. Through time and in different social classes, the quota argument might shift from a racial issue to a gender issue.

In the 1994 congressional campaign, for example, attack ads on quotas were everywhere, in part because the Clinton White House showed its seriousness in creating opportunities for women, and Hillary Clinton personified the capable, educated professional who was such a threat to male advantage. The gender gap returned with a vengeance: angry males turned out for the Republicans, while females rested on their 1992 laurels with a lower than normal turnout. Men voted 57 percent Republican and 43 percent Democratic; women voted 54 percent Democratic and 46 percent Republican. The turnout of women decreased 6 percent from 1990, while the turnout of men increased 7 percent. Final polls and exit polls captured a sullen mood, particularly among men who voted. A larger-than-normal mobilization for a congressional election was found especially among evangelicals. This too favored the Republicans and was based on a rejection of Hillary and Bill Clinton's values.

For the first time a substantial number of avowedly antifeminist Republican women were elected to the House, including six who had gotten their start in anti-abortion organizations (Melich 1996, 284). These types of women had come a long way from the anti-ERA and anti-abortion drives of the 1970s. Now they would enter the den of the enemy, the well of the House floor. All were well funded by religious political action committees. Some moved into leadership roles in a freshman class that promised to shape American politics for some time to come. The spotlight now focused on *competing* groups of women: (1) those speaking for an emerging moral order on gender and (2) those seeking to preserve an earlier moral order on gender.

Many analysts had spoken of the early Clinton years as a co-presidency. Hillary Rodham came to symbolize to many women and men what a woman can and should do in the public arena. She was an advocate and a role model. She had deep roots in Methodism, with its social transformationist ethic. However, to other women and men she was an object lesson of compromised values that result when men's specialized roles and women's specialized roles are mingled. Some fundamentalist Christians argued for a return to the "order of creation" where males were clearly dominant. For his part, Bill Clinton never successfully dispelled the perception of him as a womanizer. During the first term, the Paula Jones charges of sexual harrassment moved in and out of the news, and there were lurid rumors of unwanted sexual advances toward one White House volunteer and of trysts with a young intern, later shown to be true. Nevertheless, the 1996 election proceeded with an undercurrent rather than a tidal wave of attention to Clinton's personal life. Instead, Clinton focused much of the attention on how his social welfare and job opportunity policies were beneficial to families, especially women and children, and how a healthy economy could contribute to healthy families, however constituted. Women's ratings of President Clinton remained at the same level in 1992 and 1996, although they declined in 1994; men's ratings dropped almost 10 points in 1994 and recouped only half of that by 1996. Most of the positivity in women's ratings could be accounted for by approval of Clinton's social welfare policies (Norrander 1999, 155–60). For many women, policy appeared to have trumped character. For other men and women, removing Clinton became almost a national obsession.

In 1996, again, the stridency of the opposition allowed the Clinton campaign to caution about the dangers of theocracy. Religion informing politics, Clinton's people said, could be healthy because it holds up a vision of social justice, forgiveness, and community. Nevertheless, when religion controls politics, it becomes coercive of behavior and disrespectful of diversity. If both the White House and Capitol Hill were controlled by the Religious Right through the Republican party, they concluded, the country would suffer for it. In that climate, gender issues became part of the core definitions of the parties.

The crystallized imagery of two parties divided by moral restorationism, as described in chapter 7, seems to be an end product of the collision among feminists' desire for a more egalitarian society, pietistic churches' sense of threat posed by changing norms, and political elites' needs to amalgamate winning coalitions. This is not to argue that ambi-

218 • Chapter Ten

tious politicians were crassly motivated by counting votes. Many, if not most, on the cultural Right believed what they were saying about moral decay; and on the cultural Left, many believed what they were saying about deprivation of opportunity or rights. Rather, it is to recognize that both symbolic and policy change do not occur without the votes. We now examine the evidence of partisan change resulting from the tangled web of gender and religious issues and groups, and politicians' themes.

THE CHANGING GENDER AND INTRAGENDER BASES OF THE PARTIES

The *gender gap* has been measured in either of two ways: (1) party identification or (2) presidential or congressional vote choice. It measures the distance between the proportion of one sex having one characteristic—e.g., proportion of men voting Republican—and the proportion of the other sex having that characteristic—e.g., the proportion of women voting Republican. Typically the proportion is calculated on the base of the characteristic—e.g., all people voting for the two parties. What such a measure does is to ignore third-party voters or those who chose not to vote. When the gender gap is based on party identification, typically it ignores independents and apoliticals.

We are introducing still another measure of the gender gap. It is the distance between men and women on the Democratic partisan advantage (or disadvantage) measure. This measure, as discussed in chapter 7, is derived from the differences between partisan yield scores. Thus, our gender gap is built on party identification, turnout, loyalty, and defection by party and sex through time. It reflects a politician's calculus of the true impact of partisanship—that is, it is the part of any party's loyalists who will faithfully vote for the party and not stay at home or defect. Contrasted with gender gap measures based on two-party identification alone, it is a far more reliable outcome measure. Contrasted with gender gap measures based on vote choice alone, it lacks information about true independents and apoliticals. We are not particularly troubled by the latter since independents and apoliticals are far less likely to vote and are a smaller part of the operative electorate than some would like to claim, and since the practice of cultural politics by politicians is aimed more at turnout and defections of partisans than at fleeting alignments by independents.

Figure 10.1 shows the white, non-Latino gender gap as measured by the distance between men and women on the partisan advantage scores. As a more comprehensive measure than the other two, the gap is not quite so large and the pattern is fairly stable, with the exception of 1964, 1992, and 1996. When partisanship, turnout, and loyalty/defections are built in, men and women were about 3 to 7 points apart throughout

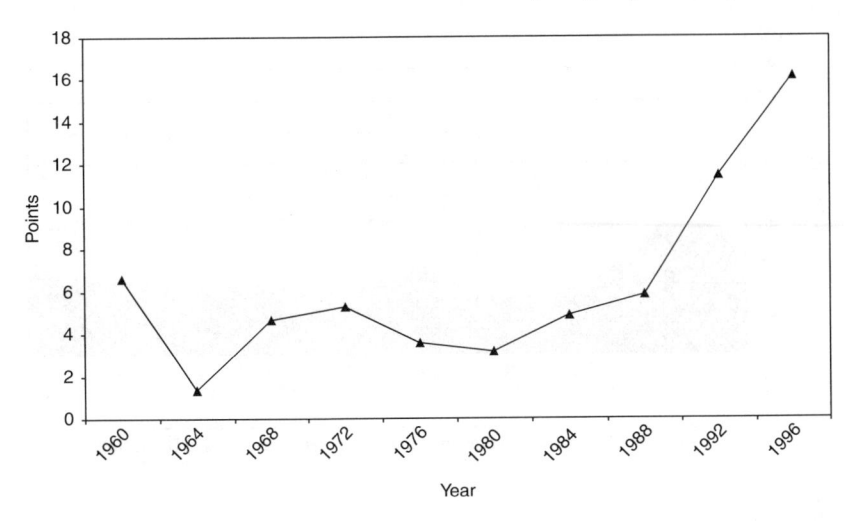

Figure 10.1. Gender Gap between Non-Latino, White Men and Women, 1960–1996

most of the post–New Deal period; consistently men were more Republican and women more Democratic. In 1992 and 1996 the gender gap grew to huge proportions, 12 to 16 points, respectively.

In data shown in figures 10.2 and 10.3, men start the period more Democratic than women and become more Republican than women beginning with the two Nixon elections of 1968 and 1972. From Reagan's first run in 1980 onward, they pull substantially ahead of women on the Republican side. In 1992 and 1996 it can clearly be said that the gender gap becomes very large by any indicator. Men went with Bush or Perot; women went with Clinton. The gap in 1992 is 12 points, reflecting the loss of patience with the Republican party by women activists. In 1996 the gap grew to a whopping 16 points, as men increased their Republican vote yield. From 1988 onward the partisan swings of men and women are so differentiated that each can be said to have its own voice. Prior to that, it appears that Republican messages, except in 1964, were considerably more attractive to men than to women; yet women, in the aggregate, swung in a similar manner. That is clearly a revisionist view of the gender gap. We need to get inside the tables to see what is happening to men and women in the campaigns that is different.

Men Versus Women

Examining figures 10.2 and 10.3 in detail, we can readily see that the New Majoritarian strategy aimed at male Democrats paid huge divi-

220 • Chapter Ten

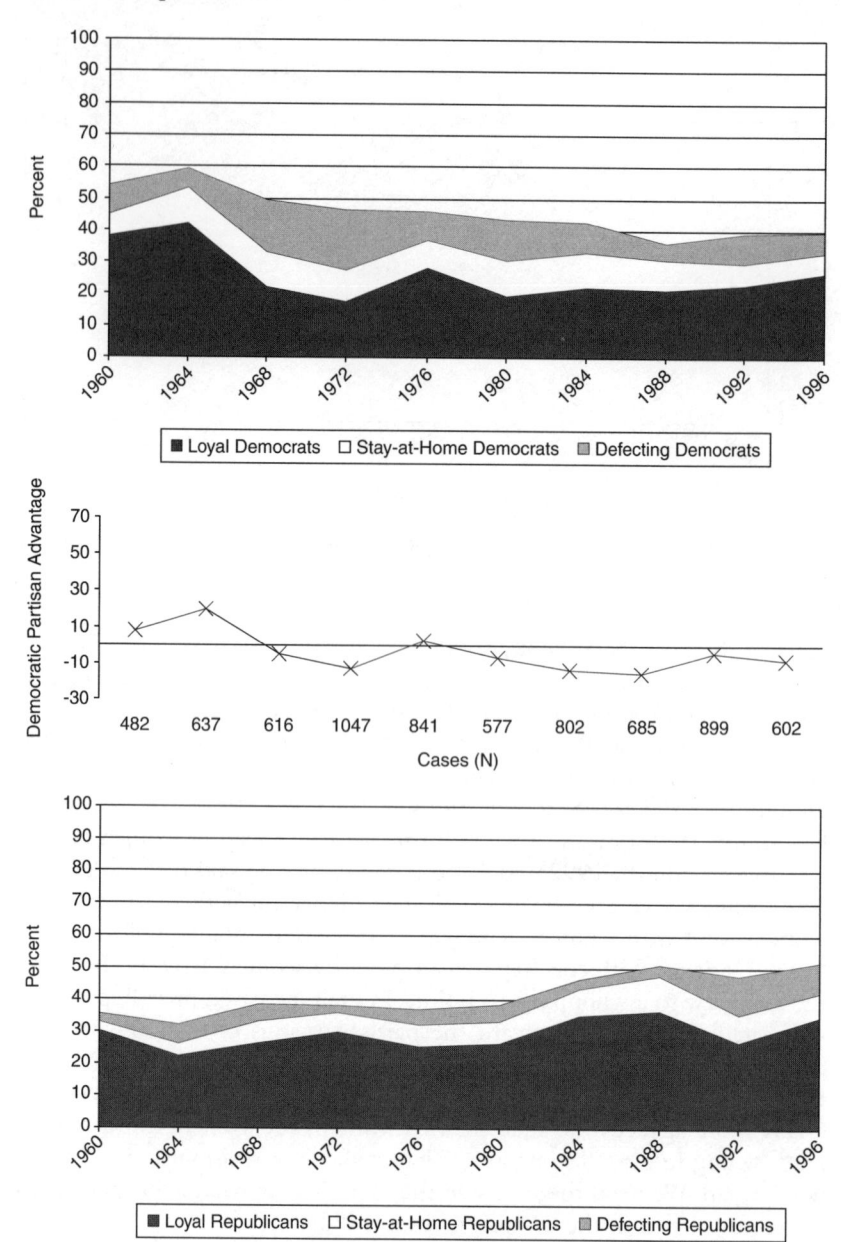

Figure 10.2. Partisan Patterns of All White, Non-Latino Men, 1960–1996

Gender, Religion, and Party • 221

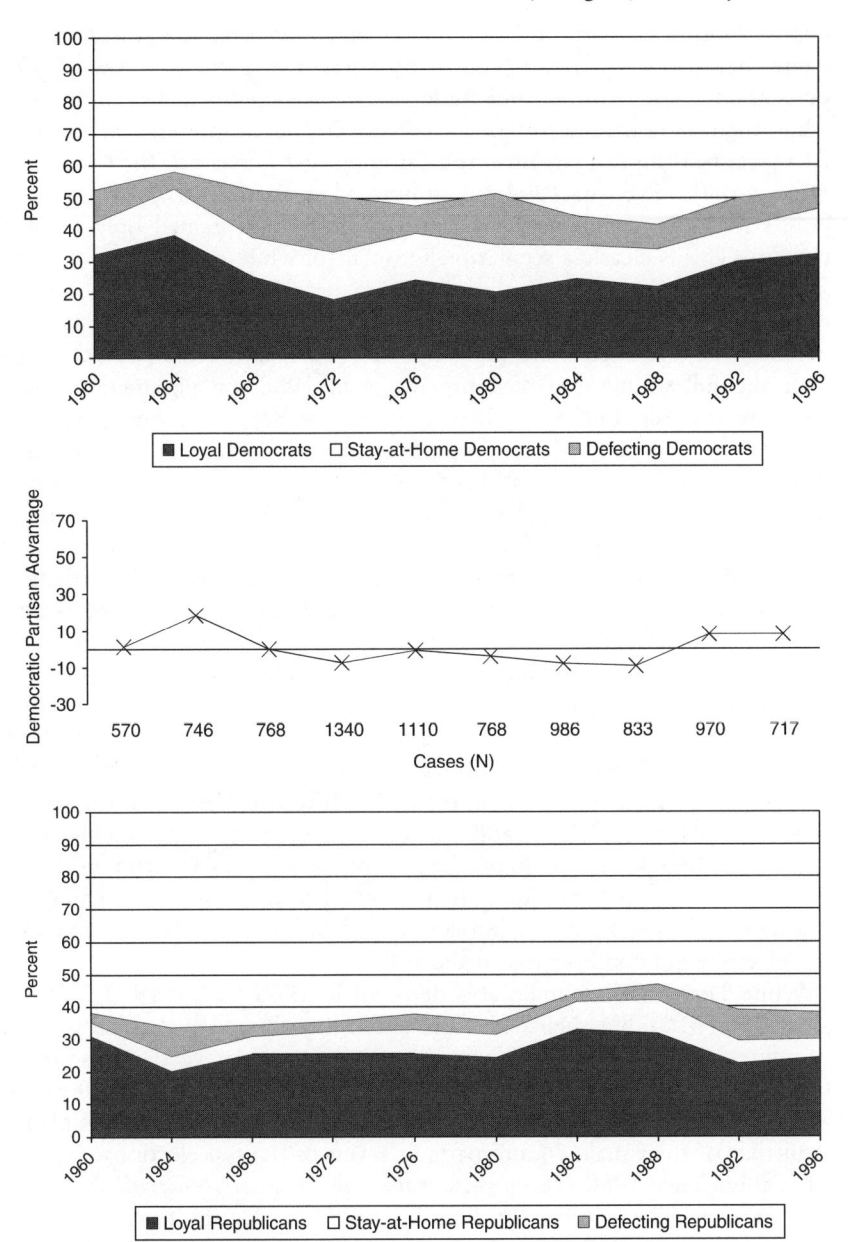

Figure 10.3. Partisan Patterns of All White, Non-Latino Women, 1960–1996

dends. During the time period, the Democratic party identification of white men dropped from a high of 59 percent in 1964 to a low of 36 percent in 1988. At the same time, Republican party identification in white men grew from a low of 32 percent in the Goldwater election to 51 percent in the Reagan-Bush transition and 52 percent in the Clinton-Dole contest. Even in 1992 Republican identification dropped only 3 points to 48 percent, and Democratic identification gained only to 39 percent. This is clearly a secular realignment of white men.

Along the way white Democratic men defected, massively in 1968 (33%), 1972 (40%), and 1980 (30%). The rate of defection among Democratic men remained quite high in 1984 (22%) and 1992 (24%), even after the full strength of realignment, as in 1988, or alignment, as in 1984, to the Republican side had set in. White Republican men, on the other hand, defected in large proportions only in 1992, when Perot was first on the ballot. Neither Wallace nor Anderson drew many white Republican men. The turnout advantage among men always favored the Republicans by about 6 or 7 points, except for near parity in 1976, 1992, and 1996, all Democratic years. In data not shown here, independents grew in size from 1972 to 1980, but Republican alignment of baby boomers was clear by Reagan's reelection in 1984.

The contrast between white women and white men is striking indeed. Democratic party identification for the women typically stayed at or above 50 percent except in the later Reagan-Bush years (44% in 1984, 42% in 1988). Republican identification stayed in the mid to high 30s and deviated to the mid to high 40s only in the later Reagan-Bush years (44% in 1984 and 47% in 1988). In contrast to men, whose secular realignment shifted them to Republican dominance by 1984, women were found on the Republican side only in 1988. The Republican strategy was not designed to make lasting inroads among women, and the outcome of the electoral era confirms that it did not.

White Democratic women also defected in 1968 (28%), 1972 (35%), and 1980 (31%), but their defections often slightly trailed the defections of white Democratic men. Their Democratic partisan yield was sometimes lower than men's because they failed to turn out. Even with lower turnout, the partisan yield among white Democratic women was higher than that of their male counterparts in seven of the ten elections and in all of them since 1980; *Democratic women did not defect or realign at the rate of men.* The pattern for Republican party identification of white women stayed much flatter than for men. Turnout was very high early in the time-series, as it was for Republican men, but it weakened, often at a slightly higher rate than for men, from 1968 on. *Defections of white Republican women, however, were much higher than the men.* In 1964, for example, 26 percent avoided Goldwater; in 1992, 25 percent avoided Bush, mainly in favor of Clinton; and in 1996, 22 percent avoided Dole.

The rate of defections among white Republican women seemed to pick up with the greater visibility of the New Right and Religious Right in their party's internal affairs and policies. In data not shown here, white women, among the boomers, were more likely to align than white men, with their rate of independence typically lower.

Close inspection of the tables reveals quite dramatic differences in the ways political strategies, policies, and events shaped the male and female electorates. Men came out of the upheavals of the 1960s looking to the Republican party. Women stayed with the Democratic party longer and by the late 1980s were even showing evidence of pulling away from the Republican party. By the 1990s the realignment of women with the Democratic party was in full bloom.

Generational Differences

When the data are examined by generation in tables not shown here, it is clear that the gender mosaic reflects realignment, dealignment, and mainly alignment. The generation that entered the electorate in the late 1960s, both men and women, entered with about the same level of Democratic identification as the New Deal generation at that time, but their rates of Republican identification were 10 points less for men and 13 points less for women because of much higher rates of independence. The first new alignment of post–New Deal women was in 1980 with 52 percent being Democrats, but 37 percent of them did not vote and 30 percent defected to Reagan or Anderson. Suddenly in 1984 Democratic identification plunged by 10 percent, and in 1988 by another 6 percent, as Republican realignment rocketed to 42 percent and 49 percent, respectively. In 1992 the temporal fragility of this realignment was evident as women flipped back to 49 percent Democratic and 38 percent Republican; this grew even further in 1996 to 54 percent Democratic and 36 percent Republican. Given such volatility, it is difficult to say what party identification means for post–New Deal white women. Yet by the mid-1990s it accounted for most of the gender gap.

The post–New Deal generation of white men did not lose most of its independents until 1984. In 1980 partisanship was at parity, 37 percent Democratic and 38 percent Republican with 23 percent independent and 3 percent apolitical. In 1984 independents plunged 11 percent and Republican identification rose 11 percent, indicating almost certainly first-time alignment with the Republicans. From there Democratic identification declined with only a 5 percent rebound in 1992 and another 3 percent in 1996; Republican identification after 1984 stayed stable between 49 percent and 52 percent. For young white males, alignment came with Reagan's Republican party; they showed substantial disloyalty only in 1992 and 1996. For young females, the Democratic party continued to be advantaged as a psychological home, but low turnout and defections rendered them very unreliable.

The New Deal generation's white men were in the eye of the New Majoritarian hurricane. Both men and women were well attached to the Democratic party going into the 1960s. But massive defections, far more for the men than for the women (36% to 29%), began in 1968. Defections peaked in 1972 (47% and 40%). Interestingly, the men came back slightly more to the party in 1976 than did the women (61% loyal to 58% loyal), and in 1980 the women defected at a slightly higher rate (33% to 30%). Then the Republican realignment started; for the men it continued by 6 percent each quadrennium through the Reagan-Bush years, but for the women it moved back in a Democratic direction the more they saw of the Reagan-Bush party. In this generation, then, the women initially looked a lot like the men, but they found a separate voice as the 1980s wore on.

The data leave little doubt that men and women in both the New Deal and post–New Deal generations are pulling apart politically. By 1996, 51 percent of New Deal women identified as Democrats while only 40 percent of their male cohort were Democrats; among post–New Dealers the gap is larger: 54 percent of women are Democrats and 40 percent of men share that identification. Their movement can be seen in figure 10.4a and figure 10.4b. Some New Deal men were attracted away from their historic party ties. Many post–New Deal men drifted politically but set anchor with the Republicans. The women of their generation started to drift Republican but abruptly set sail back toward the Democrats.

As much as generational and gender analysis can tell us, the explanations for this differential movement are found in finer groupings of women and men by occupational subculture, region, and religious tradition. We learned, for example, that men needed do little to halt the ratification of the ERA; cultural conflict between different types of women helped it stall. We learned that the "Southern strategy," aimed especially at Southern segregationists and evangelicals, was expanded to the "New Majoritarian" strategy aimed at Catholic and blue-collar voters, especially men. Finally, we learned that the Democratic counterthreats of control by theocrats were aimed at mainline Protestants, emancipated women, and the well-educated. To such categories we now direct our analysis of the appeals and counterappeals surrounding moral restorationism.

Housewives versus Women in Professional/Managerial Roles

The conflict over the ratification of the Equal Rights Amendment and over reproductive freedoms involved pitched battles between women employed in the professional and managerial ranks and women who re-

Gender, Religion, and Party • 225

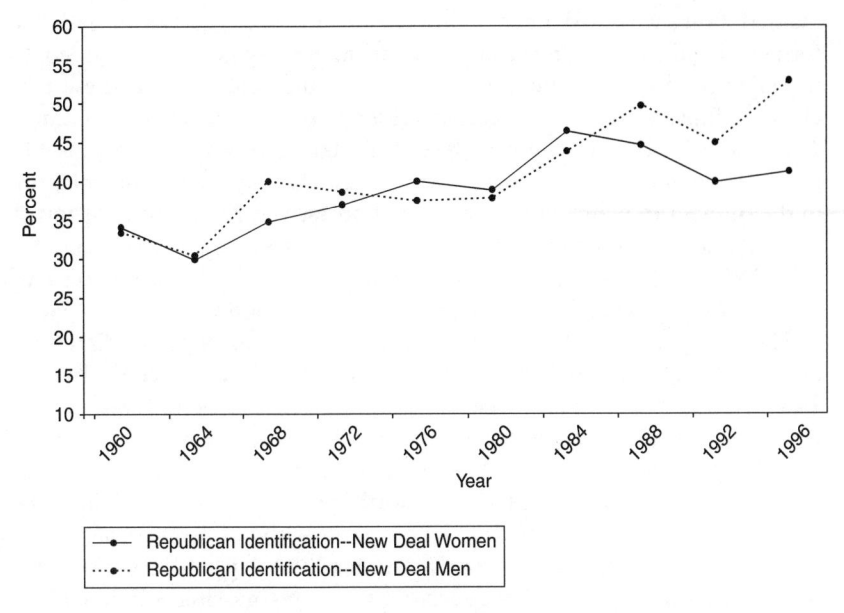

Figure 10.4a. Republican Identification by Sex, New Deal Generation, 1960–1996

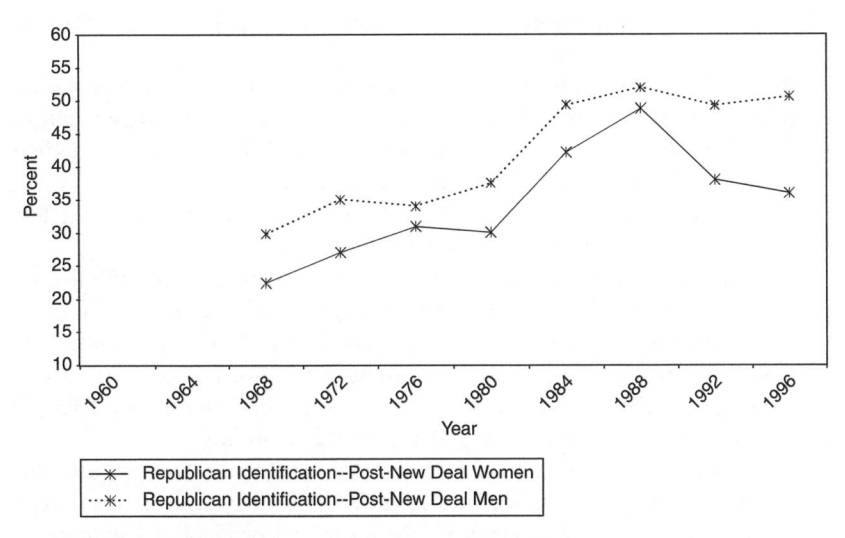

Figure 10.4b. Republican Identification by Sex, Post–New Deal Generation, 1960–1996

mained housewives. Women's movement organizations mobilized the former. Traditionalist and evangelical women's organizations tended to mobilize the latter. In the data on rank-and-file voters within these two classifications, we see considerable evidence of partisan change. Figures 10.5 and 10.6 present the evidence. Note conspicuously the decline between 1976 and 1980, after the great oil shocks and exorbitant inflation, in the number of white women who are housewives. Note also the growth of white women employed in professional and managerial occupations after 1968, a decade earlier. These alone are vivid evidence not only of the changing generations but of the changed economy.

The two groups under comparison have moved in opposite directions in their politics. Housewives began the era solidly Democratic but by 1984 moved solidly Republican and concluded the period with a 14-point advantage in Republican identification. Professional women responded to different forces. Over the period as a whole, the loyalties of professional women flipped back and forth between the parties. While the rest of the country was moving Democratic with Johnson, professional women were moving Republican; yet a lot (27%) defected. As the country was moving Republican with Nixon, they were moving solidly Democratic with McGovern's party; again, a lot (34%) defected. In 1980 Democratic defections, mainly to Anderson, some to Reagan, ballooned to 41 percent, the highest in the time-series. In 1992 the defection rate of Republican professional/managerial women was 36 percent, mainly to Clinton but many to Perot.

Professional and managerial women seldom called themselves "independents," and they voted at very high rates. Yet their partisan alignments themselves were volatile, and they defected in patterns that defied their new realignments. They were actually more independent than most other sectors of the electorate, in that the party appeared to be a less important reference group than was something else.

In general, the partisan yield of the white housewives was quite similar to the partisan yield of white men. Turnout was very low among the Democrats; their defection rate was also high, thus diminishing any Democratic partisan advantage. The Republican housewives turned out well except for the period from 1972 to 1984, and they seldom defected like their sisters who worked at the top of the economy.

Generational cohorts interact with occupational categories in quite different ways among white women. Figure 10.7 maps the partisan vote yields for each of the four groups. Business and professional women of the New Deal generation are generally found on the Republican side of the ledger, except in 1960 and 1988 and 1992. New Deal housewives yield votes heavily for the Democratic party in the early 1960s, but by 1972 they swing just as heavily to the Republicans, with the exception of

Gender, Religion, and Party • 227

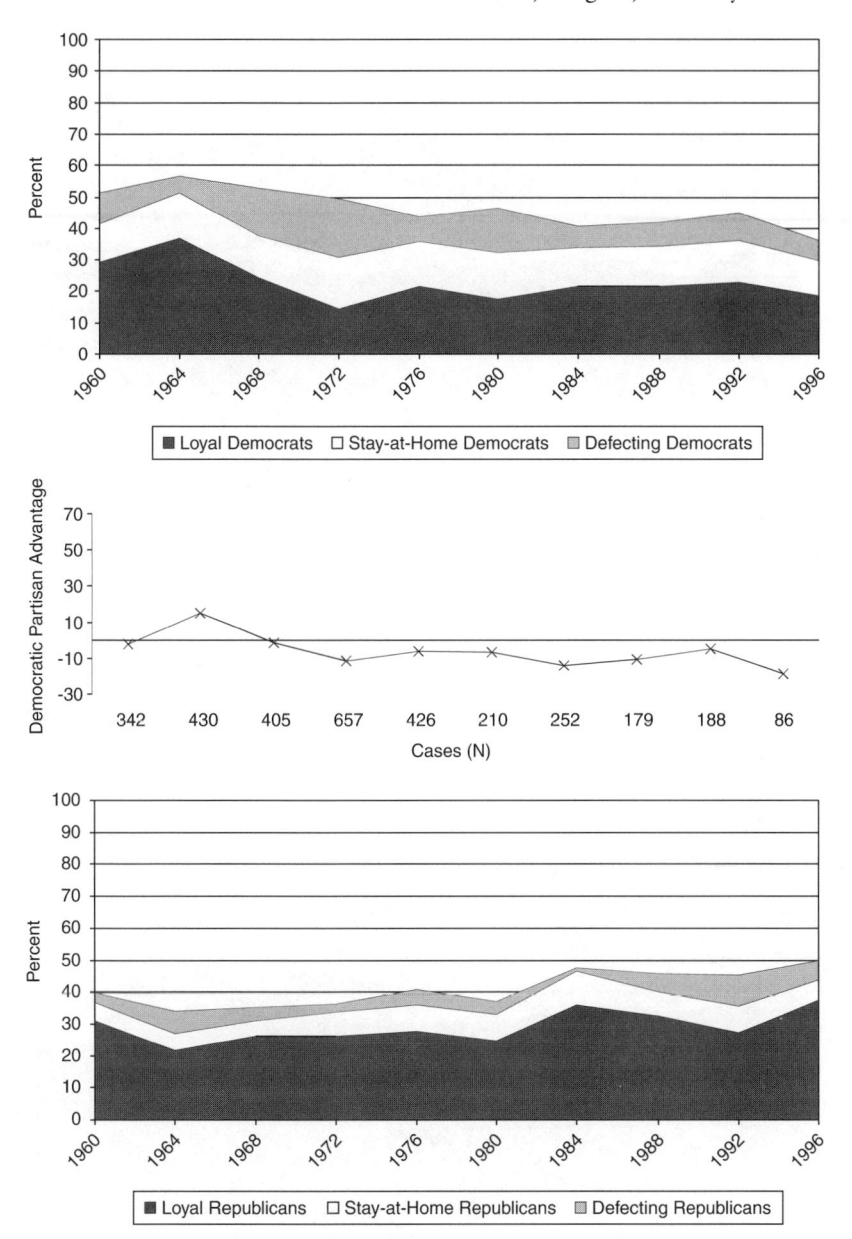

Figure 10.5. Partisan Patterns of All White, Non-Latino Housewives, 1960–1996

228 • Chapter Ten

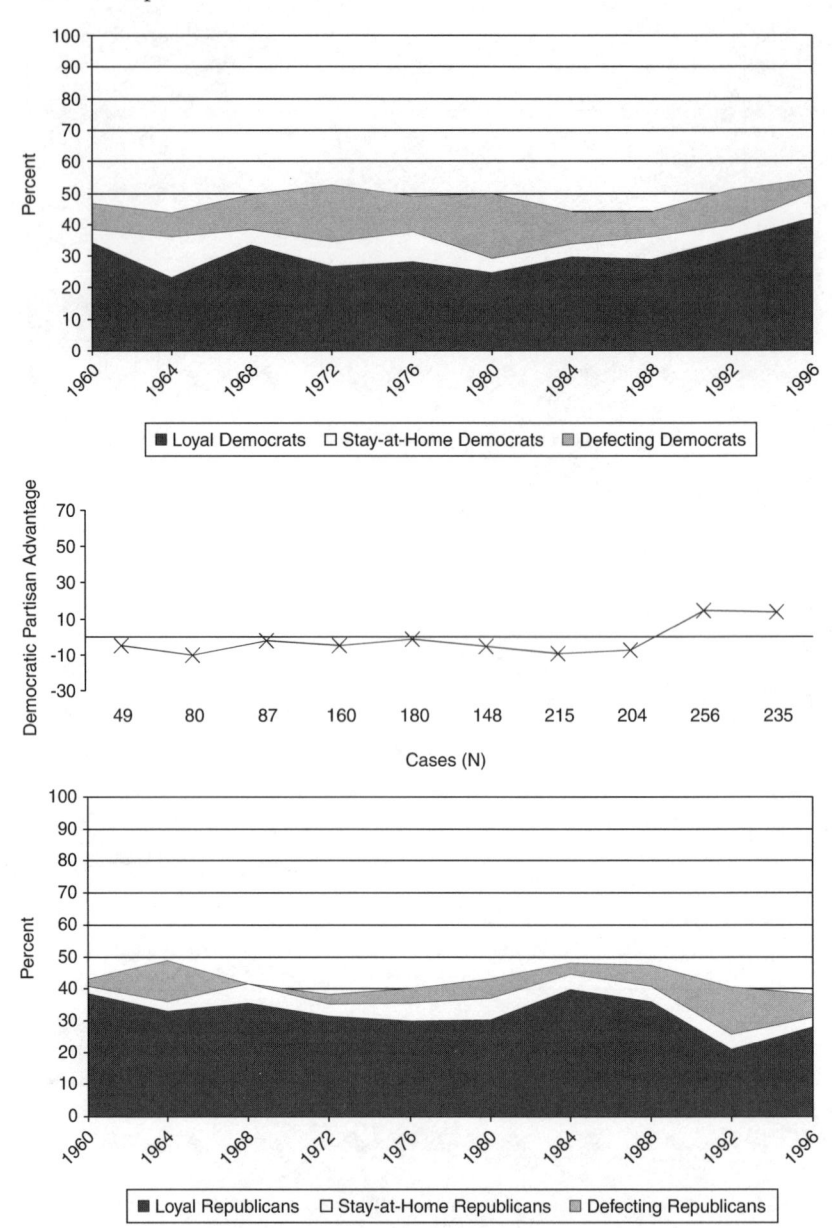

Figure 10.6. Partisan Patterns of White, Non-Latino Women in Business or Professional Occupations, 1960–1996

Gender, Religion, and Party • 229

[Figure: line chart showing Democratic Partisan Advantage from 1960 to 1996 for four groups: New Deal Housewives, New Deal Business and Professional Women, Post-New Deal Housewives, Post-New Deal Business and Professional Women]

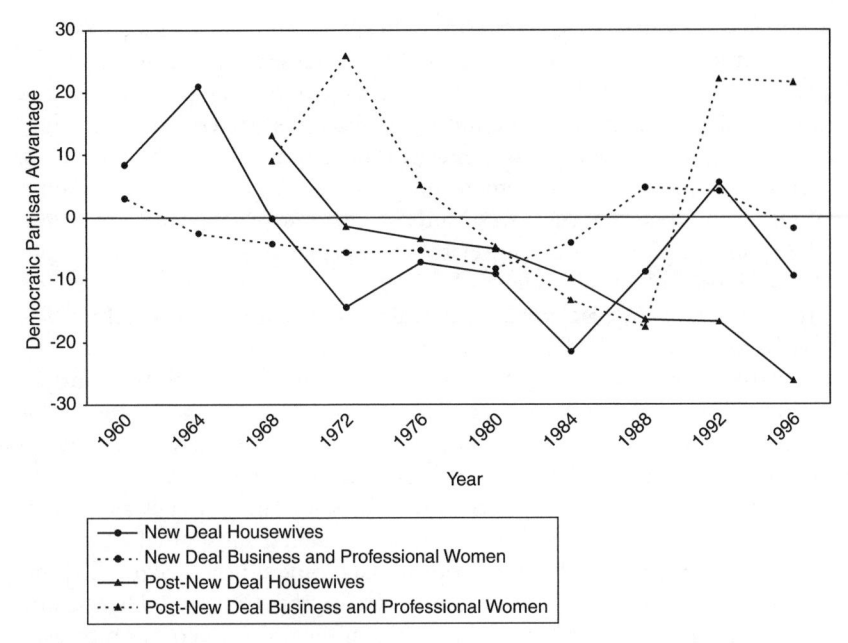

Figure 10.7. Partisan Vote Yields among White Women, by Generation and Occupational Classification, 1960–1996

1992. Younger housewives start on the Democratic side in 1968 but shift quickly to the Republicans and now deliver to them the most reliable vote bloc of any women's group. Younger business and professional women, on the other hand, peak heavily Democratic on three occasions—McGovern, and the two Clinton elections. Precisely the candidates whom Republicans have pilloried as countercultural or morally degraded are the Democrats who have heavily attracted younger business and professional women.

The largest gap of any kind found in our data on cultural politics is evident in 1996 between white business and professional women and homemakers from the post–New Deal generation—nearly a 50-point difference in partisan yields. The rift first evident at the time of the ERA has grown into a huge chasm. It outstrips the gender gap and exceeds even racial differences. It is probably the greatest cultural conflict currently evident in the electorate—the young housewives finding fulfillment in motherhood, and the young, educated business and professional women pursing success outside the home. To the factor analyses we now turn to find what kinds of issue and group differences account for this widening gap.

In tables too numerous to show here, we have compared Republican and Democratic business and professional women and Republican and

Democratic housewives. *Democratic* business and professional women defected in 1972 and from 1984 to 1992 because they did not like their party's stands on racial issues and the racial groups they perceived at the core of the party. In 1996 the moral restorationist factor depressed their turnout but had only a modest effect on defection. Although *Republican* business and professional women remained very loyal to their party until 1980, from then on they were almost the mirror opposite. In 1980, 1988, and 1992 they were upset by the Reagan-Bush party's racial policies and uses of racial codewords. But they were also among the first groups to leave the party over its appeals to the Religious Right. In 1984, 1992, and 1996 their defections can be accounted for almost entirely by the party's conservative positions on gender and family lifestyle, and by the visibility it gives to its evangelical religious core. By the 1990s defection was huge, almost half as much as party loyalty. They seemed to accept the Democratic cultural appeals that the Republican party is now more interested in a homogeneous definition of family values and career success, one that differs from their own. Further, a substantial portion of them, particularly the younger professional women, now realigned Democratic. They were at the emerging core of the Clintons' Democratic party. And their proportion of the total number of women has increased each decade.

Democratic homemakers, on the other hand, were especially responsive to Republican cultural appeals during the first two decades of the post–New Deal period. Initially they stayed at home or defected to the Republicans out of concern for U.S. resolve against communism (1960 and 1964), by 1968 they had lost trust in Democratic government, and from 1968 to 1976 they responded to Republican appeals on the racial agenda. Concern over moral decay and the pace of social change initially depressed the turnout of these Democratic homemakers in 1976 and 1980, and there was modest defection to Reagan in the latter year. But from 1980 their story is told on the Republican side of the ledger. They realigned Republican, with the party that reaffirmed respect for homemakers. The diminishing number who remained Democratic were affected by racial concerns in 1988 and moral decay in 1992, but in each case it suppressed turnout rather than encouraging defection. In most years, demographic factors are better at explaining turnout failures.

In summary, Republican appeals along the family values issues and their pillorying of groups that fail to live appropriate moral lives have reached many homemakers—so much so that a considerable realignment occurred. The same appeals and negative outgroup targeting, however, led to major backdoor losses among a natural constituency of the Republican party through history—business and professional women. For older women in this category, defection was high. For younger women, realignment occurred in the 1990s. Given the opposite growth curves of the two groups, the party that attracts the business and professional women on a more permanent basis probably has the brighter future; there are far fewer housewives.

Patterns of Ethnoreligious Group Behavior

How did the major religious groups respond to the tumultuous cultural politics of the postwar era? Table 10.1 traces the partisan habits of the major religious traditions over time. Many generalizations can be drawn from this table, only some of which match the conventional wisdom (Leege 1993a). When turnout becomes part of the political calculus, we learn from table 10.1 that white Protestants from both the mainline and evangelical traditions have contributed the most to the Republican vote.[13] The other religious groups—Catholics, Jews, Hispanics, African American Christians and seculars—gave the bulk of their support to the Democratic ticket. Party loyalty is almost always stronger on the Republican side within these ethnoreligious traditions than on the Democratic side. Mainline Protestants wavered in the 1964 Johnson landslide and in the presidential elections of the 1990s. Catholic Republicans found it harder to resist Kennedy's successor, Lyndon Johnson, and were far less loyal in the 1990s. There simply are not many black Republicans after 1964, and the volatility of the Hispanic figures reflects small samples. With the single exception of 1964, the white mainline Protestants were arrayed on the Republican side of the partisan identification continuum. That election also marked the only occasion when this category actually yielded a net voting advantage to the Democrats. The 1964 post-assassination pattern was the product of a short-term, pro-Democratic shift in partisan identification, with unprecedented levels of loyalty among Democrats, and large defections to Johnson (22%) among self-identified Republicans (specific defection and turnout data not shown). The Republican advantage was also narrowed appreciably in 1992 when 31 percent defected, and in 1996 when 21 percent defected. Although there was a modest increase in the level of defection to Clinton among Republican mainliners, most of the defectors ended up in the Perot column.

White evangelicals provide one of the big surprises of the time-series. Contrary to the conventional wisdom, they have provided a net voting advantage to Republicans for most of the period under study. In part, the

[13] The classification scheme, particularly the coding judgments that separate white evangelical Protestants from white mainline Protestants, results from the collective efforts of several scholars under the lead of Lyman Kellstedt. These are summarized in Kellstedt and Green (1993). The extension of this work to ethnoreligious traditions is described in Leege (1993a). The latter scheme is used here.

TABLE 10.1
Partisanship of Ethnoreligious Traditions, 1960–1996: Party Identification, Party Loyalty, Partisan Vote Yield, and Partisan Advantage

	1960	1964	1968	1972	1976	1980	1984	1988	1992	1996
Mainline Protestants, White Non-Latino										
% Dem	40	47	43	39	37	38	38	36	36	41
% Loyal	63	70	45	40	58	48	50	53	61	73
Yield	25	33	19	16	21	17	19	19	22	30
% Rep	51	46	49	47	49	47	54	55	52	51
% Loyal	90	68	76	79	72	71	76	72	54	69
Yield	45	31	37	37	35	33	41	39	28	35
Dem. Advantage	−21	1	−18	−21	−14	−16	−22	−20	−6	−6
Evangelical Protestants, White Non-Latino										
% Dem	59	68	52	48	46	52	37	39	39	40
% Loyal	41	53	28	19	49	39	43	40	46	52
Yield	24	36	14	9	23	20	16	15	18	21
% Rep	30	23	32	36	35	33	49	48	50	52
% Loyal	80	58	60	66	68	68	71	69	66	69
Yield	24	12	19	23	24	23	35	33	33	36
Dem. Advantage	0	22	−5	−14	−1	−2	−19	−18	−15	−15
White Roman Catholics, Non-Latino										
% Dem	73	69	63	62	61	54	52	45	53	52
% Loyal	87	79	61	39	58	45	60	67	64	65
Yield	64	55	39	24	35	25	31	30	33	33
% Rep	19	22	25	25	26	31	36	45	36	41
% Loyal	60	65	72	77	66	68	83	73	60	67
Yield	11	14	18	19	17	21	30	33	22	27
Dem. Advantage	53	40	21	5	18	4	1	−3	12	6
Black Christians										
% Dem	51	83	92	76	88	83	79	82	77	81
% Loyal	56	68	68	64	65	69	62	62	69	66
Yield	29	57	62	49	57	57	49	51	53	54
% Rep	23	8	2	11	6	8	10	11	8	8
% Loyal	32	0	33	22	0	20	17	10	24	8
Yield	7	0	1	2	0	2	2	1	2	1

TABLE 10.1
Continued

	1960	1964	1968	1972	1976	1980	1984	1988	1992	1996
Dem. Advantage	21	57	61	57	57	55	47	50	51	53
Hispanic Christians										
% Dem						55	54	60	57	66
% Loyal						41	42	65	53	63
Yield						22	23	39	30	42
% Rep						25	23	27	29	24
% Loyal						33	61	77	37	67
Yield						8	14	50	11	16
Dem. Advantage						14	9	18	20	26
Jews										
% Dem	73	76	76	75	64	88	73	55	87	78
% Loyal	93	93	85	74	77	44	73	73	84	87
Yield	68	70	64	56	49	39	54	40	74	68
% Rep	14	11	7	13	25	10	19	26	9	13
% Loyal	60	25	0	71	58	60	70	43	75	33
Yield	8	3	0	9	15	6	13	11	6	4
Dem. Advantage	59	67	64	47	34	33	40	29	67	64
Seculars										
% Dem	59	56	50	53	50	46	48	39	51	57
% Loyal	63	56	48	62	46	30	63	71	61	55
Yield	37	32	24	33	23	14	30	28	31	32
% Rep	29	25	24	24	25	29	30	37	31	29
% Loyal	50	64	46	67	29	62	61	33	35	43
Yield	14	16	11	16	7	18	18	21	11	12
Dem. Advantage	22	16	13	17	15	−4	12	7	20	19

slow erosion of Democratic partisan identification has disguised the pattern. The table documents that evangelicals' substantial Democratic identification began to erode as early as 1968 but did not produce a Republican surplus in party identification until 1984. Since then the preponderance of evangelicals have identified as Republicans. Despite the gradual decline of Democratic partisanship, evangelicals ceased to provide a Democratic voting advantage much earlier. In fact, they constituted a Democratic voting bloc only in 1964. When the ticket was headed by a fellow evangelical and Southerner in 1976 and 1980, evangelicals came close to giving the Democrats a majority of their vote yield. In 1960, despite a 2–1 Democratic advantage in party identification, massive defections among Democrats and record high levels of cohesion among Republicans balanced out, leaving evangelicals evenly divided between the two presidential candidates. The patterns returned to New Deal levels in 1964, the last election when evangelicals provided a significant electoral advantage to the Democrats. Since then, excepting only the near ties in 1976 and 1980, partisan yields have solidly favored Republicans. In the 1990s evangelicals became more reliable Republican coalition partners than were mainline Protestants.

We first examined the behavioral trends among non-Hispanic, white Catholics in chapter 8. As we saw there, white Catholics began the post–New Deal time-series with predictably (and artificially) high partisan vote yields for fellow Catholic Kennedy and his torch-bearer Johnson. Party identification was highly Democratic, and Democratic loyalty approximated or exceeded the level to which Republicans were accustomed. Then, in quick succession, came the debacle of Mayor Daley's Chicago convention, followed by the reform takeover in 1972. A slight but evident decline in party identification was coupled with a party loyalty score that bottomed out in 1972 at 39 percent. If the new Democratic party rejected the recognizably Catholic big-city leaders, rank-and-file white Catholics would take a walk. Some Catholics did not walk en masse to the Republican side of the aisle, where the increase in identification and yield was still modest, but simply avoided voting altogether (19%) or, more likely, defected to Nixon (42%). Democratic identification continued to drop and Republican identification to surge during the Reagan era. George Bush managed actually to increase the level of Catholic Republican identification in 1988, but his support among Catholics hemorrhaged in 1992. This was particularly true among Catholic Republicans who had not been so disloyal to a Republican presidential candidate since 1960 and 1964. Those defections, coupled with the rise in Democratic identification, brought the Catholic vote sharply back into the Democratic column in 1992, with a slight drop in 1996.

Because African Americans remain overwhelmingly Christian in religious affiliation, the story of their political evolution was effectively told in chapter 9. The Hispanic Christian data are limited to years after 1976 and rest on small samples. Nonetheless, Hispanics are somewhere in between blacks and white, non-Latino Catholics in their high levels of Democratic identification, loyalty, and Democratic yield. Like blacks, the net electoral advantage to the Democrats is diminished by very low turnout. As noted by Verba and associates (1995), the church has functioned as a political resource for African Americans but is barely beginning to play the same role for Latinos. Worth noting, however, is that since 1984 the Democratic partisan advantage among Latinos has risen steadily from 9 points to 26 points in 1996. The increase is largely the result of fewer defections by Latino Christian Democrats and greater defection by Latino Christian Republicans.

The small number of Jewish respondents contribute to some of the volatility exhibited by that subsample. Nonetheless, the Democratic identification of Jewish respondents nearly matches the post-1964 level among African American Christians, and the party loyalty measure among Democrats is the highest recorded within any religious group. Those African Americans who vote may be just as loyal, but Jewish turnout is so much higher that the Democratic yield of the two groups is nearly equal. However, the recognizable Republican presence among Jews and the slightly higher rate of independence depress the net Democratic advantage, bringing it slightly below the figure recorded for African Americans in some years. In both 1976 and 1980, the Carter years, the Democratic partisan advantage was depressed; recalling that evangelical Protestant Carter called for a more "balanced" foreign policy toward Israel and the Palestinians helps to explain the 44 percent defection rate among Jewish Democrats in 1980. The Democratic yield was low in 1988, as well, as Democratic identification took a plunge, but it returned to historic highs in the Clinton years, as the Republican party became the party of the Religious Right.

Although not an organized religious tradition, seculars present patterns worth noting simply because they constitute a growing proportion of the total electorate. Throughout the time-series, seculars display a Democratic advantage in party identification and partisan vote yield. Low turnouts, however, affect the magnitude of the yields for both parties. Seculars who are disloyal are less likely to have voted at all than to have crossed over to the opposition party. The seculars' partisan yield may advantage the Democrats, but it is considerably less valuable than Catholics' partisan yield. It is least likely of all the religious groupings to show either volatility or a stable trend. The most striking aspect of secular voting was the pro-Democratic surge in 1972 when the Democrats embraced the "New Politics" standard by nominating George McGovern.

Higher turnout among Democratic seculars raised the Democratic partisan yield among this group by 9 points. In the same election, other core Democratic groups were significantly reducing their contribution to the Democrats. Like Jews in 1980, however, secular Democrats deserted the party of Jimmy Carter in droves; party identification dropped 4 percent, 32 percent did not vote, and 38 percent defected, leaving the only instance in the time-series when partisan advantage favored Reagan's Republican party—among seculars. When it was clear in the 1990s that evangelical Protestants formed the principal base of the Republican party, secular yields substantially favored the Democrats. But then it was because of low turnout and high defections by secular Republicans.

Another Great Reversal

Figure 10.8 reports the *Republican partisan advantage*[14] for the two largest groups of Protestants, the mainline and the evangelicals, documenting first the erosion of the political differences between these two groups and then their reversal. Through the election of 1980, the two Protestant groups had moved in tandem, but always with a gap that made the mainline Protestants 10–15 percent more Republican. In the elections of 1984 and 1988, the differences between them eroded and they converged on a common level of Republicanism. The convergence was mostly the product of change among the evangelicals who became appreciably more Republican in partisanship and more loyal to the GOP, while the shrinking Democratic remnant has been less likely to act on its partisanship in the voting booth. In the two Clinton elections, the mainline and evangelical Protestants scissored apart. What now makes evangelicals a more reliable coalition partner than the mainline Protestants? If we disaggregate the loyalty measures into their two components—nonvoting and defection to another candidate—it becomes clear that greater evangelical commitment to the Republican party was blunted for many years by the appreciably lower voter turnout within this community. Relatively few evangelical Republicans defected, especially when compared to their mainline counterparts, but they were still much less likely to vote at all. By the 1990s, however, evangelicals had only slightly lower turnout rates than mainliners, and these were balanced by higher defection rates among mainliners. Thus, the religious center of gravity has shifted in the Republican party to the evangelicals.

---

[14] This measure is similar to the Democratic partisan advantage described above except that it subtracts the Democratic yield from the Republican yield.

Gender, Religion, and Party • 237

[Figure: line chart showing Republican Partisan Advantage from 1960 to 1996 for Non-Latino, White Mainline Protestants (solid line) and Non-Latino, White Evangelical Protestants (dashed line).]

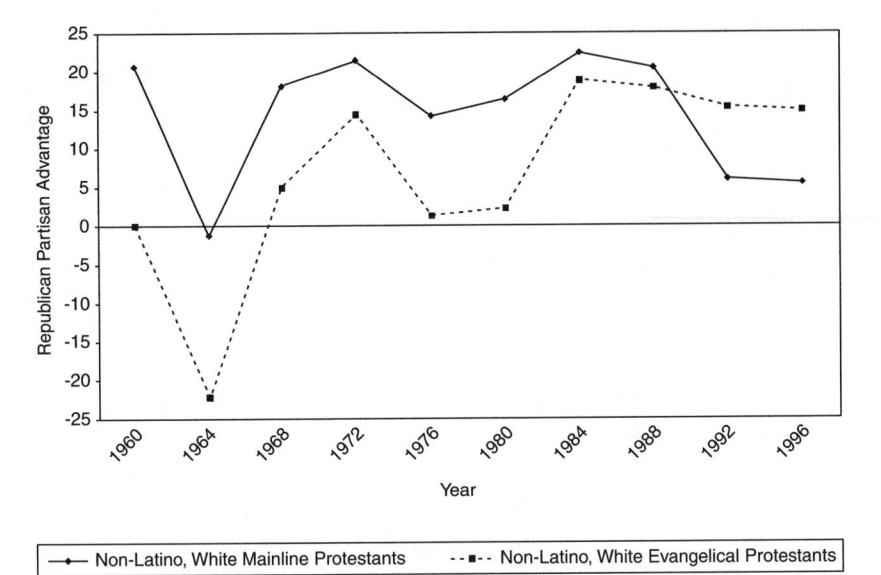

Figure 10.8. Republican Voting Tendencies of Mainline and Evangelical Protestants, 1960–1996

The Declining Significance of Catholics vs. Protestants

Another major change captured by the data is the shift in the magnitude of the Catholic-Protestant cleavage. With the decline in what we have called confessional politics, we anticipated a drop in the significance of this cleavage, and that expectation was confirmed by the data. In figure 10.9, we have charted the shifts in the *Democratic partisan advantage* for all Catholics and Protestants regardless of region or race and have extended the time-series back to 1952 in order to place the 1960 result in historical perspective. Because it is based on measures that factor in defection and nonvoting, this cumulative measure of partisan advantage takes into account the net contribution of each group to the electoral outcome. Figure 10.9 shows that the differences between Catholics and Protestants have certainly declined. Discounting the atypical case of 1960 when partisan polarization reached a historic peak, the general pattern was for the differential to hover in the 20 percent range through 1980 and then to descend to the 10 percent level, where it has remained ever since. On the one hand, the figure attests that the traditional dividing line of Catholic vs. Protestant is not as salient as it once was. To a degree, there has been a convergence to a common Christian partisanship. But on the other hand, the cleavage still is there.

238 • Chapter Ten

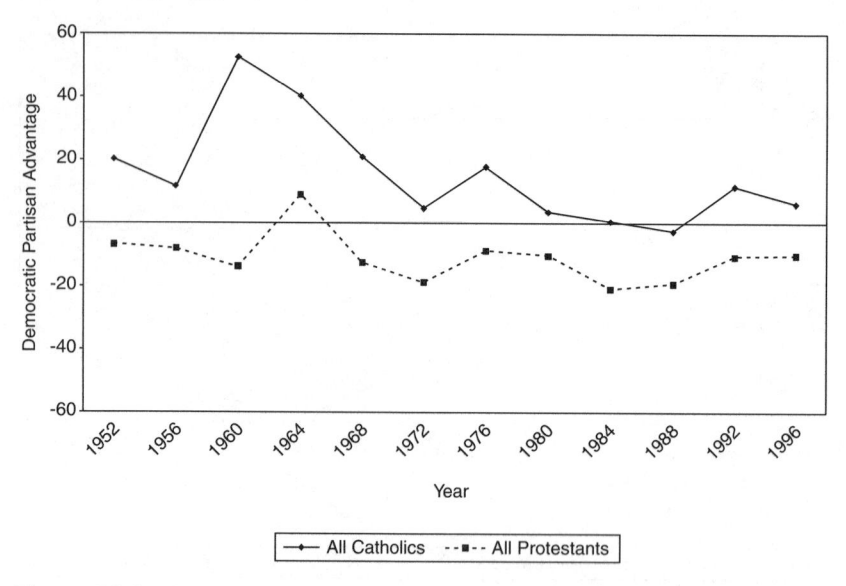

Figure 10.9. Democratic Partisan Advantage of Catholics and Protestants, 1952–1996

Group Affinity

Figure 10.10, which focuses on the behavior of white Southern evangelicals, illustrates another important cultural force in post-1960 electoral patterns—the tug of group affinity. Parties may find themselves capable of withstanding even strong electoral surges if they continue to be perceived as the "natural" home for voter groups. Just such a cognitive linkage between the Democratic party and the South enabled that party to draw reliably on Southern votes for years after the New Deal. As we have observed in chapters 8 and 9, this linkage weakened appreciably in 1960, when the party first nominated a Catholic, and began a long period of decay shortly thereafter. But in 1976 the party took a decisive step that appeared, even if temporarily, to call Southern Democrats home. The nomination of Jimmy Carter, a professed born-again evangelical, does appear to have interrupted the Republican realignment among his fellow Southern evangelicals (see 1976 and 1980).

From its artificially high point in 1964, Democratic identification among white Southern evangelicals began a free-fall that reduced support by a third in just eight years. Carter's nomination in 1976 and second run in 1980 halted the trend. The growing impact of abortion, affirmative action, and other wedge issues, particularly race, became more divisive and ultimately proved more than many Southern evangelicals could

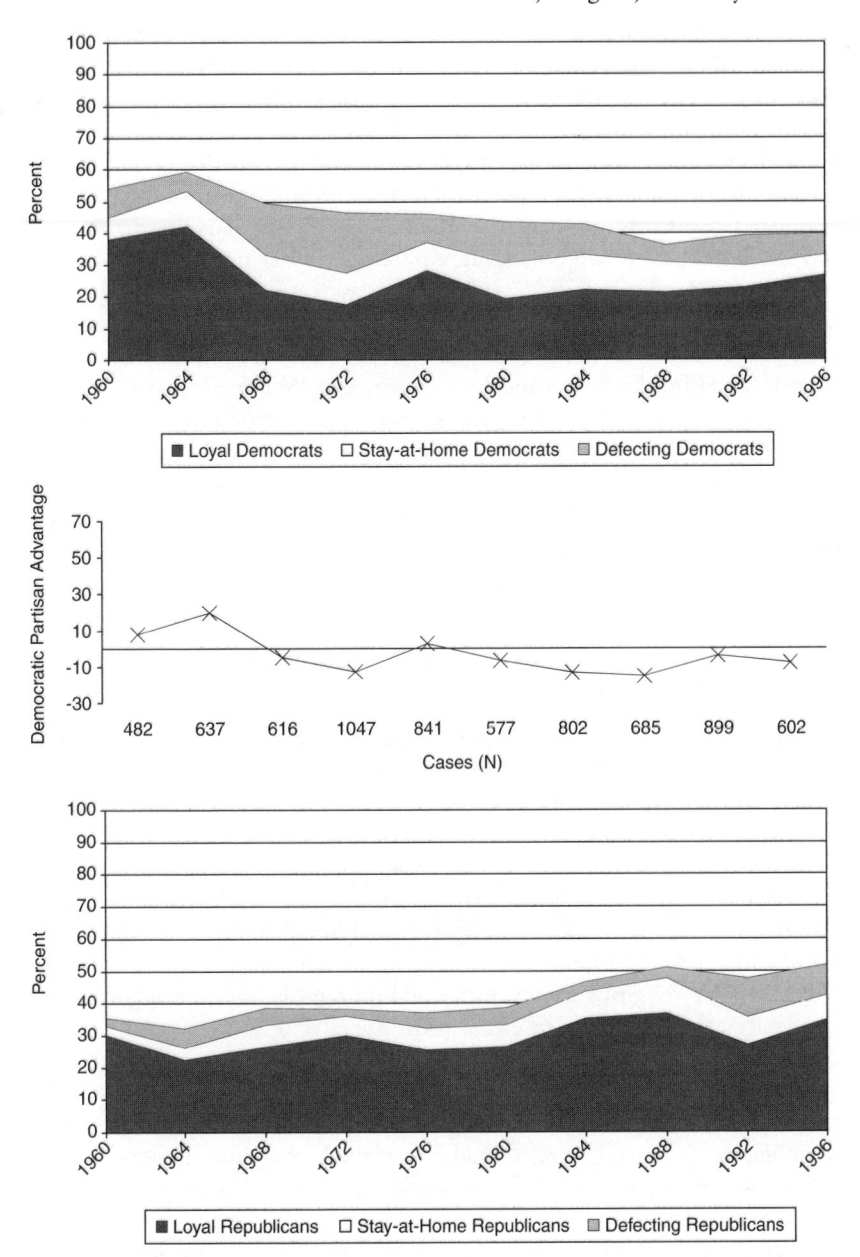

Figure 10.10. Partisan Patterns of White, Non-Latino Southern Evangelical Protestants, 1960–1996

240 • Chapter Ten

accept. The Democratic identification slope resumed its downward trend in 1984 when Carter was no longer on the ticket. Carter's nomination also stanched for a time the hemorrhage of electoral defection among those evangelicals still nominally in the Democratic tent. In the two presidential elections prior to his 1976 nomination, two-thirds and three-fourths of the putative Democrats defected to the opposition or failed to vote. In 1976 Carter managed to keep Democratic disloyalty down near the 1964 level even while winning a much narrower popular vote victory than his 1964 counterpart. Carter's image as "one of our own" may not have lasted long, but it exerted sufficient force to keep Southern evangelical Democrats closer to the fold than did such Northern liberal nominees as Hubert Humphrey, George McGovern, and Walter Mondale. In data not shown, there was no comparable movement among Southern mainline Protestants. Although Carter lessened the Republican advantage over 1972, as he did for virtually all voter groups, the swing was smaller and had less staying power among Southerners from the mainline denominations. Apparently a shared regional identity was not as strong as the combined impact of both regional and religious commonality.

Explanations for Change among Religious Groups: Race or Moral Restoration?

Change of this magnitude, we must expect, has its roots in the appeals that ambitious politicians and the parties they have captured make to the voters. At a minimum, over a period of three short decades the voters are perceiving the parties differently on gender issues and family values. But we have already seen the power of racial appeals in the 1960s through the 1980s. When does moral restorationism assert itself in the religious groups? We will summarize the factor analyses displayed in tables 8.1, 10.2, and 10.3.

Each major religious group responded differently to the moral restorationist appeals that pervaded elections in the later post–New Deal period. We will focus on the three target groups that assumed particular importance in the thinking of party strategists. Democrats periodically tried to break off mainline Protestants from the Republican coalition while the Republicans, adopting Kevin Phillips's model of a new majority, used cultural symbols to detach Catholics and evangelical Protestants from the Roosevelt coalition.

Over the course of the post–New Deal era, white evangelical Protestants made a wholesale shift. By every measure of moral restorationism—opposition to abortion, support for school prayer, opposition to civil rights for homosexuals, hesitance about women's roles outside the home, etc.—evangelicals are the most culturally conservative religious group in

TABLE 10.2
White, Non-Latino, Evangelical Protestant Democrats, 1960–1996

Factors	Stay at Home	Defect	Controls	Stay at Home	Defect
1960					
Govt Role/Social Spending	0.788***	0.784****	Education	−1.154	−0.917*
Cynicism/Trust in Govt	0.583****	−0.068	Gender	0.760	0.907*
Strength of U.S.	0.462	0.305	Income	−0.431	0.293
Isolationism/Internationalism	0.005	−0.162	Cohort	1.556***	−0.463
Race/Civil Rights	0.370	0.060	South	−1.510**	0.032
			Constant	−0.904	−0.415
N	136		LR χ² [20]	50.94	
1964					
Old Social Cleavages	0.044	−0.085	Education	−0.015	0.633
Party Ideology	0.455*	1.139****	Gender	0.561*	0.196
Cynical American First/Anticommunism	0.459***	0.710***	Income	0.008	0.263
			Cohort	0.208	−0.361
			South	−0.211	0.685
			Constant	−1.544	−2.994*
N	202		LR χ² [16]	42.33	
1968					
Race Based Party Ideology	0.451	0.989****	Education	0.599	0.947**
Cynicism/Trust in Govt	0.769****	0.734****	Gender	0.537	0.348
Anticommunism/Law & Order	−0.050	−0.195	Income	−0.866****	−0.410*
Antinativism/Prominorities	0.061	0.035	Cohort	1.826****	0.888*
			South	0.571	0.221
			Constant	−2.956**	−2.217*
N	162		LR χ² [18]	61.84	
1972					
Conservative Reaction to Social Change	0.087	0.691**	Education	−0.401	0.204
Cultural Populism	0.283	−0.011	Gender	0.569	−0.265
Elite Religious Liberals	0.066	0.389*	Income	0.097	0.327*
			Cohort	−0.018	−0.839***
			South	0.195	0.480
			Constant	−0.221	1.143
N	242		LR χ² [16]	53.08	
1976					
Opposition to Racial/Social Change	0.086	0.331	Education	−0.472	0.295

TABLE 10.2
Continued

Factors	Stay at Home	Defect	Controls	Stay at Home	Defect
Cynical Isolationism/ Moral Restorationism	0.368*	−0.298	Gender	0.278	−0.282
Cultural Populism	0.115	0.285	Income	−0.176	−0.401*
Race-Based Party Ideology	−0.082	0.745***	Cohort	0.200	−0.261
			South	0.358	0.486
			Constant	−0.552	0.216
N	185		$LR\ \chi^2\ [18]$	37.01	
1980					
Race-Based Party Ideology	0.779**	1.371****	Education	−0.604	0.402
Retreatist Racial Populism	−0.705***	−0.119	Gender	0.257	−0.019
Moral Restorationism	0.232	−0.040	Income	−0.407*	−0.114
			Cohort	0.616	0.626
			South	−0.626	−0.382
			Constant	0.248	−1.954
N	132		$LR\ \chi^2\ [16]$	34.65	
1984					
Race-Based Party Ideology	0.628*	3.016****	Education	−0.671	0.361
Race, Rights, Taxes	−0.123	0.020	Gender	0.325	2.215****
Moral Restorationism	−0.147	−0.167	Income	−0.778****	−0.203
			Cohort	1.460****	0.431
			Constant	0.077	−0.227
			South	−1.002	−5.185****
N	133		$LR\ \chi^2\ [16]$	80.06	
1988					
Race-Based Party Ideology	0.238	1.511****	Education	−0.940***	−0.037
Cynical Isolationism	0.791****	0.984****	Gender	0.147	0.576
Moral Restorationism	0.464**	0.313	Income	−0.391*	−0.106
Racial Interests	0.099	−0.047	Cohort	0.717*	0.344
			South	1.090**	0.848
			Constant	−0.449	−2.605
N	146		$LR\ \chi^2\ [18]$	56.34	
1992					
Race/Class/International Order-Based Party	−0.527	0.165	Education	0.244	1.052****
Cynicism/Trust in Govt	−0.158	0.210	Gender	−0.277	0.086
Millennial Hopes	0.338	0.006	Income	−0.497**	0.018

TABLE 10.2
Continued

Factors	Stay at Home	Defect	Controls	Stay at Home	Defect
Morally Restorationist-Based Party	1.182****	1.183****	Cohort	1.426****	1.189****
			South	0.608	−0.661
			Constant	−3.273***	−4.930****
N	175		LR χ² [18]	65.85	
1996					
Morally Restorationist-Based Party	0.706*	1.713****	Education	−1.169****	−0.175
Embrace of Internationalism	−0.132	0.092	Gender	0.721	−0.780
Outgroup Antagonism	−0.485*	−0.342	Income	−0.468*	0.439
			Cohort	1.126**	0.439
			South	0.389	−0.255
			Constant	−1.843	−1.475
N	127		LR χ² [18]	51.49	

Source: American National Election Studies (1960–1996)
Note: Multinomial-Logit Regression estimated via maximum likelihood, with voting Democratic as the base category. *Indicates $p < .1$ (two-tail) **Indicates $p < .05$ (two-tail) ***Indicates $p < .025$ (two-tail) ****Indicates $p < .01$ (two-tail) The LR χ² [df] statistic is the difference between likelihood ratios of a model estimated simply with a constant and the models reported above. This is similar to the joint F test of OLS regression.

the electorate. Antipathy toward the Catholic Kennedy affected their vote in 1960, but only since 1968 have they increasingly favored the Republican party. Given their cultural conservatism, we would expect the Republican appeal for moral restoration to explain their displeasure with Democrats and their shift to the Republican party. But the facts are more ambiguous.

Although Senator Barry Goldwater made heavy use of moral restorationist themes in 1964, statistically significant shifts of evangelicals to the Republican party for these reasons do not occur until 1972. Why? White evangelical opposition to federal civil rights policies and negative feelings toward blacks outweighed their concerns over moral issues linked to gender, sexuality, or school prayer. In fact, from 1968 to 1988 almost the entire story of the white evangelical shift from Democrats to Republicans is anchored in race and the role of the federal government in seeking to assure greater opportunity for minorities. After all, this was the basis of Nixon's famous "Southern strategy." "Big government" became a racially charged code word, as did phrases like, "liberal," "tax and spend,"

TABLE 10.3
White, Non-Latino, Mainline Protestant Republicans, 1960–1996

Factors	Stay at Home	Defect	Controls	Stay at Home	Defect
1960					
Govt Role/Social Spending	−0.300	−0.698*	Education	−1.493*	0.221
Cynicism/Trust in Govt	1.022****	−0.077	Gender	1.182	−0.252
Strength of U.S.	0.195	−0.141	Income	−0.283	−0.292
Isolationism/Internationalism	−0.014	−0.154	Cohort	1.851*	−0.519
Race/Civil Rights	−0.564	−0.383	South	1.933***	−0.149
			Constant	−5.429****	−1.214
N	240		LR χ^2 [20]	38.63	
1964					
Old Social Cleavages	0.063	−0.676***	Education	−0.264	−0.285
Party Ideology	−1.207****	−1.277****	Gender	0.221	0.681*
Cynical American First/ Anticommunism	−0.069	−0.283	Income	0.534***	0.179
			Cohort	−0.433	0.316
			South	0.299	−1.461*
			Constant	−2.067	−1.804*
N	240		LR χ^2 [16]	72.53	
1968					
Race Based Party Ideology	−0.271	−0.613*	Education	−0.232	0.021
Cynicism/Trust in Govt	0.793****	0.304	Gender	−0.323	0.239
Anticommunism/Law & Order	0.162	−0.094	Income	−0.607****	−0.149
Antinativism/ Prominorities	0.197	−0.198	Cohort	1.026***	0.050
			South	0.640	−0.175
			Constant	−0.862	−1.818
N	251		LR χ^2 [18]	44.43	
1972					
Conservative Reaction to Social Change	−0.152	−1.024****	Education	−0.502**	−0.468
Cultural Populism	0.355*	−0.420	Gender	0.120	0.458
Elite Religious Liberals	−0.347**	−0.423	Income	−0.431****	−0.050
			Cohort	0.438*	−0.209
			South	0.405	−0.412
			Constant	−0.665	−1.815
N	387		LR χ^2 [16]	64.56	

TABLE 10.3
Continued

Factors	Stay at Home	Defect	Controls	Stay at Home	Defect
1976					
Opposition to Racial/ Social Change	−0.410	0.026	Education	−0.040	−0.347
Cynical Isolationism/ Moral Restorationism	0.993****	0.289	Gender	0.243	−0.066
Cultural Populism	−0.199	−0.095	Income	−0.693****	−0.052
Race-Based Party Ideology	−0.765****	−0.595**	Cohort	0.868****	0.178
			South	−0.613	−0.512
			Constant	−1.192	−0.769
N	289		LR χ^2 [18]	71.90	
1980					
Race-Based Party Ideology	−0.504	−0.554*	Education	−0.892***	−0.149
Retreatist Racial Populism	0.018	0.176	Gender	0.221	−0.344
Moral Restorationism	−0.860****	−1.160****	Income	−0.437*	−0.141
			Cohort	0.331	0.633
			South	0.472	−0.394
			Constant	0.381	−1.557
N	186		LR χ^2 [16]	50.04	
1984					
Race-Based Party Ideology	−0.869****	−1.318****	Education	−0.476	−0.792*
Race, Rights, Taxes	0.239	0.404	Gender	−0.297	0.120
Moral Restorationism	−0.219	−1.318****	Income	−0.155	−0.456*
			Cohort	0.334	0.012
			Constant	0.376	−0.898
			South	−0.177	0.971
N	282		LR χ^2 [16]	69.37	
1988					
Race-Based Party Ideology	−0.859***	−1.283****	Education	−1.341****	−0.720**
Cynical Isolationism	−0.678***	−1.390****	Gender	−0.214	0.162
Moral Restorationism	−0.079	−0.461*	Income	−0.466**	−0.164
Racial Interests	0.063	−0.161	Cohort	2.096****	0.324
			South	1.417***	−0.240
			Constant	−2.452	−0.290
N	241		LR χ^2 [18]	124.30	

TABLE 10.3
Continued

Factors	Stay at Home	Defect	Controls	Stay at Home	Defect
1992					
Race/Class/International Order-Based Party	−0.770**	−0.856****	Education	−0.875****	−0.281
Cynicism/Trust in Govt	0.196	0.027	Gender	−0.634	−0.420
Millennial Hopes	−0.223	−0.827****	Income	−0.622****	0.105
Morally Restorationist-Based Party	−0.389	−0.684***	Cohort	1.256****	0.944****
			South	0.284	−0.719
			Constant	0.821	−1.075
N	219		LR χ^2 [18]	86.66	
1996					
Morally Restorationist-Based Party	−1.600****	−1.833****	Education	−0.554	−0.654*
Embrace of Internationalism	0.188	−0.479	Gender	−0.521	−0.811
Outgroup Antagonism	−0.270	0.041	Income	−1.052****	−0.514*
			Cohort	0.850	0.297
			South	0.141	0.069
			Constant	1.647	2.847*
N	154		LR χ^2 [16]	65.79	

Source: American National Election Studies (1960–1996)
Note: Multinomial-Logit Regression estimated via maximum likelihood, with voting Democratic as the base category. *Indicates $p < .1$ (two-tail) **Indicates $p < .05$ (two-tail) ***Indicates $p < .025$ (two-tail) ****Indicates $p < .01$ (two-tail) The LR χ^2 [df] statistic is the difference between likelihood ratios of a model estimated simply with a constant and the models reported above. This is similar to the joint F test of OLS regression.

"welfare," "crime," "law and order," "gun control," and "local control of schools."

While the *moral restorationist* factor is modestly evident in our analyses throughout the 1970s and the Reagan years, the embrace of moral traditionalism by the Republicans begins to bear fruit in 1988 and becomes the dominant factor undermining evangelical Democratic loyalty to party in both 1992 and 1996. There is also a striking cohort effect through virtually the entire period. Older evangelical Democrats are less likely to vote (and often more likely to defect) in six of the ten postwar contests. Thus the declining Democratic fortunes among evangelicals are attributable not only to alignment but also to the disenchantment of older partisans.

Only in the 1990s can we say unequivocally that a religious vote concerned with state-encouraged morality in our daily lives has dominated the political outlooks and behavior of white evangelicals. This religious tradition, heavily anchored in the South but spreading throughout the country, kept its century-old animus toward the federal government and attached it to race and social spending. Ever since Nixon, evangelicals have found the Republican party more hospitable than the Democrats. Currently, however, the family values themes are more evident than the racial codewords in anchoring evangelicals in the Republican core.

White mainline Protestants, such as Methodists, Presbyterians, Episcopalians, and Congregationalists, have always been at the core of the Republican party, and traditionally have been civic-minded and reformist in their political impulses. Their modest movement toward the Democratic party, however, mirrors those factors that attracted white evangelical Protestants to the Republicans. In 1964 mainline Republicans resented the takeover of the party by Goldwater conservatives. In fact, Republican defections over race and gender issues were a far greater cause of Goldwater's defeat than was fear of his strident anticommunism. In Nixon's 1972 victory against George McGovern, there also was substantial defection to the Democrats by white mainline Republicans because they are committed to change on race and gender issues. Such defections to the Democrats over Republican racial policies continued until 1992.

Nevertheless, white mainline Protestants were the first religious group to take notice of the moral restorationist themes deployed during the Reagan years. This became the dominant reason some voted Democratic from 1980 until 1996 (with the exception of 1988, when the use of the Willie Horton ad made race dominant again). Older cohorts, apparently dismayed by the Republicans' increasing social conservatism, began to sit out elections in increasing numbers. In 1988 they demobilized. In 1992 they demobilized and defected, accounting in large part for the decline in Republican partisan advantage among mainliners in that election. The attempt to return to the moral center in 1996 reduced these tendencies but did not erase them. As the Republican party increased efforts to harness social conservatives, the Republican base among mainliners fractured along generational lines. Although white mainline Protestants have remained Republican, they have become unreliable coalition partners.

Finally, let us look at white, non-Hispanic Catholics. There are two important things to remember about Catholics as a potential vote on moral restorationist themes. First, they are the largest single church body in the American electorate and have been the principal target for campaign themes from Dwight Eisenhower on. Second, forty years ago Catholics had the highest church attendance levels of any religious tradition, but this has changed. Today Catholics over age fifty display the high level of attendance that characterizes evangelicals. Catholics below fifty have the infrequent attendance patterns of mainline Protestants. This means that younger Catholics are less often exposed to sacramental rites and social teachings. Younger men attend Mass less frequently and are predominantly Republican, economically conservative, and culturally liberal. Younger women attend Mass slightly more frequently than younger men and are predominantly Democratic and slightly more liberal both economically and culturally. Recall that the largest gender gap of any religious group opened up in the 1990s among younger Catholics. Their elders continue to look a lot more like each other: they attend Mass quite regularly, are economically liberal, and are somewhat more conservative culturally. Given these differences and divisions, is there any basis for thinking that moral restorationist themes would sway Catholics?

It is not clear that family values issues dramatically affect the way Catholics vote. Race, for example, has had a much stronger impact on voting patterns. From 1968 to 1992 racially charged issues were far and away the dominant reason why white Catholics left the Democratic party. In this respect Catholics followed patterns similar to evangelical Protestants. To be sure, Catholics are generally more willing than other religious groups to use the government to resolve problems of equal opportunity. They also show more warmth toward minorities and the poor. Still, many of those Catholics who moved to the Republicans showed less receptiveness to government action and less warmth toward minorities and the poor. Only in 1996, after four years of the Clintons, did the cluster of issues and group feelings that constitute a moral restorationist program significantly push Catholics in a Republican direction. And here it was limited to the generation of Mass-attending women over fifty.

Furthermore, when we examine a set of four characteristics that signal deeper identification with the Catholic community—frequent Mass attendance, the importance of religion in daily life, feeling close to other Catholics, and the interaction of the first two—we find a religious impact with some regularity on two issues: opposition to abortion and opposition to the death penalty. These are both human life issues where the church has offered clear proscriptive teaching.

On the other hand, when prescriptive teachings about social justice, equal opportunity, and preferential options for the poor are involved, those who have a deeper identification with the Catholic community show greater ambiguity. For the most part, being Catholic or even being a good Catholic predicts little about a person's views about social justice and government programs. Finally, the depth of identification with the Catholic community also predicts very little about warmth toward minorities or the poor. The only exception is among older Catholic women. This is also the segment of the church that is slightly more favorable toward government involvement in social support and equal opportunity

Gender, Religion, and Party • 249

programs; yet it is the only segment of the Catholic Democratic population that showed substantial responsiveness to moral decay arguments used by Republicans. Perhaps this is a religious sector most likely to feel cross-pressure. When cross-pressure occurs, turnout often declines. Indeed this is evident in that, starting in 1968, older Democratic Catholics were much more likely to abstain from voting in six out of eight presidential elections.

The effects of cultural politics along the racial divide led many to desert their historic party. The concern over moral decay has had similar effects. Yet the generations of church affiliates seem to have responded very differently. The literature of political science has strongly argued that partisan older voters are relatively immune to the blandishments of the opposing party. But they appear more likely than the young to respond to changing party images by sitting out elections altogether. This was true for mainline Republicans, Catholic Democrats, and evangelical Democrats as well. By decomposing disloyalty into demobilization and defection, we have uncovered a pattern that suggests the need for some revision in the "immunization" model that dominates studies of age and voting. Older voters seem to react to dissatisfaction with their party by embracing half-measures (abstention) rather than sleeping with the enemy. Younger voters, on the other hand, tend to get swept into the partisan cultural themes by taking leave of their party identification. We cannot tell whether they hear and feel the cultural conflict more deeply than their elders, or whether they lack the anchor that repeated partisan behavior has given their parents. Whatever the case, generational differences in response to cultural appeals are clearly evident across all three of the religious traditions whose affections the parties have contested.

SUMMARY

In the past three chapters we have shown how the clash between settled and emerging moral orders produced both cultural and political transformations in the post–New Deal era. Ambitious politicians learned early lessons using patriotic and nationalistic appeals to divide and shape the electorate. Clearly, racial themes dominated the era's political strategies, at least until late in the period when most citizens had already realigned on race. Without the obvious fodder of the Cold War, or the past impact of race, the late post–New Deal period's party alignment centered on proper gender roles and issues of moral decline. Rooted in the economic and cultural changes of World War II and later crystallized during the civil rights struggles, this conflict pitted traditional moralistic churches against women (and men) who found long-established gender roles and sexual mores restrictive and unjust.

The much-publicized gender gap widened late in the period as gender and traditional moral issues dominated perceptions of the differences between the two parties. Albeit much of this increased gap can be attributed to the larger proportion of post–New Deal men and women in the electorate—whose individual cohort gap is greater than that of the older generation.

Just as men and women moved independently into different party homes throughout the period, the partisan dynamism among ethno-religious groups helped reshape both the perceptions and the composition of the partisan coalitions. The start of the period found mainline Protestants, and to a lesser extent evangelicals, dominating the Republican coalition. On the other hand, Catholics, Jews, African American Christians, and seculars formed the base of the Democratic party. Now, conversely, evangelicals dominate the Republican coalition rather than the shrinking and sometimes disloyal mainliners. Jews, seculars, black Christians, and, increasingly, Latinos continue to form the base of the Democratic coalition. Yet the ethno-religious base of the Democratic coalition has lost some strength. Catholics, who started the early period overwhelmingly Democratic, moved progressively more Republican as their integration into the American mainstream quickened. Catholics still provide Democrats with a party advantage, but it pales when contrasted to past support.

Not surprisingly, then, the parties' campaign strategies reflect these coalitional changes. Often using extra-denominational religious organizations as mobilization devices, the Republican party made appeals to Democratic housewives, Catholics, and evangelicals. The effect of these attempts varied. Evangelical Democrats moved to the Republican party chiefly because of racial themes throughout most of the period. However, by 1988 and into the 1990s socially conservative concerns drove disloyalty and realignment. Catholics also moved mostly because of race throughout the period—that is, until 1996, when moral restoration became an important influence, especially among older women.

Other groups, such as Democratic housewives, also moved to the Republican party in the late 1980s and 1990s because of concerns with the moral direction of their party. However, the number of housewives continues to dwindle, so the Republican realignment carries little advantage.

Democratic leaders sought to hive off factions of the Republican coalition, or at least create enough anxiety so that some would stay at home on Election Day. They deployed fears of religious extremism, threats to women's rights, and intolerance of nontraditional families. Targeted Republican groups included professional women, mainline Protestants, and other socially liberal Republican groups. As the former core of the Republican party, mainline Protestants increasingly became marginalized party coalition members. Along with business and professional women, they were the first group to move away from Republican voting because of the emergence of moral traditionalist appeals in the early 1980s, and they continued to do so throughout the latter part of the time-series. Remaining a "Republican" group, mainliners became increasingly inconsistent coalition partners.

While mainliners' exodus from the partisan coalition hurt, the Republicans have been even less successful keeping professional women enthusiastic about the Republican nominee on Election Day. By the end of the time-series, many younger professionals realigned with the Democrats, and many older professional Republican women consistently chose to stay at home rather than vote for either party's nominee, because of concerns about the expanded power of social conservatives in their party.

CHAPTER ELEVEN

Cultural Politics: Some Conclusions and Practical Implications

THE STUDY OF contemporary electoral behavior needs to recover the level of cultural awareness that was once apparent in voting studies and has long been central to the historical study of American political development. We have sought to show that a culturally informed approach has the potential to illuminate processes that are slighted in existing theories of mass political behavior. Social choice models of the electoral process often begin by assuming that voters have preferences, but the nature and origin of those preferences are treated as exogenous forces beyond the bounds of the analysis (Wildavsky 1987). In our judgment, the nature of electoral alignments depends heavily on voter preferences that are, in turn, largely the products of ambitious politicians seeking issues that will carry them to victory. The social-psychological model of voting, the chief rival of the social choice approach, differs from the social choice perspective by emphasizing that the sociodemographic cleavages that divide the electorate are related to partisanship. But this approach, too, says relatively little about how those cleavages are politicized in the campaign process. A cultural model has the virtue of both putting preference formation back into voting studies and elucidating the processes by which politicians manage those preferences through their electoral appeals.

This book has developed a cultural approach to campaign processes and electoral behavior. In this final chapter, we attempt to draw together the strands of the argument into a coherent statement about culturally based campaign politics. The first part of the chapter recapitulates the theoretical arguments made in chapters 1–5. Then, we mine the group-based analysis of patriotism, race, religion, and gender in chapters 6–10 and generate a number of conclusions with practical political implications. The focus of this section is on the psychological mechanisms that enabled parties to make salient appeals to specific electoral groupings. Next, we explore how these themes were condensed into efficient symbols and attached to the parties. Some observations about Election 2000 follow. The chapter, then, offers a brief exploration of the normative dimension of cultural politics. To what extent does a strategy of group-based polarization threaten democratic stability, inhibit the policy options considered by the electorate, and offer "space" for new parties to enter the electoral universe? If, as we believe, cultural themes are central to contemporary political life, it is essential to understand their impact upon the broader political system. The chapter concludes with suggestions for future research.

A Definition of Cultural Politics

During the post–New Deal period, political elites have utilized a variety of techniques to mobilize or destabilize the partisanship of segments of the American electorate. Cultural conflict is behind the success of these appeals. Through the manipulation of various psychological mechanisms rooted in primary group attachments, political elites attempted to frame issues in such a way as to mobilize specific portions of the electorate and demobilize other portions. This form of cultural politics remains a durable strategy that has been consistently used from one election to the next. Yet, as numerous examples display, the use of an electoral strategy that divides the electorate on cultural values and identities is not guaranteed to work.

In understanding culture, we have drawn most heavily upon history, anthropology, and sociology, disciplines in which culture has been central to scholarly discourse. The object of culture, much like science, is to make life easier by simplifying a complex world. We make sense of natural and social phenomena so that we can either control nature (science) or maneuver with some predictability among fellow humans (culture). Because any one set of cultural norms competes among many, the chosen culture needs justification and legitimation. Both scientific and transcendent rationales are used to legitimate cultural norms.

Culture consists of a set of control mechanisms for governing behavior. It identifies and labels actors, defining who we are and who we are not. By providing norms and boundaries for thinking and acting, culture tells us who is like us and who is not. This is tested through the observation of others' behavior in domains such as family, group, religion, and polity. Through this demarcation process, individuals define who is acceptable and unacceptable, as well as what is and is not acceptable behavior.

This designation of acceptable groups extends to our analysis of contemporary American politics. While some scholars posit that modern societies have high levels of cultural consensus, we are more hesitant. Perhaps especially in the plural United States, subcultures persist, new ones develop, and they lie at the heart of modern political conflicts. Further, many scholars have limited culture to a small domain of issues such as abortion, homosexuality, and drug use. Here, however, we argue that political conflicts do not warrant the label of cultural conflicts just because of the issue at stake.

Cultural conflict is best described as an argument about how we as a people should structure our lives. Thus, political conflict becomes "cultural" when it involves disagreements about what the society and government prescribe and proscribe as the appropriate way of life. This style of argumentation does not limit itself to a specific set of cultural issues, though some issues are more easily captured by the style of discourse employed in cultural politics.

The cultural style of politics is symbolic, not technical. Cultural politics generally deals with ends instead of means. Further, the issues most frequently engaged by cultural politicians are *positions* rather than *valences*. Because of the tendency of practitioners of cultural politics to occupy an issue space that is nonnegotiable, divisive political conflict often ensues. The black-and-white framing of one's own and, more importantly, one's opponents' issue position may be used to separate portions of an electoral coalition. If an issue can be framed properly to carry enough fundamental moral weight, then compromise or support of a candidate holding the "wrong" position is unthinkable.

Politicians seek to avoid placing collective blame on society. Instead, they often simplify and overemphasize which groups are to blame for the problems of the country. The two parties' debate over school shootings and youth violence provides a recent example of this strategy. Conservatives claim that "Hollywood" has poisoned the culture and prescribe content-based restrictions on the media. Liberals emphasize the availability of tools of violence due to the gun lobby. By defining outgroups negatively, political elites attempt to claim that the shortcomings of American society lie in the growing absence of a cultural consensus. If all people were to accept their vision of what it means to be a true American, then these problems would be mitigated. Even further, elites claim that some nonconforming groups receive unfair advantage in the current system. They conduct research to identify strategic audiences where such arguments will resonate. Cultural politicians, through the use of *relative deprivation*, argue that American society may not be restored until this impropriety is rectified.

Cultural appeals cannot be crafted independently, and they resonate only because they tie into real or perceived social tensions and conflicts. Cultural politics thus stems from elite responses to and management of long-term social change and episodic events. Long-term social change disturbs the normal social order, the *moral order*, and provides raw material for elites to lead various kinds of ideological movements. Long-term social change also defines what public and private behavior is acceptable and unacceptable, influencing how we evaluate a candidate's character. This can often create problems for politicians who find themselves trapped between an old and emerging social consensus (see, for example, the contrast in the response to the sexual escapades of Gary Hart versus those of John Kennedy).

Episodic events, on the other hand, offer situations for strategic politicians to create symbols that dramatize group differences. These events, such as, urban riots, may offer plausible evidence to substantiate the claims of strategic politicians. Events that make evident, for example, religious persecution or gender maltreatment may also temporarily raise the salience and political relevance of a particular group identity. Alternately, episodic events, such as the collapse of Soviet Union, reduce issues and "enemies" available to strategic politicians. This may force political elites to search for new enemies against which to mobilize a bloc. Both long-term social change and episodic events provide the necessary material for elites to manipulate cultural symbols; the former resembles an ocean current, dynamic yet lethargic, and the latter a wave, powerful yet fleeting.

The connection between culture and politics goes deeper than simply providing resources during elections. Just as religious and subcultural leaders need politics to shape society into their conception of the proper moral order, political leaders and the political system need religious and cultural symbols to legitimate the system and its inherent choices and inequalities. Religion, however, is not simply an opiate of the masses; at times it makes prophetic judgments about the norms of society and delegitimizes the outcomes of the political system, as was evident in the civil rights era.

Cultural politics legitimates the uses of political power by selected leaders. Campaigns and elections provide the rituals for society to define itself and choose its leaders. The outcome of this process decisively (and divisively) tells us who we are as a people and who we are not. At the center of the confluence of culture and politics lies the election of the president, our principle cultural icon. The dramaturgic ritual of presidential elections reinforces the commonalties as well as the dividing lines within American society. The "core values" that play an important role in defining party differences also suggest the groups within society that comprise each party's electoral coalition. Through the manipulation of symbols attached to these "core values" and social groups, party elites are able to maintain a coalition, attract new members, and effectively dissemble portions of the opposition party's coalition through outgroup appeals.

General Themes

Throughout the post–New Deal period, roughly 1960 to 1996, the electorate has remained attached through long-term group loyalties to one or the other of the main parties. Yet because American parties consist of many diverse groups and espouse a large number of sometimes inconsistent issue positions, groups within these party coalitions can become vulnerable to countermobilization strategies implemented by the other party. In terms of party identification, the Democrats were the majority party throughout this period. For the Republicans to win the White House, they needed to shape the size and composition of the active electorate. To do this, the minority party used well-founded psychological mechanisms to create anxiety and disaffection in troubled groups within the Democratic partisan coalition and encourage some of them either to vote for the Republican ticket or to stay at home. At the same time, the prospect of victory created enthusiasm and mobilization among its own coalition members. Three themes or currents were evident during this period—patriotism/nationalism during the Cold War, race and the aftermath of the civil rights era, and the conflict generated where the aspiration of feminists met the purposes of organized religion.

Cultural Roots of Cold War Politics

The Nixon-McGovern race best demonstrates the success of negative outgrouping based on foreign policy appeals. Hard-working, play-by-the-rules Democratic groups whose fathers and sons had fought the wars watched as the young, highly educated antiwar protesters from the 1968 convention fracas became institutionalized delegates in 1972. Even worse, these former fringe elements changed the rules and secured the nomination for George McGovern. The Democratic party no longer consisted of people like us. Nixon, reminiscent of Goldwater's earlier appeals, offered an alternative. He pointed out the weakness and radical peacenik ideology of McGovern, while claiming to carry the flag for all real Americans willing to take a stand for their way of life against godless communism. The end of the Vietnam War would only come with the dignity the soldiers and all "real" Americans deserved. Not surprisingly, all Democratic groups that Republican research identified as targetable with these foreign policy appeals (such as Catholics, Southerners, and the less educated) did set aside their Democratic predispositions in 1972.

The Southern realignment, perhaps the greatest story of the post–New Deal period, was fed largely by long-term changes in race relations. The moral order of American apartheid was diminished in the civil rights reforms of the 1960s. However, to say that Southerners moved to the Republicans in this period only because of racial change would be a vast oversimplification. Southerners, throughout the 1960s and into the 1970s, consistently defected to the Republicans also because of foreign policy appeals. Many Southern Democrats were convinced that the national Democratic party no longer supported the Southern patriotic-military tradition. "Pinkos, peaceniks, and protestors," according to Republican claims, increasingly became attached to the Democratic party and its candidates. Southerners saw the Democratic party giving control of domestic policy to African Americans while simultaneously giving control of its foreign policy agenda to "fellow travelers."

While the Republican party garnered great gains through its use of the Cold War countermobilization strategy, it was not without its own risks. A strategy based on negative outgroup affect to generate anxiety within the Democratic coalition, and the propagation of stereotypes to generate Republican victory, had the risk of driving portions of the core Republican constituency away from the party. The uses of Cold War cultural symbols by Goldwater and Nixon clearly alienated portions of Republican identifiers with higher levels of education. Defection by this group from the Republican coalition grew throughout Reagan's classic Cold Warrior campaigns and actions. His successor, Bush, continued this trend in his two campaigns, by attacking first a Snoopy-like character riding a tank and then a noninhaling draft-dodger reminiscent of the peaceniks involved in the 1968 and 1972 conventions. With the collapse of the Soviet Union during Bush's tenure, and Clinton's aggressive foreign policy agenda, the Cold War ceased to provide the necessary raw cultural material for either party to co-opt portions of its opponent's partisan coalition. Recent attacks on American soil masterminded by Osama bin Laden and supported by a variety of non-Christian rogue states lurking on the periphery of the current world order may indeed provide strategic politicians with powerful new symbols and "easy issues" to define what it means to be an American for future cultural appeals.

Race

Starting with Truman's halting first steps toward racial integration and continuing with Kennedy's strategic call to Corretta Scott King, nationally the Democrats moved beyond the party of social welfare to the party of civil rights in the post–New Deal period. Southerner President Johnson—partially out of respect to the nation's fallen prince—was not about to change this trend, and the nation's first serious civil rights legislation became law. African Americans noted which party was now leading the effort and realigned their party identification abruptly in 1964 Not surprisingly, throughout the 1960s and 1970s Southerners gradually realigned to the Republicans in response to changes within the Democratic party. Further, an analysis of the regressions throughout this period indicates that racial concerns worked to demobilize or create defections in each election among white Southern Democrats. Republican candidates mined the Democrats' growing impotence among white Southerners, who felt they lost control of "their" party and subsequently their way of life. It was Westerners like Goldwater, Nixon, and Reagan, not Southerners like Johnson and Carter, who were able to speak fluently the Southern language of states' rights, law and order, welfare spending, gun rights, and limited government, the codewords for slowing the pace of change in the moral order surrounding race. Realignment finally stabilized throughout the 1980s; explicit racial concerns no longer seemed to enter the white Southern Democrats' voting calculus—even with the racial focus of the 1988 campaign; now it was pushed aside by concern over moral decadence. Through the previous two decades of realignment, Southern Democrats who had consistently defected to Republican candidates based on racial concerns finally found their natural home in the reoriented Republican party.

The effectiveness of racial appeals was not limited to Southerners. Many observers noted that, with increased regional immigration by African Americans, working-class whites outside the South should also be sensitive to racial scapegoating. Many in the working class, alienated by a Democratic party that seemed to care more about social justice than about New Deal economic justice, felt that blacks and other minorities received unfair advantages through the Democrats' social programs. Keenly aware that, as the minority party, they needed to reshape the size and composition of the electorate in order to win the presidency, Republicans were quick to notice and exacerbate the working class's anxiety through both overt and covert racial appeals. Our multivariate analyses indicate that this strategy seemed to have worked consistently throughout the post–New Deal period for the working class, and to a lesser extent for the middle class and Catholics. Unlike for Southerners, however, no major realignment took place among working-class whites outside the South. Partly because of this, racial appeals continued to be effective throughout the 1980s in hiving off portions of the non-South working class from the Democratic coalition.

Those groups once known as Lincoln Republicans, who perceived the party as a vehicle for racial progress, moved away from the GOP due to its changing positions on race. African Americans realigned abruptly in the period 1964–1968, as the Democratic party turned to strategies to mobilize them in successive elections. It took longer, however, for the educated portion of the Republican party to react in backlash against its party's visceral racial appeals. Starting in 1972, moderately to highly educated Republicans often stayed at home or deserted their party because of the racial appeals. Just as Southern Democrats found their party deserting its natural position on race, many Lincoln Republicans felt alienated by their party's stance on racial issues.

Religion and Gender

Apart from the confessional religious conflict in the 1960 election, religious appeals throughout the post–New Deal era most often used gender and sexual mores as a referent. World War II first upset the general gender and sexual consensus, but the parties would not successfully use gender or sex to divide their opponent's coalitions until the 1980s. Why use gender when patriotic and racial symbols were effective (and easy) in the early days of the post–New Deal period? After Watergate, however, Republicans saw opportunity in the growing divide over the role of women, abortion, and sexual standards. Nevertheless, until the mid-1980s, both men and women as groups were moving into the Republican party, but women were usually about six points behind men.

Having already succeeded with those in the Democratic coalition irked by the changing racial consensus, Republicans drew attention to the consequences of changing gender roles, and to recent Supreme Court decisions on school prayer and abortion. Grass-roots evangelical Christian leaders, working to oppose the Equal Rights Amendment, homosexuality, and abortion, were approached in the late 1970s by conservative Republicans who wanted to move the GOP further to the right. If these religious leaders' resources could be combined with the forces of secular conservatism, a powerful force could be forged. Local movements largely made up of traditional women (and to a lesser extent men) could be trained to produce the necessary votes for the New Majoritarians to regain office, in exchange for the Christian Right having access to national policymakers. Gender and sexual traditionalists, disturbed by changing social mores, had been at home in the Democratic party for economic reasons but now could be convinced to convert or temporally depart for "moral" reasons.

Jimmy Carter, a self-professed born-again Christian who often talked in biblical language, had mobilized many evangelicals in 1976. Although vulnerable to many appeals, he could not be pinned with deviant sexual morals; his problem was that he had appointed too many liberals, Jews, and women to high executive and judicial posts. In Reagan's second election, however, a liberal Northeast *woman* won the right to represent the Democrats on the national ticket. This classic case of an episodic event— the nomination of a liberal woman—provided the necessary raw material for the Republicans to play cultural politics. Abortion, including unfaithfulness to her own church's teaching, lesbianism (guilty by association), not showing proper respect for the high calling of motherhood— well-placed Republican rhetoric—made her suspect on all counts. For those already leery of the Democratic party and its convention in San

260 • Chapter Eleven

Francisco, these became plausible stories. Sectors of the Democratic coalition targeted for these appeals (homemakers, Catholics, and evangelicals) reacted by disengaging politically or deserting to Reagan. For the rest of the time-series Republicans would use "family values" to drive a wedge between traditional Democrats and their party. Though the examples are too numerous to report here—Robertson's run in 1988, the Houston convention in 1992, Clinton's sex life, the 1994 election and subsequent embrace of the Contract with the American Family—all worked to solidify the Democrats as the party of loose sexual morals and the Republicans as the defenders of traditional mores. Joining already disaffected men, evangelical women and mobilized housewives became a new mainstay of the Republican party. Both affirmative action and childcare were seen as destroying the solidarity of the family.

The increased emphasis on traditional gender roles and sexual morals did not go unnoticed by moderate members of the Republican coalition. As early as 1980 mainline Protestant Republicans bolted from the Republican nominee out of a reaction to the growing presence of evangelicals in the party. It was their party, not the evangelicals'. Throughout the next two decades, mainline Protestants, once the core of the Republican party, consistently found reason to desert the Republican candidate because of the emphasis on moral-cultural concerns. Unlike mainline Protestants who largely defected during this period, many Republican business and professional women realigned throughout this period, as well as defected from the Republican nominee based on gender-related matters. What was once a 7-point partisan gap favoring the Republicans among business and professional women in 1964 became nearly a 20-point gap in favor of the Democrats by 1996. For both these groups, the Republican party has been their natural economic home; yet the spectre of theocracy from within drove many in these groups temporarily and some more permanently into the Democratic fold.

These three currents flowed simultaneously in the river of post–New Deal politics. Often coalition members seeking more attention to their agenda will assert that their "issue" was dominant. For example, *Crisis* magazine, a conservative Catholic fortnightly, has argued (Wagner 1998) that Catholics realigned with the Reagan Republican party already early in the 1980s because of abortion, respect for the family, and moral degradation in general. Our analyses, however, show that for Democratic Catholics in the aggregate, race and the role of the federal government in assuring opportunity for minorities was the dominant factor in defections from 1968 to 1992, and only in Clinton's 1996 run did moral restorationism predominate among Catholic defectors. Further most of the realignment occurred during the Nixon years, while new alignment of younger voters predominated under Reagan. They liked his economic policies, his racial policies, and his philosophy of limited government. Finally, at various points during the Nixon and Reagan years, patriotic anticommunism drew Catholics from their Democratic moorings.

Perhaps one of the best ways to summarize our findings is to underscore the strength of the racial current in the river. Race quickly overtook patriotism as the dominant force. And even though moral restorationism was a current introduced as early as 1964, not until the late 1980s and particularly the 1990s did it overtake race. Race remains a powerful current, but more recently it is harder to distill from the dominant current of character/family values. In some respects Clinton was able to stanch the Republican advantage of the racial current, but he gave greater force to the moral restoration current. This latter force was felt so deeply that it was never far below the surface of campaign rhetoric in 2000.

The Development of Efficient Party Symbols

Throughout the post–New Deal period, our multivariate analyses indicate that feelings toward the parties consistently rank as the best predictor of defection from the Democratic coalition. As the time-series progresses, strategic Republican politicians are able to influence individuals' perceptions by attaching meaning to the Democratic party. The notion of party image is constantly in flux, dependent on party legislative action and elite appeals in specific campaigns, and also conditioned by long-term social change. By attaching negative groups and issues to a rival party, politicians can create anxiety among those who feel that their party no longer respects members like them. These anxious feelings generally promote abstention or defection to the opposite party. Through our factor analyses we are able to identify those issues and groups that individuals connect with the parties. What emerges is a pattern of evolutionary change; issues and groups slowly become politically salient and then wane, being replaced by other packages of issues and groups.

Given the context of politics in the United States, the development of efficient symbols becomes necessary to communicate with citizens. Strategic politicians are limited in the types of appeals that they can make at two levels. First, and perhaps most importantly, strategic politicians wish to minimize backlash against their campaign from the use of visceral images. Appeals that were once socially acceptable to the general population often lose their mass acceptability due to changing social consensus. While some types of campaign rhetoric no longer remain acceptable to the mass electorate, some divisive imagery still resonates within significant pockets of the electorate who are key to electoral success. A new way to reach these groups must be found.

Second, the average citizen spends little time collecting and processing information critical to voting decisions. Political psychology and rational-choice theory both suggest that individuals use cognitive shortcuts to make the voting decision as "cheap" as possible, collecting political information that satisfices. When this is coupled with the media's proclivity to cover campaigns as horse races, only highlighting a day's reel of activity, politicians must find an easy way to communicate broad campaign themes within the context of a six-second sound-bite.

The solution to both problems is the development of efficient symbols—a package of codewords that can be easily communicated by the politician to the electorate. These codewords remind loyalists of who the party is and is not. They give the faithful cognitive reinforcement sufficient to mobilize. Additionally, these codewords only hint at anxiety-producing imagery that should resonate in selected targets among the opposition.

At the beginning of the post–New Deal period, our analyses show, individuals generally viewed the parties through the lens of the New Deal. Labor, conservatives, and the government's role in the economy dominated citizens' perceptions of the parties' allies and key cleavages. Despite changes within each party, prior perceptions from the New Deal took time to update—though race did show initial signs of becoming embedded in the Democratic party in 1964. By 1968 race fully entered as a core component of the party image. Civil rights and race emerged here and became fully attached to the Democratic party image for the next twenty years. Not only could Republicans explicitly blame the Democrats for pushing racial change at unsafe speeds, but they also could implicitly point to the Democrats' position on race, by discussing government transfer programs. Big government meant aid to "undeserving" minorities. These appeals were especially helpful in more progressive areas where Republicans could talk in the principled language of laissez-faire economics while at the same time projecting negative racial symbols on the Democrats. By 1972 crime and law-and-order themes carried similar racial weight. Being tough on crime meant that while Democrats coddled black criminals and rioters, Republicans protected law-abiding (white) Americans.

The election of 1972 provided further illumination on the development of efficient party symbols. In this year, the Democratic symbol also became attached to questionable patriotism and the women's movement. These three negative attachments coalesced in 1972 to form the triumvirate of negative symbols used by Republicans to varying degrees of success throughout the post–New Deal period. Generally relying on one or two dominant themes, no other election so successfully combined all the culturally divisive strategies like the Nixon-McGovern race did. All the necessary cultural planets lined up just so. Long-term social change created underlying anxiety, countless dramatic episodic events provided the raw material for strategic elites, a personally vulnerable Democratic candidate provided the perfect target, and an ambitious Republican candidate had the resources and skill to close the deal.

The next two elections would return to party images primarily based on race. Along with feelings toward minorities, social spending and crime continued to load heavily on higher-order party factors. Covert racial appeals continued to be used to good effect. Also at this time, a new word packaging all the negative cultural baggage associated with Democrats first became popular. Tagging a Democratic candidate as "liberal" enabled the strategic politician to indict the opponent on all counts. Appearing in 1976 and more so in 1980, the newly defined liberals became permanently attached to the core of the Democratic party by 1984.

As early as 1976 and with greater effect in 1980, a new moral traditionalism dimension emerged and foreshadowed future partisan rifts. For the next decade, moral traditionalism and race competed for the center of the party image. During Reagan's second campaign, gender and moral traditionalism edged out race as the dominant characteristic of party image—not surprising given the Democratic vice presidential nominee. Race-based politics returned in 1988 with Jesse Jackson's primary run, the Horton frenzy, weak positions by the Democratic nominee on the death penalty, and a strong critique of Dukakis as a "tax-and-spend liberal."

A moral-cultural-based party, symbolized by the Houston convention, first dominated the party image in 1992. In Houston even the party elite spoke of a cultural war, a monumental struggle for the soul of America. This image, reinforced by the 1994 midterm elections and the early attention given to the Christian Coalition by Republican presidential hopefuls, resurfaced with even more force in 1996. Former crossover Democrats, many of them conservative Christians, ascended to the core of the Republican party. This visibility provided Democrats an opportunity to steal pages from the Republican playbook, creating anxiety within the Republican coalition. The Democrats effectively manipulated the electorate by negatively outgrouping evangelicals as religious zealots within the Republican coalition, attributing to them the party's apparent preference for social over economic conservatism. Mainline Protestants, business and professional Republican women, and other educated groups became anxious, often defecting or staying at home on Election Day.

Cultural Politics in Presidential Year 2000

In the 2000 presidential contest, Republicans faced an opportunity fraught with risk. The incumbent president had been caught in the pantry with his pants down, lied about it for a long time, and then was hit by impeachment. Yet the overwhelming majority of the public did not feel the Senate should convict him and remove him from the White House. Most analysts felt the GOP was hurt in the 1998 congressional elections by the decision to pursue Bill Clinton relentlessly.

Having been burned by the stridency of its culture wars rhetoric in 1992 and continuing to suffer fallout from Democratic uses of it in 1996 and 1998, Republicans had to find a way to make character an issue in 2000 without appearing overly judgmental. They had to recapture mainline Protestants and centrist Catholics as reliable members of the party coalition. The challenge was all the greater because George W. Bush had to turn to evangelical voters when his path to the nomination was nearly blocked by the surprising success of John McCain in the early primaries. The solution involved the genius of Karl Rove and other handlers of Bush.

In his acceptance speech, Bush offered litanies to civil religion. He professed dependence on a higher power and saw religion as the source of goodness in America. The unique twist, however, was with the notion of tolerance. He described his generation, the baby boomers, as slow learners of central American values, but "we are almost back." He spoke for a *prodigal generation*, prevailing on the forgiveness of another generation to welcome it to leadership and responsibility. Throughout the campaign Bush, who had a longer than normal adolescence and an acknowledged drinking problem, readily confessed to the mistakes of his "youth." Careful to avoid the "born-again" language of evangelicals, he testified to a calling by a higher power, an experience that made it possible for him to avoid drink and find meaning in his life. Not only was his a prodigal generation, but he was a prodigal son. Late in the campaign when his conviction at the age of thirty for drunk driving was disclosed, he was immunized from recrimination. Few biblical parables match the power of the prodigal son for American Christians.

For his part, Vice President Al Gore recognized the strategy and tried to checkmate it with the selection of running mate Senator Joseph Lieberman, an observant Jew who spoke frequently about the importance of religious faith in the public square and had been an early critic of Clinton's immorality and Hollywood's culture of gratuitous sex and violence. Gore's acceptance speech assured the nation that "I am my own man," he kept Clinton for the most part off the campaign trail, and he too spoke frequently of the importance of faith-based organizations in American civil society. But in humility before God and the American people, Gore was no match for Bush. He showed a propensity for embellishment, never owned up to lies told during the Clinton years, and projected a condescending demeanor.

By avoiding the sectarian aspects of religion—failing to attend the annual meeting of the Christian Coalition and downplaying his opposition to abortion—and assuming the role of prodigal son, Bush actually expanded a "religious vote." Of the 38 percent of voters who said honesty and trustworthiness were the most important factor in selecting a presidential candidate, 78 percent voted for Bush and 16 percent voted for Gore (Benedetto 2000). Further, of those who considered likability an important trait, 58 percent voted for Bush and 39 percent Gore. The Rove-Bush solution kept Clinton fatigue and Gore's proximity to Clinton in the foreground, while asking the country to be tolerant of a sinful man who had seen the error in his ways and converted. The negative judgment did not need explicit voicing. It remained an embarrassment for Democrats.

For his part, Gore embraced cultural politics wholeheartedly. He sought to mobilize the party's base by animosity toward the rich. Over and over, he warned that Bush's politics were unjust, benefiting "the richest 1 percent," big oil, the polluters, and greedy pharmaceuticals. A less frequently intoned staple of his campaign was the fear of theocracy: Bush would appoint to the bench judges who "threatened a woman's right to choose" (note how the labeling employed a central cultural value—choice—rather than addressing the issue, abortion). As our theory has suggested, his strategy on the latter was to dissemble business and professional women, mainline Protestants, and young Catholic women from the potential Republican coalition. Also as predicted by our theory, as the parties approach parity in identifiers, the former majority party's candidate will use cultural politics strategies with the same vigor as the minority party does.

Political parties have available two fundamental strategies. One is the classic Downsian strategy of attempting to occupy the same issue space as the opposition. The other strategy is that, when opposing a sizable majority coalition, the minority party must practice cultural politics to reduce the size of the electorate. If the Republican party is successful in establishing itself as the majority party in the future, we should expect the Democrats to face some difficulties in countering with cultural politics on the Republican majority. Democrats are historically less mobilized and united by a central faith than is the Republican party. It will be both more difficult to mobilize a minority base of Democrats and to hive off no-shows and defectors from the Republicans. More importantly, the Democrats in recent times have seen themselves more as a pluralist collection of groups practicing identity politics than as a party united in central principle.

Because of the success of the Republican party in shaping the size and composition of the electorate, and in successfully alienating parts of the Democratic majority while co-opting other parts of it, perhaps the Republicans' rush to the moral middle after the 2000 primary season and the Democrats' embrace of negative cultural politics in this general election campaign signaled the end of one era of cultural politics and the development of a new period. Democrats may have to dislodge Republican majorities. As detailed earlier, Democrats, through the use of relative deprivation, seem to be targeting the elderly as well as the working poor. More subtly, it seems that the Democrats will attempt to outgroup the religiously judgmental.

Opportunities for Left and Right Third-Party Campaigns

Cultural politics can provide an opportunity for third-party campaigns. In 1992, after twelve consecutive years of exile from the White House, the Democrats shifted their political strategy to the right. Since the McGovern-Fraser reforms after the 1968 election, Democrats had typically nominated candidates from the liberal wing of the party. With the move to the center, the Republican strategy was not nearly so effective. The picture for Democrats becomes further complicated because they no longer enjoy the advantage (especially among likely voters) of being solidly the majority party. As we noted elsewhere, the Republicans eventually countered the Clinton shift by moving leftward and converging with the Democrats on many political issues.

Unlike the third-party movement of Ross Perot that attempted to occupy the vacuous center between the Democrats and the GOP, however, the shift to the center by both parties provides room on the ideological dimension for Left parties as well as Right parties. Not surprisingly the 2000 election, with its competition for the median voter by both the parties, made the Left and Right flanks of the Democratic party and Republican party, respectively, somewhat vulnerable to third-party attacks. Long-time consumer advocate Ralph Nader ran under the Green party label and eked out close to 4 percent of the popular vote, drawing most from leftist Democrats and disenfranchised youth. He has drawn considerable blame for Gore's electoral college plight. On the Right, Pat Buchanan, former Nixon speechwriter and communitarian almost in the 1930s European sense, managed about 1 percent of the popular vote running under the Reform party label. If the two major parties continue to scrum for the median voter, look for the continued viability of third parties such as the Green party and a successor to the Reform party to attempt to capture the ideological tails away from the Democrats and Republicans.

Some Implications of Cultural Politics

Cultural politics suggests a particular style of electioneering. Though a cultural strategy based on within-group mobilization and negative outgrouping may be an effective electoral strategy, problems may arise from its divisive appeals. In this section we consider the implications of the politics of cultural differences.

Several extant electoral systems encourage the creation of broad electoral coalitions (see Horowitz 1991 for alternatives) requiring the support of the opposition in order to legitimize elected officials. Such systems encourage campaign strategies that emphasize similarities within society. However, the American first-past-the-post, winner-take-all system largely constrains issues to one ideological continuum but often—through elite manipulation—exacerbates cultural group differences. One particular campaign style used to fragment and divide the electorate is what we describe as the politics of cultural differences.

The politics of cultural differences emphasizes campaign rhetoric that creates anxiety and fear through scapegoating, assigning blame, and outgrouping. Through repeated application of this strategy, efficient party symbols emerge, while portions of the electorate are essentially removed from the game. As particular groups become attached to a party, democratic theory would suggest that the party should respond to the policy demands of such a group. A party's relative ability to represent an outgroup's interests compared to those of other members of its coalition decreases when its opponent uses cultural politics. If the party does give equal weight to this outgroup member, it cripples itself by substantiating the claims of its opponent that the party has become the handmaiden to cultural deviance. Therefore, the party must be extra cautious when addressing the needs of the outgroup. A loss of policy choice ensues. This does not imply a normal regression to the median policy opinion within a democracy through deliberation and compromise. Instead, because voter preferences are largely endogenous to ambitious politicians' cultural strategy, policy constrictions are made at the emotional level, having little to do with the merits of the actual policies.

In some situations, such as the threat of certain electoral failure, no party will allow a cultural outgroup into its coalition. This action by the parties results in de facto disenfranchisement and loss of citizenship for members of the group. To be sure, most partisan coalition members targeted as an outgroup by the opposition will probably still receive partial benefits from the party. Nevertheless, if enough groups, with enough similarities, become fully or partially disenfranchised, they could provide the necessary electoral support for third-party candidates.

So far we have looked at cultural politics from a "glass half-empty" perspective. It is also possible to see cultural politics in a more positive light. While the development of efficient party symbols is cultural politics at its most refined—visceral imagery tightly packaged in what appears to be harmless boxes—the development of efficient symbols also tells us precisely what a party is and is not. Politicians who choose to identify with a particular party are constrained by these symbols, often forcing them to be more responsible party members than they would otherwise be. It is perhaps deliciously ironic that a responsible party system may be encouraged by an emotive-based campaign style largely developed for entrepreneurial politicians to shape and manipulate the electorate. On the other hand, as we acknowledged early in the book, many politicians really believe the cultural scripts they are deploying.

Directions for Future Research

We conclude by discussing the implications of this work for future scholarship in political science. We have written this book as a challenge to scholars: our goal is to inspire others to take up their tools on behalf of a more culturally aware form of electoral analysis. To a considerable degree our book has attempted to model one way in which electoral analysis can incorporate such a cultural dimension. What central questions or issues might a reader take away from the exercise?

The most original feature of the electoral analysis in part 2 was the manner in which voting behavior was conceptualized and measured. In conventional electoral analysis, it has been customary to measure voter choice, whether at the individual or group level, as a simple dichotomy of voting Democratic or Republican (or trichotomously in three-party contests). As intuitively obvious as this approach to the dependent variable may seem, it misses some of the central cultural dynamics of the electoral process. At the base level, it omits those eligible voters who choose not to exercise the franchise in response to cultural appeals. The resulting statistical model of voter choice identifies the forces that influenced for whom respondents voted but fails to capture the issues and forces that pushed voters out of the electorate altogether. To further compound the problem, this voter-choice approach fails to take into account the phenomenon of defection, the movement of some voters out of their customary partisan home. Consider a hypothetical regression analysis that might have resulted in an election year where one party succeeded in dividing a previously monolithic social group relatively equally between the parties. This would produce a nonsignificant coefficient for the variable representing that group, leading to the conventional interpretation that group membership had no impact on vote choice. In fact, under these circumstances, the absence of a customary cleavage may well be the story of the campaign. Yet this complex reality is submerged because voters are treated as political free agents rather than as people with social locations and associated partisan dispositions.

Both turnout and defection are central to the mobilization of cultural differences because parties make strenuous efforts to demobilize and convert significant components of the opposing party's electoral coalition. The relatively simple alternative proposed in chapter 7 partitioned voters into social categories and then further allocated them to subgroups based on their partisan propensities. The dependent variable was coded such that coefficients reflected the tendency of voters to remain loyal to their stated party, sit out an election, or cross the aisle by supporting the opposing candidate for office. Although we do not suppose that this is the last word in conceptualization and measurement, this mode of analysis has the virtue of capturing the effects associated with cultural mobilization and demobilization.

Subsequent research may well improve upon this approach in several respects. The relatively simple technical approach we have used in this volume could doubtless be enhanced by alternate formulations. But more important, we believe, is the resolve to pay attention to electoral conditions that lead to the phenomena of depressed turnout and high levels of voter defection. Choice includes the option to abstain, and the choices of those voters who do participate must be approached from the baseline of underlying partisan dispositions. That is the first area where we would like to see electoral scholars extend this analysis.

The second unique aspect of the analysis in part 2 involved bringing politicians back into the electoral process. This is overstatement, of course, because electoral research has paid increasing attention to candidates in recent years. In particular, strong scholarship by political psychologists has shown how emotional reactions to candidate traits condition vote choice. This moved beyond the classic American voter studies from the 1960s and 1970s, where candidate likability was included along with party images and issues as the major determinants of vote choice. But it does not yet specify what candidates do to shape emotional arousal.

In our judgment, politicians need to be incorporated in another way. We have argued that ambitious politicians attempt to determine the salience of the issues in a campaign. They frame issues with the explicit intent to forge linkages in the voter's mind among parties, groups, and issue positions and thus to activate the abstention and conversion dynamics. Although we devoted considerable space to the linkages in the theoretical section of the book, we have not directly measured them in part 2 but have relied instead on inferences from the data-mapping exercises involving social groups. If the cultural analysis of elections is to progress, scholars must develop techniques that permit the empirical study of interactions among candidates, issues, groups, and party images. This will of course require scholars to measure more reproducibly the campaign strategies of the major parties.

The final domain where we see the need for additional research involves scholars seeking guidance outside the profession. In particular, we call upon electoral analysts to pay closer attention to the work of political journalists. In understanding voter dynamics over the post–New Deal era, we have benefited enormously from the work of writers such as Samuel Lubell, Kevin Phillips, Thomas Edsall, E. J. Dionne, Michael Barone, and David Broder. In this work and many of the post-mortems that now appear routinely following elections, we can find remarkably explicit accounts of how ambitious politicians understood and conceptualized the electorate and the strategies they pursued in order to forge a winning coalition. For example, the reporting on the 1998 congressional elections made it very clear that the goal of Republicans was to fire up their base constituency—social conservatives—and hope that core Democratic voter groups stayed home out of disgust about the behavior of President Clinton. By contrast, the Democrats hoped that backlash against the Starr investigation would stimulate much higher than normal turnout among such key Democratic constituencies as African Americans, liberals and unionized workers. The party leadership did not simply hope for these outcomes but actively pursued them by crafting specific tactics in political advertising, get-out-the-vote drives, and other such means. The insights of the political journalists often direct us to specific issues that might well affect the propensities of voters to demobilize or vote for what they normally perceive as the opposition.

Over the past half-century, political scientists have grappled with the role of culture in voting behavior. As we noted in the opening pages of this book, that effort has been fraught with problems because of the seeming intractability of culture and the difficulty of applying such a vague and amorphous concept to empirical tests. In this book, we have tried to demonstrate what can be gained by utilizing an explicit formulation of cultural theory in the study of mass electoral behavior. In part, this has meant recovering elements from earlier voting theories such as the Columbia school and weaving them together with the insights of more recent rational-choice and political psychological models of electoral choice. We are acutely aware that this volume offers only one take on the problem of cultural politics and that subsequent research will do much to amplify and tighten the arguments we have put forward. If that is the outcome, this reconnaissance will have more than served its purpose.

References

Abramowitz, Alan I. 1995. "It's Abortion, Stupid: Policy Voting in the 1992 Presidential Election." *Journal of Politics* 57 (1):176–86.
Abramson, Paul R., and John H. Aldrich. 1982. "The Decline of Electoral Participation in America." *American Political Science Review* 76 (3):502–21.
Abramson, Paul R., John H. Aldrich, and David W. Rohde. 1994. *Change and Continuity in the 1992 Elections.* Washington, DC: CQ Press.
———. 1998. *Change and Continuity in the 1996 Elections.* Washington, DC: CQ Press.
Almond, Gabriel A., and Sidney Verba. 1963. *The Civic Culture: Political Attitudes and Democracy in Five Nations.* Princeton: Princeton University Press.
Amos, S. Karin. 1995. *Alexis De Tocqueville and the American National Identity: The Reception of De La Démocratie en Amérique in the United States in the Nineteenth Century.* Frankfurt am Main: P. Lang.
Balmer, Randall Herbert. 1996. *Grant Us Courage: Travels along the Mainline of American Protestantism.* New York: Oxford University Press.
Banfield, Edward C., and James Q. Wilson. 1963. *City Politics.* Cambridge: Harvard University Press.
Barnes, Fred. 1995. "The Orthodox Alliance." *American Enterprise* (November/December 1995): 70–71.
Barone, Michael. 1990. *Our Country: The Shaping of America from Roosevelt to Reagan.* New York: Free Press.
Bashevkin, Sylvia. 1998. *Women on the Defensive.* Toronto: University of Toronto Press.
Baumgartner, Frank R., and Beth L. Leech. 1998. *Basic Interests: The Importance of Groups in Politics and in Political Science.* Princeton: Princeton University Press.
Beck, Paul Allen. 1979. "The Electoral Cycle and Patterns of American Politics." *British Journal of Political Science* 9 (1):129–56.
Belli, Robert, Santa Traugott, and Steven J. Rosenstone. 1984. *Reducing Over-Reporting of Voter Turnout: An Experiment Using a Source Monitoring Framework.* Ann Arbor: National Election Studies.
Benedetto, Richard. 2000. "Vote Seemed to Be Split Sharply." *USA Today,* November 8, 2000, 8A.
Benson, Lee. 1961. *The Concept of Jacksonian Democracy; New York as a Test Case.* Princeton: Princeton University Press.
———. 1979. "Marx's General and Middle-Range Theory of Social Conflict." In *Qualitative and Quantitative Social Research: Papers in Honor of Paul F. Lazarsfeld,* edited by R. K. Merton, J. S. Coleman and P. H. Rossi. New York: Free Press.
Bentley, Arthur F. 1908. *The Process of Government.* Cambridge: Belknap Press of Harvard University Press.
Berelson, Bernard R., Paul F. Lazarsfeld, and William N. McPhee. 1954. *Voting: A Study of Opinion Formation in a Presidential Campaign.* Chicago: University of Chicago Press.
Berger, Peter L., and Thomas Luckmann. 1966. *The Social Construction of Reality: A Treatise in the Sociology of Knowledge.* Garden City, NY: Doubleday.

Bloomfield, Lincoln P. 1974. *In Search of American Foreign Policy: The Humane Use of Power.* New York: Oxford University Press.

Blumenthal, Sidney. 1986. *The Rise of the Counter-Establishment: From Conservative Ideology to Political Power.* New York: Times Books.

———. 1990. *Pledging Allegiance: The Last Campaign of the Cold War.* New York: HarperCollins.

Bonk, Kathy. 1988. "The Selling of the 'Gender Gap': The Role of Organized Feminism." In *The Politics of the Gender Gap*, edited by C. M. Mueller. Newbury Park, CA: Sage Publications.

Boynton, George R., and John S. Nelson. 1995. "Communicating Feeling: Music in Campaign Ads." Paper presented at the Annual Meetings of the Midwest Political Science Association, Chicago.

Brady, Henry E., and Paul M. Sniderman. 1985. "Attitude Attribution: A Group Basis for Political Reasoning." *American Political Science Review* 79 (4):1061–78.

Brint, Steven G. 1994. *In an Age of Experts: The Changing Role of Professionals in Politics and Public Life.* Princeton: Princeton University Press.

Buchanan, Pat. 1992. "The Election Is about Who We Are." *Vital Speeches* 58 (September 15, 1992):712–15.

Burdick, Eugene. 1956. *The Ninth Wave.* Boston: Houghton Mifflin.

———. 1964. *The 480.* New York: McGraw-Hill.

Burdick, Eugene, and Arthur J. Brodbeck. 1959. *American Voting Behavior.* Glencoe: Free Press.

Burnham, Walter Dean. 1970. *Critical Elections and the Mainsprings of American Politics.* New York: Norton.

Burris, Val. 1980. "Capital Accumulation and the Rise of the New Middle Class." *Review of Radical Political Economics* 12:17–34.

Byrnes, Timothy A. 1991. *Catholic Bishops in American Politics.* Princeton: Princeton University Press.

Campbell, Angus, Philip E. Converse, Warren E. Miller, and Donald E. Stokes. 1960. *The American Voter.* New York: Wiley.

Carmines, Edward G., and Geoffrey C. Layman. 1997. "Issue Evolution in Postwar American Politics: Old Certainties and Fresh Tensions." In *Present Discontents: American Politics in the Very Late Twentieth Century*, edited by B. E. Shafer. Chatham, NJ: Chatham House Publishers.

Carmines, Edward G., and James A. Stimson. 1980. "The Two Faces of Issue Voting." *American Political Science Review* 74 (1):78–91.

———. 1989. *Issue Evolution: Race and the Transformation of American Politics.* Princeton: Princeton University Press.

Carmody, Denise L., and John T. Carmody. 1990. *The Republic of Many Mansions: Foundations of American Religious Thought.* New York: Paragon House.

Churchill, Winston. 1974. *Winston S. Churchill: His Complete Speeches, 1897–1963.* Edited by R. R. James. New York: Chelsea House Publishers.

Clinton, Bill. 1992. "Acceptance Address." *Vital Speeches* 58 (August 15, 1992):642–45.

Clubb, Jerome M., William H. Flanigan, and Nancy H. Zingale. 1980. *Partisan Realignment: Voters, Parties and Government in American History.* Beverly Hills, CA: Sage Publications.

Conover, Pamela Johnston, and Stanley Feldman. 1981. "The Origins and Meaning of Liberal/Conservative Self-Identifications." *American Journal of Political Science* 25 (4):617–45.

———. 1984. "How People Organize the Political World: A Schematic Model." *American Journal of Political Science* 28 (1):95–126.

Converse, Phillip E. 1966. "Religion and Politics: The 1960 Election." In *Elections and the Political Order*, edited by A. Campbell, P. E. Converse, W. E. Miller, and D. E. Stokes. New York: Wiley.

Costain, Anne N. 1992. *Inviting Women's Rebellion: A Political Process Interpretation of the Women's Movement*. Baltimore: Johns Hopkins University Press.

Crawford, Alan. 1980. *Thunder on the Right: The "New Right" and the Politics of Resentment*. New York: Pantheon Books.

Dawidowicz, Lucy S., and Leon J. Goldstein. 1963. *Politics in a Pluralist Democracy: Studies of Voting in the 1960 Election*. New York: Institute of Human Relations Press.

Dawson, Michael C. 1994. "Ideological Tendencies in the 1993 Black Public Map." Paper presented at the Annual Meetings of the American Political Science Association, New York.

De Vries, Walter, and V. Lance Tarrance. 1972. *The Ticket-Splitter: A New Force in American Politics*. Grand Rapids, MI: Eerdmans.

Delli Carpini, Michael, and Lee Sigelman. 1986. "Do Yuppies Matter? Competing Explanations of Their Political Distinctiveness." *Public Opinion Quarterly* 50 (4):502–18.

Diamond, Edwin, and Stephen Bates. 1992. *The Spot: The Rise of Political Advertising on Television*. 3d ed. Cambridge: MIT Press.

DiMaggio, Paul. 1997. "Culture and Cognition." *Annual Review of Sociology* 23:263–87.

Dionne, E. J. 1996. *They Only Look Dead: Why Progressives Will Dominate the Next Political Era*. New York: Simon & Schuster.

Dowd, Maureen. 1996. "Daddy in Chief." *The New York Times*, June 2, 1996, E15.

Downs, Anthony. 1957. *An Economic Theory of Democracy*. New York: Harper.

Durkheim, Emile. 1965. *The Elementary Forms of the Religious Life*. New York: Free Press.

Easton, David. 1953. *The Political System: an Inquiry into the State of Political Science*. New York: Knopf.

Eckstein, Harry. 1988. "A Culturalist Theory of Political Change." *American Political Science Review* 82 (3):789–804.

Edsall, Thomas B. 1992. "GOP Plans a 'Family Values' Offensive." *Washington Post*, August 19, 1992.

———. 1997. "The Cultural Revolution of 1994: Newt Gingrich, the Republican Party, and the Third Great Awakening." In *American Politics in the Very Late Twentieth Century*, edited by B. E. Shafer. Chatham, NJ: Chatham House.

———. 1998. "GOP's Own Successes Weaken Its Draw, Strategists Say." *Washington Post*, November 25, 1998, A4.

———. 1999. "GOP Aims Wedge at Democratic Issues." *Washington Post*, November 8, A1.

———. 2000. "NRA Puts Faith in Turnout." *Washington Post*, May 22, A4.

Edsall, Thomas B., and Mary D. Edsall. 1991. *Chain Reaction: The Impact of Race, Rights, and Taxes on American Politics*. New York: Norton.

Eisenstein, James. 1977. *Felony Justice: An Organizational Analysis of Criminal Courts*. Boston: Little, Brown.

Enelow, James M., and Melvin J. Hinich. 1984. *The Spatial Theory of Voting: An Introduction*. New York: Cambridge University Press.

Fiorina, Morris P. 1981. *Retrospective Voting in American National Elections.* New Haven: Yale University Press.

———. 1983. "Who Is Held Responsible? Further Evidence on the Hibbing-Alfred Thesis." *American Journal of Political Science* 27 (1):158–64.

Flanigan, William H., and Nancy H. Zingale. 1994. *Political Behavior of the American Electorate.* 8th ed. Washington, DC: CQ Press.

Foley, Michael. 1980. *The New Senate: Liberal Influence on a Conservative Institution, 1959–1972.* New Haven: Yale University Press.

Formisano, Ronald P. 1971. *The Birth of Mass Political Parties, Michigan, 1827–1861.* Princeton: Princeton University Press.

———. 1983. *The Transformation of Political Culture: Massachusetts Parties, 1790s–1840s.* New York: Oxford University Press.

Fox-Genovese, Elizabeth. 1996. *Feminism Is Not the Story of My Life: How Today's Feminist Elite Has Lost Touch with the Real Concerns of Women.* New York: Nan A. Talese.

Freedman, Samuel G. 1996. *The Inheritance: How Three Families and America Moved from Roosevelt to Reagan and Beyond.* New York: Simon & Schuster.

Freeman, Jo. 1975. *The Politics of Women's Liberation.* New York: McKay.

———. 1983. *Social Movements of the Sixties and Seventies.* New York: Longman.

———. 1993. "Feminism vs. Family Values: Women at the 1992 Democratic and Republican Conventions." *PS: Political Science & Politics* 26:21–28.

———. 1999. *Waves of Protest: Social Movements since the Sixties.* Lanham, MD: Rowman and Littlefield.

Gallup, George, Jr., and Jim Castelli. 1987. *The American Catholic People: Their Beliefs, Practices, and Values.* Garden City, NY: Doubleday.

Geertz, Clifford. 1973. *The Interpretation of Cultures: Selected Essays.* New York: Basic Books.

Germond, Jack, and Jules Witcover. 1981. *Blue Smoke and Mirrors: How Reagan Won and Why Carter Lost the Election of 1980.* New York: Viking.

———. 1985. *Wake Us When It's Over: Presidential Politics of 1984.* New York: Macmillan.

———. 1989. *Whose Broad Stripes and Bright Stars?: The Trivial Pursuit of the Presidency, 1988.* New York: Warner Books.

———. 1993. *Mad as Hell: Revolt at the Ballot Box, 1992.* New York: Warner Books.

Gerstle, Gary, and Steve Fraser. 1989. "Introduction." In *The Rise and Fall of the New Deal Order, 1930–1980,* edited by S. Fraser and G. Gerstle. Princeton: Princeton University Press.

Gilens, Martin. 1999. *Why Americans Hate Welfare.* Chicago: University of Chicago Press.

Ginsberg, Benjamin, and Martin Shefter. 1990. *Politics by Other Means: The Declining Importance of Elections in America.* New York: Basic Books.

Glenn, Norval D. 1987. "Social Trends in the U.S.: Evidence from Sample Surveys." *Public Opinion Quarterly* 51 (Supplement, part 2):S109–S126.

Glock, Charles Y. 1972. "Images of 'God,' Images of Man, and the Organization of Social Life." *Journal for the Scientific Study of Religion* 11 (1):1–15.

Gould, Julius, and William Lester Kolb. 1964. *A Dictionary of the Social Sciences.* New York: Free Press of Glencoe.

Greeley, Andrew M. 1989. *Religious Change in America.* Cambridge: Harvard University Press.

Green, John C., and James L Guth. 1991. "The Bible and the Ballot Box: The

Shape of Things to Come." In *The Bible and the Ballot Box: Religion and Politics in the 1988 Election*, edited by J. L. Guth and J. C. Green. Boulder: Westview.

Green, John C., James L. Guth, Corwin E. Smidt, and Lyman A. Kellstedt. 1996. *Religion and the Culture Wars: Dispatches from the Front*. Lanham, MD: Rowman and Littlefield.

Guth, James L., John C. Green, Lyman A. Kellstedt, and Corwin E. Smidt. 1994. "Onward Christian Soldiers: Religious Activist Groups in American Politics." In *Interest Group Politics*, edited by A. Cigler and B. Loomis. Washington, D.C.: CQ Press.

Hadden, Jeffrey K. 1969. *The Gathering Storm in the Churches*. Garden City, NY: Doubleday.

Hammond, Phillip E. 1992. *Religion and Personal Autonomy: The Third Disestablishment in America*. Columbia: University of South Carolina Press.

———. 1998. *With Liberty for All: Freedom of Religion in the United States*. Louisville: Westminster John Knox Press.

Harrison, Cynthia. 1988. *On Account of Sex: The Politics of Women's Issues, 1945–68*. Berkeley: University of California Press.

Harvey, Anna L. 1998. *Votes without Leverage: Women in American Electoral Politics, 1920–1970*. New York: Cambridge University Press.

Hausman, Jerry, and Daniel McFadden. 1984. "Specification Tests for the Multinomial Logit Model." *Econometrica* 52 (5):1219–40.

Hays, Samuel P. 1980. *American Political History as Social Analysis: Essays*. Knoxville: University of Tennessee Press.

Hertzke, Allen D. 1992. *Echoes of Discontent: Jesse Jackson, Pat Robertson, and the Resurgence of Populism*. Washington, DC: CQ Press.

Higham, John. 1970. *Strangers in the Land: Patterns of American Nativism, 1860–1925*. 2d ed. New York: Atheneum.

Himmelfarb, Gertrude. 1995. *The De-Moralization of Society: From Victorian Virtues to Modern Value*. New York: Knopf.

Himmelstein, Jerome L. 1990. *To the Right: The Transformation of American Conservatism*. Berkeley: University of California Press.

Homans, George Caspar. 1950. *The Human Group*. New York: Harcourt Brace.

Horowitz, Donald L. 1991. *A Democratic South Africa?: Constitutional Engineering in a Divided Society*. Berkeley: University of California Press.

Huckfeldt, Robert, Paul Allen Beck, Russel J. Dalton, and Jeffrey Levine. 1995. "Political Environments, Cohesive Social Groups, and the Communication of Public Opinion." *American Journal of Political Science* 39 (4):1025–54.

Hunter, James Davison. 1991. *Culture Wars: The Struggle to Define America*. New York: Basic Books.

Hunter, James Davison, and Tracy Fessenden. 1992. "The New Class as Capitalist Class: The Rise of the Moral Entrepreneur in America." In *Hidden Technocrats: The New Class and New Capitalism*, edited by H. Kellner and F. W. Heuberger. New Brunswick, NJ: Transaction.

Hurwitz, Jon, and Mark Peffley. 1997. "Public Perceptions of Race and Crime: The Role of Racial Stereotypes." *American Journal of Political Science* 41 (2):375–401.

Isserman, Maurice, and Michael Kazin. 2000. *America Divided: The Civil War of the 1960s*. New York: Oxford University Press.

Jackson, Kenneth T. 1967. *The Ku Klux Klan in the City, 1915–1930*. New York: Oxford University Press.

Jacoby, William G. 2000. "Issue Framing and Public Opinion on Government Spending." *American Journal of Political Science* 44 (4):750–67.

Jamieson, Kathleen Hall. 1992. *Packaging the Presidency: A History and Criticism of Presidential Campaign Advertising.* 2d ed. New York: Oxford University Press.

———. 1996. *Packaging the Presidency: A History and Criticism of Presidential Campaign Advertising.* 3d ed. New York: Oxford University Press.

Jensen, Richard J. 1971. *The Winning of the Midwest: Social and Political Conflict, 1888–1896.* Chicago: University of Chicago Press.

Johnson-Cartee, Karen S., and Gary Copeland. 1991. *Negative Political Advertising: Coming of Age.* Hillsdale, NJ: L. Erlbaum Associates.

———. 1997. *Manipulation of the American Voter: Political Campaign Commercials.* Westport, CT: Praeger.

Jorgenson, Lloyd P. 1987. *The State and the Non-Public School, 1825–1925.* Columbia: University of Missouri Press.

Katz, Michael. 1989. *The Undeserving Poor: From the War on Poverty to the War on Welfare.* New York: Pantheon Books.

Katzenstein, Mary Fainsod, and Carol McClurg Mueller, eds. 1987. *The Women's Movements of the United States and Western Europe: Consciousness, Political Opportunity, and Public Policy.* Philadelphia: Temple University Press.

Keith, Bruce E., David B. Magleby, Candice J. Nelson, Elizabeth A. Orr, Mark C. Westlye, and Raymond E. Wolfinger. 1992. *The Myth of the Independent Voter.* Berkeley: University of California Press.

Kellstedt, Lyman A., and John C. Green. 1993. "Knowing God's Many People: Denominational Preference and Political Behavior." In *Rediscovering the Religious Factor in American Politics*, edited by D. C. Leege and L. A. Kellstedt. Armonk, NY: M. E. Sharp.

Kellstedt, Lyman A., John C. Green, James L. Guth, and Corwin E. Smidt. 1994. "It's the Culture Stupid! 1992 and Our Political Future." *First Things* 42 (1):28–33.

Kennedy, John F. 1964. *John Fitzgerald Kennedy: A Compilation of Statements and Speeches Made during His Service in the United States Senate and House of Representatives.* Washington, DC: United States Government Printing Office.

Kessel, John H. 1984. *Presidential Campaign Politics.* 2d ed. Homewood, IL: Dorsey Press.

Key, V. O., Jr. 1955. "A Theory of Critical Elections." *Journal of Politics* 17 (1):3–18.

———. 1959. "Secular Realignment and the Party System." *Journal of Politics* 21 (2):198–210.

———. 1966. *The Responsible Electorate: Rationality in Presidential Voting, 1936–1960.* Cambridge: Belknap Press of Harvard University Press.

Kinder, Donald R., and Roderick Kiewiet. 1981. "Sociotropic Politics: The American Case." *British Journal of Political Science* 11 (2):129–61.

Kinder, Donald R., and David O. Sears. 1985. "Whites' Opposition to Busing: On Conceptualizing and Operationalizing Group Conflict." *Journal of Personality and Social Psychology* 48 (5):1141–47.

Kinder, Donald R., and Lynn M. Sanders. 1996. *Divided by Color: Racial Politics and Democratic Ideals.* Chicago: University of Chicago Press.

Klein, Ethel. 1987. "The Diffusion of Consciousness in the United States and Western Europe." In *The Women's Movements of the United States and Western Europe: Consciousness, Political Opportunity, and Public Polic*, edited by M. F. Katzenstein and C. M. Mueller. Philadelphia: Temple University Press.

Kleppner, Paul. 1970. *The Cross of Culture: A Social Analysis of Midwestern Politics, 1850–1900.* 2d ed. New York: Free Press.
———. 1979. *The Third Electoral System 1853–1892: Parties, Voters, and Political Cultures.* Chapel Hill: University of North Carolina Press.
Krueger, Brian S. 1998. "The Unintended Consequences of Campaign Themes: Seculars' Reaction to the 1992 Presidential Campaign." Paper presented at the Annual Meetings of the Midwest Political Science Association, Chicago.
Kusnet, David. 1992. *Speaking American: How the Democrats Can Win in the Nineties.* New York: Thunder's Mouth Press.
Ladd, Everett Carll. 1981. "The Brittle Mandate: Electoral Dealignment and the 1980 Presidential Election." *Political Science Quarterly* 96 (1):1–25.
———. 1991. "Like Waiting for Godot: The Uselessness of 'Realignment' for Understanding Change in Contemporary American Politics." In *The End of Realignment?: Interpreting American Electoral Eras*, ed. B. E. Shafer. Madison: University of Wisconsin Press.
———. 1993. "The 1992 Vote for President Clinton: Another Brittle Mandate?" *Political Science Quarterly* 108 (1):1–28.
Lasswell, Harold D. 1958. *Politics: Who Gets What, When, How.* New York: Meridian Books.
Lasswell, Harold D., and Abraham Kaplan. 1950. *Power and Society: A Framework for Political Inquiry.* New Haven: Yale University Press.
Lau, Richard R., and David O. Sears. 1986. *Political Cognition: The 19th Annual Carnegie Symposium on Cognition.* Hillsdale, NJ: L. Erlbaum Associates.
Lazarsfeld, Paul F., Bernard Berelson, and Hazel Gaudet. 1948. *The People's Choice: How the Voter Makes Up His Mind in a Presidential Campaign.* 2d ed. New York: Columbia University Press.
Leege, David C. 1988. "Catholics and the Civic Order: Parish Participation, Politics, and Civic Participation." *Review of Politics* 50 (4):704–36.
———. 1992. "Coalitions, Cues, Strategic Politics, and the Staying Power of the Religious Right, or Why Political-Scientists Ought to Pay Attention to Cultural Politics." *PS: Political Science & Politics* 25 (2):198–204.
———. 1993a. "The Decomposition of the Religious Electorate: A Comparison of White, Non-Hispanic Catholics with Other Ethnoreligious Groups, 1960–1992." Paper presented at the Annual Meetings of the American Political Science Association, Washington, DC.
———. 1993b. "Religion and Politics in Theoretical Perspective." In *Rediscovering the Religious Factor in American Politics*, edited by D. C. Leege and L. A. Kellstedt. Armonk, NY: M. E. Sharpe.
Leege, David C., Lyman A. Kellstedt, and Kenneth D. Wald. 1990. "Religion and Politics: A Report on Measures of Religiosity in 1989 NES Pilot Study." Paper presented at the Annual Meetings of the Midwest Political Science Association, Chicago.
Lerner, Robert, Althea K. Nagai, and Stanley Rothman. 1996. *American Elites.* New Haven: Yale University Press.
Levine, Myron A. 1995. *Presidential Campaigns and Elections: Issues and Images in the Media Age.* 2d ed. Itasca, IL: F. E. Peacock.
Lienesch, Michael. 1997. "The Origins of the Christian Right: Early Fundamentalism as a Political Movement." In *Sojourners in the Wilderness*, edited by C. E. Smidt and J. M. Penning. Lanham, MD: Rowman and Littlefield.
Lincoln, C. Eric, and Lawrence H. Mamiya. 1990. *The Black Church in the African American Experience.* Durham: Duke University Press.

Lodge, Milton, and Ruth Hamill. 1986. "A Partisan Schema for Political Information Processing." *American Political Science Review* 80 (2):505–20.

Lowi, Theodore J. 1979. *The End of Liberalism: The Second Republic of the United States.* 2d ed. New York: Norton.

Luce, R. Duncan, and Arnold A. Rogow. 1956. "A Game Theoretic Analysis of Congressional Power Distributions for a Two-Party System." *Behavioral Science* 1 (2):83–95.

Luker, Kristin. 1984. *Abortion and the Politics of Motherhood.* Berkeley: University of California Press.

Lupia, Arthur, and Mathew D. McCubbins. 1998. *The Democratic Dilemma: Can Citizens Learn What They Need to Know?* New York: Cambridge University Press.

McAdam, Doug. 1982. *Political Process and the Development of Black Insurgency 1930–1970.* Chicago: University of Chicago Press.

McClosky, Herbert, and John Zaller. 1984. *The American Ethos: Public Attitudes toward Capitalism and Democracy.* Cambridge: Harvard University Press.

McCormick, Richard L. 1974. "Ethno-Cultural Interpretations of the Nineteenth Century American Voting Behavior." *Political Science Quarterly* 89 (2):351–77.

———. 1986. *The Party Period and Public Policy: American Politics from the Age of Jackson to the Progressive Era.* New York: Oxford University Press.

McGinniss, Joe. 1969. *Selling of the President, 1968.* New York: Trident Press.

MacKuen, Michael B., Robert S. Erikson, and James A. Stimson. 1989. "Macropartisanship." *American Political Science Review* 83 (4):661–89.

McWilliams, Wilson Carey. 2000. *Beyond the Politics of Disappointment: American Elections, 1980–1998.* New York: Chatham House.

Mansbridge, Jane J. 1986. *Why We Lost the ERA.* Chicago: University of Chicago Press.

Manza, Jeff, and Clem Brooks. 1999. *Social Cleavages and Political Change: Voter Alignments and U.S. Party Coalitions.* New York: Oxford University Press.

Marcus, George E., W. Russell Neuman, Michael B. MacKuen, and John L. Sullivan. 1996. "Dynamic Models of Emotional Response: The Multiple Roles of Affect in Politics." In *Research in Micropolitics*, edited by R. Y. Shapiro, M. Delli Carpini and L. Huddy. Greenwich, CT: JAI Press.

Matalin, Mary, and James Carville. 1995. *All's Fair: Love, War, and Running for President.* New York: Random House.

Matthews, Donald G., and Jane S. De Hart. 1990. *Sex, Gender, and the Politics of ERA: A State and the Nation.* New York: Oxford University Press.

May, Ernest R., and Janet Fraser, eds. 1973. *Campaign '72; the Managers Speak.* Cambridge: Harvard University Press.

Melich, Tanya. 1996. *The Republican War against Women: An Insider's Report from Behind the Lines.* New York: Bantam Books.

Mendelberg, Tali. 1997. "Executing Hortons: Racial Crime in the 1988 Presidential Campaign." *Public Opinion Quarterly* 61 (1):134–57.

Michener, James A. 1961. *Report of the County Chairman.* New York: Random House.

Miller, Arthur H., and Christopher Wlezien. 1993. "The Social Group Dynamics of Partisan Evaluations." *Electoral Studies* 12 (1):5–22.

Miller, Warren E. 1990. "Party Identification and the Electorate of the 1990s." In *The Parties Respond: Changes in the American Party System*, edited by L. S. Maisel. Boulder: Westview Press.

Miller, Warren E., and J. Merrill Shanks. 1996. *The New American Voter.* Cambridge: Harvard University Press.

Mueller, Carol McClurg. 1988. "The Empowerment of Women: Polling and the Women's Voting Bloc." In *The Politics of the Gender Gap*, edited by C. M. Mueller. Newbury Park, CA: Sage Publications.

Neuhaus, Richard John. 1984. *The Naked Public Square: Religion and Democracy in America.* Grand Rapids, MI: W. B. Eerdmans.

Newman, Bruce I. 1994. *The Marketing of the President: Political Marketing as Campaign Strategy.* Thousand Oaks, CA: Sage Publications.

Norrander, Barbara. 1999. "Is the Gender Gap Growing?" In *Reelection 1996: How Americans Voted*, edited by H. F. Weisberg and J. M. Box-Steffensmeier. New York: Chatham House Publisher of Seven Bridges Press.

Oestreicher, Richard. 1988. "Urban Working-Class Political Behavior and Theories of American Electoral Politics, 1870–1940." *Journal of American History* 74 (4):1257–86.

Peffley, Mark, Jon Hurwitz, and Paul M. Sniderman. 1997. "Racial Stereotypes and Whites' Political Views of Blacks in the Context of Welfare and Crime." *American Journal of Political Science* 41 (1):30–60.

Petrocik, John R. 1981. *Party Coalitions: Realignment and the Decline of the New Deal Party System.* Chicago: University of Chicago Press.

———. 1994. "Issue Ownership in Political Elections." Paper presented at the Annual Meetings of the American Political Science Association, New York.

Phillips, Kevin P. 1969. *The Emerging Republican Majority.* New Rochelle, NY: Arlington House.

———. 1990. *The Politics of Rich and Poor: Wealth and the American Electorate in the Reagan Aftermath.* New York: Random House.

———. 1993. *Boiling Point: Republicans, Democrats, and the Decline of Middle-Class Prosperity.* New York: Random House.

Pinderhughes, Dianne M. 1987. *Race and Ethnicity in Chicago Politics: A Reexamination of Pluralist Theory.* Urbana: University of Illinois Press.

Popkin, Samuel L. 1991. *The Reasoning Voter: Communication and Persuasion in Presidential Campaigns.* Chicago: University of Chicago Press.

Powell, Michael. 1998. "One Nation, Torn Apart: The '60s Culture Clash Underlies a New Crisis." *Washington Post*, December 19, 1998, C1.

Pratt, John Webb. 1967. *Religion, Politics, and Diversity: The Church-State Theme in New York History.* Ithaca: Cornell University Press.

Putnam, Robert D. 2000. *Bowling Alone: The Collapse and Revival of American Community.* New York: Simon & Schuster.

Pye, Lucian W. 1968. *The Spirit of Chinese Politics: A Psychocultural Study of the Authority Crisis in Political Development.* Cambridge: MIT Press.

Quayle, Dan. 1992a. "The Family Comes First." *Vital Speeches* 58 (September 15, 1992):711–12.

———. 1992b. "Restoring Basic Values." *Vital Speeches* 58 (June 15, 1992): 517–20.

Ranney, Austin, and Willmoore Kendall. 1956. *Democracy and the American Party System.* New York: Harcourt Brace.

Reading, Hugo F. 1977. *A Dictionary of the Social Sciences.* London and Boston: Routledge and Kegan Paul.

Reimer, Samuel H. 1995. "A Look at Cultural Effects on Religiosity: A Comparison between the United States and Canada." *Journal for the Scientific Study of Religion* 34 (4):445–57.

Rieder, Jonathan. 1985. *Canarsie: The Jews and Italians of Brooklyn against Liberalism.* Cambridge: Harvard University Press.

Riker, William H., and Peter C. Ordeshook. 1973. *An Introduction to Positive Political Theory.* Englewood Cliffs, NJ: Prentice-Hall.

Roof, Wade Clark. 1993. *A Generation of Seekers: The Spiritual Journeys of the Baby Boom Generation.* San Francisco: Harper.

Rosenstone, Steven J., and John Mark Hansen. 1993. *Mobilization, Participation, and Democracy in America.* New York: Macmillan.

Runkel, David R. 1989. *Campaign for President: The Managers Look at '88.* Dover, MA: Auburn House.

Scammon, Richard M., and Ben J. Wattenberg. 1970. *The Real Majority.* New York: Coward-McCann.

Schattschneider, E. E. 1956. "United States: The Functional Approach to Party Government." In *Modern Political Parties*, edited by S. Neumann and F. C. Barghoorn. Chicago: University of Chicago Press.

Schlesinger, Joseph A. 1966. *Ambition and Politics: Political Careers in the United States.* Chicago: Rand McNally.

Sears, David O., and Jack Citrin. 1982. *Tax Revolt: Something for Nothing in California.* Cambridge: Harvard University Press.

Seelye, Katharine Q. 1996. "New Dole Speech Stresses Ideology and Personality." *New York Times*, May 16, 1996, B10.

Shafer, Byron E. 1989. "The Election of 1988 and the Structure of American Politics—Thoughts on Interpreting an Electoral Order." *Electoral Studies* 8 (1):5–21.

Shafer, Byron E., and William J. M. Claggett. 1995. *The Two Majorities: The Issue Context of Modern American Politics.* Baltimore: Johns Hopkins University Press.

Shannon, W. Wayne. 1982. "Mr. Reagan Goes to Washington: Teaching Exceptional America." *Public Opinion* 4:13–17, 55.

Sharp, Elaine B. 1999. *The Sometime Connection: Public Opinion and Social Policy.* Albany: State University of New York Press.

Simon, Herbert A. 1957. *Models of Man: Social and Rational.* New York: Wiley.

Smith, Larry D. 1994. "The New York Convention: Bill Clinton and 'a Place Called Hope.'" In *Bill Clinton on Stump, State, and Stage*, edited by S. A. Smith. Fayettville: University of Arkansas Press.

Sniderman, Paul M., Richard A. Brody, and Philip Tetlock. 1991. *Reasoning and Choice: Explorations in Political Psychology.* New York: Cambridge University Press.

Sniderman, Paul M., and Thomas Leonard Piazza. 1993. *The Scar of Race.* Cambridge: Belknap Press of Harvard University Press.

Sobel, Lester. 1967. *Civil Rights 1960–66.* New York: Facts on File.

Stanley, Harold W., William T. Bianco, and Richard G. Niemi. 1986. "Partisanship and Group Support over Time: A Multivariate Analysis." *American Political Science Review* 80 (3):969–76.

Swidler, Ann. 1986. "Culture in Action: Symbols and Strategies." *American Sociological Review* 51 (2):273–86.

Swierenga, Robert P. 1977. "Ethnicity in Historical Perspective." *Social Science* 52 (1):31–44.

———. 1990. "Ethnoreligious Political Behavior in the Mid-Nineteenth Century: Voting, Values, Cultures." In *Religion and American Politics: From the Colonial Period to the 1980s*, edited by M. A. Noll. New York: Oxford University Press.

Tate, Katherine. 1993. *From Protest to Politics: The New Black Voters in American Elections.* Cambridge: Harvard University Press.
———. 1995. "Structural Dependence or Group Loyalty? The Black Vote in 1992." In *Democracy's Feast: Elections in America*, edited by H. F. Weisberg. Chatham, NJ: Chatham House.
Taylor, Shelley E., Letita Anne Peplau, and David O. Sears. 1994. *Social Psychology.* 8th ed. Englewood Cliffs, NJ: Prentice Hall.
Thomas, Cal. 1996a. "GOP Adopts the Green Bay Sweep." *Gainesville Sun*, February 14, 1996.
———. 1996b. "Testing the Faith of the 'Religious Right.'" *Gainesville Sun*, July 9, 1996.
Times-Mirror. 2000. *The Times Mirror News Interest Index: 1989–1995.* The Pew Research Center for the People & the Press, 1995 [cited November 15, 2000]. Available from www.people-press.org/niidata.htm.
Traugott, Michael W., Santa Traugott, and Stanley Presser. 1992. "Revalidation of Self-Report Vote." Paper presented at the Annual Meetings of the American Association of Public Opinion Research, St. Petersburg Beach, Florida.
Truman, David B. 1951. *The Governmental Process: Political Interests and Public Opinion.* New York: Knopf.
Turner, John C. 1982. "Toward a Cognitive Redefinition of the Social Group." In *Social Identity and Intergroup Relations*, edited by H. Tajfel. New York: Cambridge University Press.
Tversky, Amos, and Daniel Kahneman. 1974. "Judgment under Uncertainty." *Science* 185:1124–31.
Verba, Sidney, and Norman H. Nie. 1972. *Participation in America: Political Democracy and Social Equality.* New York: Harper & Row.
Verba, Sidney, Kay Lehman Schlozman, and Henry E. Brady. 1995. *Voice and Equality: Civic Voluntarism in American Politics.* Cambridge: Harvard University Press.
Wagner, Steven. 1998. "The Catholic Voter Project." *Crisis*, November, C2–C8.
Wald, Kenneth D. 1990. "The New Christian Right in American Politics: Mobilization Amidst Modernization." In *Religious Resurgence and Politics in the Contemporary World*, edited by E. F. Sahliyeh. Albany: State University of New York Press.
Wald, Kenneth D., Lyman A. Kellstedt, and David C. Leege. 1993. "The Public Dimension of Private Devotionalism." In *Rediscovering the Religious Factor in American Politics*, edited by D. C. Leege and L. A. Kellstedt. Armonk, NY: M. E. Sharpe.
Wald, Kenneth D., Dennis E. Owen, and Samuel S. Hill, Jr. 1988. "Churches as Political Communities." *American Political Science Review* 82 (2):531–48.
———. 1990. "Political Cohesion in Churches." *Journal of Politics* 52 (1):197–215.
Walters, Ronald W. 1988. *Black Presidential Politics in America: A Strategic Approach.* Albany: State University of New York Press.
Walton, Hanes, Jr. 1990. "Black Presidential Participation and Critical Election Theory." In *The Social and Political Implications of the 1984 Jesse Jackson Presidential Campaign*, edited by L. Morris. New York: Praeger.
Watanuki, Joji. 1977. *Politics in Postwar Japanese Society.* Tokyo: University of Tokyo Press.
Weber, Max. 1946. *From Max Weber: Essays in Sociology.* Translated by H. H. Gerth and C. W. Mills. New York: Oxford University Press.

Webster v. Reproductive Health Services. 1989. 492 U.S. 490.
Weiner, Tim. 1999. "In Tapes, Nixon Talks of Plans for Foreign Embassy Break-Ins." *New York Times*, February 26, A11.
Weisberg, Herbert F. 1980. "A Multidimensional Conceptualization of Party Identification." *American Behavioral Scientist* 2 (1):33–60.
West, Darrell M. 1997. *Air Wars: Television Advertising in Election Campaigns, 1952–1996.* 2d ed. Washington, DC: Congressional Quarterly.
White, John Kenneth. 1990. *The New Politics of Old Values.* 2d ed. Hanover, NH: University Press of New England.
——. 1997. *Still Seeing Red: How the Cold War Shapes the New American Politics.* Boulder: Westview Press.
White, Theodore H. 1962. *The Making of the President, 1960.* New York: Atheneum Publishers.
——. 1965. *The Making of the President, 1964.* New York: Atheneum Publishers.
——. 1969. *The Making of the President, 1968.* New York: Atheneum Publishers.
——. 1973. *The Making of the President, 1972.* New York: Atheneum Publishers.
Wilcox, Clyde. 1996. *Onward Christian Soldiers? The Religious Right in American Politics.* Boulder: Westview Press.
Wilcox, Clyde, Lee Sigelman, and Elizabeth Cook. 1989. "Some Like It Hot: Individual Differences in Responses to Group Feeling Thermometers." *Public Opinion Quarterly* 53 (2):246–57.
Wildavsky, Aaron. 1987. "Choosing Preferences by Constructing Institutions: A Cultural Theory of Preference Formation." *American Political Science Review* 81 (1):3–21.
Wills, Garry. 1979. *Nixon Agonistes: The Crisis of the Self-Made Man.* New York: New American Library.
——. 1998. "Whatever Happened to Politics? Washington Is Not Where It's At." *New York Times Magazine*, January 25, 1998, 26–35.
Wirthlin, Richard B. 1978. "The Republican Strategy and its Electoral Consequences." In *Party Coalitions in the 1980s*, edited by S. M. Lipset. San Francisco: Institute for Contemporary Studies.
Witcover, Jules. 1970. *The Resurrection of Richard Nixon.* New York: Putnam.
——. 1977. *Marathon: The Pursuit of the Presidency, 1972–1976.* New York: Viking Press.
Wolfe, Alan. 1998. *One Nation, after All: What Middle-Class Americans Really Think about God, Country, Family, Racism, Welfare, Immigration, Homosexuality, Work, the Right, the Left, and Each Other.* New York: Viking.
Wright, Gerald C. 1993. "Errors in Measuring Vote Choice in the National Election Studies, 1952–88." *American Journal of Political Science* 37 (1):291–316.
Wright, James E. 1973. "The Ethnocultural Model of Voting: A Behavioral and Historical Critique." *American Behavioral Scientist* 16:653–74.
Wuthnow, Robert. 1987. *Meaning and Moral Order: Explorations in Cultural Analysis.* Berkeley: University of California Press.
——. 1988. *The Restructuring of American Religion: Society and Faith since World War II.* Princeton: Princeton University Press.
——. 1998. *After Heaven, Spirituality in America since the 1950s.* Berkeley: University of California Press.

Index

abortion, 10, 124, 211
Abramson, Paul, and John Aldrich, 131; and David Rhode, 4, 60, 86, 131
acceptable behavior, 261
accommodationism, 69
advocacy explosion, 34
AFDC. *See* Aid to Families with Dependent Children
affective bonds, 92
African American churches, 111, 184
African Americans, 59, 142, 187; radicals as targets, 111, 112, 136, 184
Aid to Families with Dependent Children, 185
Ailes, Roger, 114, 125
alignment, 187
Almond, Gabriel, and Sidney Verba, 25
ambition theory, 10, 56
American National Election Studies, 131, 138
The American Voter, xi, 4
ANES, *see* American National Election Studies
anticommunism, 160
Atwater, Lee, 125

Banfield, Edward, and James Wilson, 67
Barnes, Fred, 20
Barone, Michael, 213
bounded rationality, 86
Brezhnev Doctrine, 116
Burdick, Eugene, 37, 106

campaign industry, 93
campaign strategy, 8, 14, 15, 75, 111, 113, 158, 179, 203, 213
Carmines, Edward, and Geoffrey Layman, 139; and James Stimson, 28, 179
Catholic leadership, 124
Catholic rank and file, 8, 10, 24, 78, 101, 108, 111, 122, 160, 192, 206, 231
character: its role in 2000 election, 23, 261, 263; mobilization of, 93; tests of, 61
cheap talk, 262

Chicago Democratic Convention (1968), 113
Christian Coalition, 69, 79, 263, 265
church, role of, 31
Churchill, Winston, 103
Civil Rights Act of 1964, 85, 112, 187
class conflict, 33
clergy, 207
coalitions, 83; as unwieldy, 78
cognitive misers, 5
cognitive structures, 137
Cold War, 103, 107, 116, 138, 158, 256; containment policy during, 105; end of, 127
Cold War consensus, 113, 118, 126
collective action, 45
collective values, 60
Colson, Charles, 115
communal identification, 52
compensations, 46
Concerned Women for America, 68
Connectionist activity, 84
Conover, Pamela, and Stanley Feldman, 84
Converse, Philip, 52
conversion strategy, 89
Costain, Anne, 120
counterculture, 20
counter-mobilization strategy, 93
counter-reform movement, 67, 69, 111, 121
critical election, 179, 187
Cuba, 107
cultural codewords, 112, 185, 200, 230, 247, 258, 262
cultural conflict, 26, 118
cultural forces, 195
cultural outgroups, 5
cultural politics, definitions of, 25, 26; development of, 30, 264; historic usage of, 17; as nonbargainable, 29; unintended consequences of, 18, 175, 199
cultural theory of politics, 91
Culture War, 7, 13, 16, 102, 263
culture, 40; concepts of, 13; definition of, 252–253; origins and functions of, 40

284 · Index

Daisy Girl, 108
deference values, 47
delegitimation, 57n
Democratic coalition, 102; changing demographics of, 78; historic elements of, 206
de Tocqueville, Alexis, 46
desexegration, 159
détente, 116
Diamond, Edwin, and Stephen Bates, 213
Dionne, E. J., 31
disabled group, 198
disciplined parties, 267
Downs, Anthony, xi, 46, 62, 265
Durkheim, Emile, 42

Eagle Forum, 209
"easy" issues, 5, 28, 257. *See also* "hard" issues
Edsall, Thomas, xiii, 9, 16, 18, 21, 94; and Mary Edsall, 5, 35, 59, 71, 179, 181
education, 168, 171, 199
efficient party symbols, 121, 143
egalitarian individualism, 211
elections, role of presidential, 39
electoral orders, 101
electoral systems, 101
emotions, 87, 106, 182, 193, 214, 267; power of, 113, theory of, xii
economy, role of, 128
episodic events, types of, 70
Equal Employment Opportunities Act, 203
Equal Pay Act, 203
Equal Rights Amendment. *See* ERA
equality, origins of, 41
ERA, 38, 74, 209, 224
estimation, 146
Evangelical Protestants, 69, 72, 205, 231
external enemies, 104, 106
extragovernmental institutions, 45
extremist groups, 112

Falwell, Jerry, 145, 210
family issues, 203
family values, 15, 16, 19, 123, 144, 160, 230
The Feminine Mystique. *See* Friedan, Betty
Fiorina, Morris, 86
forecasting models, xiii
Fox-Genovese, Elizabeth, 119
Freedman, Samuel, 123, 192

Freeman, Jo, 204
Friedan, Betty, 119, 204
friendship networks, 92

Gallup, George, and Jim Castelli, 192
Geertz, Clifford, 25, 40, 42
gender, 10, 59, 68, 118, 125, 142, 204, 218
gender gap, 211, 218; evolution of, 120
generational replacement, 163, 223
Gilens, Martin, 184
Glock, Charles, 45
government, role of, 44, 179, 181
Greeley, Andrew, 192
Green, John, and James Guth, 207
group affinity, 238
group consciousness, 1, 76, 189
group salience, 53
group-based heuristics, xi

"hard" issues, 5, 29. *See also* "easy" issues
Himmelfarb, Gertrude, 43
history, ownership of, 44
homosexuality, 20, 211
honesty, 63
Huckfeldt, Robert, and John Sprague, 92
Hunter, James D., 6, 102, 207

ideological development, six forms of, 66
ideological labels, 84
ideological movements, 77
ideology, 46, 62
independent voters, 4
in-group symbols, 72
integration, 109
internal enemies, 177
Iranian Revolution, 117
issue framing, 269
issue images, 59, 159
issue ownership, 1, 84, 86
issue positions, 254
issue space, 266
issue voting, 4

Jamieson, Kathleen Hall, 125, 182, 213
Jarvis, Howard, and Paul Gann, 183
Jews, 24, 59, 101, 117, 122, 206, 231, 235

Keith, Bruce, David Magleby, Candice Nelson, Elizabeth Orr, Mark Westlye, Raymond Wolfinger, 131

Kellstedt, Lyman, and John Green, 231n
Kennedy assassination, impact of, 112
Key, V. O., 4, 86
Kinder, Donald, and Lynn Sanders, 179
King, Coretta Scott, 110
King, Martin Luther, Jr., 110
knowledge elite, 32
Kristol, Irving, 128

Laborem Exercens, 104
Ladd, Everett, 130
LaHaye, Beverly, 68
Lasswell, Harold, 45; and Abraham Kaplan, 47
Latinos, 8, 59, 234
"law 'n' order," 114, 115, 181
Lazarsfeld, Paul, 92; and Bernard Berelson and Hazel Gaudet, 86
legitimating material, 63
legitimation, 51
liberals, called "tax and spend," 71, 115, 142
Lienesch, Michael, 36n
limited government, 59
Lowi, Theodore, 32
Luker, Kristen, 43

mainline Protestants, 78–79, 121, 205, 231
Mansbridge, Jane, 43, 68, 124, 141, 209
Manza, Jeff, and Clem Brooks, 7
Marcus, George, 87
Marx, Karl, 49
McGovern-Fraser reforms, 266
meaning, 50
Melich, Tanya, 119, 174, 216
Mendleberg, Tali, 184
Middle East policy, 117
migration, 109
Miller, Warren, and J. Merrill Shanks, 4, 83, 131
minority strategies, 83
mobilization/countermobilization strategy, 89
modernity, effects of, 79; impact of, 35, 36, 208; traditionalist responses to, 43
moral decay, 213
moral issues, 112
Moral Majority, 210
moral order, 1, 25, 39, 47, 61, 65, 254; restoration of, 22

moral restorationism, 240, 243, 246, 247, 260
moral traditionalism, 23, 203, 259
multinomial logit, 146
mythology, role of, 41

National Education Association, 124
National Rifle Association, 186
National Organization for Women, 204
nationalism, 102. *See also* patriotism
nationalities Division, 158
NEA. *See* National Education Association
negative outgroup symbols, 71, 94, 267
neofederalism, 183
New Christian Right, 125
New Covenant, 18
New Deal coalition, 89; collapse of, 101
New Deal party system, 101
new majoritarian strategy, 78, 219, 224
new middle class, 32, 208
new South, 70
Niemi, Richard, 7
Norrander, Barbara, 217
NOW. *See* National Organization for Women
NRA. *See* National Rifle Association

oil crises, 117
opportunistic appeals, 180

parallel culture, 36, 66
Parsons, Talcott, 8
partisan advantage, 132, 133, 190, 218, 236, 237
partisan disloyalty, 135
partisan realignment, 130, 187
partisan schema, 88
partisan yield, 132, 135
party coalitions, evolution of, 108, 168, 174, 187, 267
party cores, 85
party identification, 4; competing models of, 92; realignment of, 4
party ideology, 143, 182
party image, 261; evolution of, 262
party loyalty, 131, 189
party symbols, 267
party systems theory, 4
party systems, 101; efficiency of, 261. *See also* party systems theory

286 • Index

patriotism, 105, 158, 252, 256
permanent campaign, 183
Persian Gulf War, 127
Petrocik, John, 7
Phillips, Kevin, 78, 174, 192
plausibility structures, 51
Pledge of Allegiance, 126
pocketbook voting, 5
political system, impacts of, 57
politicians, cardinal rules of, 10
politics of righteousness, 22
politics, group basis of, 49
polling apparatus, 114
Popkin, Samuel, 19, 84
principled appeals, 180
prodigal generation, 264
Putnam, Robert, 6

racial imagery, impact of, 167
race, 108, 179
reactive symbols, 59
reality, construction of, 50
relative deprivation, 1, 75, 94, 204, 216, 254
religion, 46, 252; definition of, 42; role in politics, 122
religious traditionalism, 7
religious war, 13
Republican coalition, emergence of, 78; impact of urban reform movement on, 67
retrospective voting, 86, 116
revitalization movements, 66
Rieder, Jonathan, 192
rights revolution, 43
Riker, William, and Peter Ordeshook, 86
RIP (revelation, investigation, and prosecution), 57n, 90
ritual, 1, 30, 56, 58, 60, 255
Roe v. Wade, 124
Roof, Wade Clark, 122
Rosenstone, Steven, and Mark Hansen, 9, 189

sanctions, 45
Scammon, Richard, and Ben Wattenberg, 203
Schattschneider, E. E., 79
schema theory, 87, 183
Schlafly, Phylis, 68, 209
Sears, David, and Jack Citrin, 179, 183

secularization forces, 208
sexual revolution, 31, 43, 61
Shafer, Byron, and William Claggett, 9, 138
Sniderman, Paul, and Thomas Piazza, 179, 186
social attribution theory, 62, 126, 141, 210
social categorization, 14
social cohesion, 50, 52, 53, 207, 210. *See also* social identification
social connectedness, 189
social conservatism, 203
social control mechanisms, 6, 45, 47
social groups, 5
social heuristics, 87
social identification, 50, 51, 52, 209, 210. *See also* social cohesion
social mobility, 31
social norms, 41
sociotropic voting, 5
solid South, 191
Southern whites, 168, 191, 208
Southern strategy, 192, 224, 243
Southernization of America, 37
strength of leadership, 8
structural dependence, 190
suburbanization of the electorate, 206
Supreme Court, 122, 143, 210–211
Swidler, Ann, 42
symbol makers, 35, 51
symbolic manipulation, 85
symbols of cultural threat, 50, 93, 254, 261

Teeter, Robert, 125
theocracy, threat of, 123, 217
"Third Disestablishment," 121
Thomas, Clarence, confirmation hearings, 73
Title VII of the Civil Rights Act, 120
Title IX of the Education Equity Act, 204
traditional values, 15, 68, 203
transformational movement, 209
Turner, John, 51
turnout, minimization of, 9

uncertainty, 62
urban reform movement, 66

valence issues, 28, 254
Vatican II, 68

Verba, Sidney, and Norman Nie, 189; and Kay Lehman Schlozman and Henry Brady, 189
veto points, 80
Vietnam, 158
Voting Rights Act, 85
voting, theories of, 92

Watergate, 72, 116, 214
Weber, Max, 71
Weisberg, Herbert, 131

welfare queen, 159, 185
welfare reform, 185
welfare values, 47
Weyrich, Paul, 210
Wilcox, Clyde, Lee Sigelman, and Elizabeth Cook, 141n
Wildavsky, Aaron, 6, 26, 252
within-group mobilization, 266
Wuthnow, Robert, 6, 25, 50, 51, 56, 58, 62, 66, 122, 207